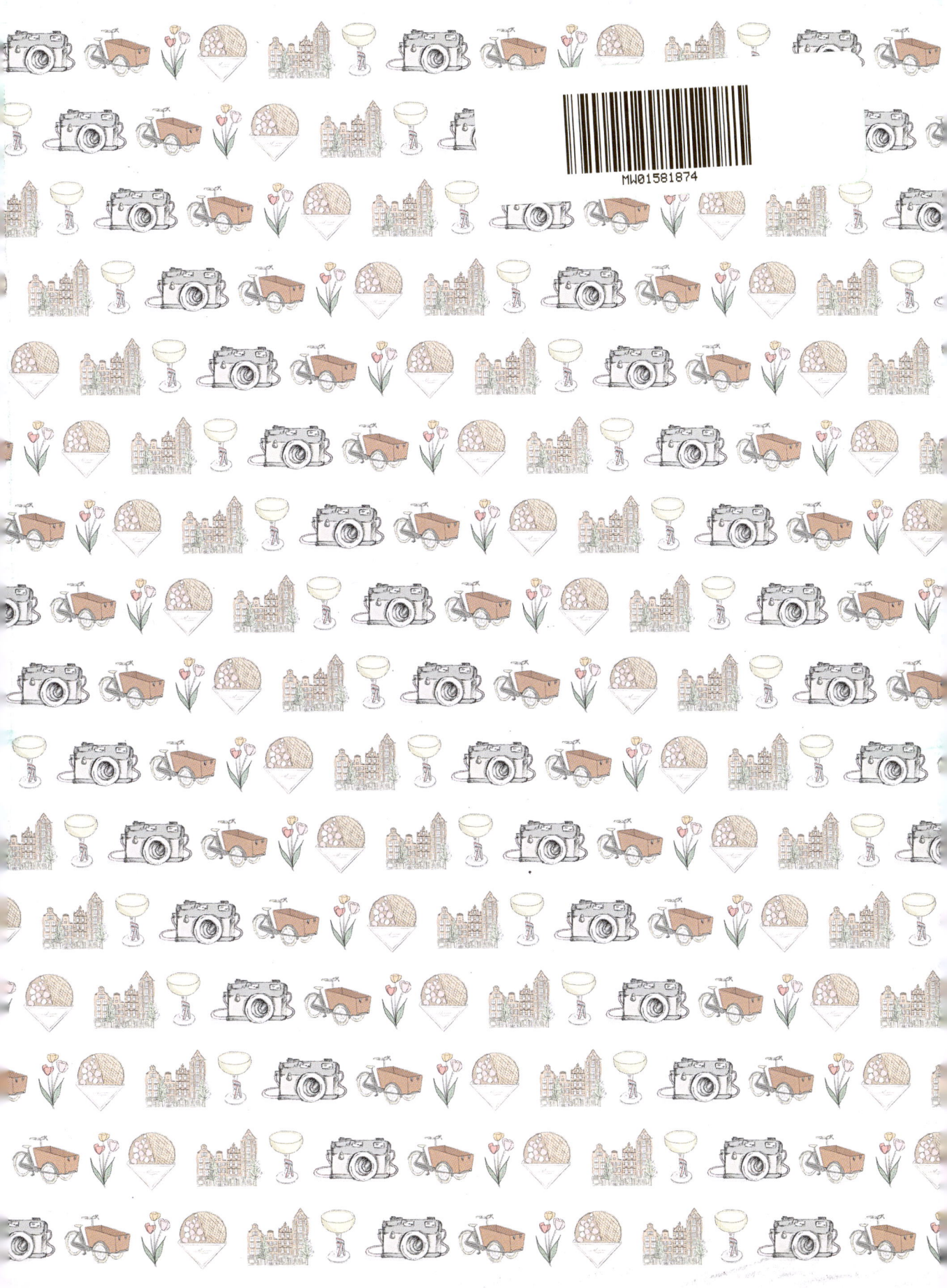

PRETTYCITYAMSTERDAM
DISCOVERING AMSTERDAM'S BEAUTIFUL PLACES

SIOBHAN FERGUSON

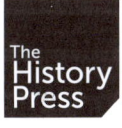

Front cover: image by Siobhan Ferguson
Back cover: bottom middle by @velvet.boulevard; all others by Siobhan Ferguson

@theprettycities and all other contributing Instagram accounts are operated independently and are not affiliated with, endorsed or sponsored by Instagram LLC.

First published 2024

The History Press
97 St George's Place,
Cheltenham GL50 3QB
www.thehistorypress.co.uk

© Siobhan Ferguson, 2024

The right of Siobhan Ferguson to be identified as the Author of this work has been asserted in accordance with the Copyright, Designs and Patents Act 1988.

All rights reserved. No part of this book may be reprinted or reproduced or utilised in any form or by any electronic, mechanical or other means, now known or hereafter invented, including photocopying and recording, or in any information storage or retrieval system, without the permission in writing from the Publishers.

British Library Cataloguing in Publication Data.
A catalogue record for this book is available from the British Library.

ISBN 978 0 7509 9523 8

Design by Katie Beard
Printed and bound in India by Thomson Press India Ltd

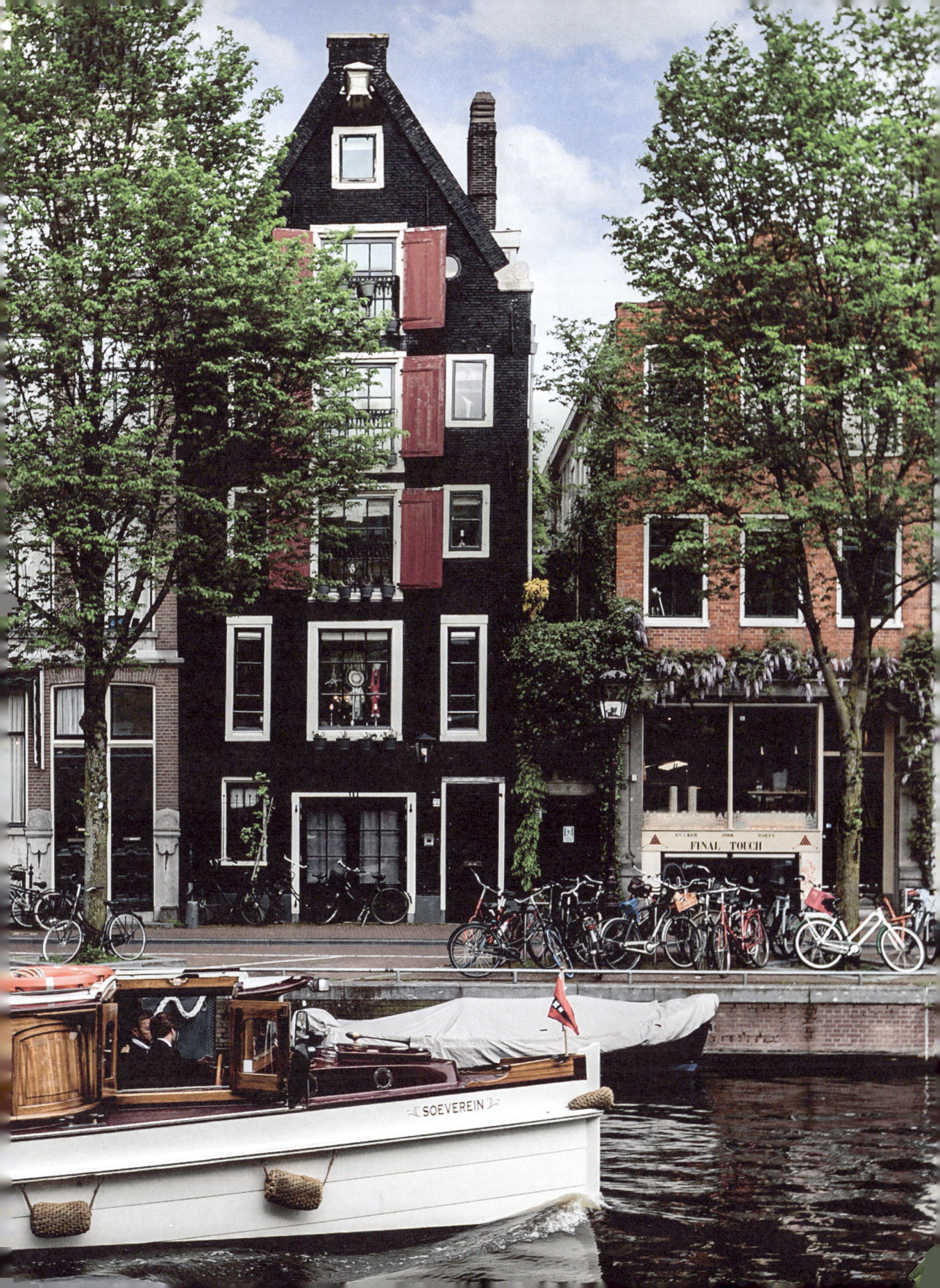

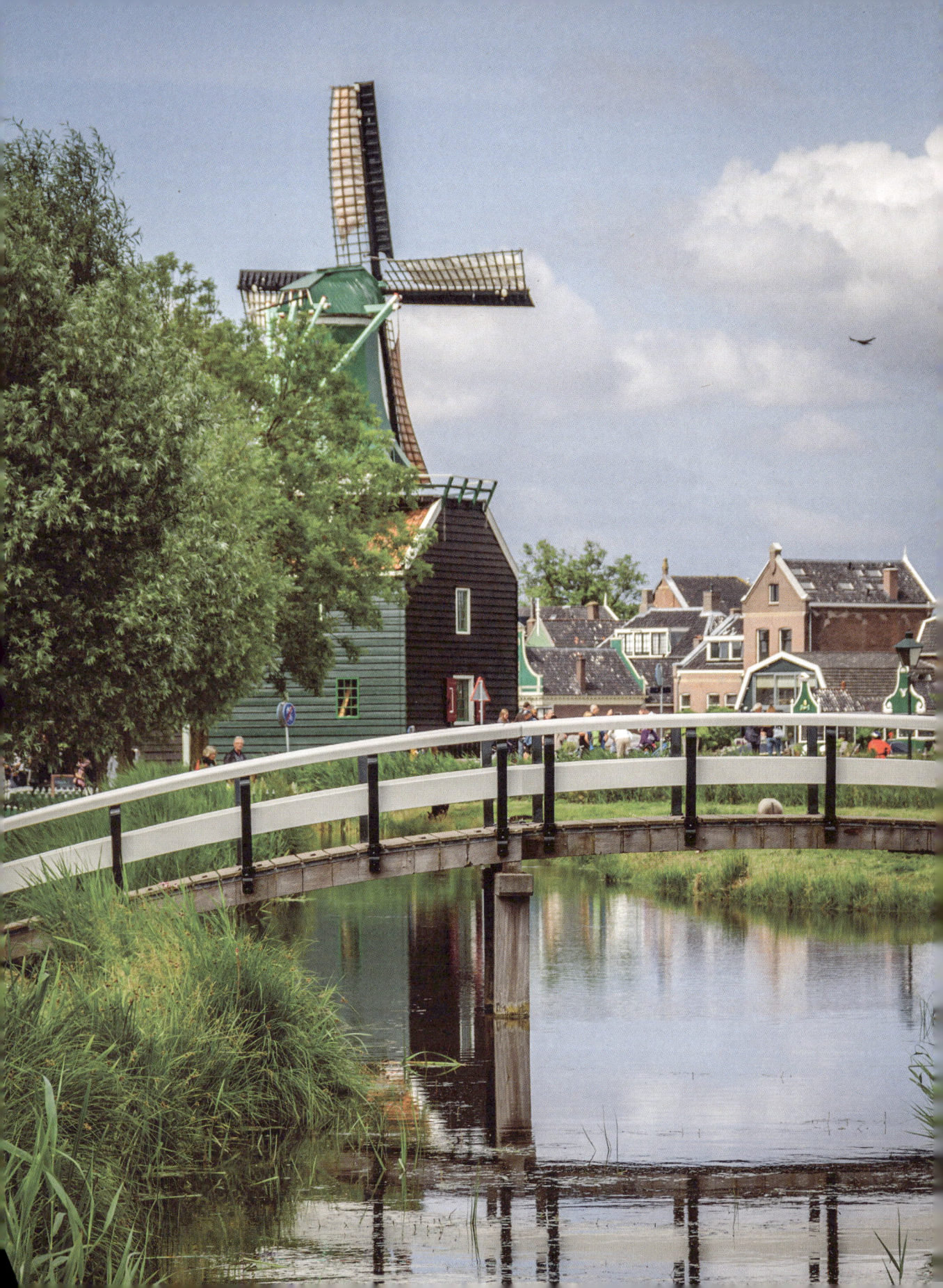

CONTENTS

Introduction 6
How to Use This book 14

Part I: Photography Tips 19

Part II: Through the History Books 29

Part III: Neighbourhoods:
Central Canal Ring: One half of the UNESCO World Heritage Site; a maze of cobbled roads with gabled canal houses and humpback bridges; home to the famous 9 Streets 38
Southern Canal Ring: The other half of the UNESCO World Heritage Site; quintessential Amsterdam with stunning architecture and picturesque canal houses; home to the Museum and Antique Quarters 66
Jordaan: Community spirit and charm in abundance: narrow streets, picturesque canals and historic buildings; home to Noordermarkt 90
De Pijp: Local and vibrant atmosphere with an eclectic mix of cultures, trendy bars, one-off shops and home to the famous Albert Cuyp Markt 118
Oud-West: A laid-back atmosphere enhanced with plenty of local bakeries, vintage shops and top-notch restaurants 130
Medieval Centrum, Oude Zijde and Nieuwe Zijde: Amsterdam's oldest quarter; busy with visitors but brimming with hidden gems 140

Part IV: Pretty City Amsterdam Through the Seasons 183

Part V: Bucket List of Things to Do in Pretty City Amsterdam 201

Contributors 220
Acknowledgements 222

INTRODUCTION

Amsterdam allures with its maze of enchanting waterways, humpback bridges and tall, skinny houses with fancy gables. It is a city of old-world charm and contemporary structures; it's a city with a rich cultural offering through its world-class museums, with a thriving art scene both here in the present and back in the past. It's a city of bohemian enclaves and a profound community spirit; of bicycles, spokes and bells and swarming cyclists with places to go. It's a city of brown bars, cosy cafes and copious coffee shops; of open green spaces, windmills and bustling markets; of culinary delights and gastronomic adventures; of bitterballen (Dutch meatballs), apple pie and stroopwafels; of poffertjes, artisanal cheese, herring and frites. It's a city of gable houses, gable stone and a gregarious curly script; a city of lights, both twinkly and notorious; of virtues and vice and open-mindedness; of tolerance and inclusivity. It is a city of contradictions and surprises around every bend.

My *Pretty City* books rarely start with a clean state. Previously, they all have had a story to tell that begins with an already-in-place connection or a well-established love story. In that sense, my London book was very straightforward as I have lived in the capital for over twenty years; I had visited New York for work and pleasure umpteen times before embarking on that book; while my connections with Dublin came from being Irish and living and working there for many years. As for Paris, well for Paris I had so many profound connections. But, when it came to Amsterdam, I was starting from scratch, and I couldn't help but agonise over it.

Marks and fragments from an underwhelming visit in my twenties formed my concerns about this city of freedom being the focus of my latest book in the *Pretty City* series. Rhythms of misconceptions of a city of coffee shops and cannabis together with visions of the gritty red-light district, the window brothels and gawkers imprinted in my brain, yet I had a book to do: I had committed to discovering the beautiful side, and I had to crack on.

And I am so pleased to say that the narrative surrounding this historic city and my journey with it swiftly transitioned. For me, it became a place

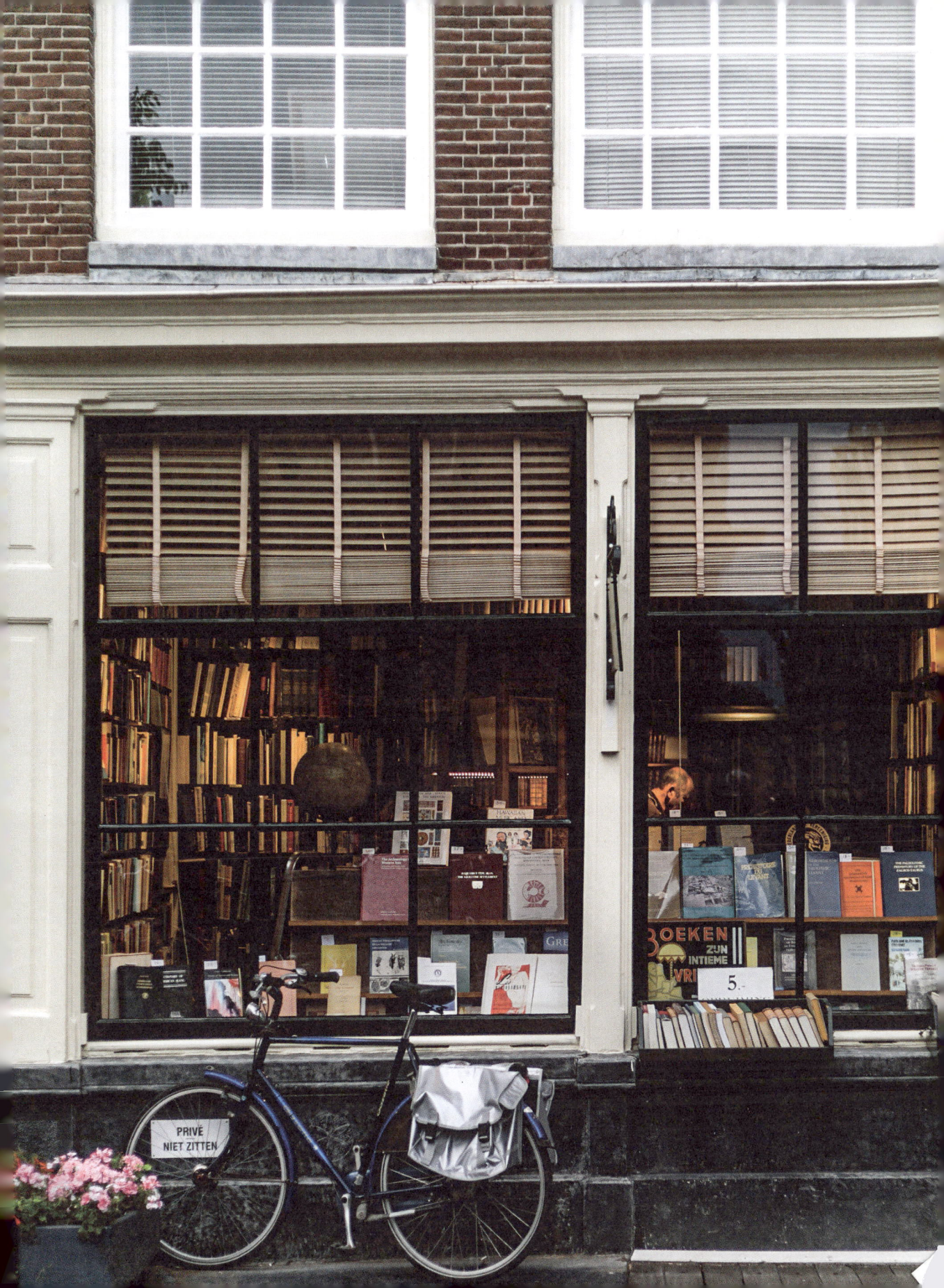

of boundless discovery, a cause for wonder and surprise, a beautiful tale, and a wonderful change of heart. I visited Amsterdam six times in 2023 to research and photograph it. Of course, it began to quickly impress. Sure, the red-light district and coffee shops still play a role but in its burgeoning enclaves, reflective golden-age canals with their little bridges, labyrinthine streets brimming with charming cafes and cultural revelations, and its beautiful warm and friendly people I found a profound connection. I must admit, it didn't take very long into my first trip during winter before I felt captivated. In fact, I think I was just one short hour in and, somewhere between emerging from an old-world alleyway on to the Singel and arriving at the nearby Negen Straatjes, I realised I was in for a joyous treat of adventure and discovery.

Admittedly, on arrival I did have to coax myself out of my warm hotel room off Dam Square, but then, when walking beneath the bare elm trees lining Prinsengracht, I started to relax; it might have had something to do with the twinkly lights reflecting on the attic windows of the crooked houses, which appear to lean on one another. As I meandered with no grander plan than to orientate myself, I was mesmerised by a swarm of bikes sweeping over the humpback bridges in a flurry of spokes and bells ...

The city is deep in its winter sleep: I feel like I have it to myself, the hush on the glassy canals soothing, with only a boat or two braving the icy temperatures. Although the waterways are blanketed in silence, they begin to enthral, and from the corner of my eye I catch a glimpse of a flickering glow of warm light and ambience drifting through the fogged windows of a little brown bar. It doesn't take very long to encourage me inside Café de Pels, and once in I find a laid-back local crowd, most enjoying a warm drink and reading around a worn communal table under the window. I take the last seat at the bar and absorb the ambience of my surroundings: art on the walls, newspapers on display. Under the advice of the friendly barman, I order a biertje and a small plate of bitterballen and, as I strike up a conversation with the lovely lady on my left and bite into my first ever local snack, my thoughts shift. I have nothing to fear; discovering the beautiful side of Amsterdam will be just fine.

Thanks to endless more experiences like that one, I found it was just fine indeed.

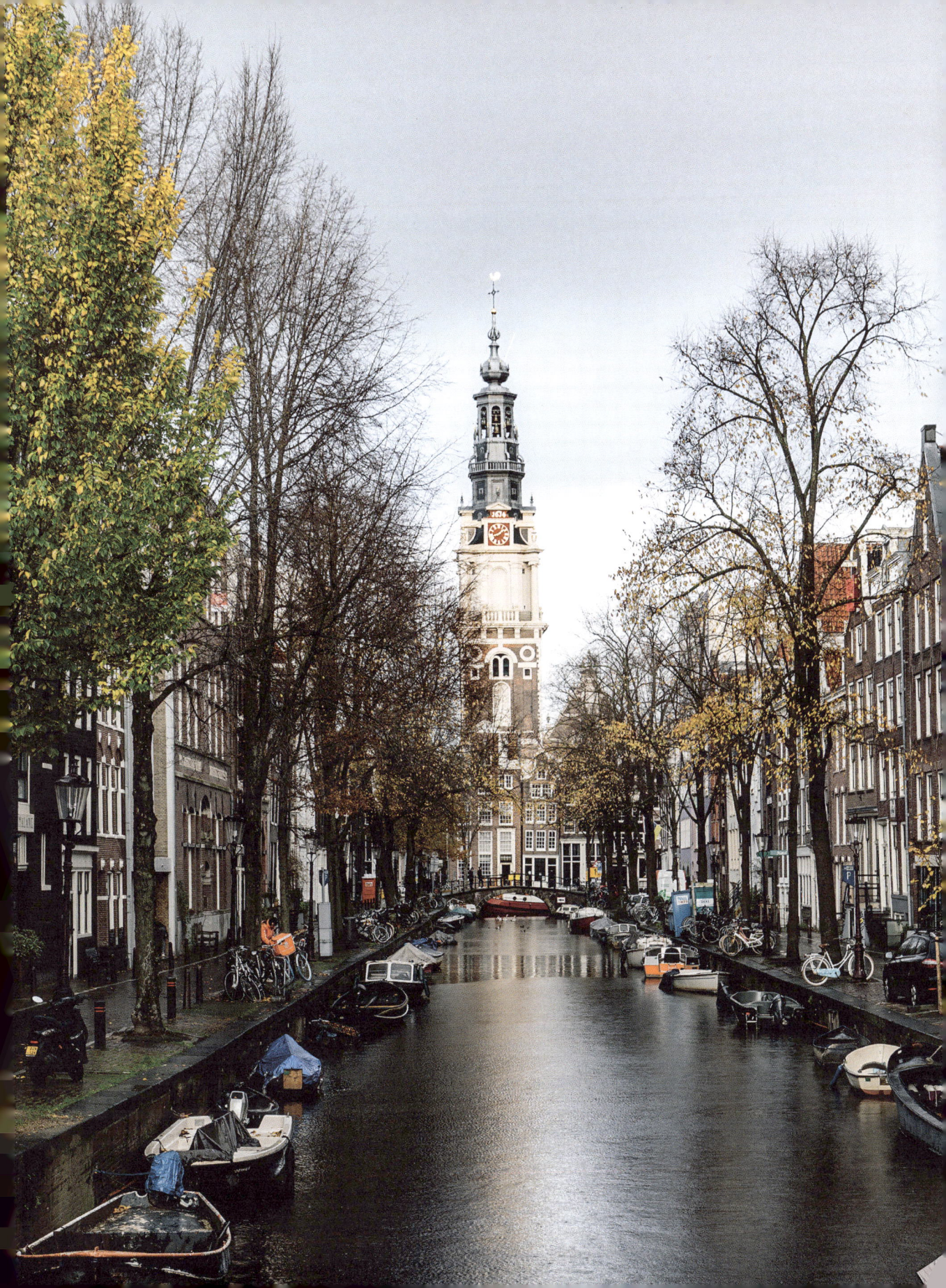

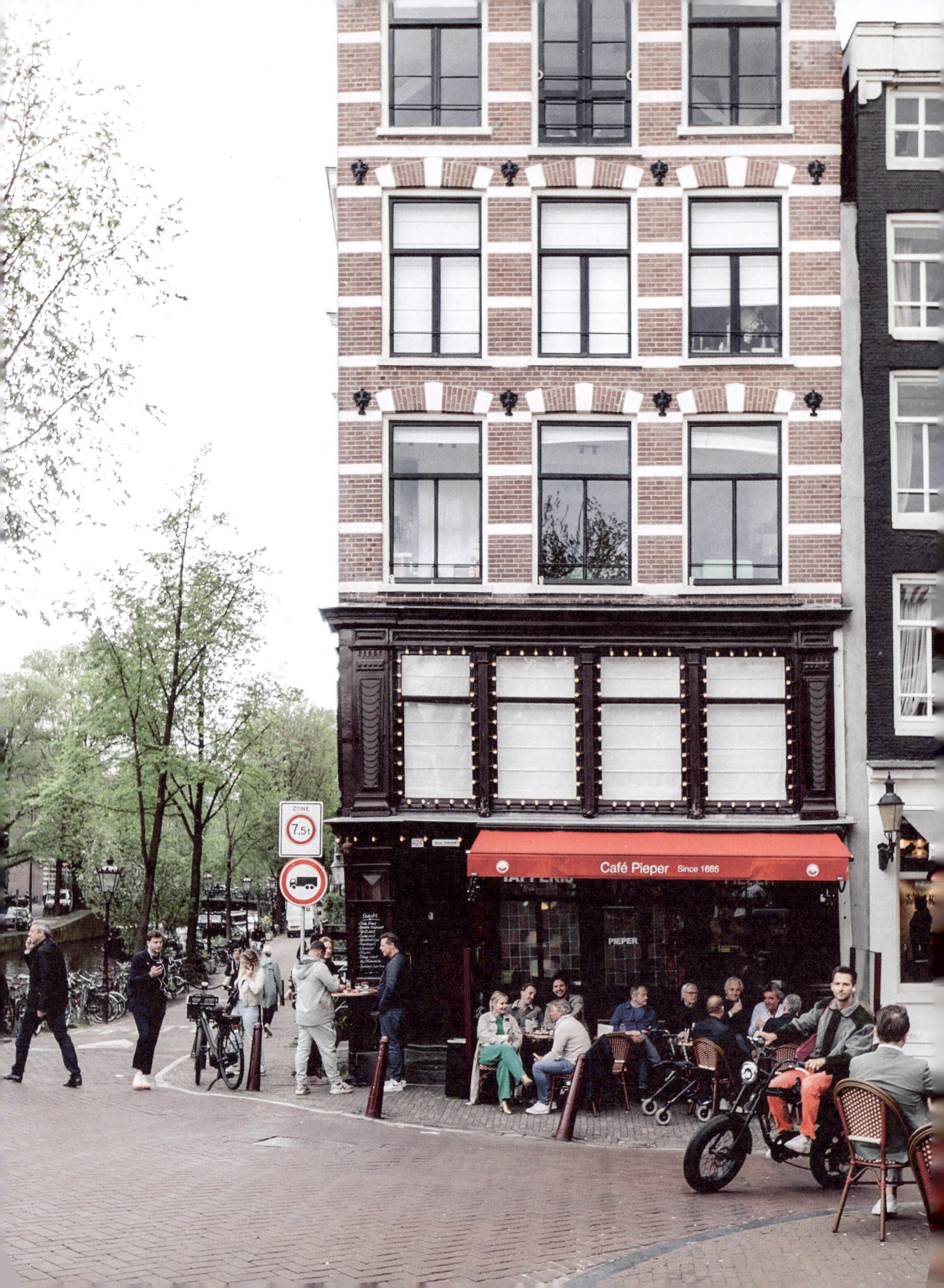

The book and its structure weren't designed overnight: I pored over maps and made five more trips, during which I explored every neighbourhood once, twice and sometimes thrice, and then retraced my steps again until I landed on a structure I was happy with. I mulled over it all, omitted a few districts and included several others until the book had the perfect balance. The result is a blend of stories, walks, experiences and photographs designed to inspire and help you practically explore the city; it also features a celebration of the city through the seasons, a discerning selection of addresses to add to your own bucket list and some tips on creating your own postcards of Amsterdam. Like the other books in the series, it is not intended to be strict or exhaustive but I really hope you like it. Better still, if you have any apprehensions about Amsterdam yourself, it might just help you too to have a change of heart.

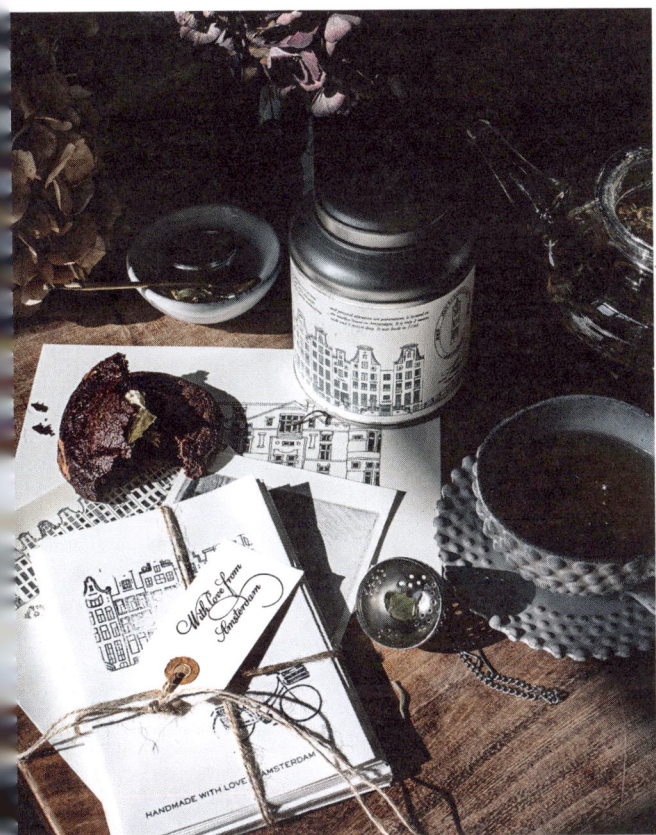
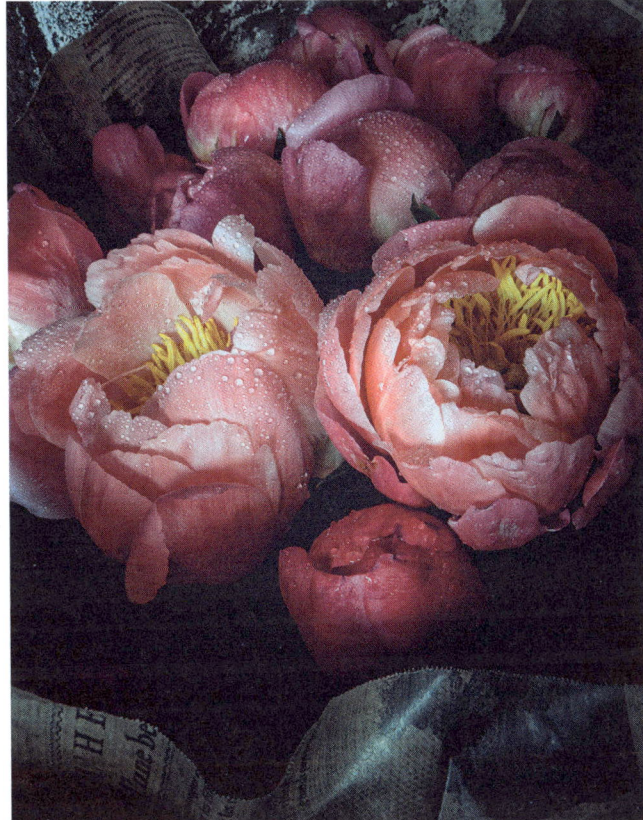

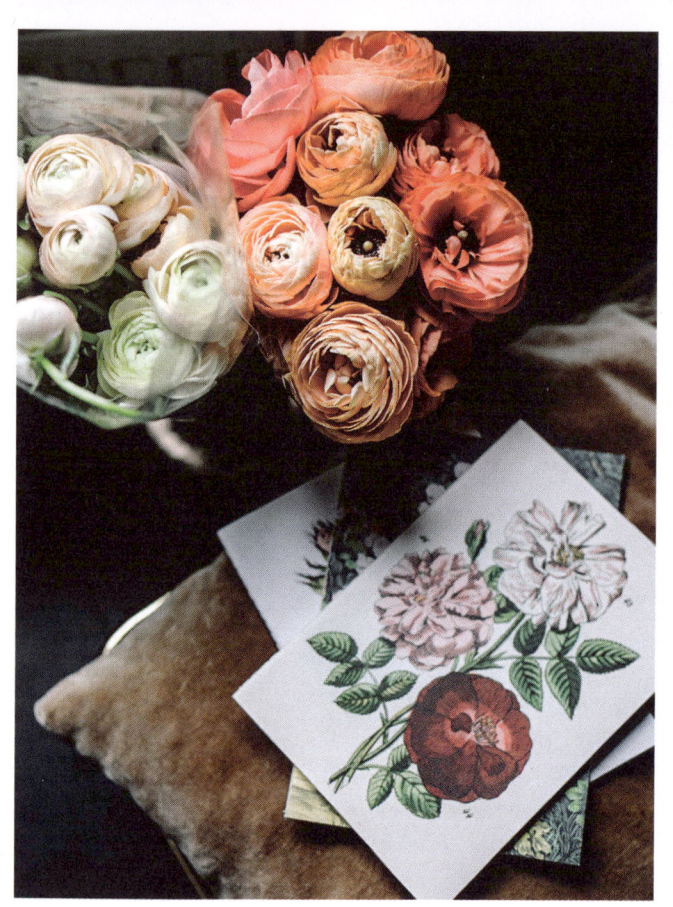
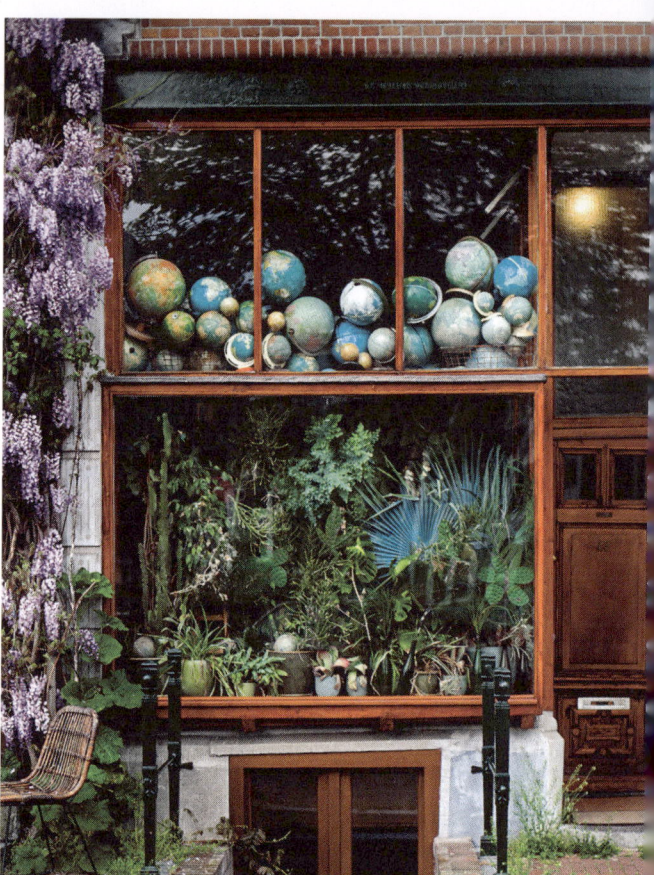

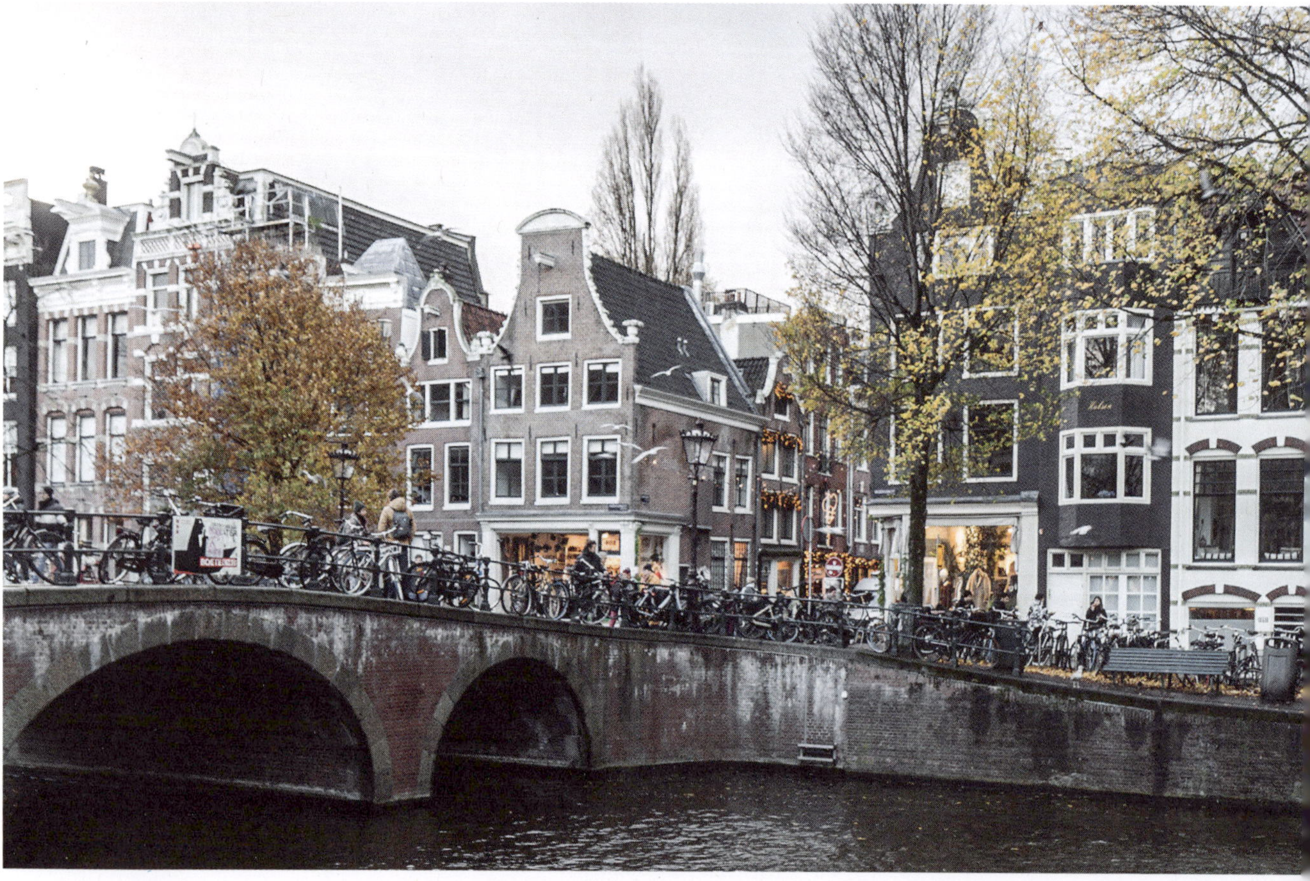

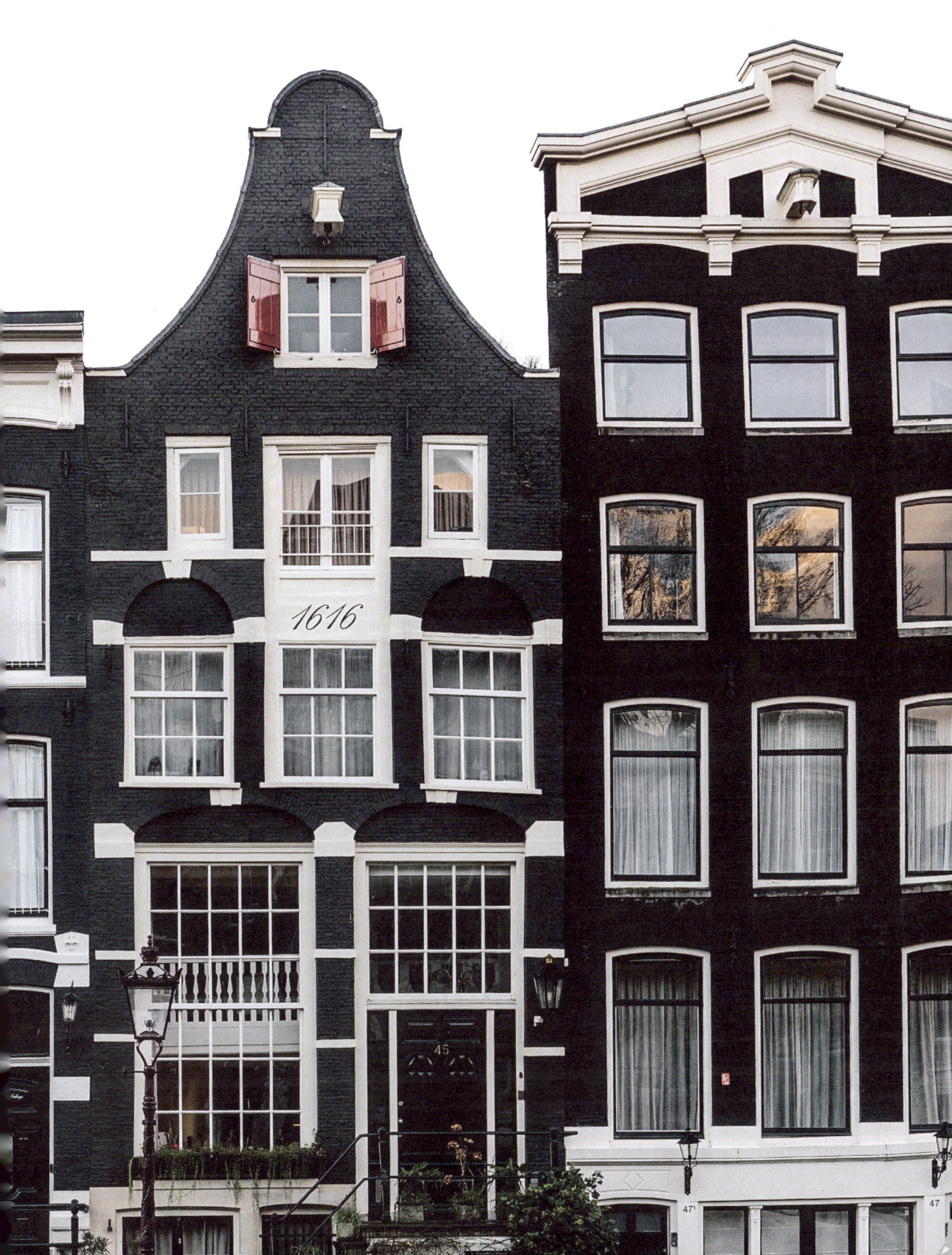

HOW TO USE THIS BOOK

For the most part, this book is a visual celebration of the most beautiful places I have discovered when exploring Amsterdam. Like the other books in the series, it is intended to be inspiring and valuable by providing the key to navigating the city by neighbourhood and hints on how to make the most of these enclaves in an accessible manner. It is not intended to be exhaustive or comprehensive, nor is it intended to be strict.

It includes five key parts: photography tips, a journey through the history books, neighbourhoods, a celebration of Amsterdam through the seasons, and a list of selected addresses to add to your bucket list.

The photography tips section includes helpful tips on taking beautiful captures to add to your memory books.

As the name suggests, the neighbourhood section is arranged by the areas of the capital that genuinely represent the Pretty City aesthetic and charm. Some neighbourhoods are grouped in one section, as exploring them together makes logistical sense and they have features that complement each other. This section also features a variety of locations worth visiting and that are easy to capture, from shops to cafes, galleries to parks. Some areas contain a sample guided walk, whereas other areas simply list the streets to visit. The maps at the beginning of each section, illustrated by Holly Webber, indicate what to expect in the area and are not to scale.

Through the Seasons is a short but beautiful section celebrating the changing seasons in the city.

Finally, the bucket list section is a curated list of ideas of what to do in the city to truly experience the essence of Pretty City Amsterdam.

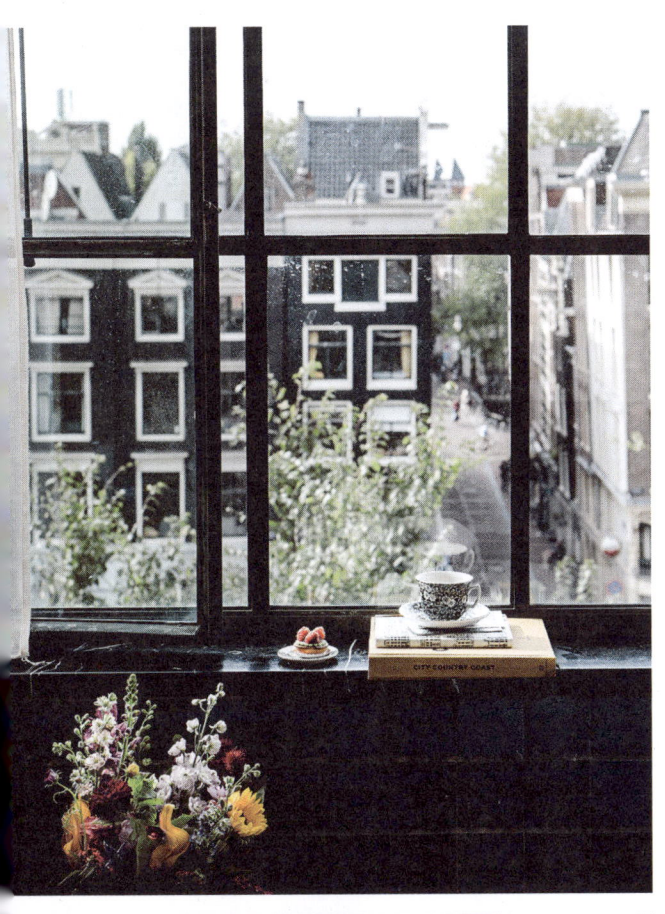
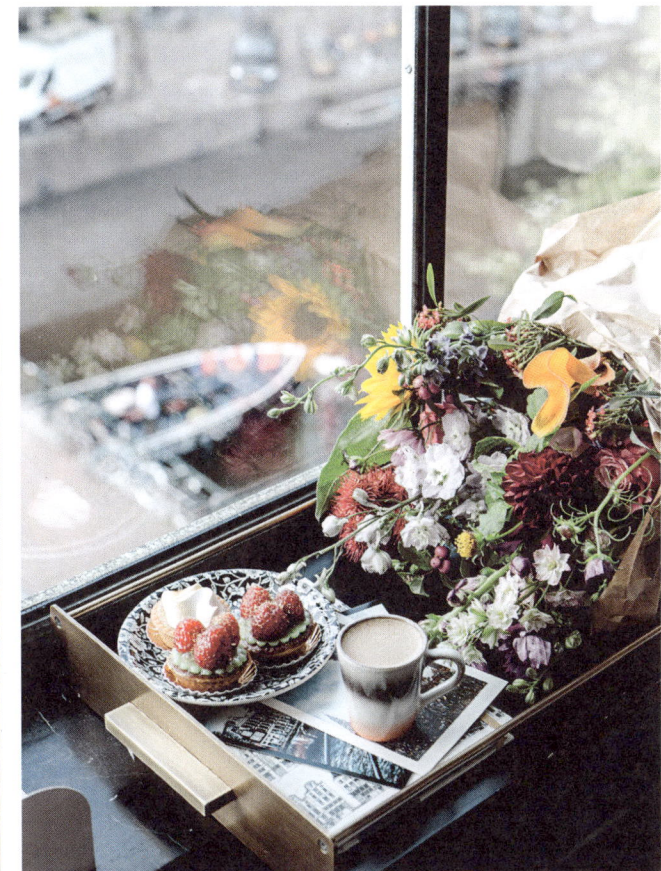
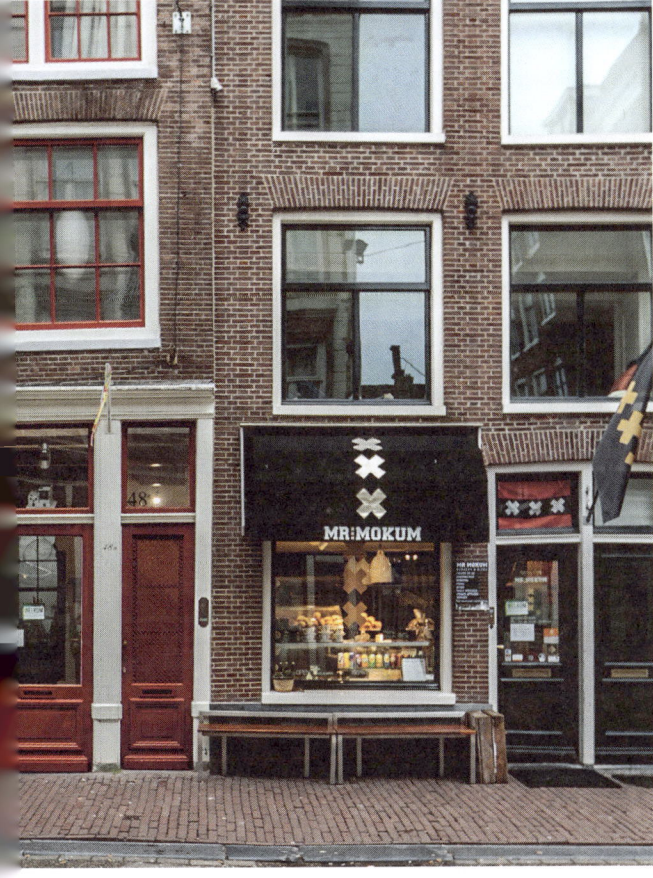
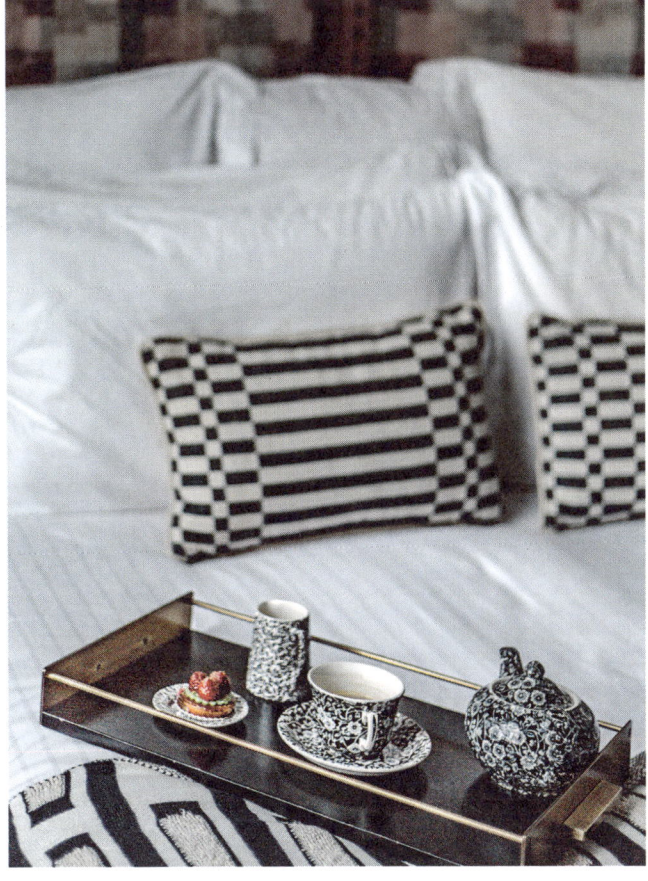

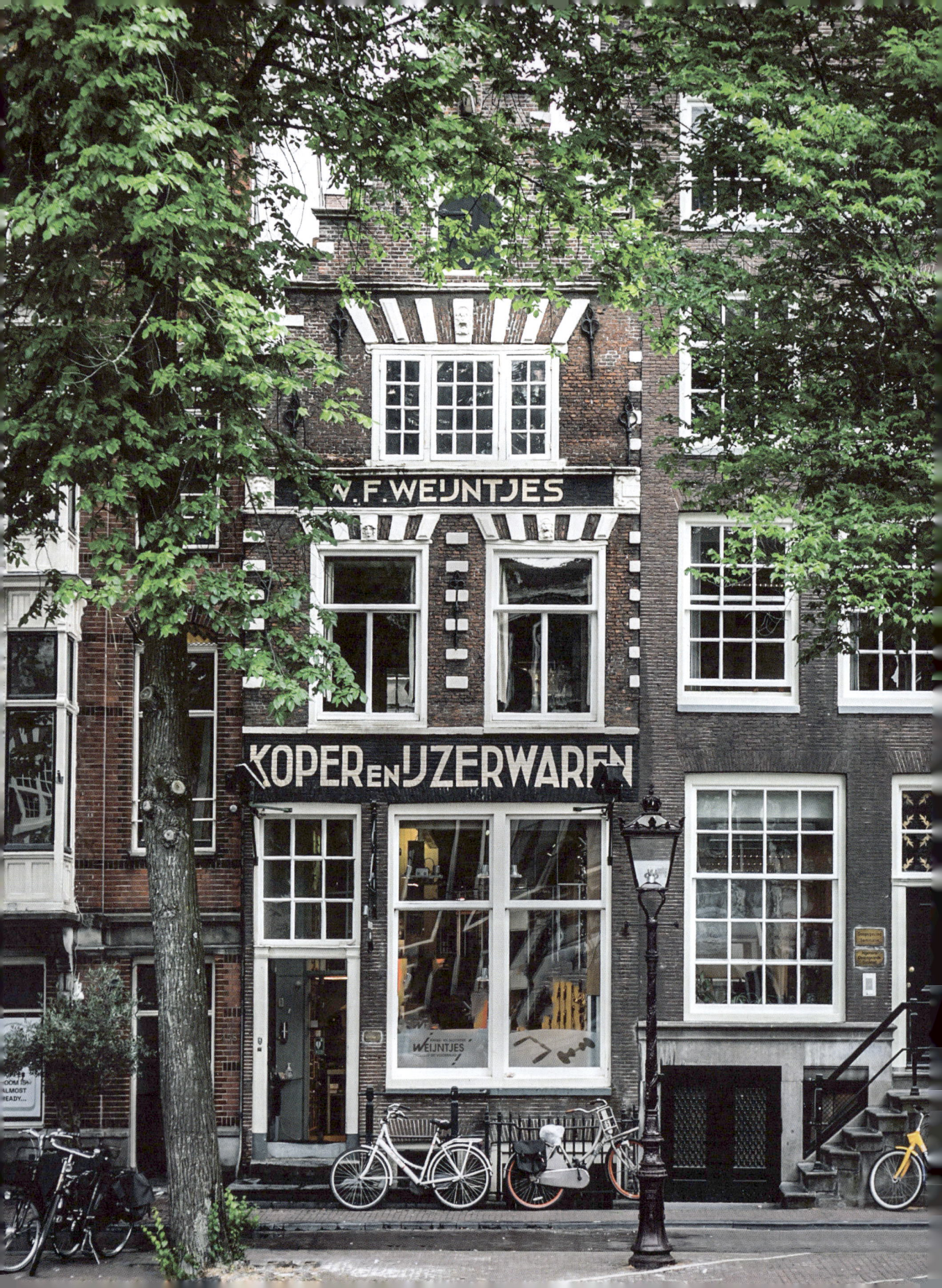

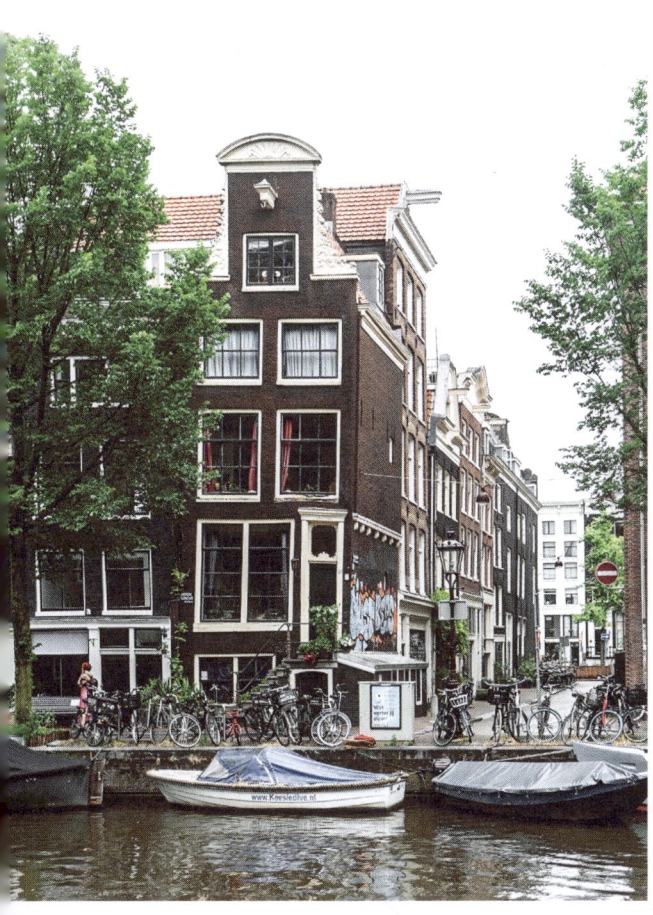
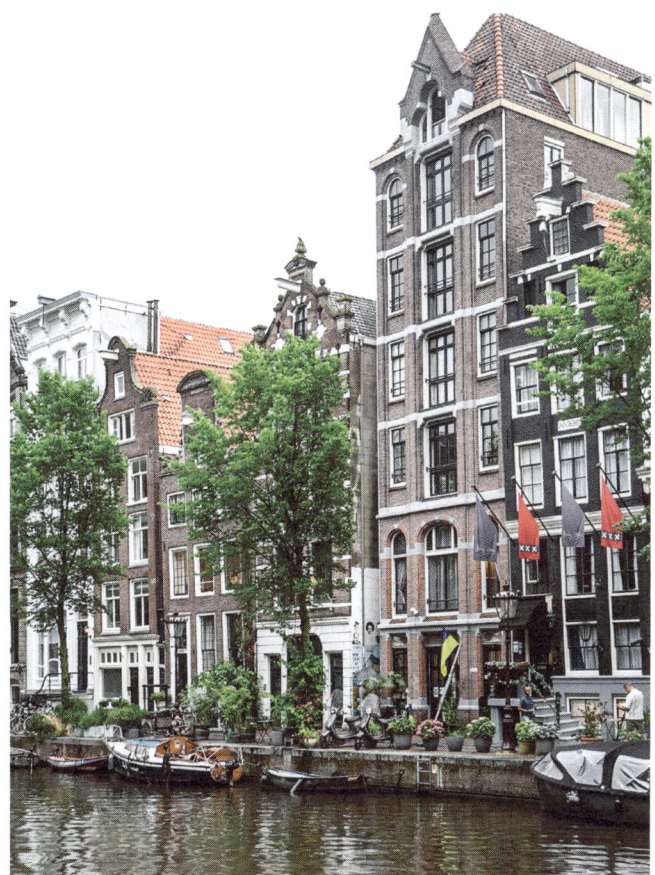
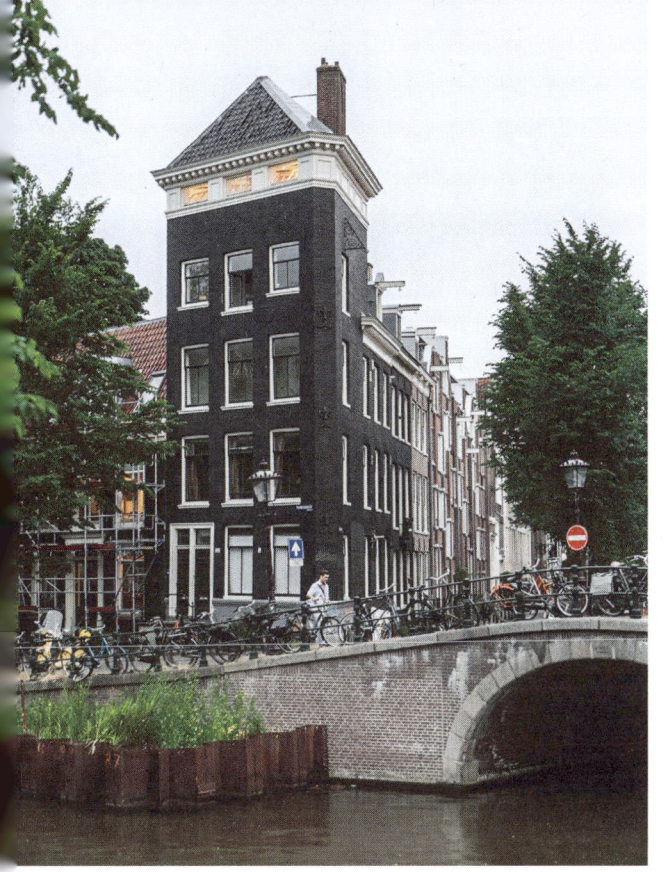
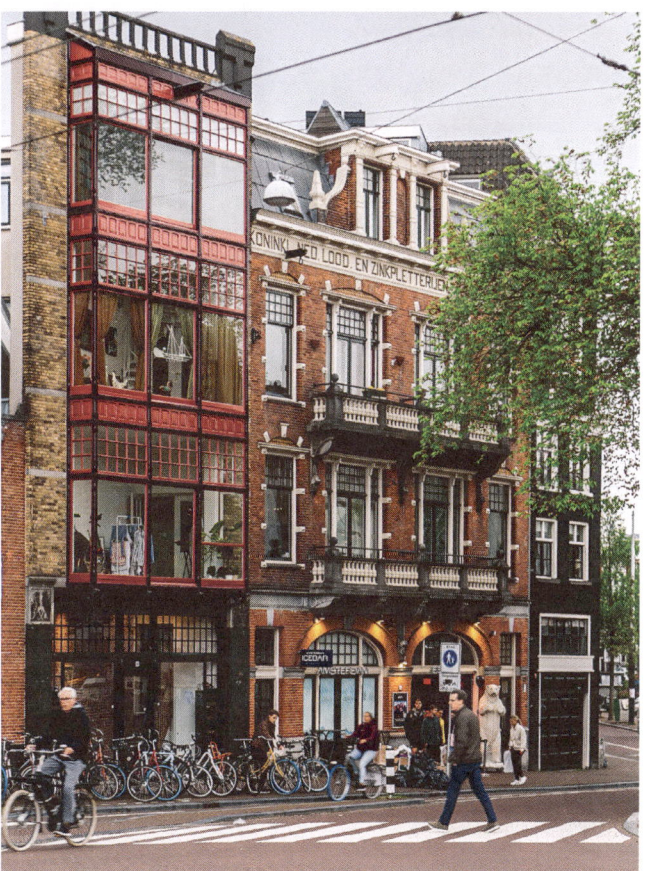

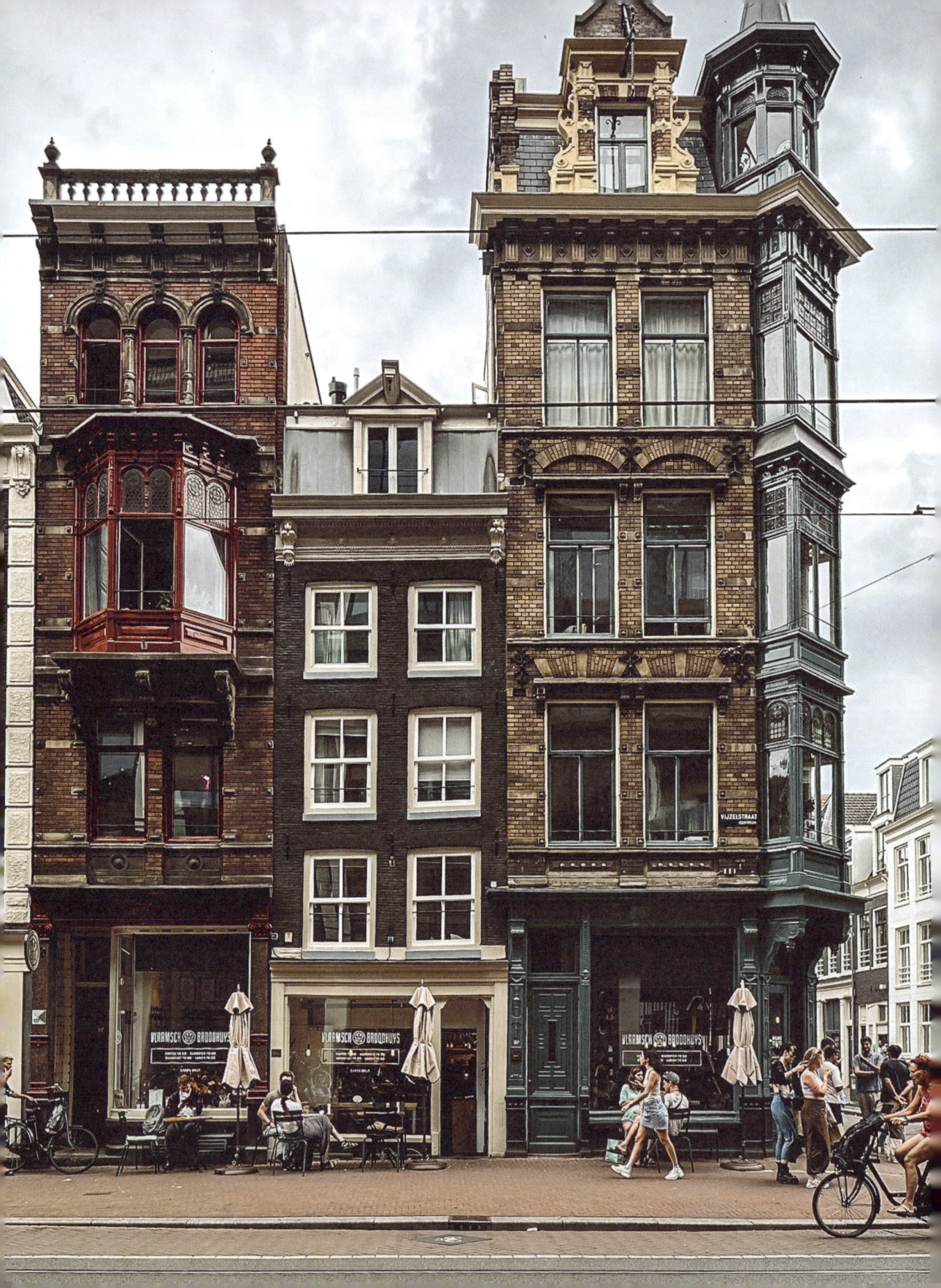

PART I

PHOTOGRAPHY TIPS

Anyone can build a memory book or start an Instagram account: you don't have to be a professional photographer, nor do you have to have a professional camera kit. Just train your eye and practise your portfolio as much and as often as you wish. The most important thing to remember is that it doesn't have to be perfect. I have had the splendid fortune to find my passion for photography and visual storytelling but, save for a short training course at the London School of Photography, I have never had any formal training. Despite having been practising for more than a decade, I still struggle to call myself a photographer, but it doesn't stop me from trying hard to get that shot. Here are some tips you might find useful in Amsterdam.

CHASE THE LIGHT

Light plays a crucial role in photographing Amsterdam and influences the overall mood, atmosphere and aesthetics of the photographs. Amsterdam is known for its beautiful canals, historic architecture and vibrant street scenes, and capturing these elements requires a good understanding of how light interacts with the subject, whether natural or artificial.

The quality and direction of light can enhance or diminish the visual impact of a photograph. For example, soft, diffused light during sunrise or sunset can create a warm and romantic mood, perfect for capturing the charm of Amsterdam's canal houses and bridges. On the other hand, harsh sunlight at midday can cast strong shadows and wash out colours, potentially making the photos less appealing. Additionally, light can highlight certain features and details in a scene. It can emphasise the texture of the buildings, reflect off the canals, or create interesting shadows and reflections. By observing and utilising the available light, we can bring out the unique characteristics of Amsterdam and make our photographs more visually captivating. Waiting for the 'golden hour', which is the time shortly after sunrise or before sunset when the light is soft and warm, can result in stunning photographs with beautiful colours and a magical feel.

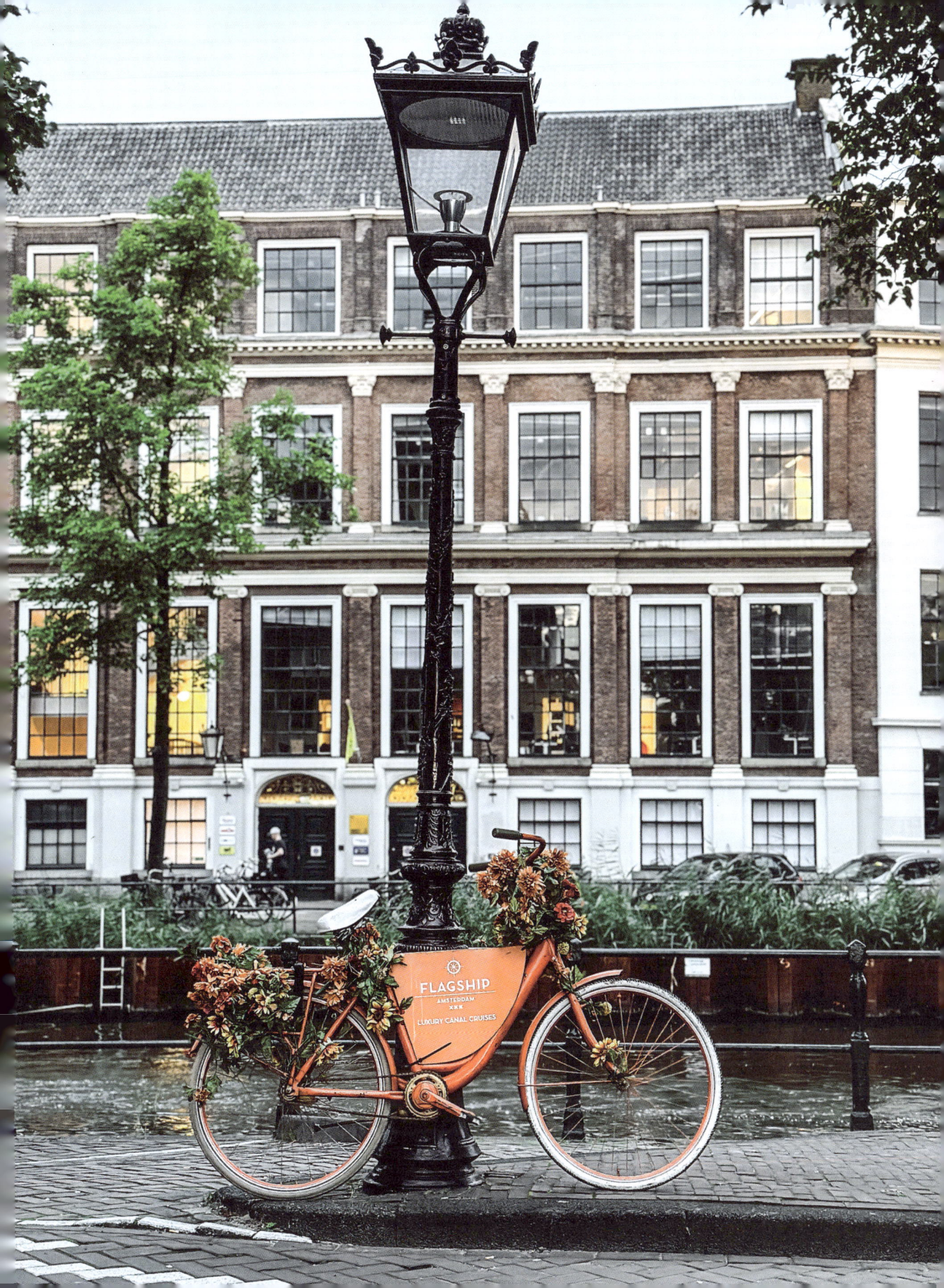

At night, Amsterdam's cityscape comes alive with illuminated bridges, buildings and vibrant nightlife. Experiment with long exposures to capture reflections on the canals.

Adapt your eye and photography to the time of year and, indeed, the time of day. Harsh midday sunlight isn't great for shooting outdoors, but it can be helpful for indoor photography. However, it is best to avoid direct sunlight through the windows, as that will give you the same problems as shooting outside in direct sunlight. Instead, seek that soft overcast of light. Train your eye to find it. Once you do, you will never look at clouds in the same way again.

A little research will tell you the best places in the city to capture the magic of sunrise and sunset along the river, but on the bridges overlooking the canals are where it is best. Plan your visit to suit and you will get some beautiful results.

HAVE YOUR CAMERA/SMARTPHONE READY AT ALL TIMES

Amsterdam is a photographer's dream, and there is always something special to capture. Capturing the details of the city with people going about their business can add an extra layer of depth to the story you tell through your photography. Capture the bicycles: Amsterdam is famous for its cycling culture, so photograph the rows of parked bikes or cyclists in motion. Look for interesting angles and compositions highlighting the bikes as a focal point. The bustling streets of Amsterdam offer endless opportunities for candid street photography. Capture locals, tourists and the vibrant street life. Blend in with the crowd and observe interesting moments or interactions.

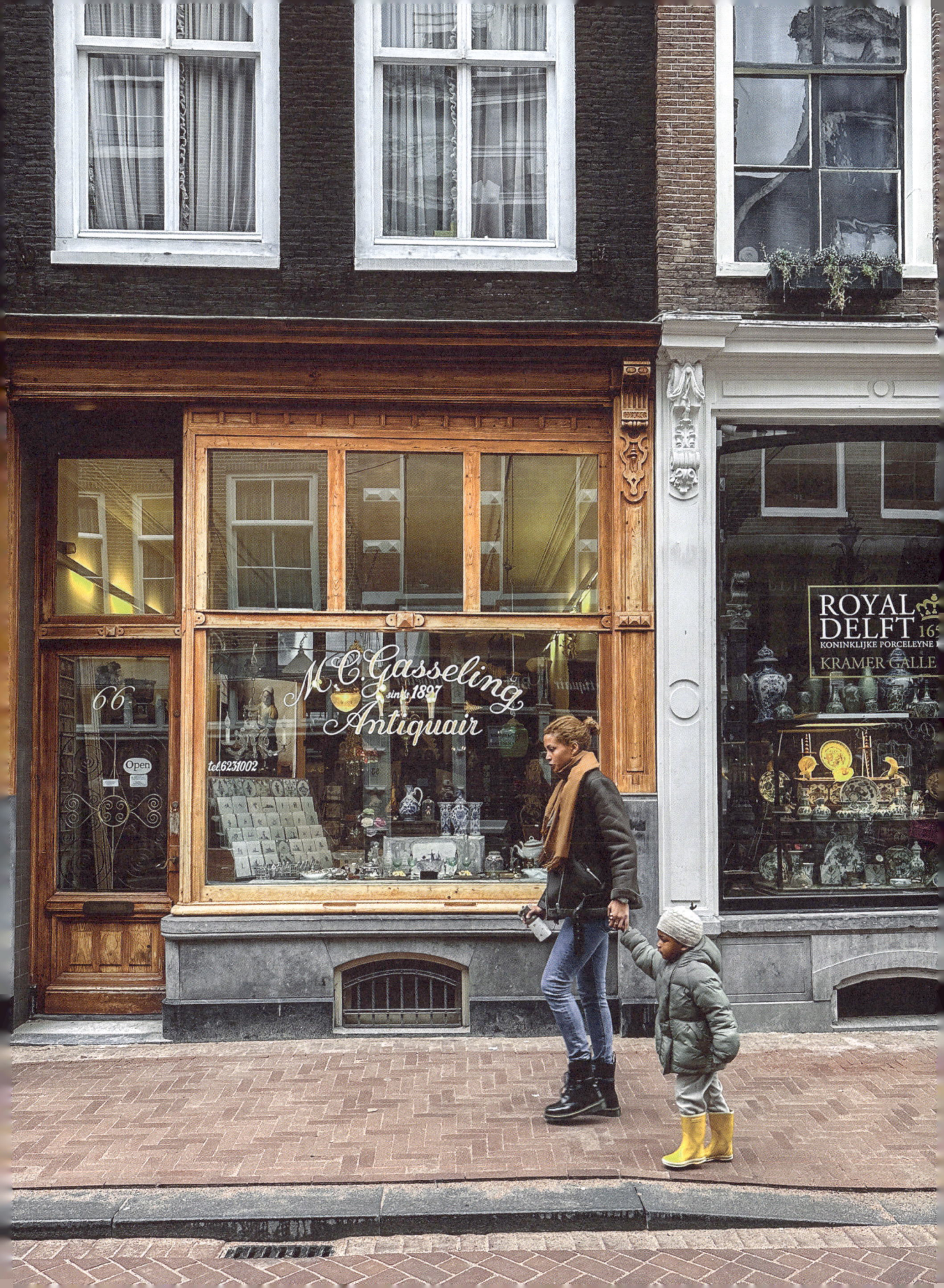

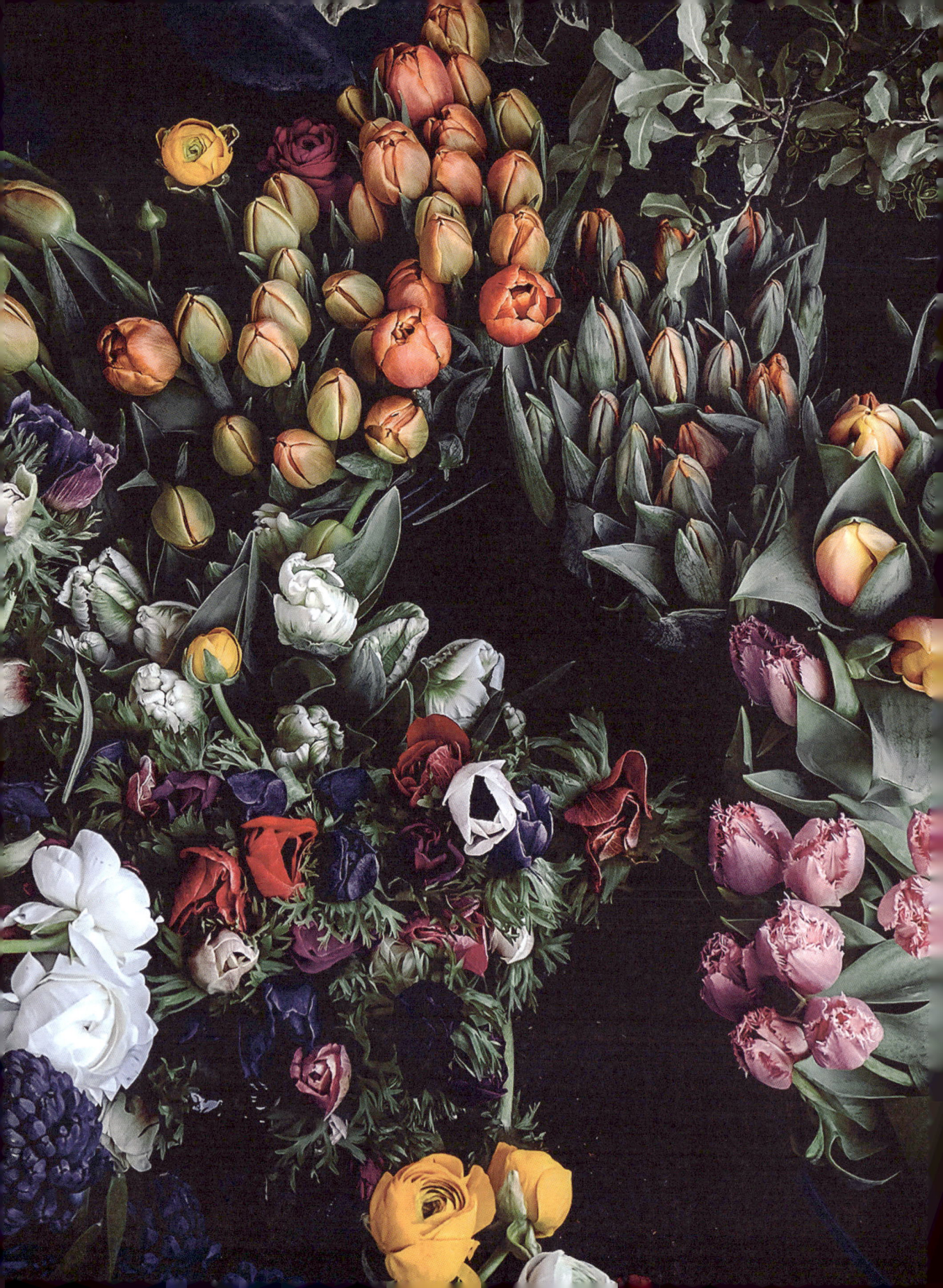

CHECK FOR THE DETAILS

Tell me you were in Amsterdam without telling me you were in Amsterdam. Give a sense of place in your shots by including typical Amsterdam details in your background or foreground, but don't let them dominate. Add context and soul to your shot by adding a human element. The characterful neighbours of Amsterdam and the canals have abundant stunning details, such as big-ticket monuments, canal houses and bridges. As mentioned, photograph the rows of parked bikes along the canals. Amsterdam is home to many historic buildings with unique architectural features. Capture the ornate details, gabled facades and distinct rooftops of structures like the Anne Frank House or the Royal Palace.

Visit the charming neighbourhoods listed in this book; these neighbourhoods are filled with narrow streets, traditional houses and colourful flowers, depending on the time of year. Wander around and capture the unique atmosphere of these enclaves.

FIND YOUR PERSPECTIVE

Perspective refers to the point of view or the angle from which a photograph is taken. Perspective plays a crucial role in photographing Amsterdam by highlighting landmarks, conveying depth, enhancing the atmosphere, emphasising symmetry and offering different viewpoints. It allows us to capture the city's essence and present it visually in a compelling and engaging way.

The role of perspective when photographing Amsterdam is essential in capturing the beauty and unique characteristics of the city. It helps determine the spatial relationships between objects in the scene and influences the photograph's overall composition and visual impact.

When photographing Amsterdam, different perspectives can showcase various aspects of the city's architecture, culture and atmosphere. Here are a few critical roles perspective plays:

Highlighting landmarks: by choosing different perspectives, we can emphasise iconic landmarks such as the Anne Frank House, the Rijksmuseum or the canals. Shooting from a low angle can make the buildings appear more imposing, while capturing them from elevated viewpoints can provide a broader context of the surrounding area.

Conveying depth: perspective can create a sense of depth in photographs, especially when capturing the canals, narrow streets and houses that characterise Amsterdam. Utilising leading lines, such as the curves of the canals or the facades of the buildings, can draw the viewer's eye into the scene, giving a three-dimensional feel to the photograph.

Enhancing atmosphere: different perspectives can help convey the unique atmosphere of Amsterdam. For instance, shooting from a bridge over a canal can capture the lively and picturesque reflections of the houses on the water. Alternatively, photographing from a cafe terrace can capture the cosy and vibrant street life.

Emphasising symmetry: Amsterdam's architecture is renowned for its symmetrical designs, particularly along the canals. By utilising perspective, we can highlight the symmetry and balance in our compositions, creating visually pleasing and captivating images.

Perspective allows us to offer our own interpretation of Amsterdam, showcasing the city from various angles. It enables creativity and the opportunity to showcase the less-explored parts of the town or capture unique scenes that may go unnoticed.

Remember, each photographer has their own unique style and perspective, so feel free to experiment and find your creative expression while capturing the beauty of Amsterdam.

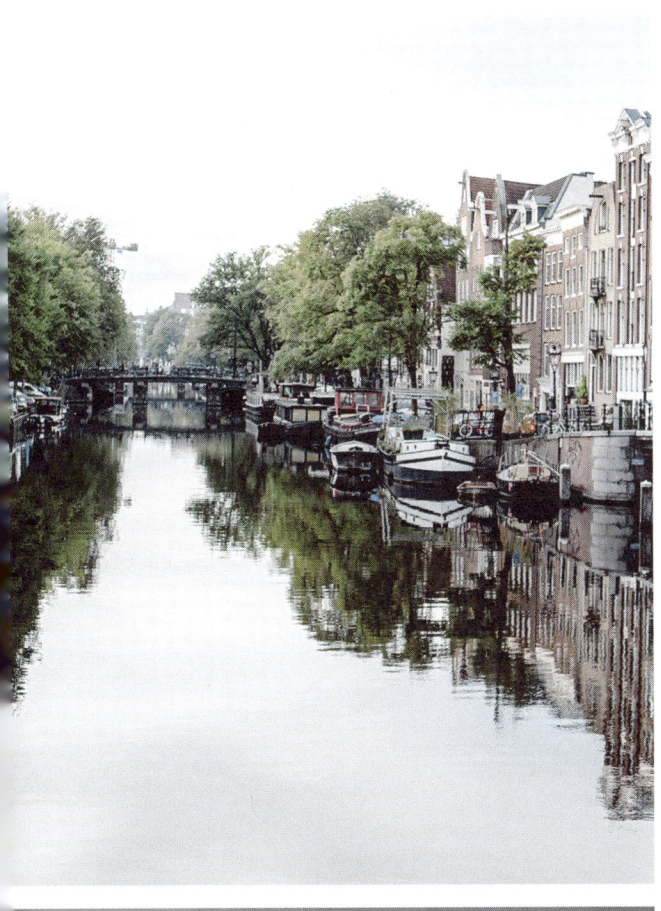
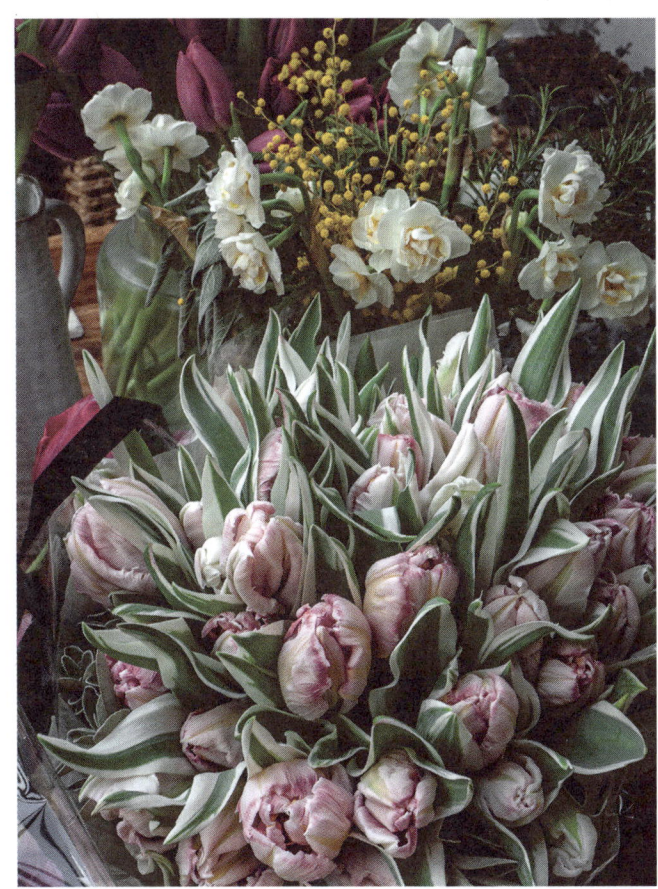
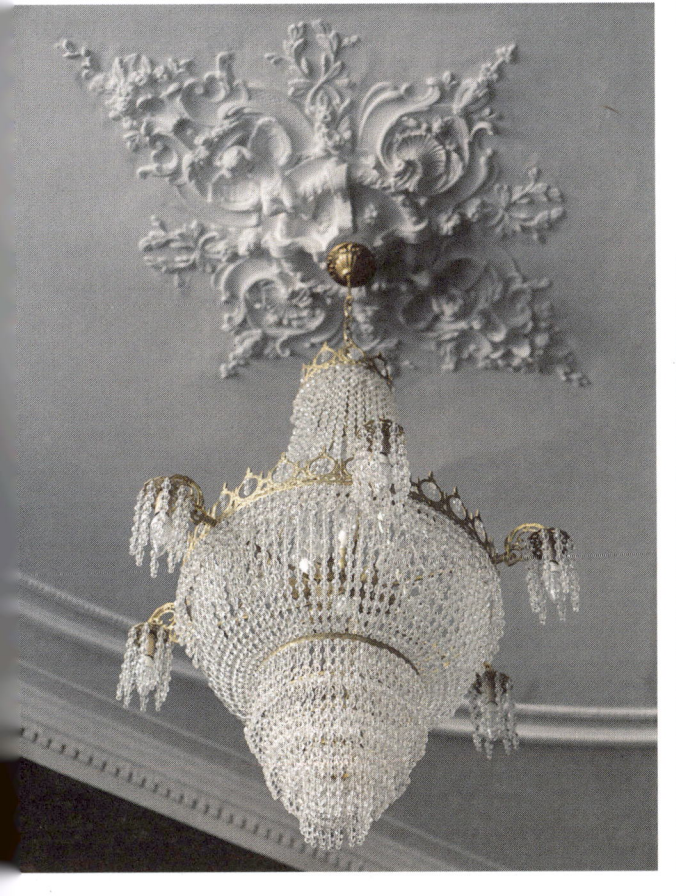
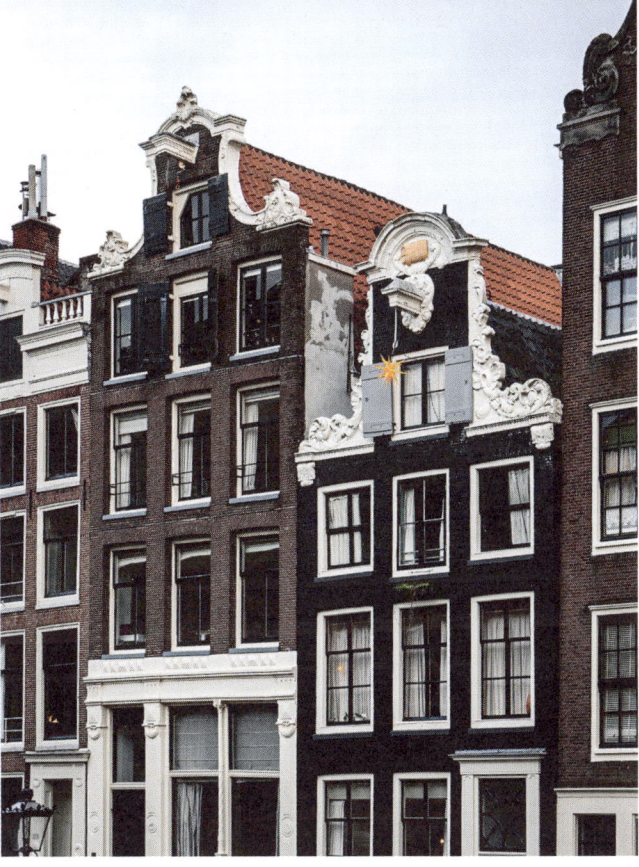

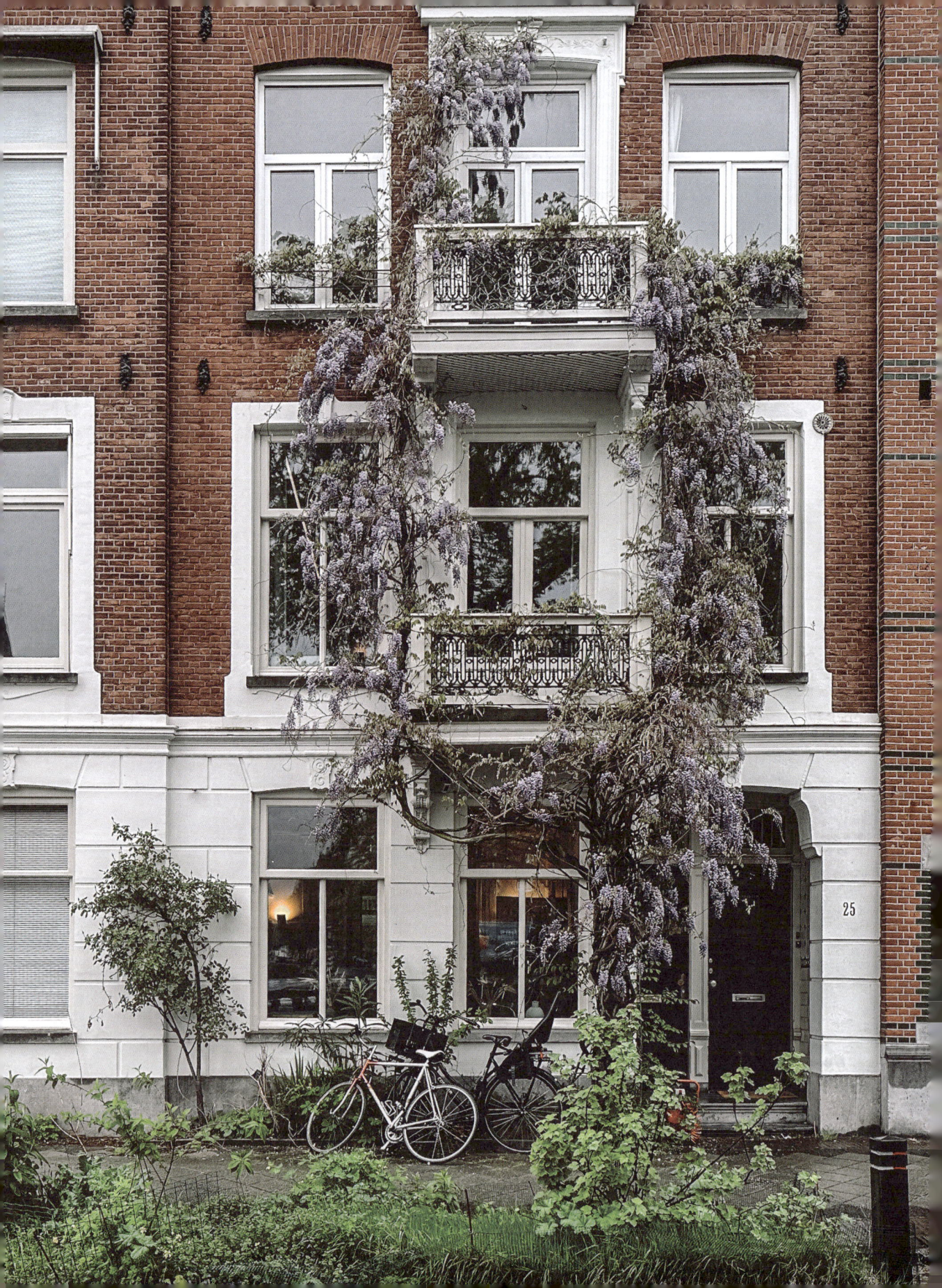

PART II

THROUGH THE HISTORY BOOKS

Amsterdam first presented itself in the thirteenth century as a small medieval settlement on boggy dykes on either side of the Amstel river, dammed to tame the floodwaters of the South Sea. In fact, the city's name derives from the Amstel dam. As part of a master plan for the city, and primarily to protect itself from flooding, Amsterdam was ringed by a defensive moat and bisected by a series of canals that provided a series of dry pockets of land on which to build. By the fourteenth century, the city had grown into a thriving port city, and in 1306 it was granted city rights by the bishop of Utrecht. By the seventeenth century, a time referred to as the Dutch Golden Age, Amsterdam was regarded as one of the world's most influential cities. Its prosperity was built on a booming naval and trading industry, particularly of spices, diamonds and textiles. This power also helped foster a rich cultural scene, with many philosophers, artists and writers calling the city home. By this time, the population had grown to almost 70,000 residents and with this growth came a demand for new land, which eventually gave way to further expansion beyond the Singel.

The first significant phase of this expansion occurred around 1612, to the west of the old city and into the area known as Jordaan, with the addition of three arcing parallel canals: the Herengracht (Gentlemen's Canal), Keizersgracht (Emperors' Canal) and Prinsengracht (Princes' Canal). Towards the end of the seventeenth century, by which time the population had more than doubled, the canals were expanded eastwards towards the Amstel river to complete the characteristic rings of concentric and radial canals that are so well known today. Beautiful gabled houses were packed into every inch of space along the canals, competing for water views. Whilst most look much the same today, they weren't always used in the same way; many were used as warehouses, with a special beam or pulley located in the attic that was used to hoist up valuable goods like cotton and spices. This city pocket, bounded by the Singelgracht, Brouwersgracht and the Amstel river, has been a UNESCO World Heritage Site since 2010.

Amsterdam covers an area of about 219.3sq. km. Often regarded as 'The Venice of the North', it has over 160 canals spanning around 75km (which, in fact, is twice that of Venice). The city is relatively flat, with no significant hills or mountains (hence all the cyclists). Amsterdam is divided into eight

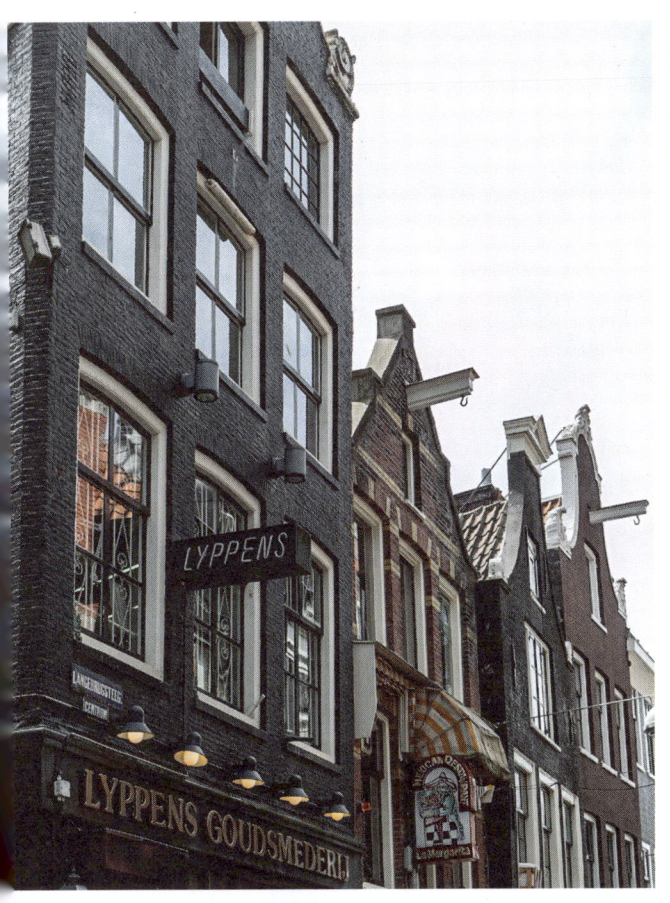
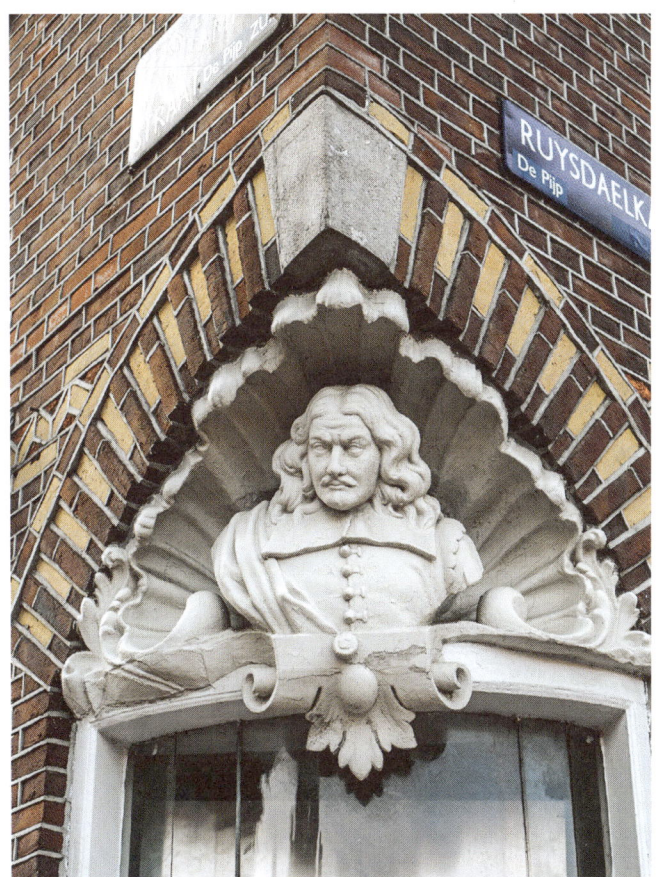
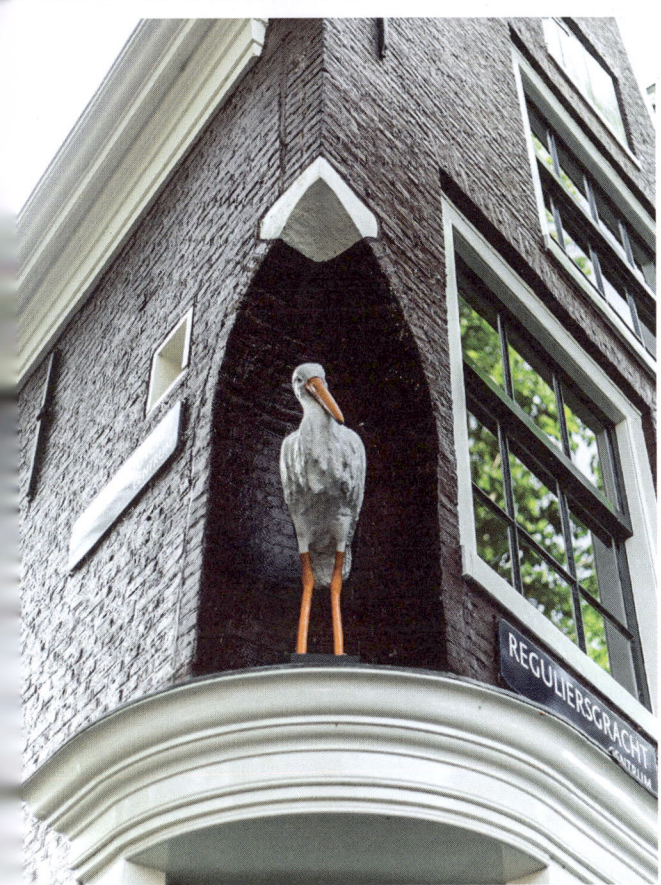
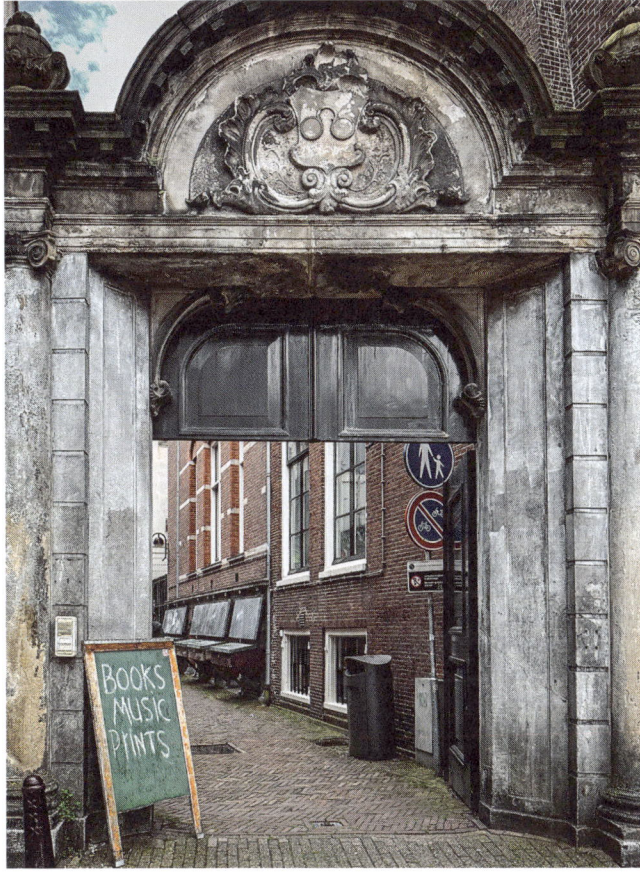

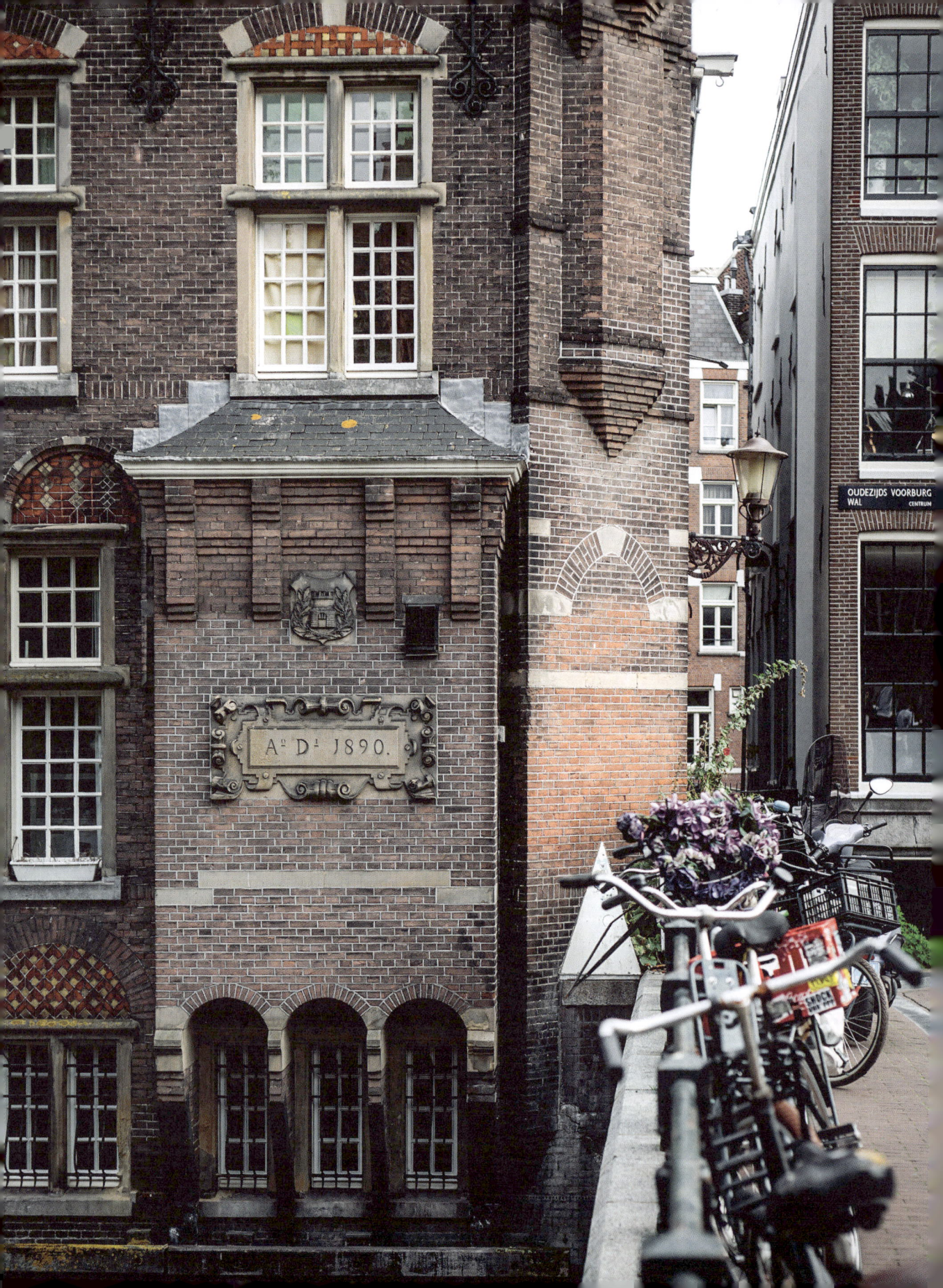

boroughs (*stadsdelen*), which are further divided into neighbourhoods: Centrum, Zuid, West, Oost, Noord, Nieuw-West, Zuidoost and Westport. Like most cosmopolitan cities, most of the neighbourhoods have their own distinctive character. As you make your way through the chapters you will see I have decided to include only the following districts: Central Canal Ring, Southern Canal Ring, Jordaan, De Pijp, Oud-West and Centrum (Oude Zijde and Nieuwe Zijde). Like the other books in the series, you will also discover that the neighbourhoods section isn't always broken down by official district but instead clustered by how I think it best to explore the area; each chapter contains an organised plan to help you make the best of your trip. You will also note that some sections spill over into several neighbourhoods, and others concentrate on just one. Providing an overview of the neighbourhoods covered in the book might be helpful, highlighting their significant icons and sharing a hint of the gems I discovered.

I got lost quite often in Amsterdam, especially in the old centre and the canal district, where waterways and paths blend into confusion, so having a little information on the layout of the critical areas of focus in the book can be helpful.

Medieval Centrum (the Old Centre): as the name suggests, this is the city's oldest quarter and is remarkably preserved. Its overall layout has mostly stayed the same since the Golden Age. It is the innermost district of Amsterdam and is a tangled maze of canals and narrow streets. Most guides are divided into the Nieuwe Zijde (New Side) on the left bank and the Oude Zijde (Old Side) on the right, separated by Damrak (the famous dancing gingerbread houses) and Rokin. I have decided to do the same.

The Nieuwe Zijde is best known for its hotels, shopping streets (Kalverstraat and Nieuwendijk), restaurants and cafes. It can get hectic, but my discerning edit will help you navigate the chaotic streets to find the charming gems of the neighbourhood. Enclaves such as Paleisstraat, Spui Square and Begijnhof provide a quiet refuge from the bustle. Walks along the Singel and around Spui to uncover the many hidden gems are amongst the many highlights of this section.

The Oude Zijde is located east of the historic centre, bounded by Prins Hendrikkade, Oudeschans and Zwanenburgwal, the Amstel river, Rokin and

Damrak. It is known for its picturesque canals, narrow streets and historic buildings. The neighbourhood is home to the famous red-light district (De Wallen) neighbourhood. It also houses several historic landmarks like the Oude Kerk (Old Church) and the Amsterdam Museum. In theory, it should not feature in my book – its crowds should be enough to deter me – but I did find some of the most beautiful and quaint places hiding in plain sight. I recommend exploring it when it is quiet, early morning, before the crowds descend.

Grachtengordel (the Canal Belt): this refers explicitly to the historic canal district in Amsterdam. It is a UNESCO World Heritage Site characterised by its concentric rings of canals, with four main canals forming semi-circular rings around the city centre. The Keizersgracht (Emperors' Canal) and Herengracht (Lords' Canal) lie between Singel and Prinsengracht. The Central Canal Ring is loved worldwide for its crisscrossing waterways, picturesque bridges, gabled canal houses, iconic humpback bridges and an inimitable charming atmosphere. It is one of the most well-preserved examples of urban planning from the seventeenth century.

My book, like most guidebooks, divides the canal belt into two:

Central Canal Ring: located between the IJ and Amstel, and the Singelgracht, Herengracht, Keizersgracht and Prinsengracht. It also incorporates the quaint enclave known as The 9 Streets (De 9 Straatjes) – a rectangle of nine tiny streets filled with vintage stores, designer boutiques and great food spots. It borders Jordaan and is one of the most loved areas of my book, thanks to its romantic air and cosy ambience.

Southern Canal Ring: known for its beautiful architecture, picturesque canal houses and historic buildings (the Anne Frank House being the most famous). The Singel canal and the Amstel river define this pocket. Bloemenmarkt, with its floating flower vendors, the Museumkwartier and the Spiegelkwartier are also covered here.

Jordaan: borders the Central Canal Ring and dates back to the early seventeenth century when its marshy farming lands were developed to house the working class and immigrants. Today, it is best known for its bohemian spirit, historic buildings, narrow streets, outdoor markets and picturesque canals. It is also here you will find Anne Frank House and Westerkerk, on its edges on the banks of Prinsengracht. Jordaan has a rich cultural and artistic history, and is brimming with many art galleries, boutiques, cafes and restaurants. It is a popular destination for locals and tourists, and offers a vibrant atmosphere with a mix of traditional and trendy establishments. Its official boundaries consist of the Prinsengracht to the east, the Lijnbaansgracht to the west, Brouwersgracht to the north and Leidsegracht to the south. This chapter will include the area just north of Brouwersgracht, including Haarlemmer and Prinseneiland.

De Pijp: located south of the canal belt. Formerly a working-class quarter built to help a 'bursting at the seams' Jordaan, today it has a very similar bohemian atmosphere. A diverse and vibrant area with a mix of cultures, offering a variety of ethnic food, stylish bars, the Albert Cuyp Markt and the Sarphatipark.

Oud-West: a residential neighbourhood close to Jordaan and Museumplein, which was created and developed for the working classes in the last quarter of the nineteenth century, with beautiful architecture, a culinary centre (Foodhallen), popular streets like De Clercqstraat and Kinkerstraat, and the vibrant Vondelpark.

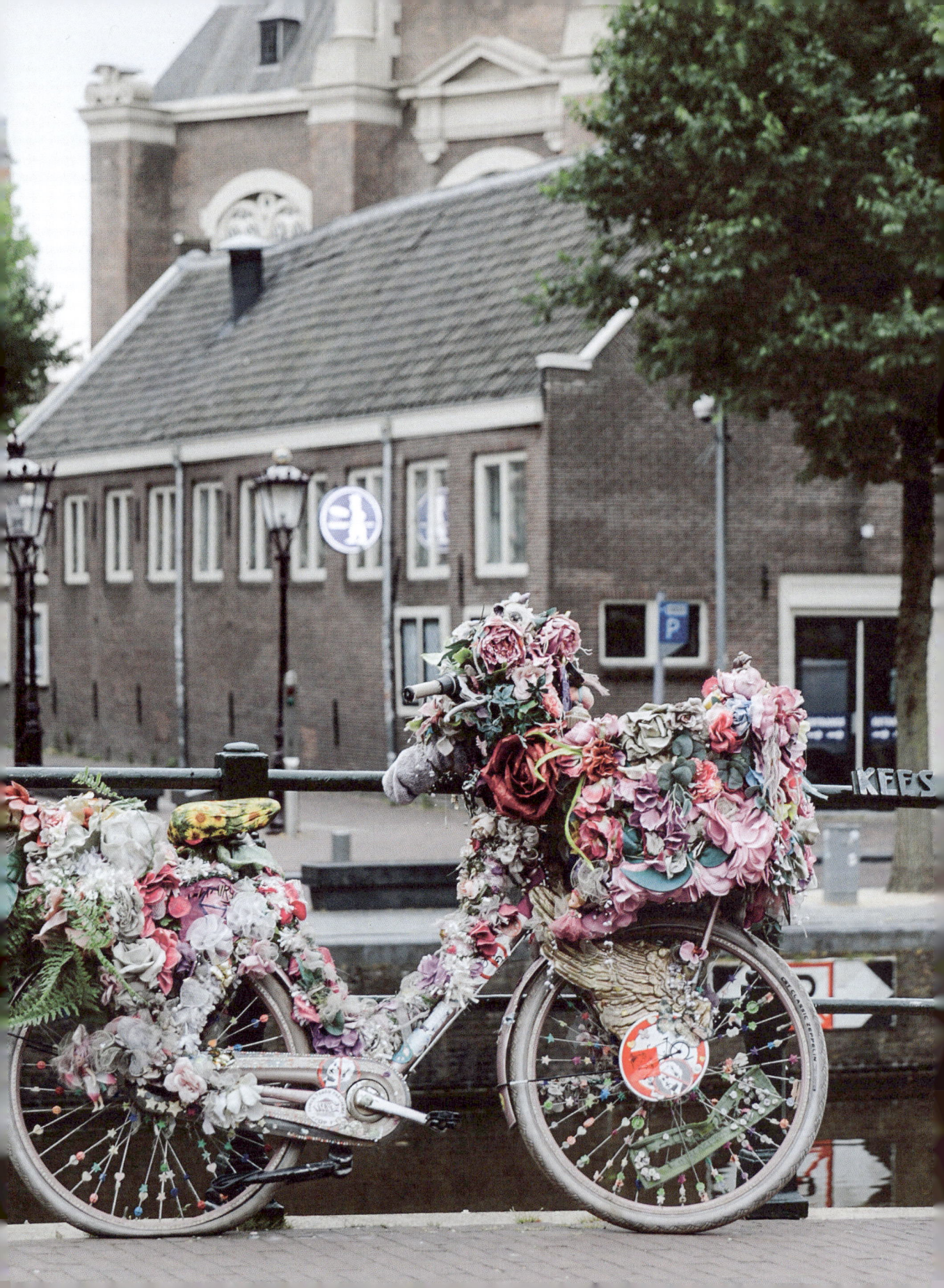

PART III

NEIGHBOURHOODS

CENTRAL CANAL RING

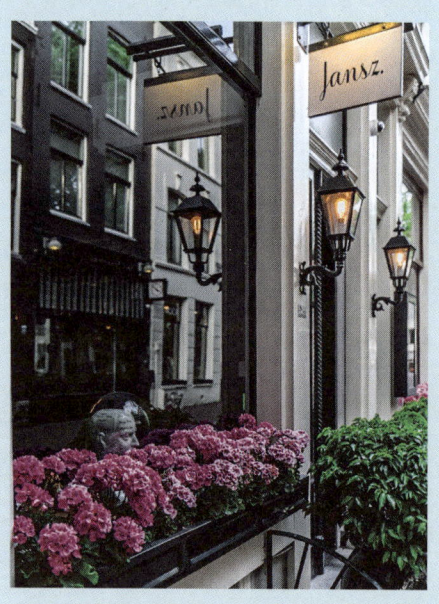

ONE HALF OF THE UNESCO WORLD HERITAGE SITE;
A MAZE OF COBBLED ROADS WITH GABLED CANAL
HOUSES AND HUMPBACK BRIDGES; HOME TO THE
FAMOUS 9 STREETS

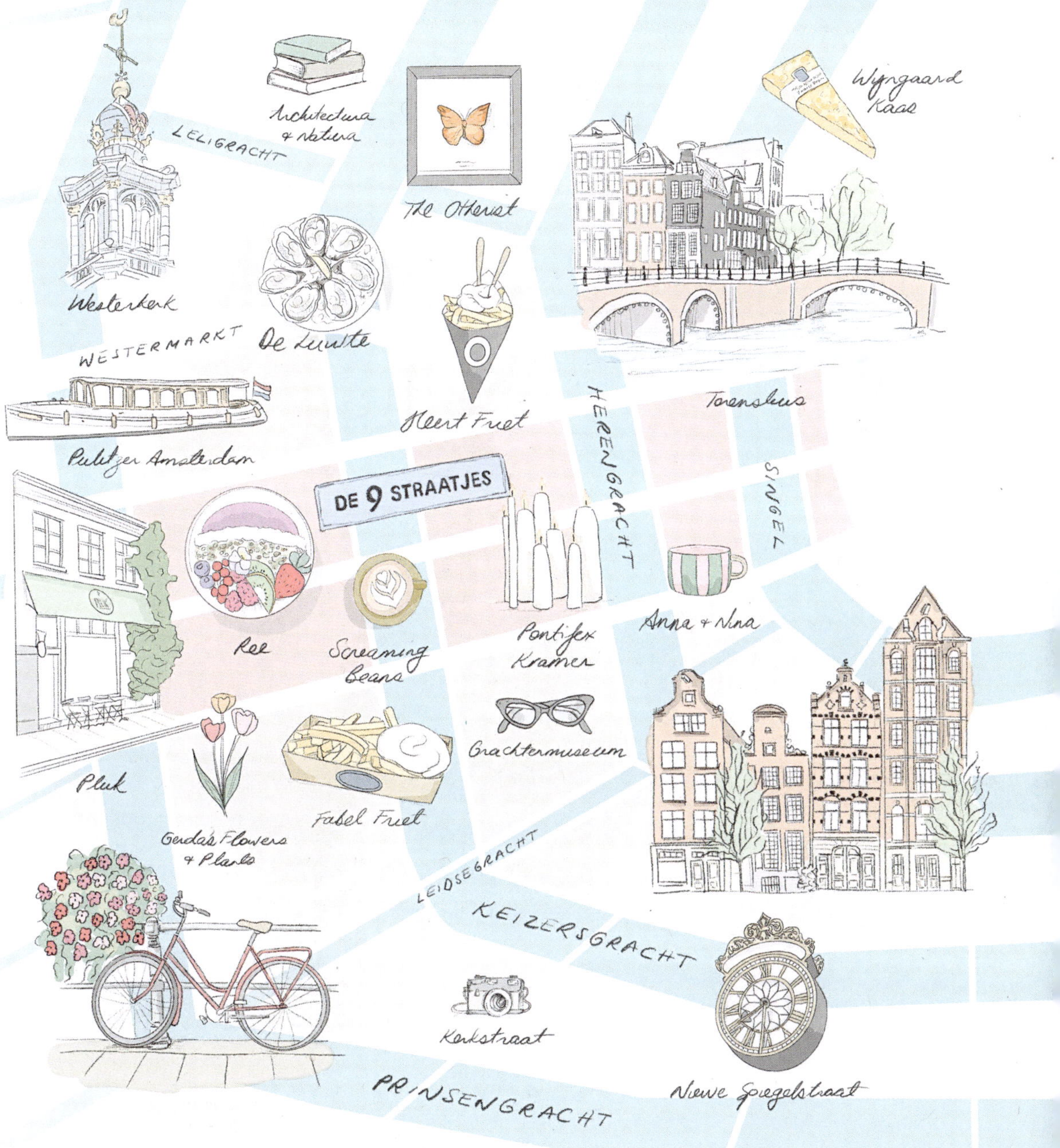

CENTRAL CANAL RING

#prettycityamsterdam

ANNA + NINA Herengracht 369
THE OTHERIST Leliegracht 6
PONTIFEX KRAMER Reestraat 20
WIJNGAARD KAAS Singel 182

PLUK Berenstraat 19
REE 7 Reestraat 7
SCREAMING BEANS Runstraat 6

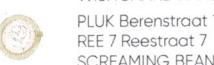
DE LUWTE Leliegracht 26-28
HEERTJE FRIET Herengracht 169
FABEL FRIET Runstraat 1

De 9 Straatjes, Herengracht, Keizersgracht, Kerkstraat, Leidsegracht, Leliegracht, Nieuwe Spiegelstraat, Prinsengracht, Torensluis, Westerkerk

ARCHITECTURA & NATURA Leliegracht 22H

GERDA'S FLOWERS AND PLANTS Runstraat 16

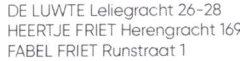
GRACHTENMUSEUM Herengracht 386

PULITZER AMSTERDAM Prinsengracht 323

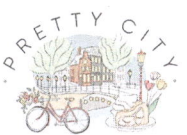

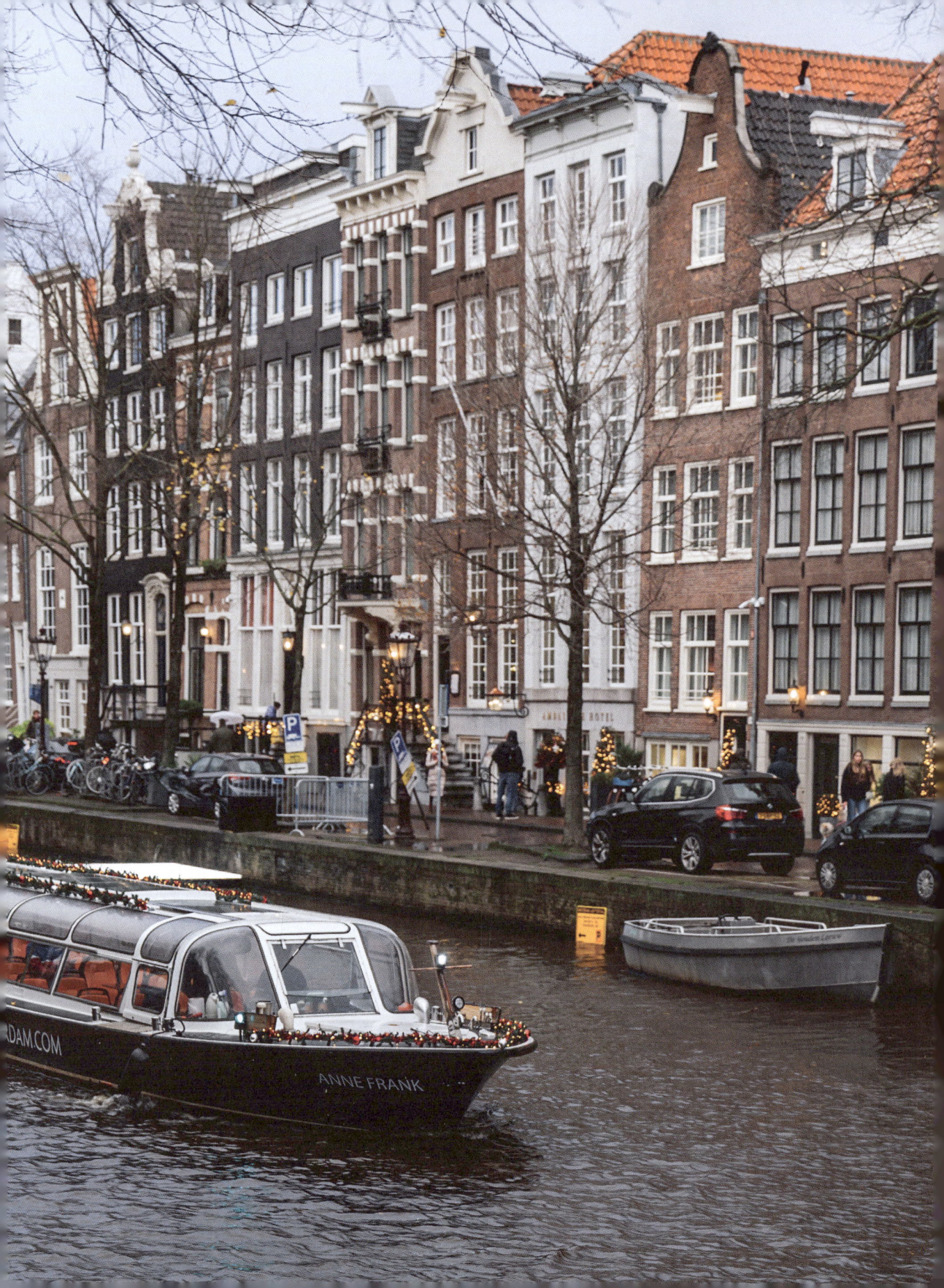

THE CANAL BELT (GRACHTENGORDEL)

Amsterdam is often regarded as the 'Venice of the Low Countries', and it's no wonder, as this beautiful city has hundreds of canals, moats and other urban waterways, but none are as famous as the Grachtengordel. You may have heard the term 'Grachtengordel', even if you have never been to Amsterdam: it refers to the fan-shaped canal area enclosing the old city centre. This most beautiful pocket – the city's defining characteristic – is over 400 years old, took over 100 years to build and was declared a UNESCO World Heritage Site in 2010. A maze of cobbled roads connects more than 1,200 bridges that elegantly arch over almost 100 canals. The heritage site covers the area between Brouwersgracht and the Amstel river and features four main canals: Singelgracht, Herengracht, Keizersgracht and Prinsengracht. These canals, along with the smaller connecting canals, form a semi-circle around the city centre.

The Canal Belt is divided into two parts by the Leidsegracht: the western canal belt runs to Brouwersgracht, while the southern runs to the Amstel river. Each is lined with beautiful historic warehouses and merchant houses, which are exquisite remnants of the city's prosperous past and integral to its architectural heritage. The canals were constructed as a way to manage the citys growing population and as a means to transport goods and people. The houses that line the canals were built by wealthy merchants who wanted to showcase their prosperity and status within the city. Due to the limited width of the canal-front plots, the houses were constructed as tall, narrow structures, typically consisting of several storeys, a gabled facade and ornate decorations. The buildings were made using a combination of brick and wood, with intricate details and carvings adorning the facades. One notable feature of these houses is big, narrow windows; another is their stepped gables, which were used to maximise the available space within the little plots of land on which they were built. The gables often feature intricate designs and sculptures, emphasising the wealth and prestige of the house owners. They also include a pulley outside to transport goods (once spices and now likely furniture) to the upper floors.

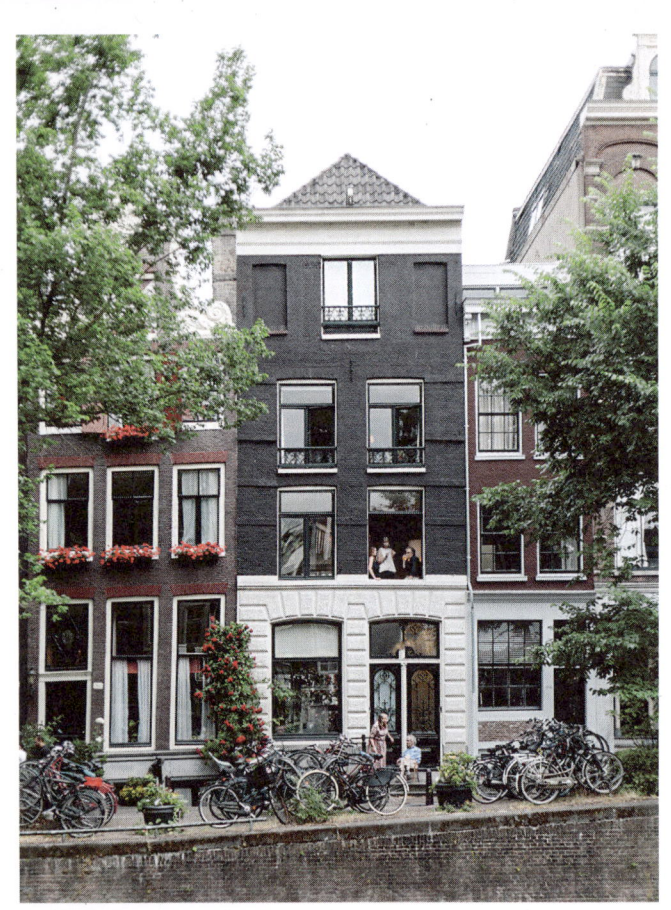
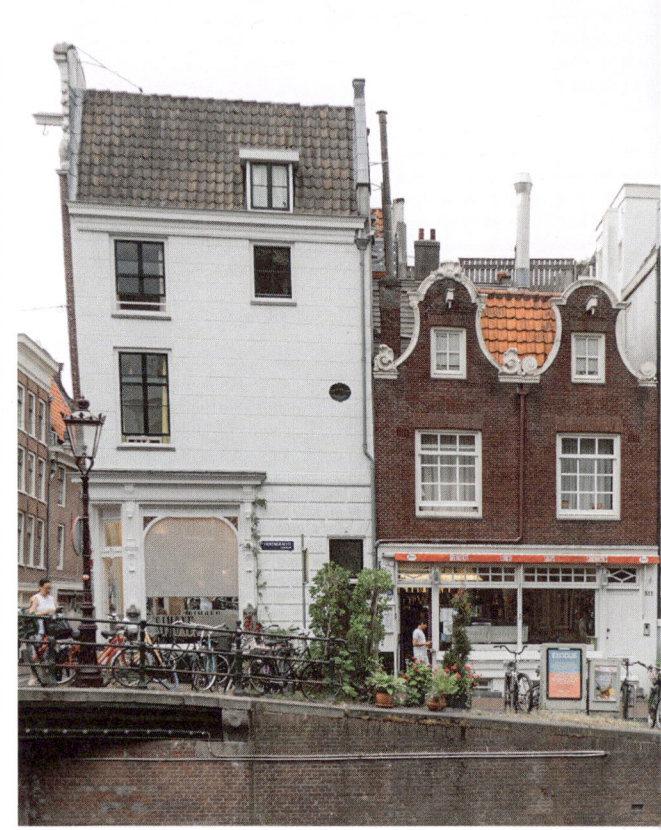
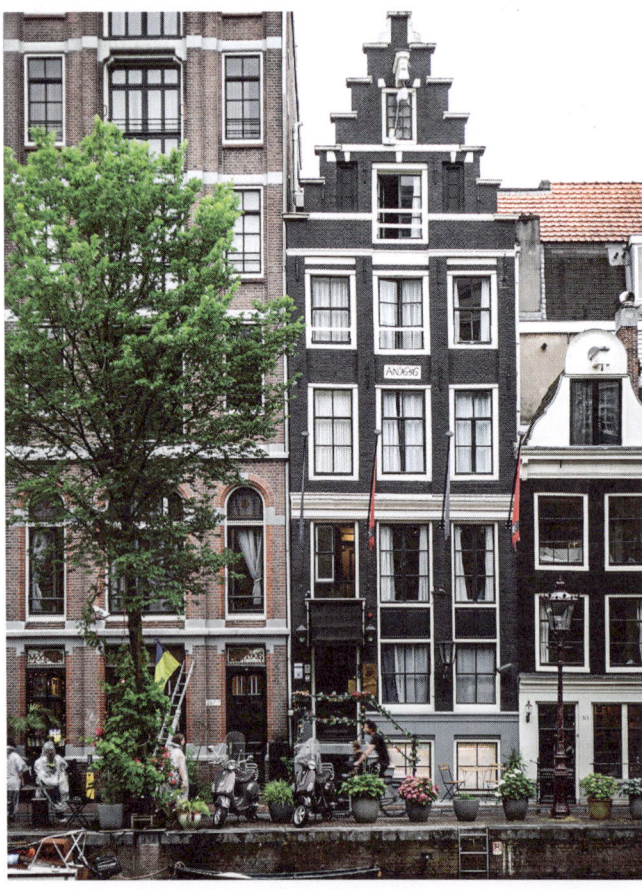
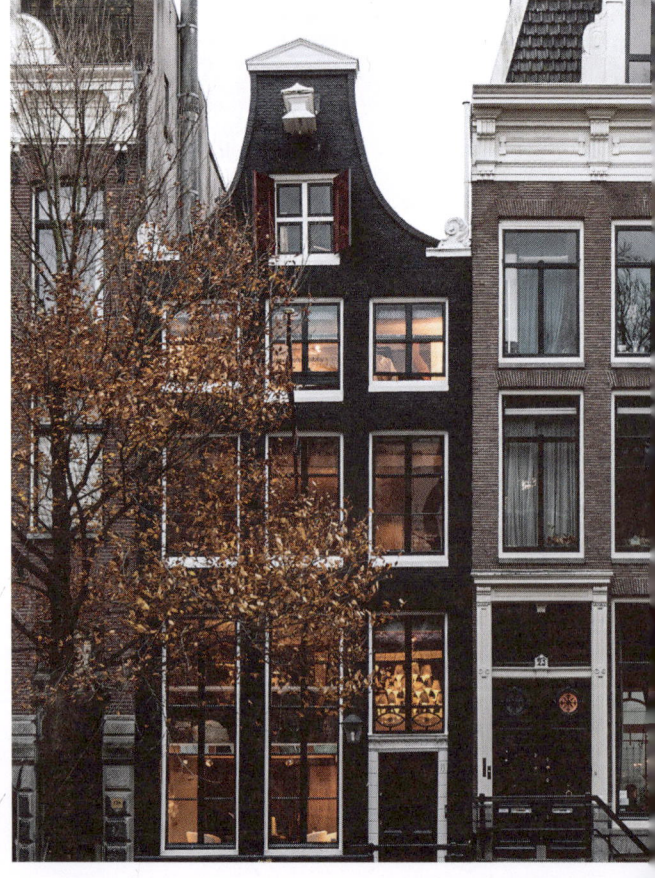

The houses were designed to accommodate the merchants' living quarters and businesses. The ground floor typically served as a shop or a warehouse, while the upper floors contained bedrooms, living areas and entertaining spaces.

Today, many Amsterdam merchants' houses have been converted into museums or office spaces, while some are still privately owned and preserved as historical landmarks. They offer a glimpse into the city's rich trading history and are a popular tourist attraction in Amsterdam. Notable examples include the Museum Van Loon, the Willet-Holthuysen Museum and Amsterdam's famous Canal Ring area.

This neighbourhood's most famous building is undoubtedly the Anne Frank House, but the area is also flanked by The 9 Streets: a charming cluster of nine streets, once the centre of the leather trade, and now brimming with one-off boutiques and great little cafes.

CENTRAL CANAL RING

The extension of Amsterdam's three main canals continued from the early seventeenth century, as the merchant class, wealthy from booming maritime trade, sought to escape the overcrowding and, indeed, squalor in the old city around the Amstel. The nucleus of the area lies along the Singelgracht, Keizersgracht, Herengracht and Prinsengracht. The striking gabled houses, tall and skinny, witnessed the city's enrichment through maritime trade, science and art during the Golden Age.

The eastern border of the Central Canal Ring goes slightly beyond the Singel canal; the western border is Prinsengracht; the northern border is around Leliegracht; and the Amstel river is its southern edge. Much of its appeal lies in its historic, gabled canal houses and mansions, as well as The 9 Streets (De 9 Straatjes) and the landmark Anne Frank House.

The four major canals in Amsterdam are:

Herengracht: The 'Gentlemen's Canal' is the innermost and most prestigious of the four canals. It is surrounded by opulent merchant houses, mansions and official buildings.

Keizersgracht: The 'Emperors' Canal' is the middle of the four canals. Keizersgracht features stunning architecture, tree-lined streets and numerous historical landmarks.

Prinsengracht: The 'Princes' Canal' is the longest and outermost of the four canals. Prinsengracht is famous for the Anne Frank House and numerous cultural institutions. It is my favourite canal in Amsterdam.

Singelgracht: Originally a city moat and the network's oldest canal, it was initially the primary route for all trade vessels coming and going from Amsterdam. It became the innermost channel after the expansion of the city. Singel is known for its charming houseboats, beautiful canal houses and floating flower market.

This side of the Canal Belt is compact but brimming with many beautiful places to explore. It is made for wandering and meandering. I felt a guided walk might feel restrictive so, instead, I will list my favourite discoveries:

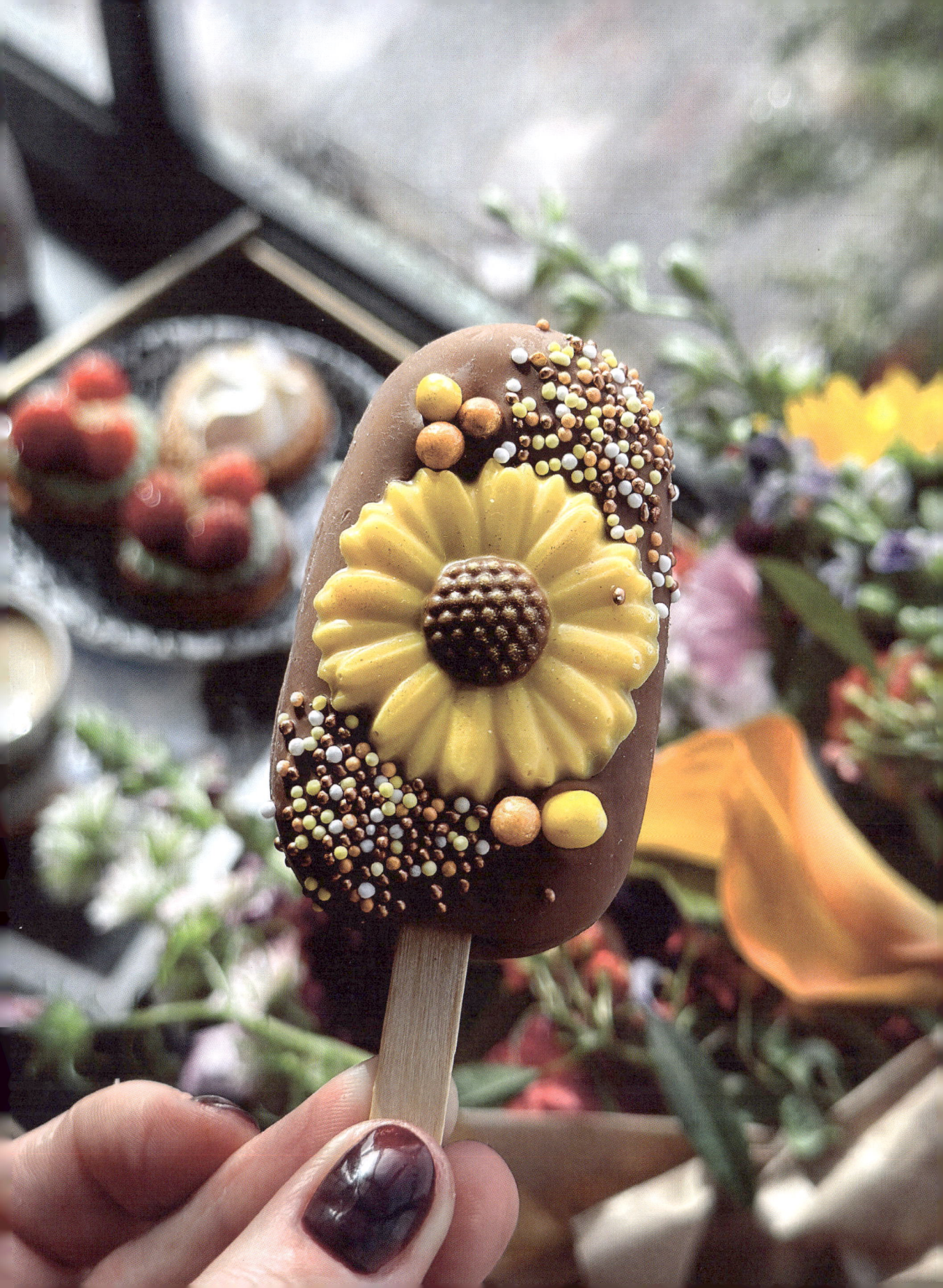

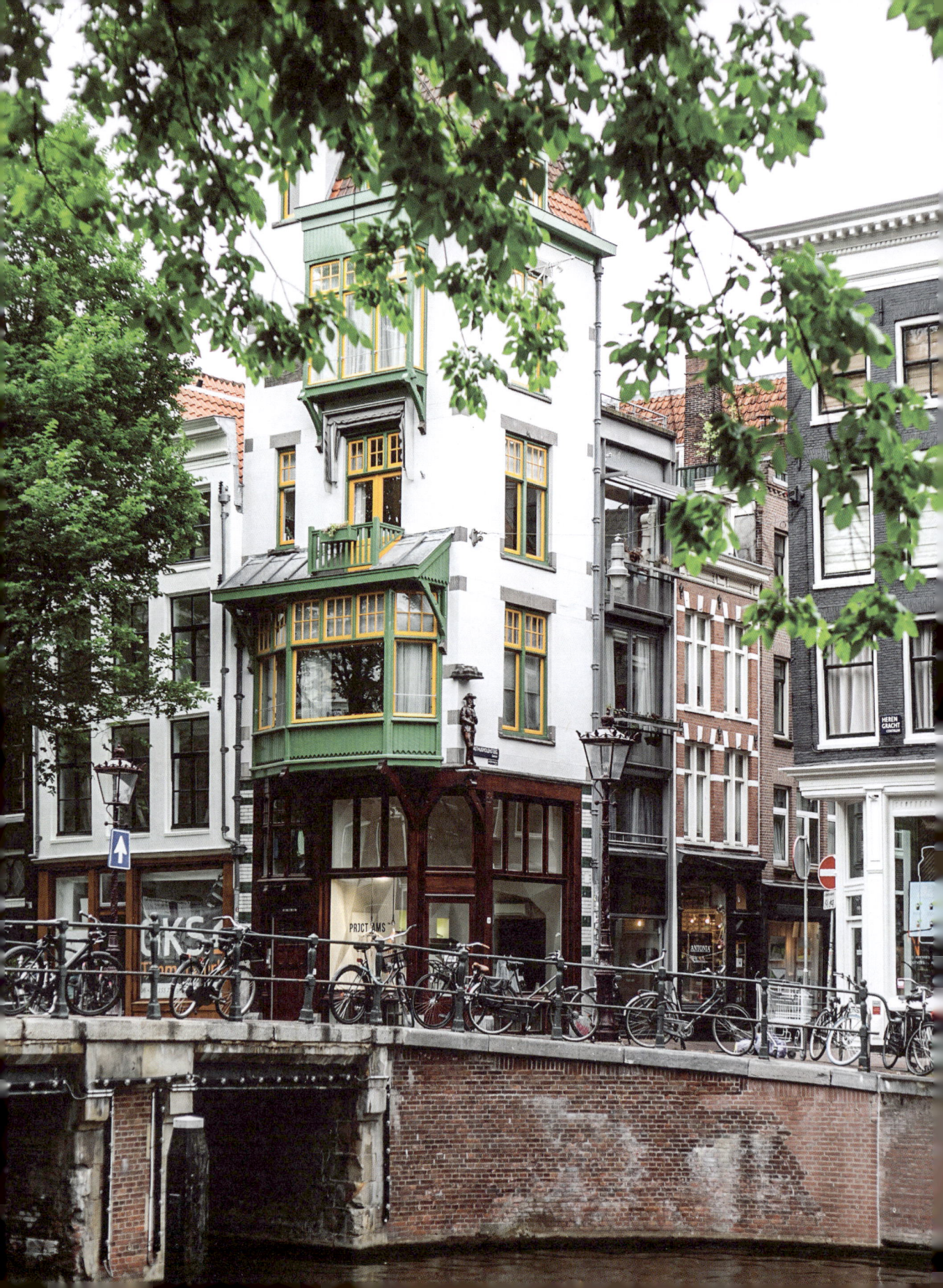

THE 9 STREETS (DE 9 STRAATJES)

The 9 Streets (De 9 Straatjes) neighbourhood is a famous shopping district offering a unique blend of international brands and local businesses. An inimitable atmosphere permeates the quaint streets, lined with independent one-off shops, hidden cafes, hotspot restaurants, bars and galleries, making it a great place to explore, shop and relax.

It is named after its nine narrow streets, which include: Hartenstraat (Hearts Street), Gasthuismolensteeg (Guest House Mill Alley), Reestraat (Roe Deer Street), Wijde Heisteeg (Wide Heath Street), Wolvenstraat (Wolf Street), Berenstraat (Bear Street), Oude Spiegelstraat (Old Mirror Street), Runstraat (Cow Street) and Huidenstraat (Skins Street).

The more prominent streets, namely Reestraat, Berenstraat, Wolvenstraat, Runstraat and Huidenstraat refer to the trade in animal skin for the leather industry. They offer a great insight into all the architectural styles of Amsterdam, with most buildings dating back to the Golden Age. From antique to contemporary, from Old Dutch to ethnic, the area is brimming with unique artisanal shops and cafes.

ADDRESSES OF NOTE

Jansz., **Reestraat 8**
Located within the leading five-star hotel Pulitzer Amsterdam, Jansz. is a beautiful, modern, Dutch all-day dining restaurant serving lunch and dinner. Housed in a seventeenth-century pharmacy, Jansz. embodies the lifestyle of seventeenth-century craftsman Volkert Jansz., who embraced the finer things in life but believed that decadence and luxury were most enjoyable when shared. Complete with a cosy atmosphere and a great menu, you can enjoy oysters, tartare and the scallops to die for. Don't leave without trying the chocolate cake with caramel. Ask for a window overlooking Keizersgracht or Reestraat.

Pluk and *Pluk Amsterdam*, **Reestraat 19 and Berenstraat 19**
Pluk and its sister, Pluk Amsterdam, are popular and healthy cafes and concept stores in the heart of The 9 Streets, founded by Iris and Tessa Zeilstra. Alongside their locally sourced seasonal menu, they offer a delicious selection of sweet treats. Downstairs, you will find various stylish home and lifestyle products on sale; upstairs, you can enjoy your meal in the most atmospheric setting. These fun and laid-back cafes and concept stores are big on style but small in size, but don't worry if you can't get a table: they have another sister cafe a stone's throw away, on Leliegracht, called Brasserie De Luwte.

Across the street from the entrance to Jansz., at number 7, is Ree7. This is a bustling little cafe, with the prettiest facade and interiors, owned by the folk behind Pluk and De Luwte. It has a similar offering and atmosphere but with an added special: the Freakshake.

Anna + Nina, **Herengracht 369**
When it comes to concept shops in Amsterdam, Anna + Nina really is one of the best. This one, in the middle of The 9 Streets, offers a smaller product selection than its sister boutique in De Pijp. It was founded in 2012 by Anna de Lanoy Meijer and Nina Poot, inspired by their shared travels to exotic places. They offer a curated home decor collection, jewellery, accessories and gifts. Their shared love of nature, film and art weaves itself into all of their designs, and their stores are much loved for their eclectic and bohemian aesthetic. Anna + Nina also has an online store, allowing customers worldwide to shop for unique products.

Screaming Beans, **Runstraat 6**
Opened here in 2018 as its flagship, Screaming Beans now has several locations in Amsterdam. All locations are well regarded for their impeccable coffee and friendly service.

In addition to their coffee offerings, Screaming Beans has a selection of pastries and light bites to accompany your drink. Whether you're stopping by for a quick caffeine boost or looking to sit down and enjoy a leisurely coffee, the skilled staff at Screaming Beans are sure to find the best coffee blend to match your requirements.

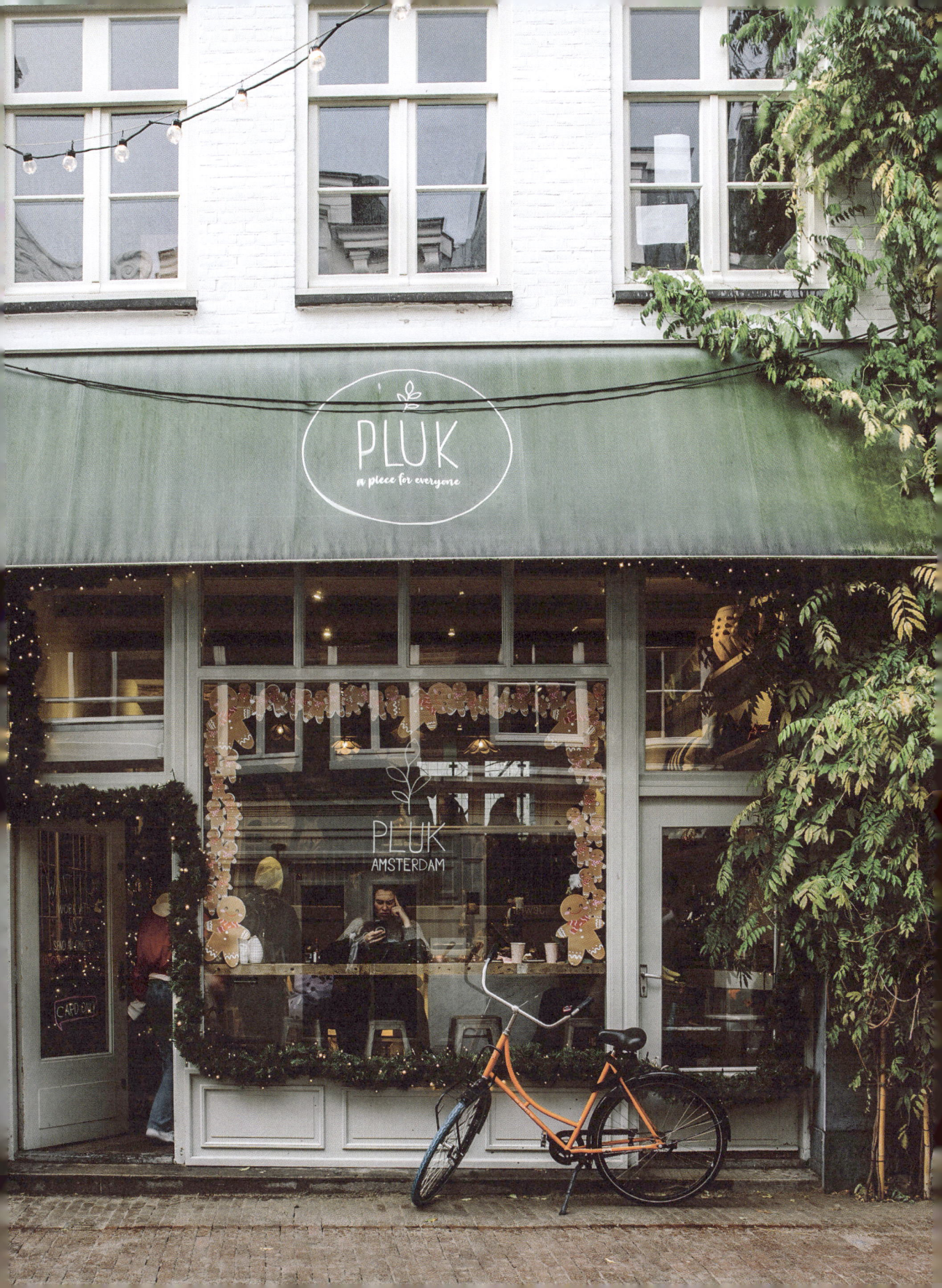

Pontifex_Kramer, **Reestraat 20**
Further along, at number 20, you will find a shop like no other. Broken dolls are brought back to life by Mr Kramer, a doctor for antique teddies and dolls who has practised here for several decades. Under the same roof, Pontifex is a traditional Dutch candle shop specialising in ritual and spiritual candles, incense sticks, resin incense and special scented oils.

Fabel Friet, **Runstraat 1**
Here the speciality is fries with freshly grated Parmesan cheese and truffle mayonnaise. Join the queue and savour your crispy fries by the canal.

Gerda's Bloemen en Planten, **Runstraat 16**
A magical florist with beautiful blooms spilling out on to the pavement. In addition to providing all the flowers for the Grachten Festival, they also offer an extensive selection of floral services, covering almost any occasion.

Café de Pels, **Huidenstraat 25**
Café de Pels, nestled in The 9 Streets, has been a concept in the city for over fifty years. It is still as popular as ever with locals and tourists alike. You could be forgiven for missing its unforgettable bland exterior, but that would be a real shame. The interior is characterised by exquisite simplicity: wooden floors and panelling; a curved metal counter; low-hanging, frosted pendant lights; and walls decorated with local artwork donated by patrons. They also have a bulging rack full of papers from all over the world and – the best bit – a big communal table in the window. Go for the renowned beer or two; if you are feeling peckish, you could order a toastie or bitterballen.

Marie-Stella-Maris, **Keizersgracht 357**
You will find the Marie-Stella-Maris flagship store on the corner of Keizersgracht and Huidenstraat. The impressive cinema light-box wall bears witness to the full range of 120 products; step in to try the broad range for yourself. The collection includes candles and fragrances as well as oils, soaps, and skin and hair products. If you decide to buy, it's nice to know that they contribute a fixed amount towards clean drinking-water projects for every purchase.

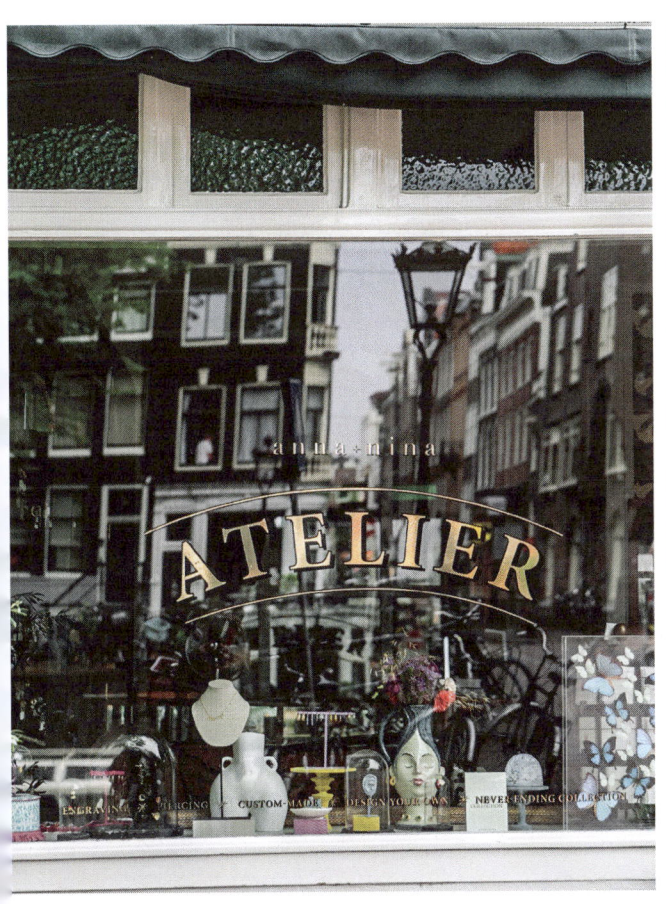
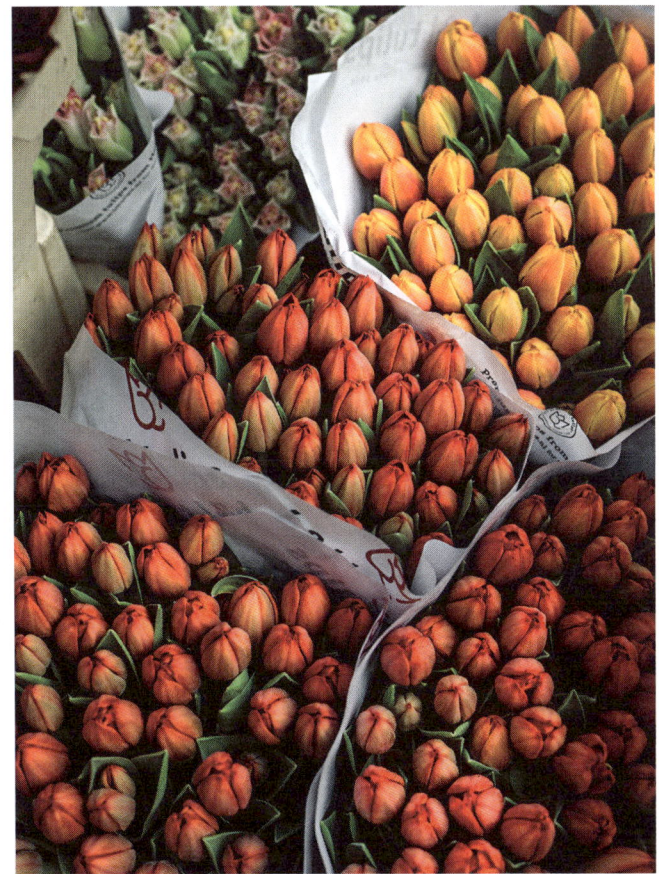
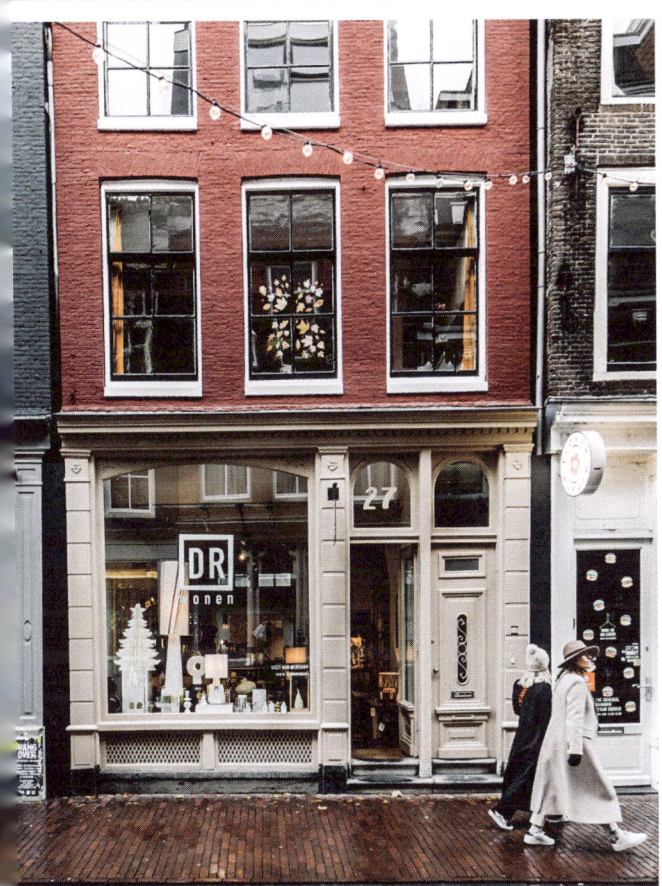
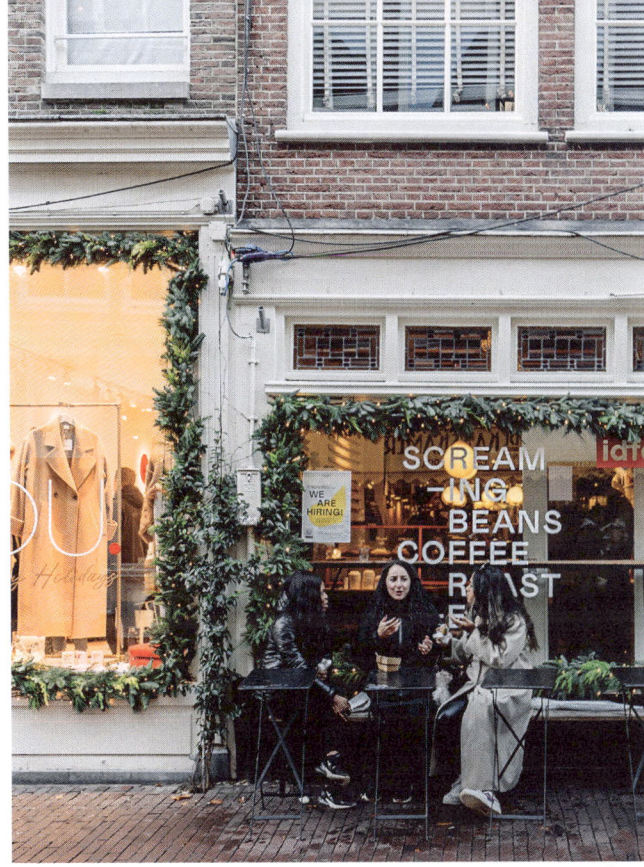

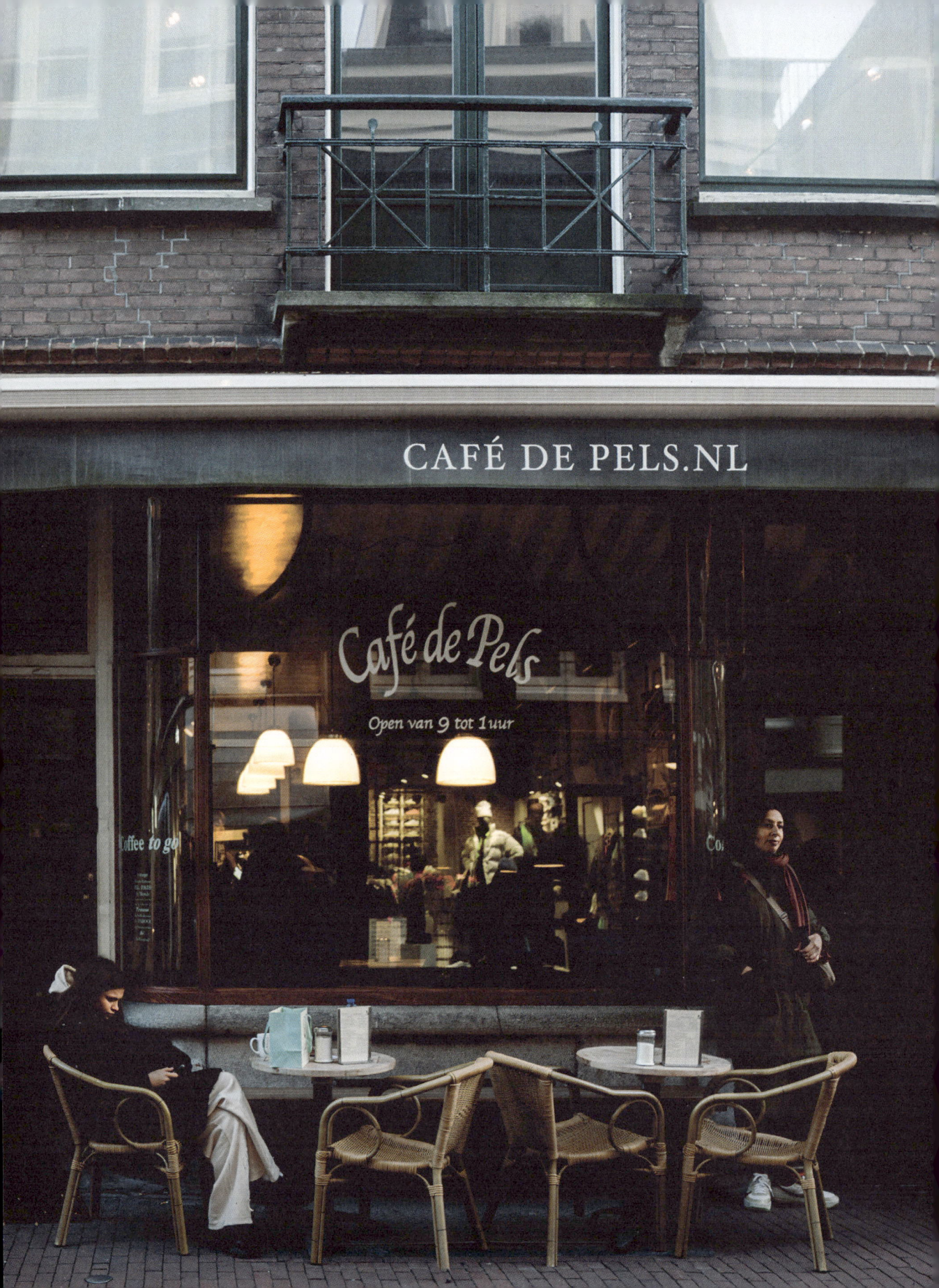

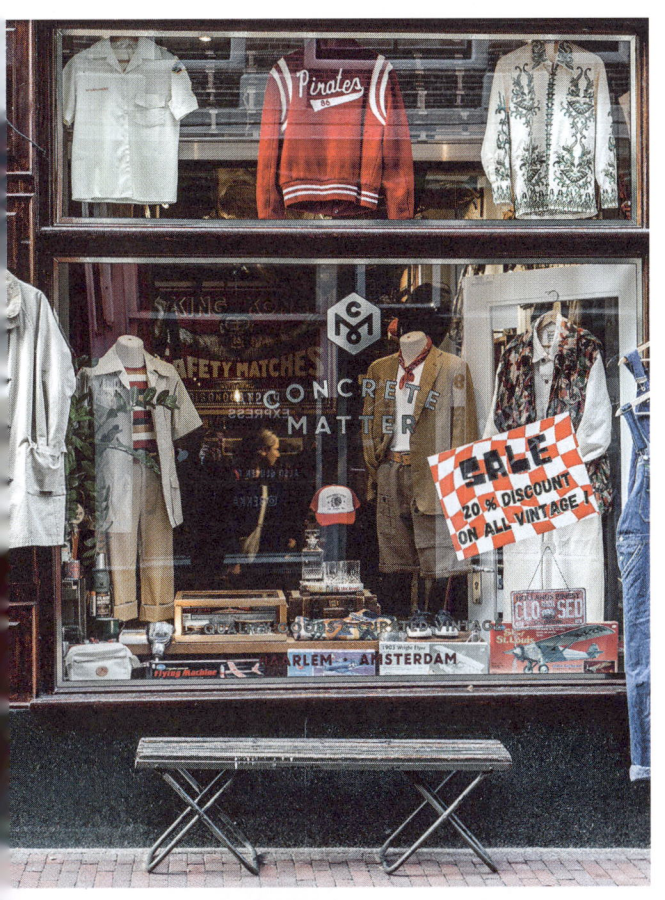
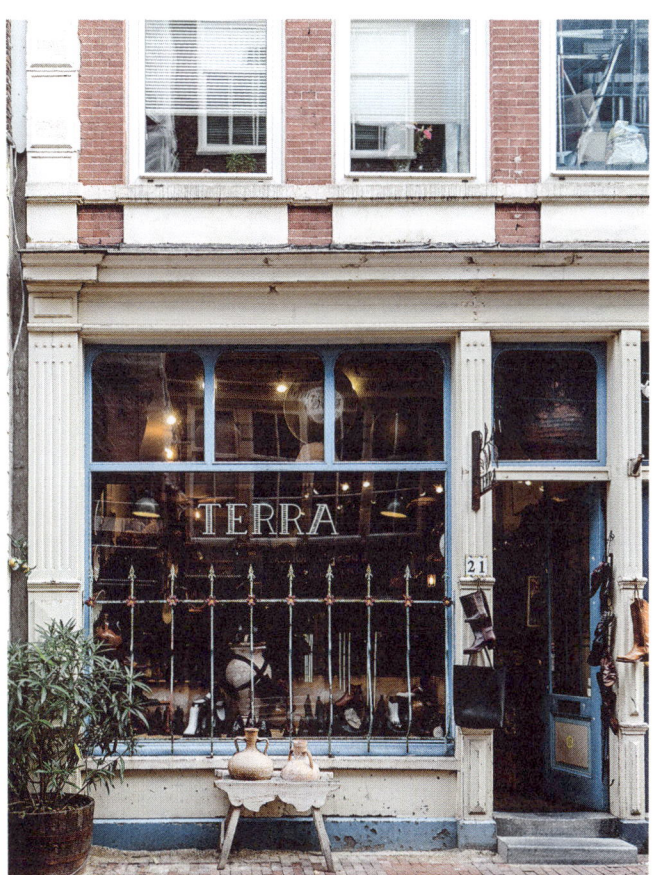
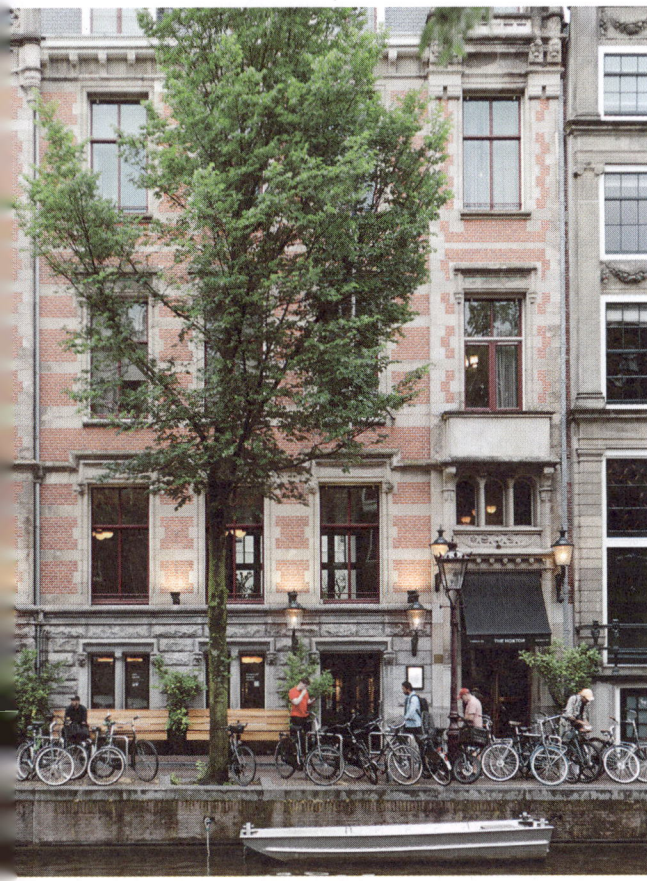
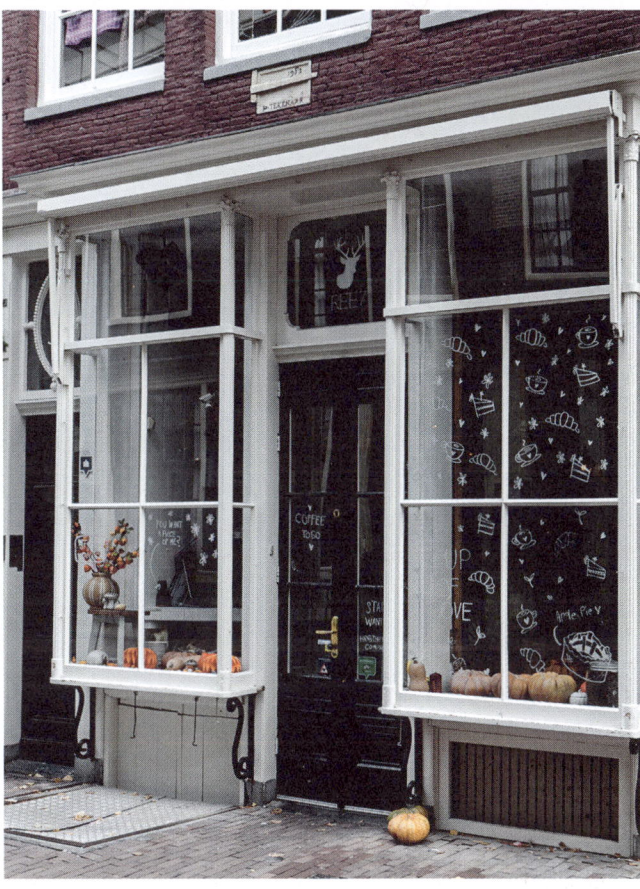

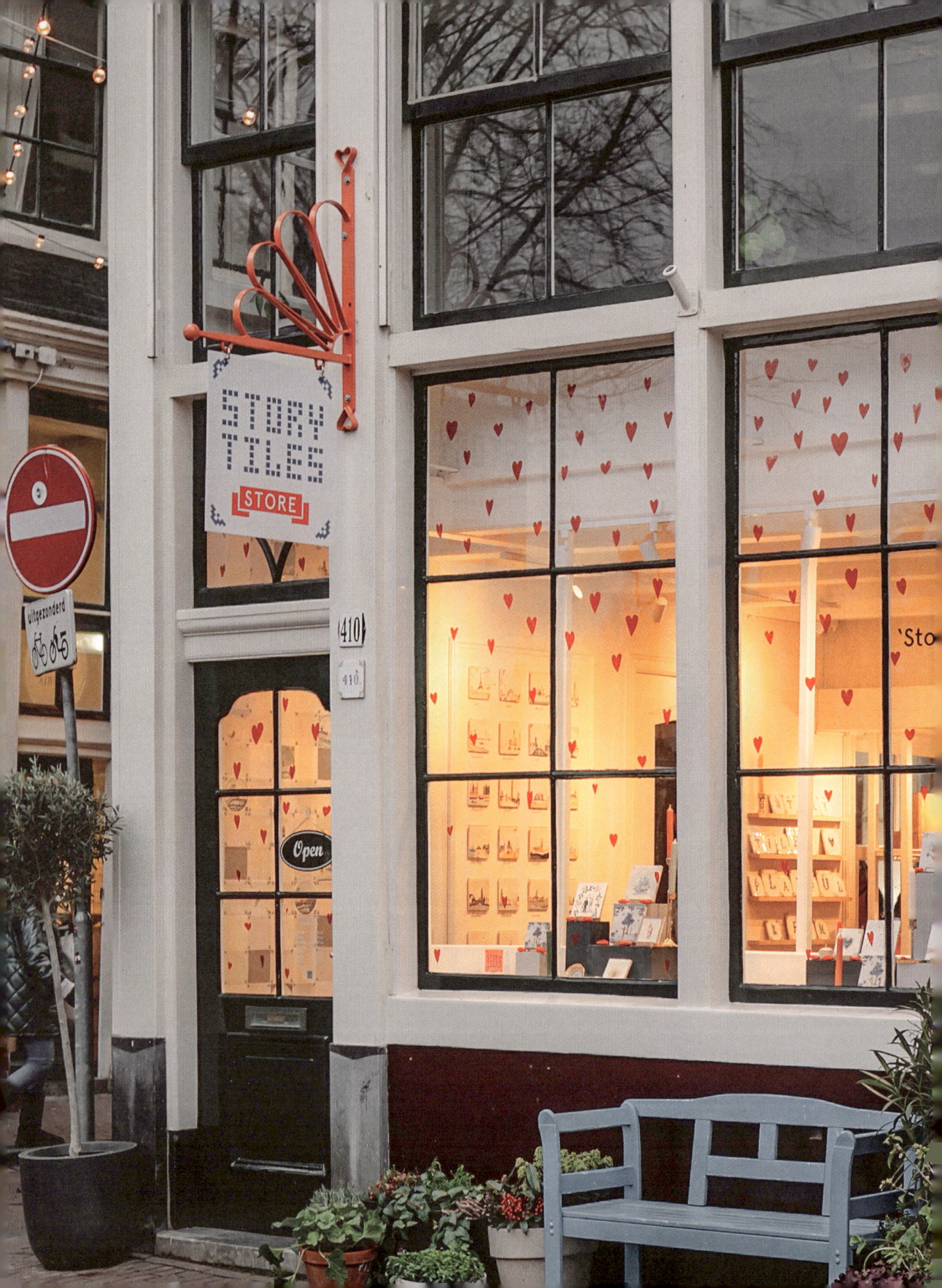

Diptyque Boutique Amsterdam, **Prinsengracht 531**
Founded in Paris in the early 1960s by three artistic friends, this cult brand is famous for its scented candles, perfumes and home fragrances. It has a beautiful, light-filled corner home on Prinsengracht.

Arden Art Gallery, **Prinsengracht 529**
Individual aerial and architectural photography by acclaimed photographer Arden is on display and for sale from his brick-and-mortar studio in The 9 Streets.

StoryTiles, **Singel 410**
StoryTiles is a small, independent ceramics studio founded in 2013 by Marga van Oers. Marga and her team of talented artists specialise in meticulously crafting unique, handcrafted ceramic tiles that tell beautiful stories. The team starts by sketching their designs on paper before transferring them on to the tiles. The illustrations are then delicately hand-painted using vibrant colours, giving life to the stories depicted.

The stories showcased on the tiles are inspired by various themes, including nature, folklore and everyday life. They draw inspiration from Dutch history and culture and other influences from around the world. Each design features a playful detail in which 'classic concepts clash with modern elements'.

In addition to their tiles, StoryTiles creates other ceramic products, such as vases, jewellery and even wallpaper. These products showcase the same attention to detail and storytelling their tiles are known for. Everything displayed in the shop contributes to a distinctive atmosphere that makes a visit an essential part of any trip to Amsterdam.

De Kaaskamer, **Runstraat 7**
This iconic speciality cheese shop and deli is much loved for its wide selection of Dutch and international cheeses, ranging from traditional gouda and edam to unique and artisanal varieties. The shop offers tastings and expert advice on pairing cheeses with wine and other accompaniments. It is a popular destination for local cheese lovers and tourists looking to sample and purchase high-quality and authentic Dutch cheeses.

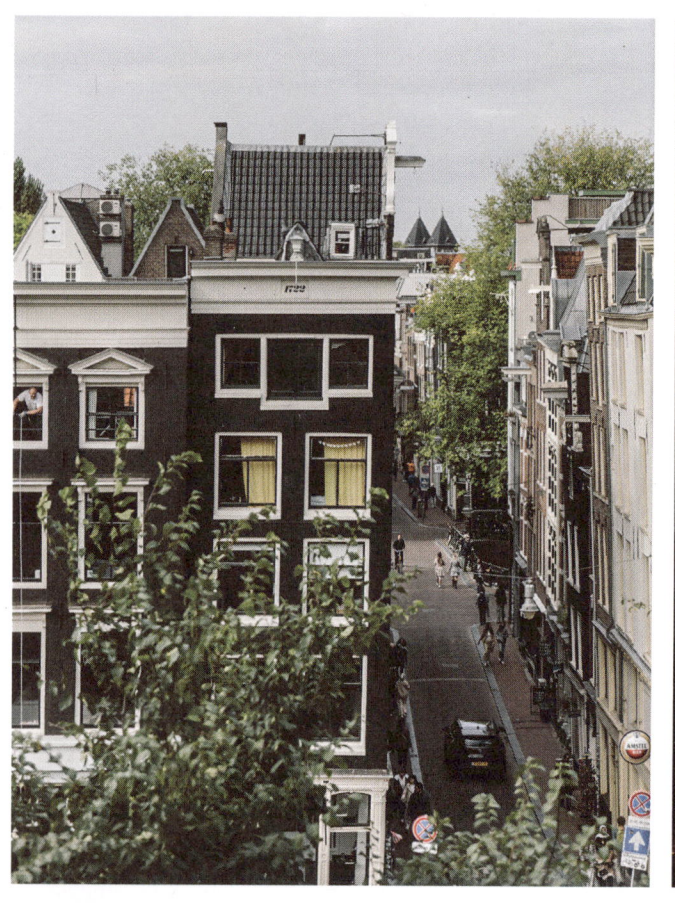
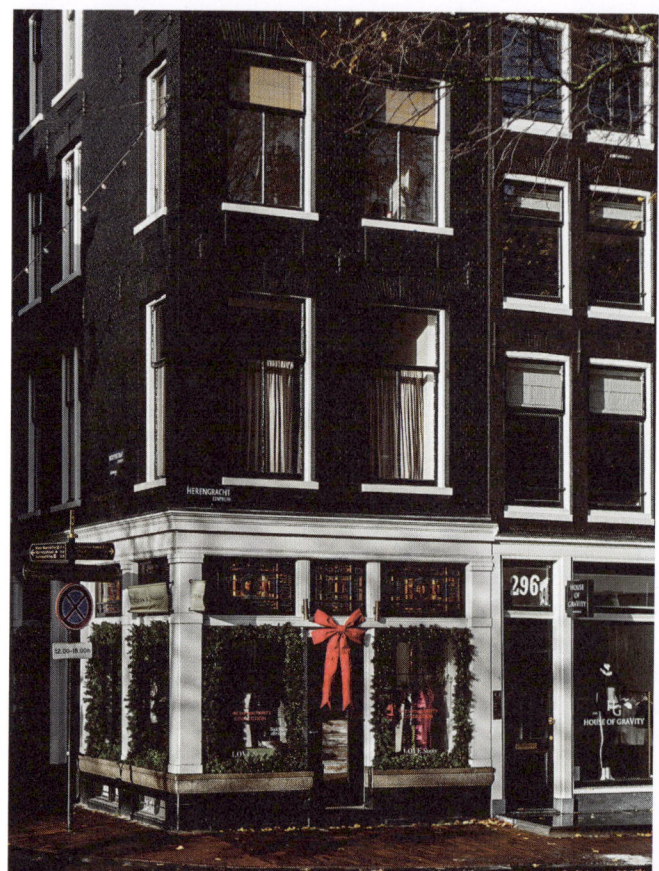
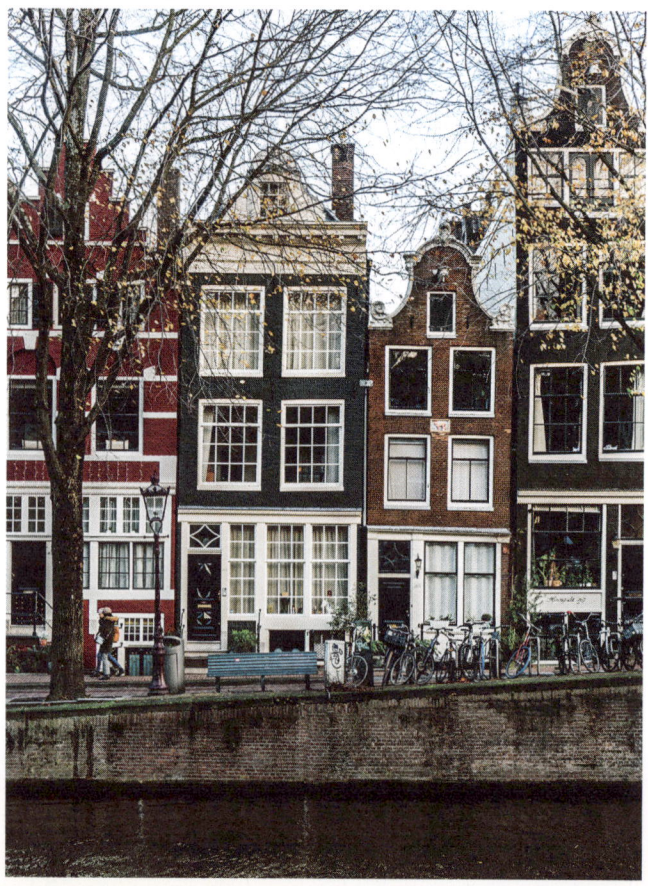
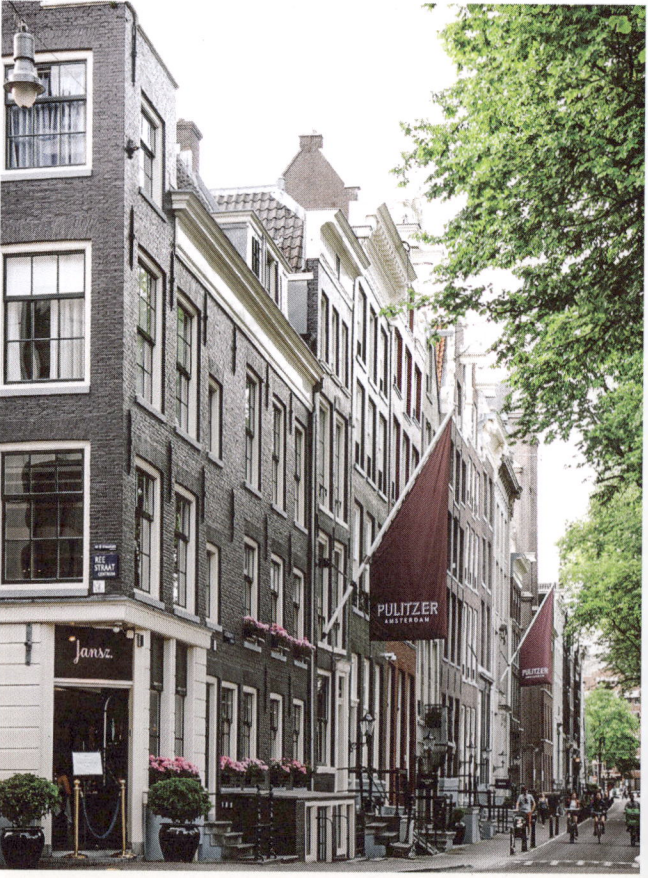

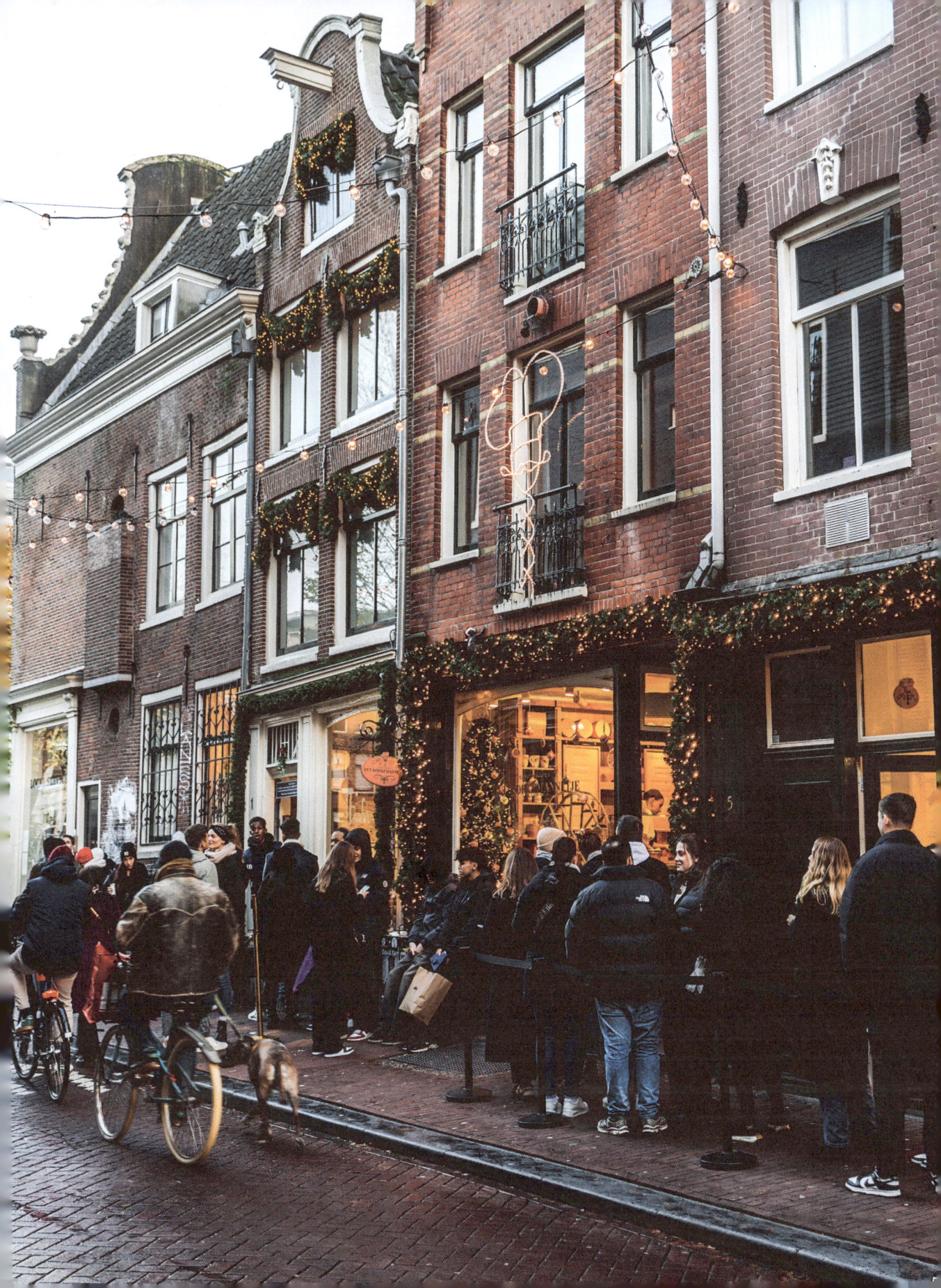

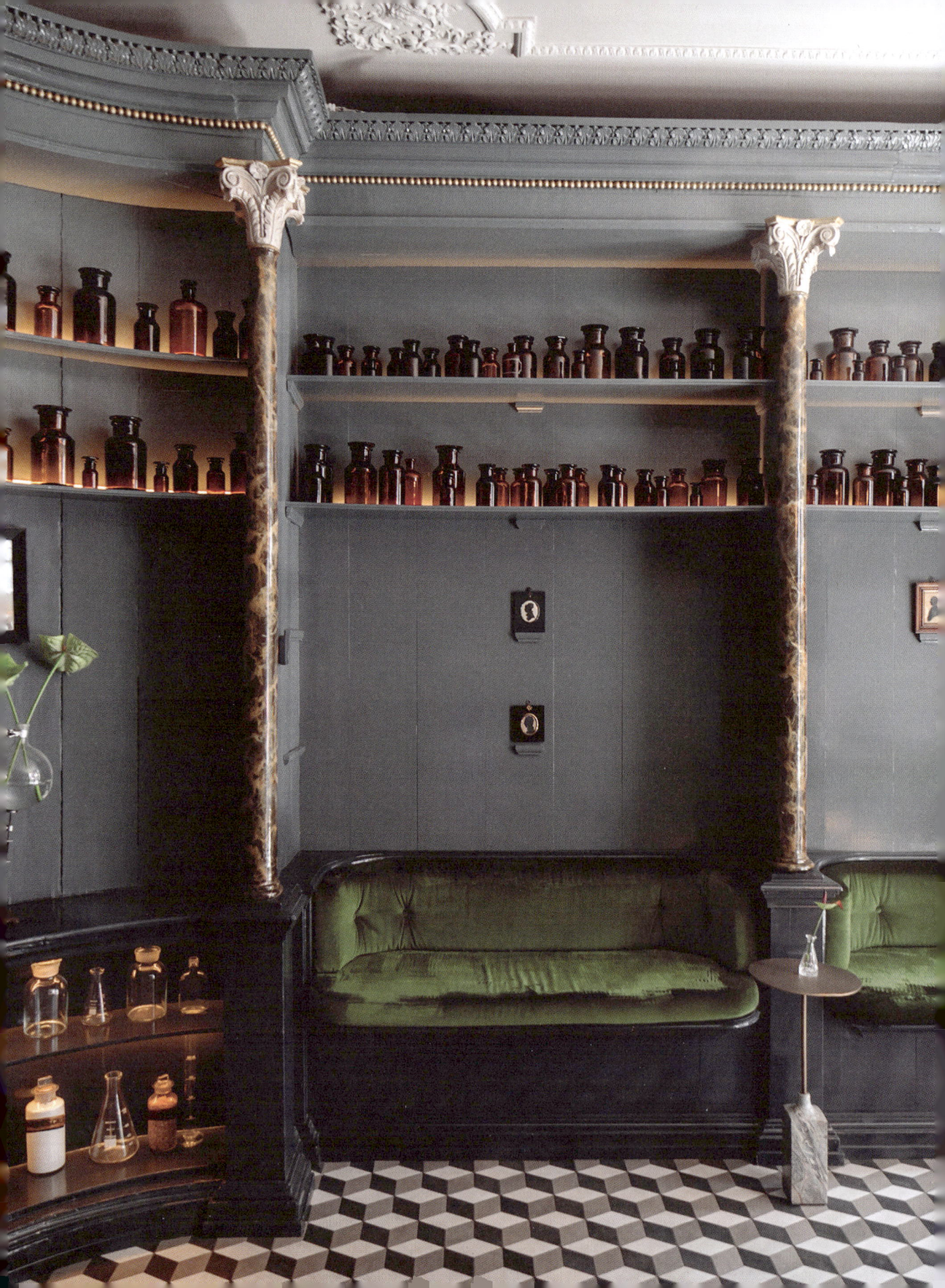

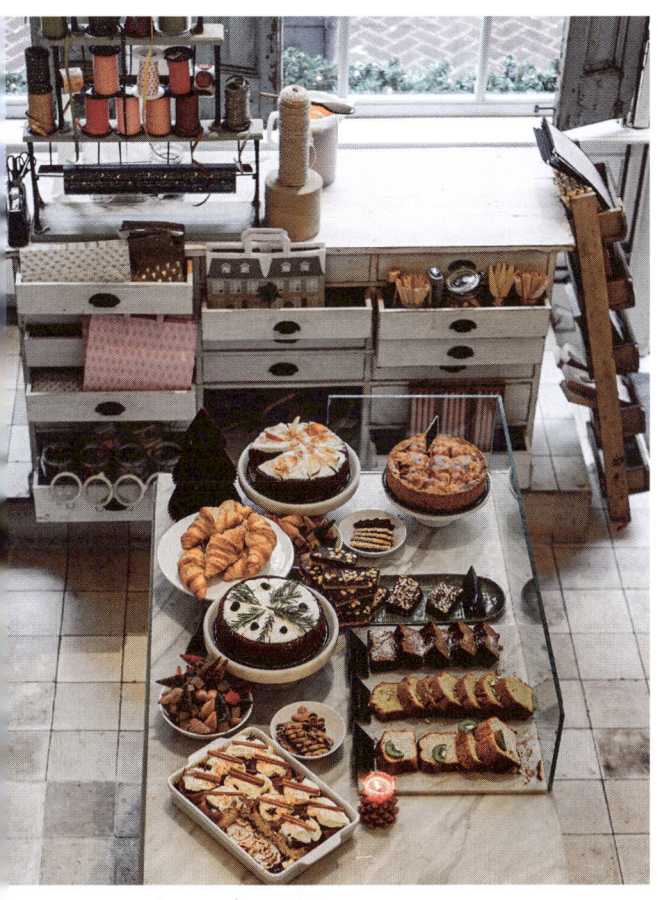
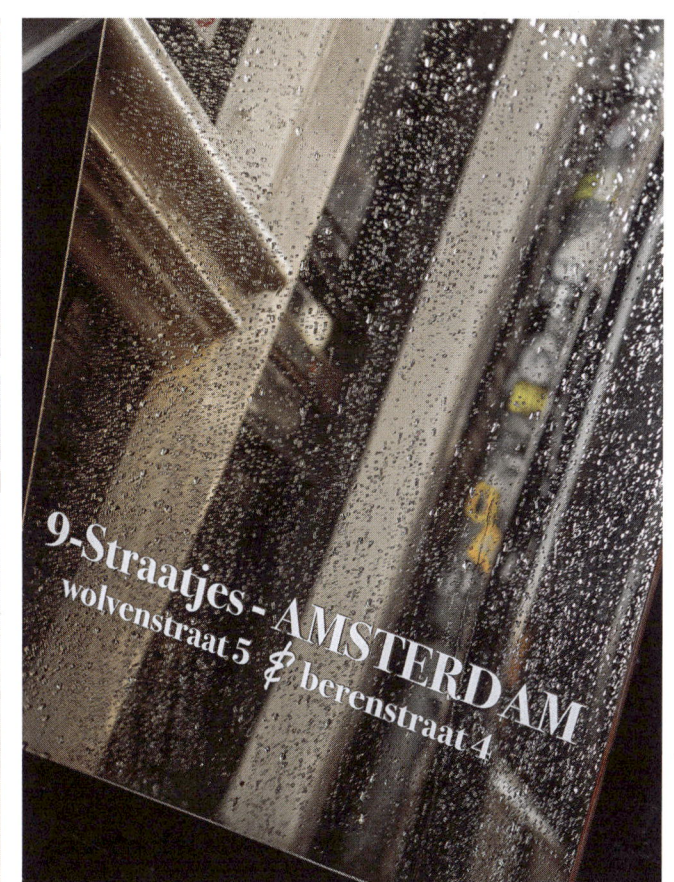
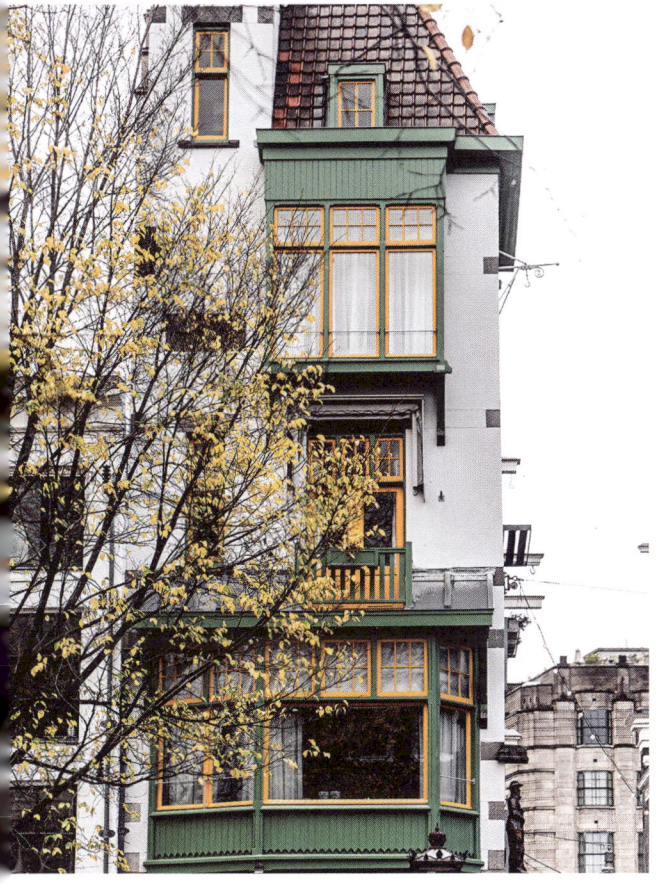
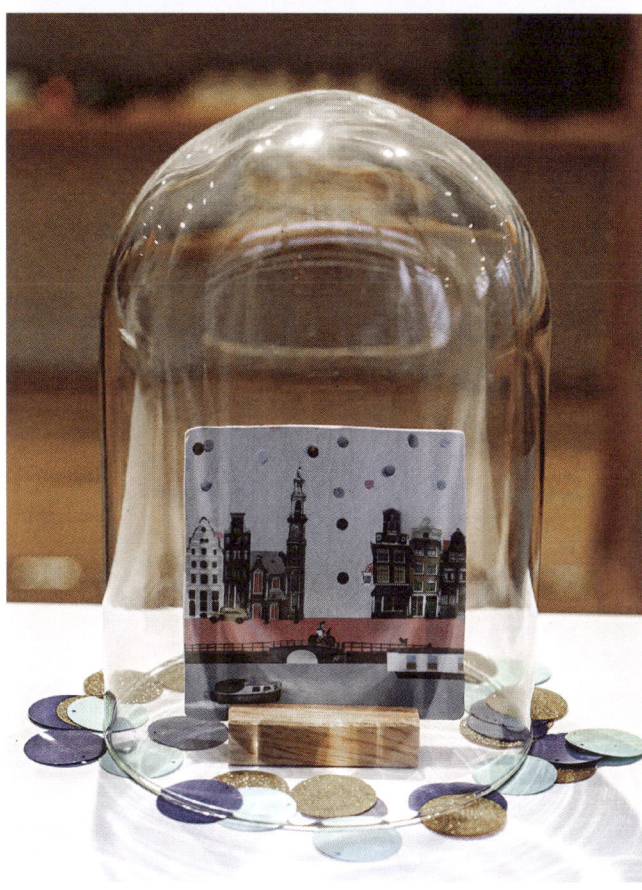

LELIEGRACHT

Walk north from The 9 Streets until you reach Leliegracht and stay connected to Amsterdam's rich history with a stroll along the picturesque canal street. Leliegracht is situated between Herengracht and Keizersgracht, making it an ideal location for a leisurely stroll along the water. The street is also studded with several art galleries and boutique shops, adding to its charm. You could while away an entire afternoon perusing the shops and sampling the food on offer in the cafes, but to capture the soul of this street, you could seek out the following areas and addresses.

ADDRESSES OF NOTE

Torensluis Bridge is Amsterdam's oldest and broadest bridge, spanning the Singel canal, and is known for its unique design and architectural features. The bridge has a rich history, having been constructed in 1648, and was initially built as a defensive structure, with two towers on either side. Unusual for the time it was built, it only has a single arch, and it also features a stone balustrade and decorative sculptures. Since its construction, the bridge has undergone several renovations.

Wijngaard Kaas, **Singel 182**
Wijngaard Cheese is a family business with a long tradition of artisan cheese-making going back over 100 years. The current Wijngaard brothers, who run the cheese business, are the third generation responsible for this delicate, award-winning gouda cheese.

The cheese prepared by the Wijngaard family is made from milk from grass-fed cows. Cows fed on fresh grass give milder and better milk, and cheese made from this milk ripens better. However, supply of this type of milk is limited since summers are short in Holland. The cheese is matured in custom-built cheese cellars in the historic town of Woerden. The unique

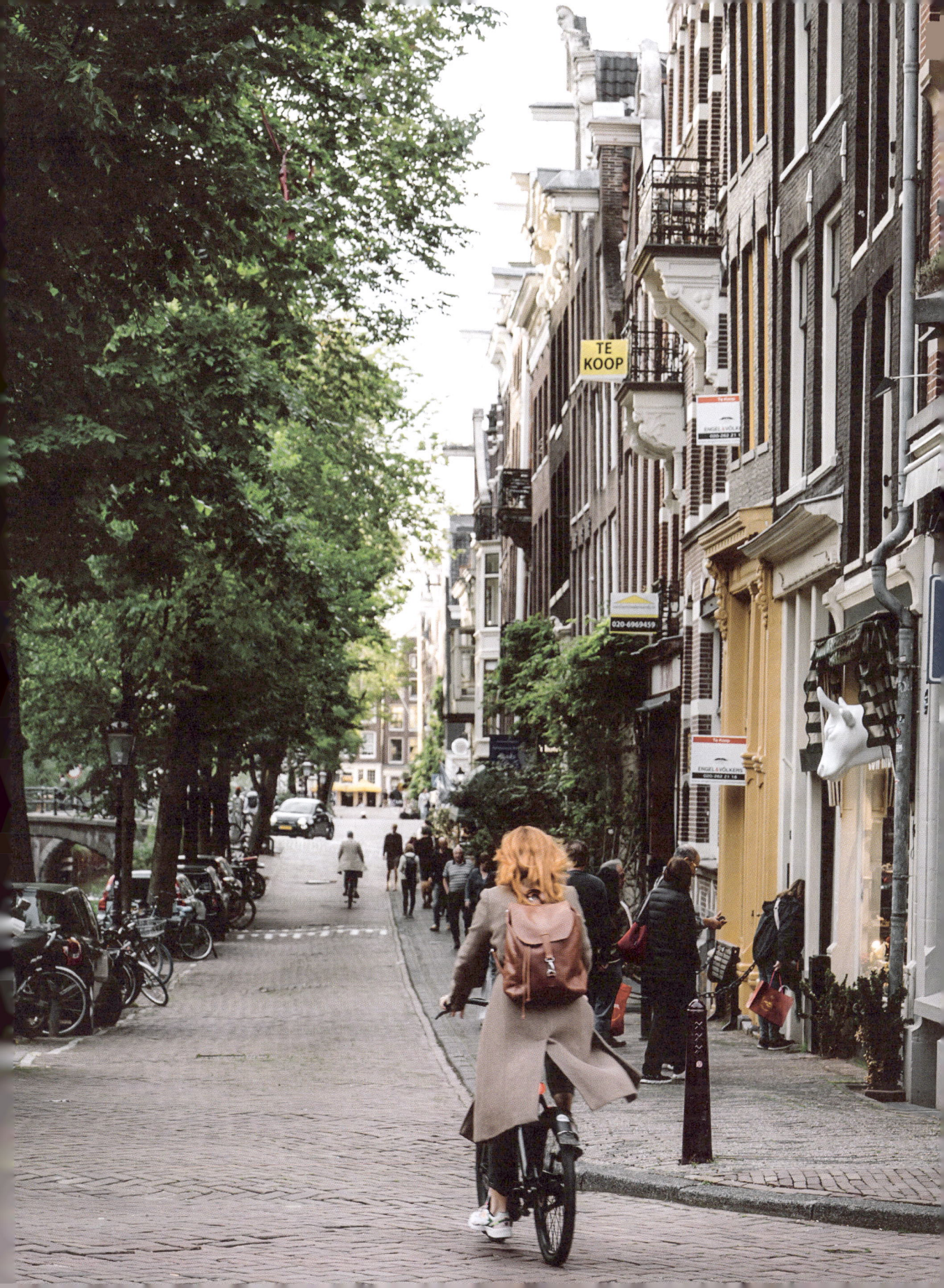

microclimate in these cellars, with fluctuating temperature and humidity, influences the cheese's flavour greatly.

Alongside cheese, they also offer a variety of other gourmet products, such as crackers, wine and preserves. The shop is known for its friendly and knowledgeable staff, who can provide guidance and recommendations based on individual preferences.

Heertje Friet, **Herengracht 169**
Fabel Friet in The 9 Streets is arguably the city's most popular chip shop, but if you can't be bothered to queue, this place is much less busy and just as lovely!

the Otherist, **Leliegracht 6**
Open the door to this quaint boutique, along one of my favourite streets, and you will find a cabinet of curiosities like no other in Amsterdam. Their focus is on the uniquely handmade, hard-to-find, one-off pieces. Peruse the shelves of framed butterflies, unique jewels and treasures, and you will find something extraordinary.

Architectura & Natura, **Leliegracht 22H**
This decades-old bookstore is meticulously stocked with specialist architecture, design and nature books.

Brasserie De Luwte, **Leliegracht 26–28**
Iris Zeilstra brings a touch of something special to all her lovely cafes and restaurants in Amsterdam, and this one is no exception. The chances are you have seen its Insta-famous cocktail tree on social media, but it's much more than that. This fuss-free neighbourhood restaurant, open from 11 a.m. to late, is a favourite amongst Amsterdam locals and tourists. In the warmer months, you can't beat a canal-side table, but it's equally as memorable inside under the glow of the candles when it gets a little colder.

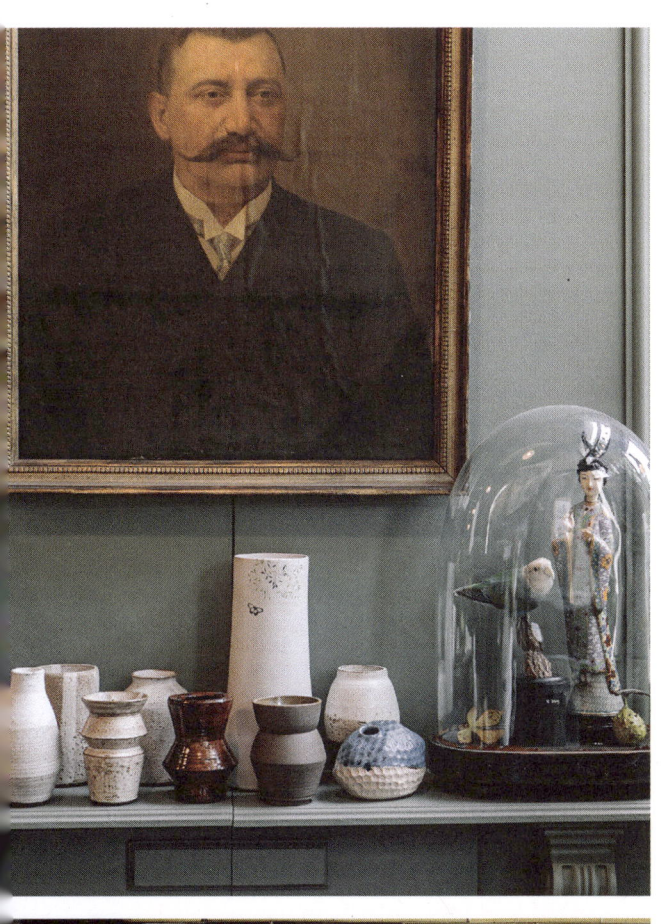
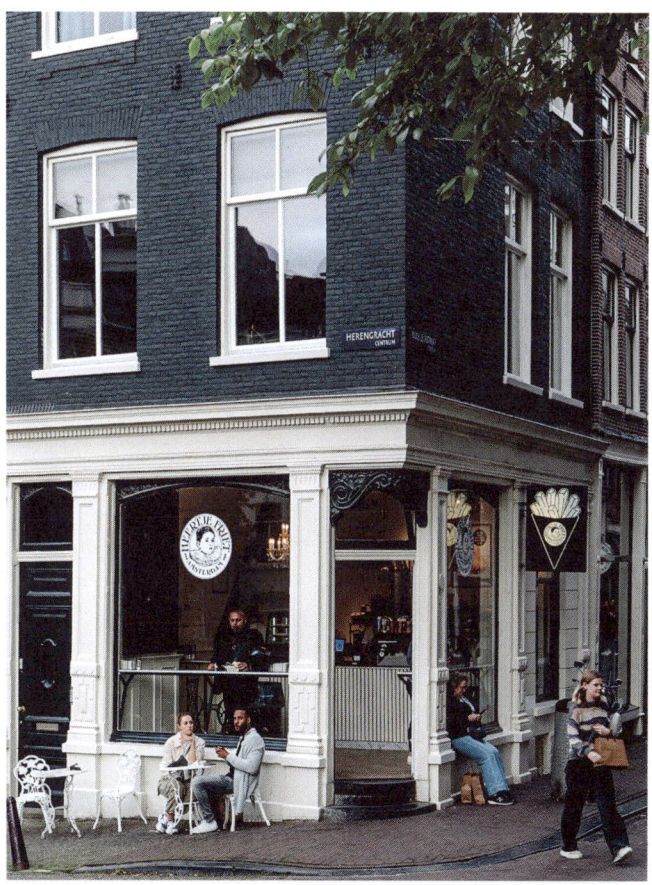
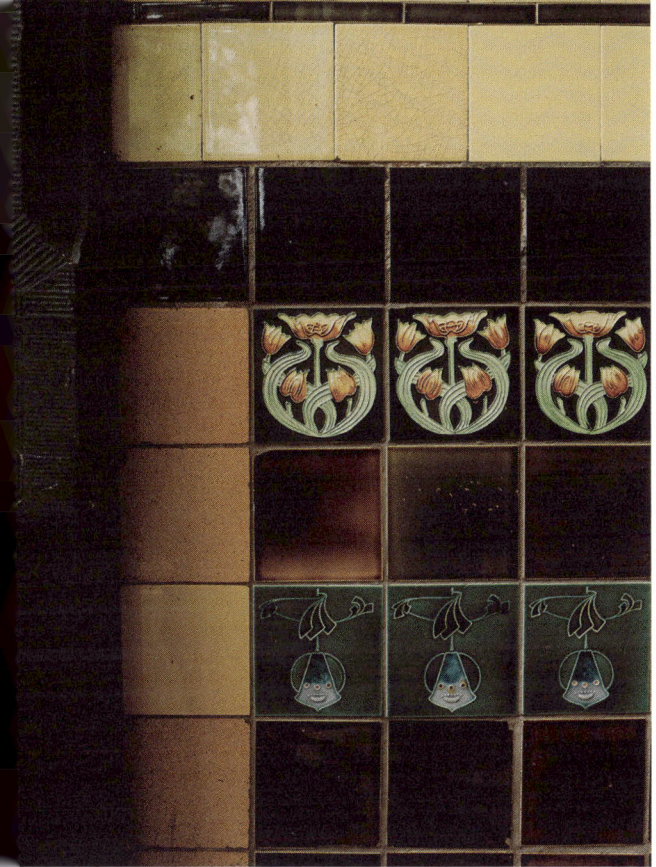
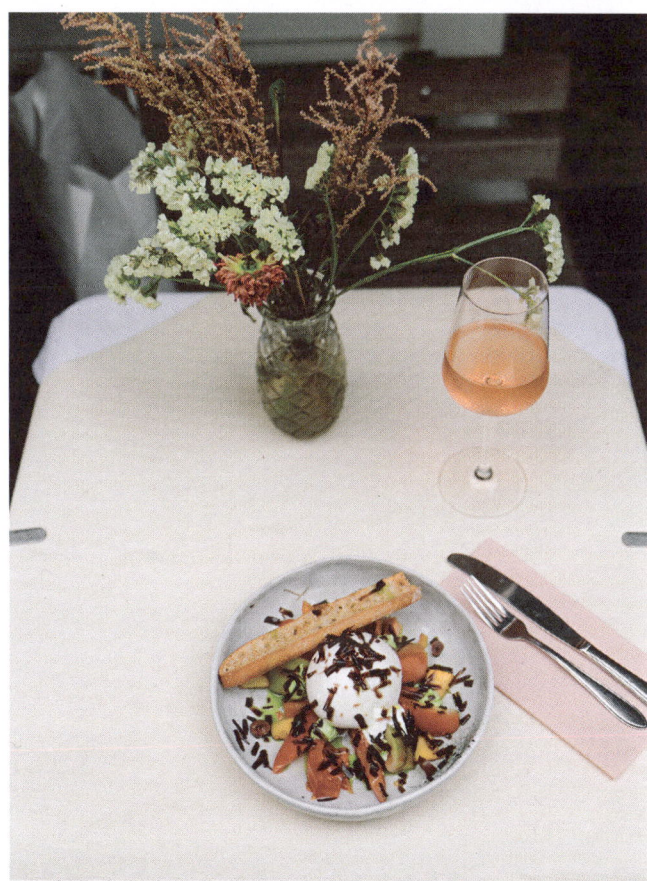

Café Brandon, **Keizersgracht 157**
A quintessential Dutch bar on the borders of the Jordaan district. Apparently one of the oldest brown bars in Amsterdam, it offers the perfect setting to watch the sun go down with a biertje or two. Go for the beer and stay for the untouched 1940s decor.

The intersection of Leliegracht and Keizersgracht is one of my favourite spots to stand to photograph the general atmosphere of the area.

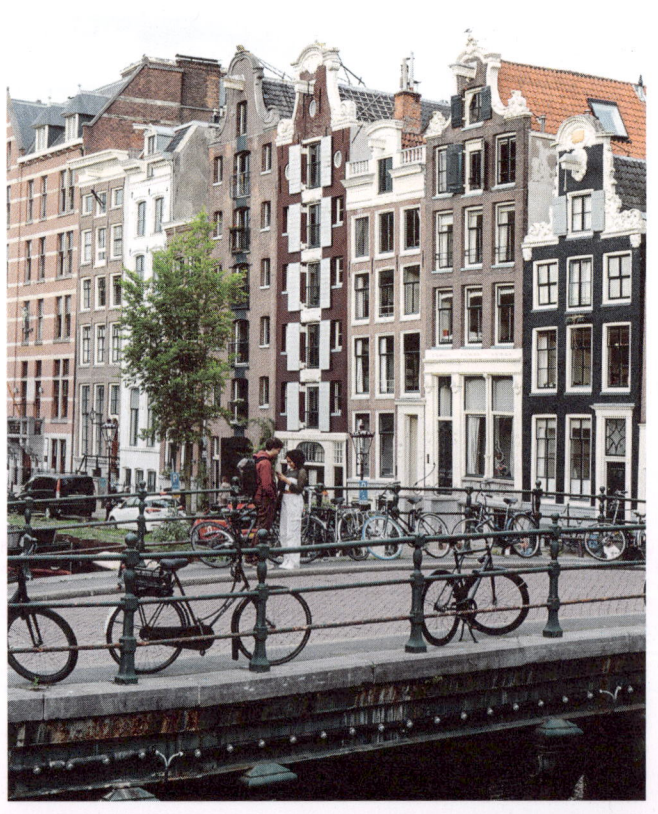
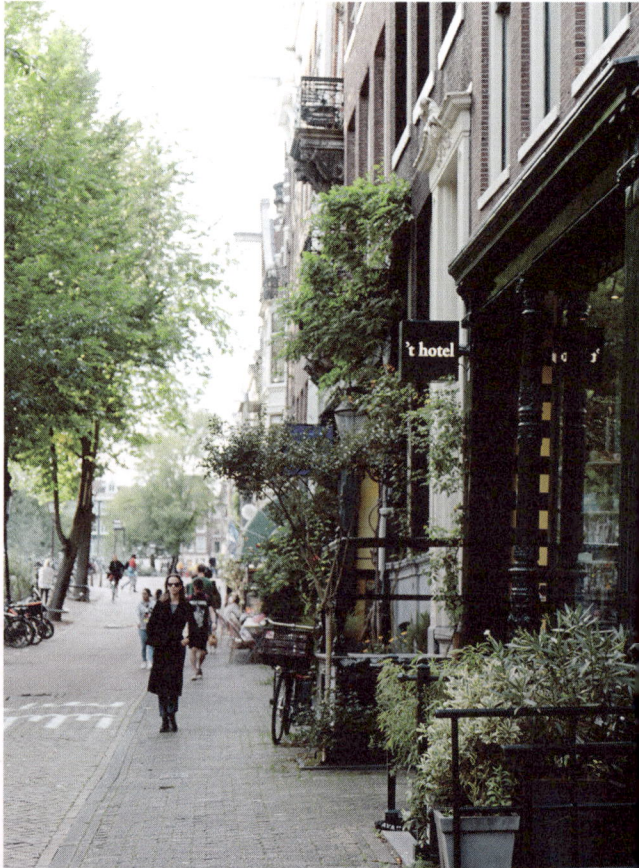

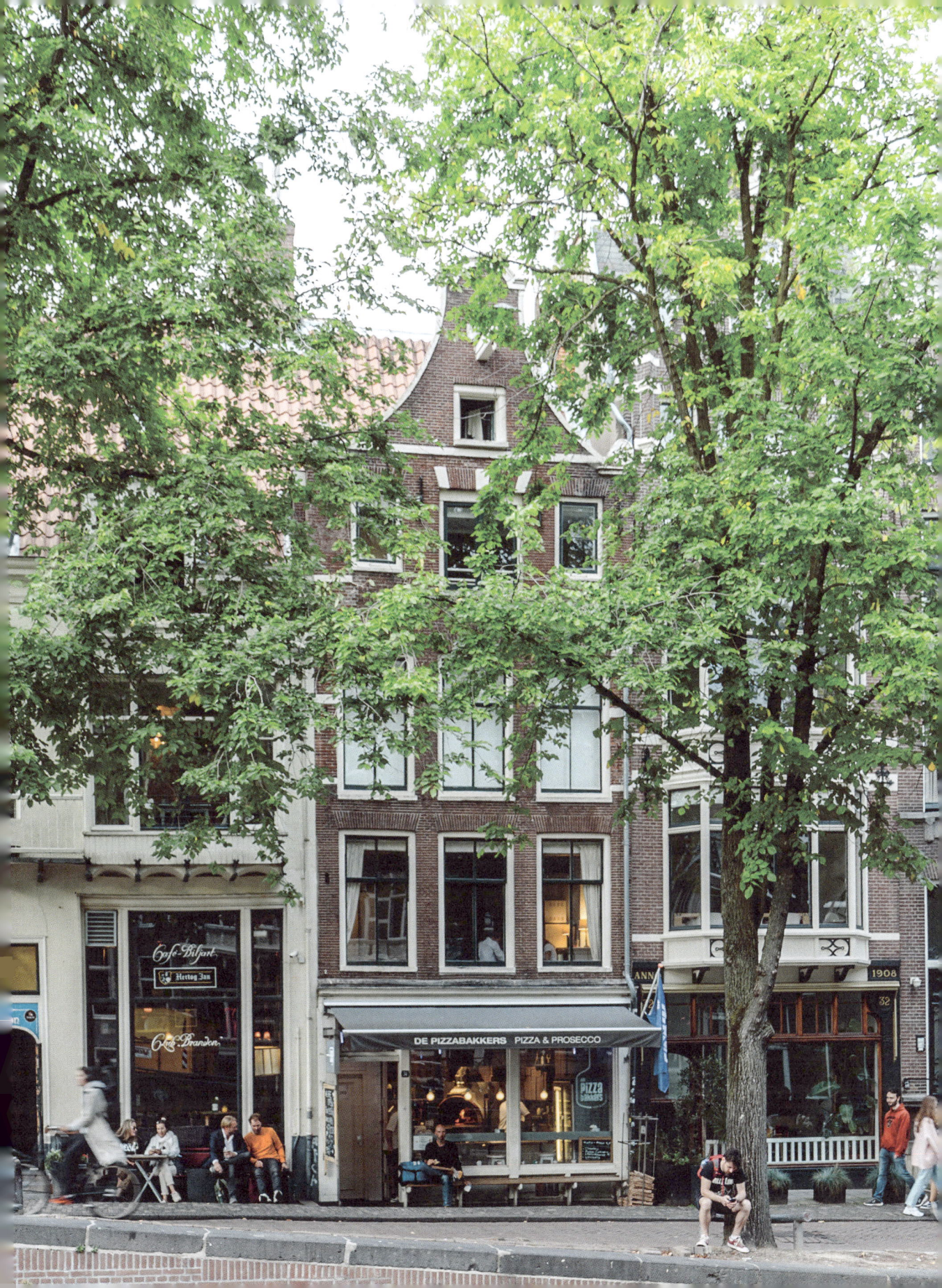

SOUTHERN CANAL RING

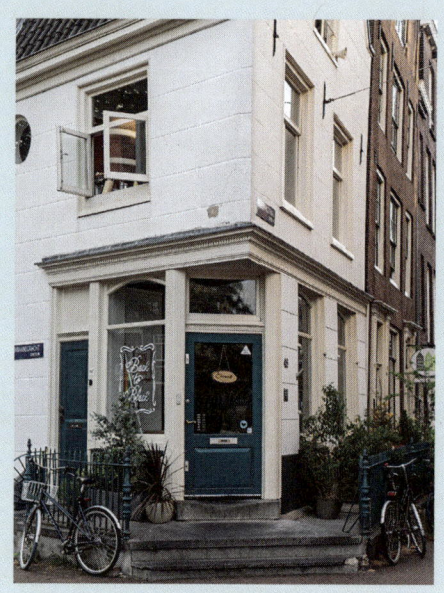

THE OTHER HALF OF THE UNESCO WORLD HERITAGE SITE; QUINTESSENTIAL AMSTERDAM WITH STUNNING ARCHITECTURE AND PICTURESQUE CANAL HOUSES; HOME TO THE MUSEUM AND ANTIQUE QUARTERS

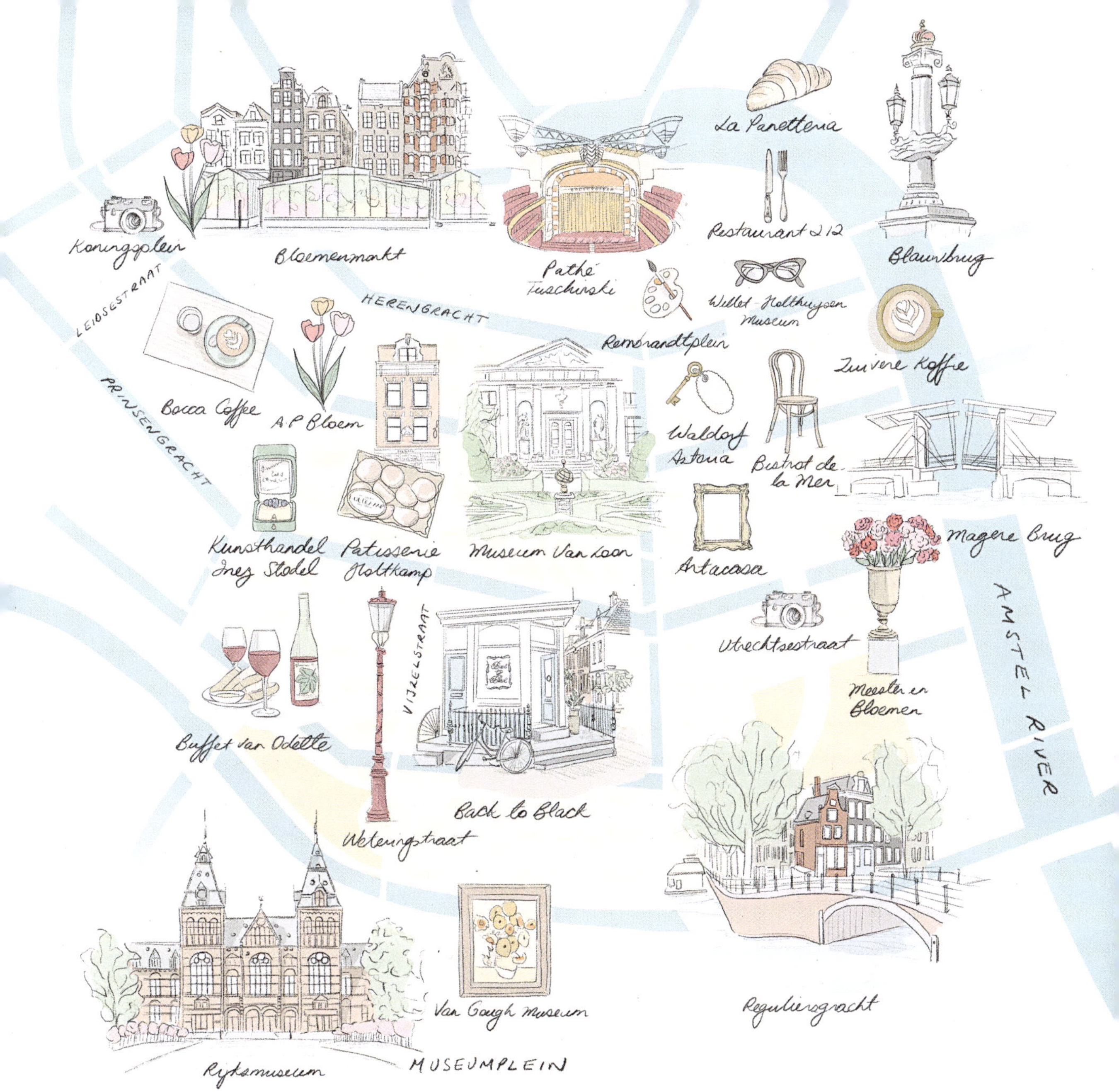

SOUTHERN CANAL RING

#prettycityamsterdam

 KUNSTHANDEL INEZ STODEL Nieuwe Spiegelstraat 65
ARTACASA Kerkstraat 411

 BACK TO BLACK Weteringstraat 48
LA PANETTERIA Amstel 200
ZUIVERE KOFFIE Utrechtsestraat 39
PATISSERIE HOLTKAMP Vijzelgracht 15
BOCCA COFFEE Kerkstraat 96H

 RESTAURANT 212 Amstel 212
BISTRO DE LA MER Utrechtsestraat 57
BUFFET VAN ODETTE Prinsengracht 598

 Magere Brug, Amstel River, Utrechtsestraat, Weteringstraat, Reguliersgracht, Rembrandtplein, Kerkstraat, Blauwbrug, Bloemenmarkt, Koningsplein

 MEESTER IN BLOEMEN Kerkstraat 408Hs
A·P BLOEM Kerkstraat 151A

 WILLET-HOLTHUYSEN MUSEUM Herengracht 605
VAN GOGH MUSEUM Museumplein 6
RIJKSMUSEUM Museumstraat 1
PATHÉ TUSCHINSKI Reguliersbreestraat 26-34
MUSEUM VAN LOON Keizersgracht 672

 WALDORF ASTORIA Herengracht 542-556

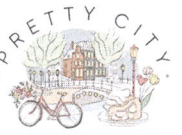
PRETTY CITY
AMSTERDAM

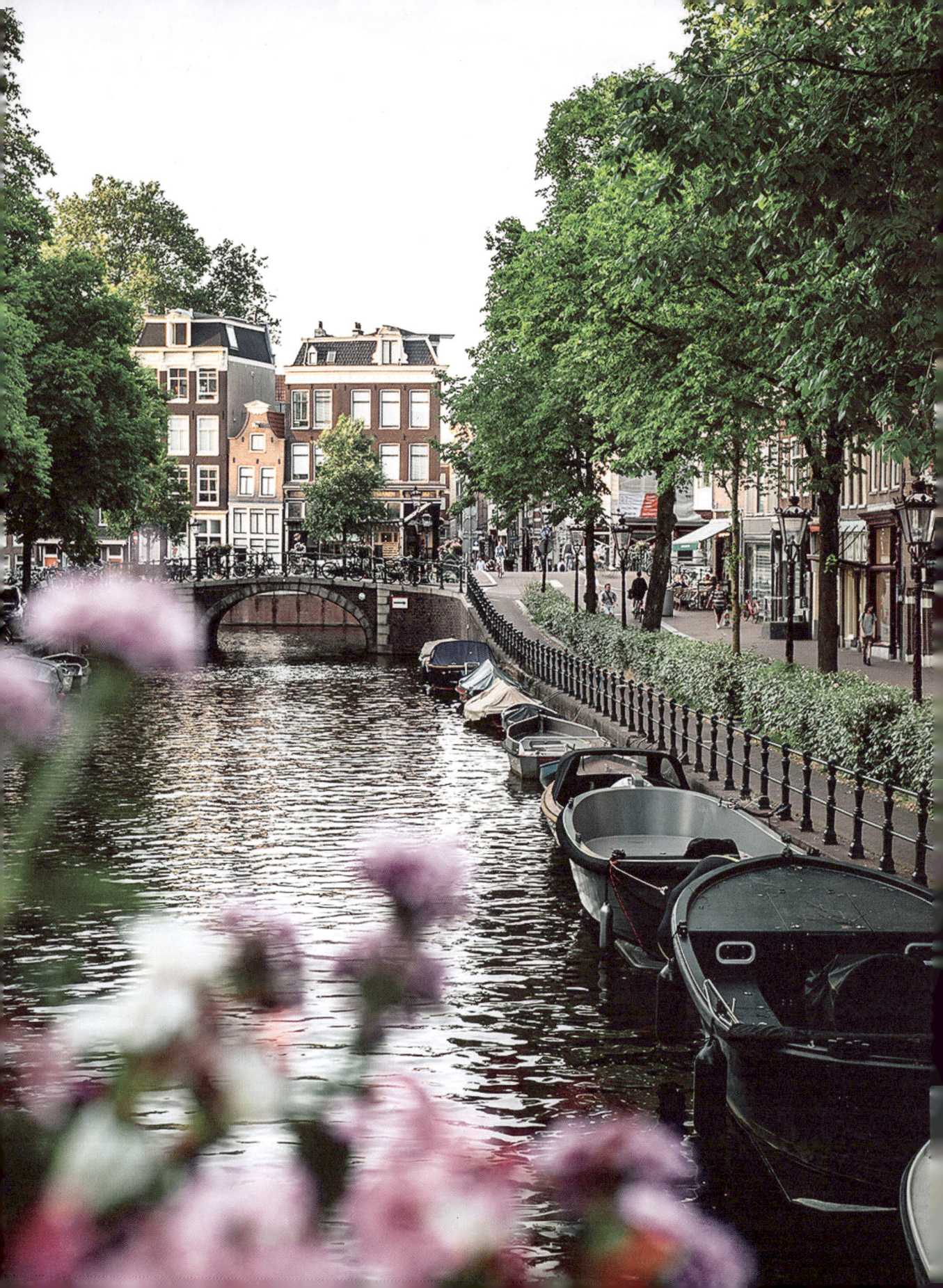

Encompassing the southern half of the Grachtengordel, from Leidsestraat to the Museumplein and the Amstel river, this district exudes shopping, art and culture like no other. Like the Central Canal Ring, this pocket of the Grachtengordel mesmerises with beauty and charm at every corner, and is best known for its picturesque canal houses, world-class museums and charming village feel. The Rijksmuseum and Van Gogh Museum draw year-round crowds. To see another face of this area, you can follow one or both of my suggested routes.

ROUTE ONE

A leisurely walk from *Bloemenmarkt* to *Rijksmuseum* via Spiegelgracht offers an opportunity to explore the picturesque canals, admire beautiful houses and visit exciting attractions.

You could begin your day at Bloemenmarkt, Amsterdam's famous floating flower market. Leave enough time to see it, but I wouldn't plan to stay too long: there are much more beautiful places to buy flowers.

Head west on Singel. The Bloemenmarkt may disappoint, but the picturesque views of the canal and the historic buildings from here surely won't. After a short walk, you will reach Leidsestraat. Turn left onto Leidsestraat and continue walking until you reach Leidsegracht.

Walk along Leidsegracht, another charming canal lined with many more lovely canal houses and several classic Dutch cafes and restaurants. Take in the scenery and immerse yourself in the local atmosphere. Continue walking along Leidsegracht until you reach Keizersgracht. Here, you will encounter the famous 'Golden Bend', which refers to Amsterdam's most prestigious stretch of canal houses. Admire these buildings' elegant architecture and grandeur, which cling to the curve of the Herengracht between Spiegelstraat and Vijzelstraat. Privileged and affluent locals overcame the construction restrictions at the time, which stipulated that plots had to be limited in size and must have gardens, by building one house with two front doors. A common feature of all these lavish houses is a double staircase. They were constructed of sandstone, greatly inspired by ancient Greece, and adorned with columns and pediments. Today, most

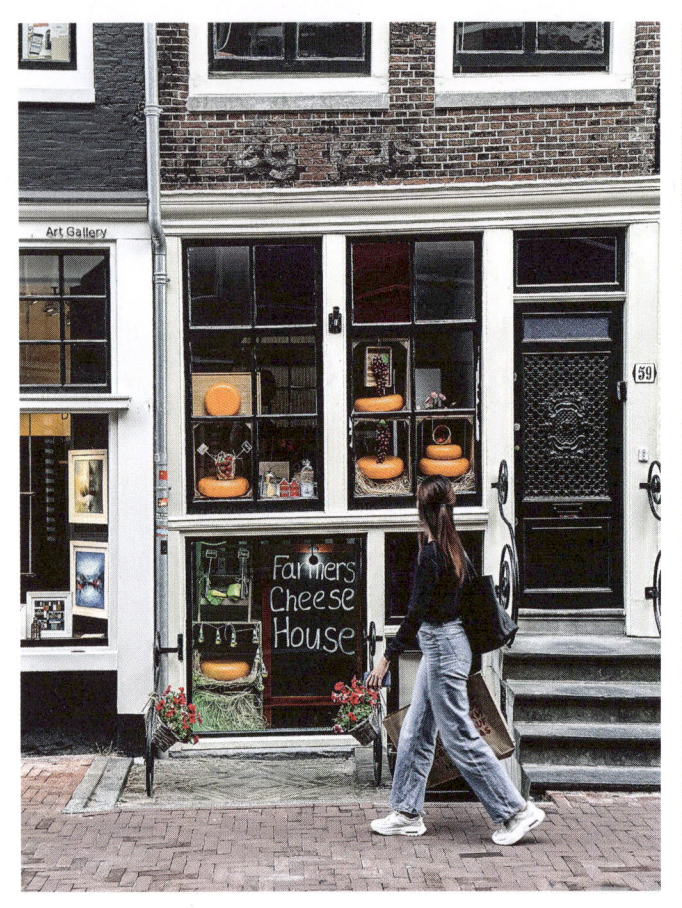
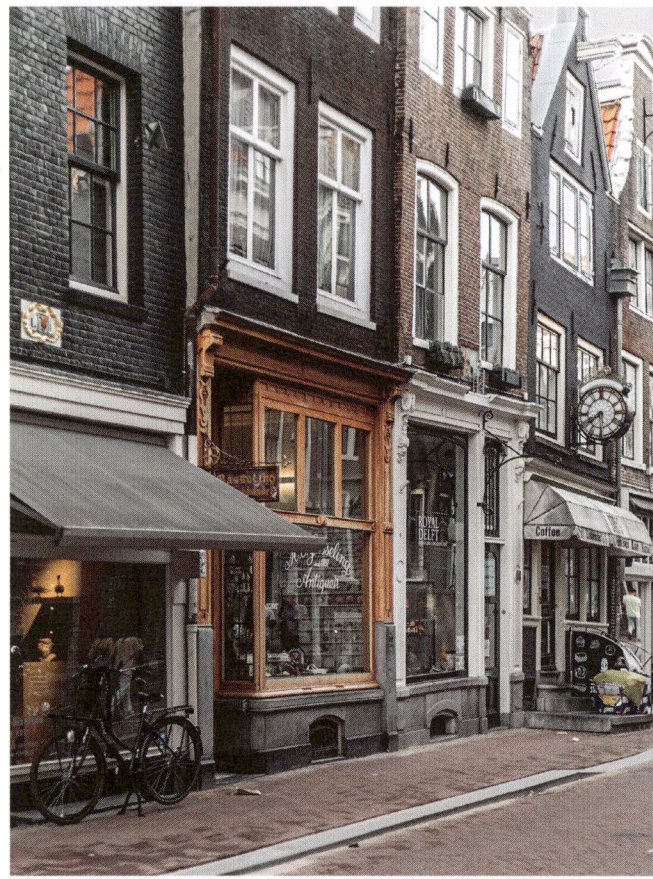
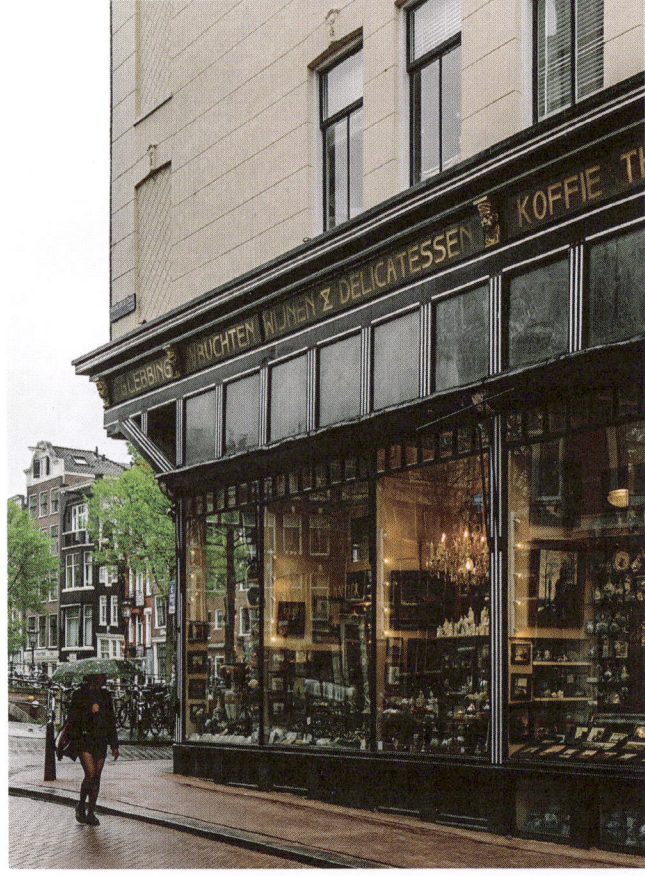
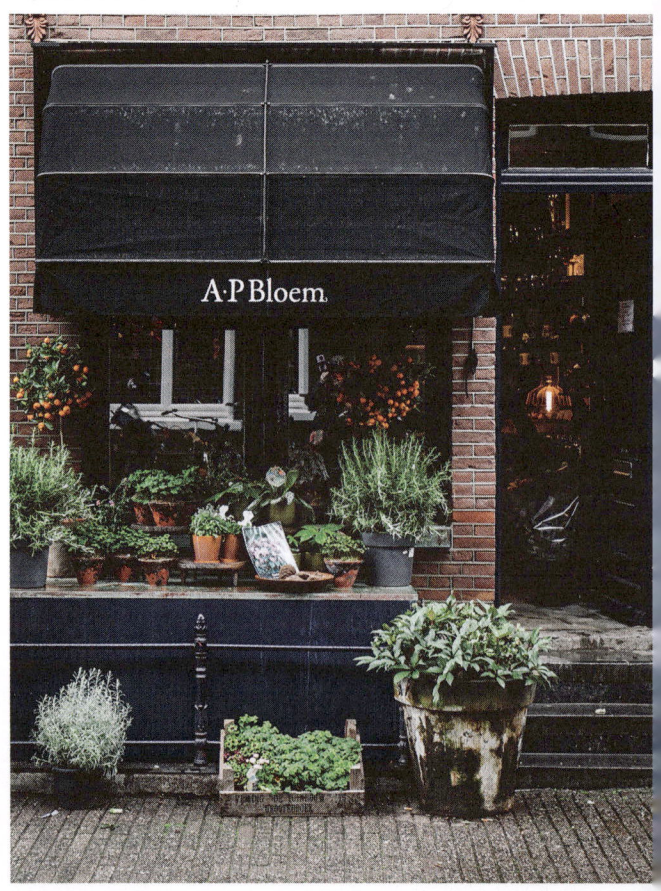

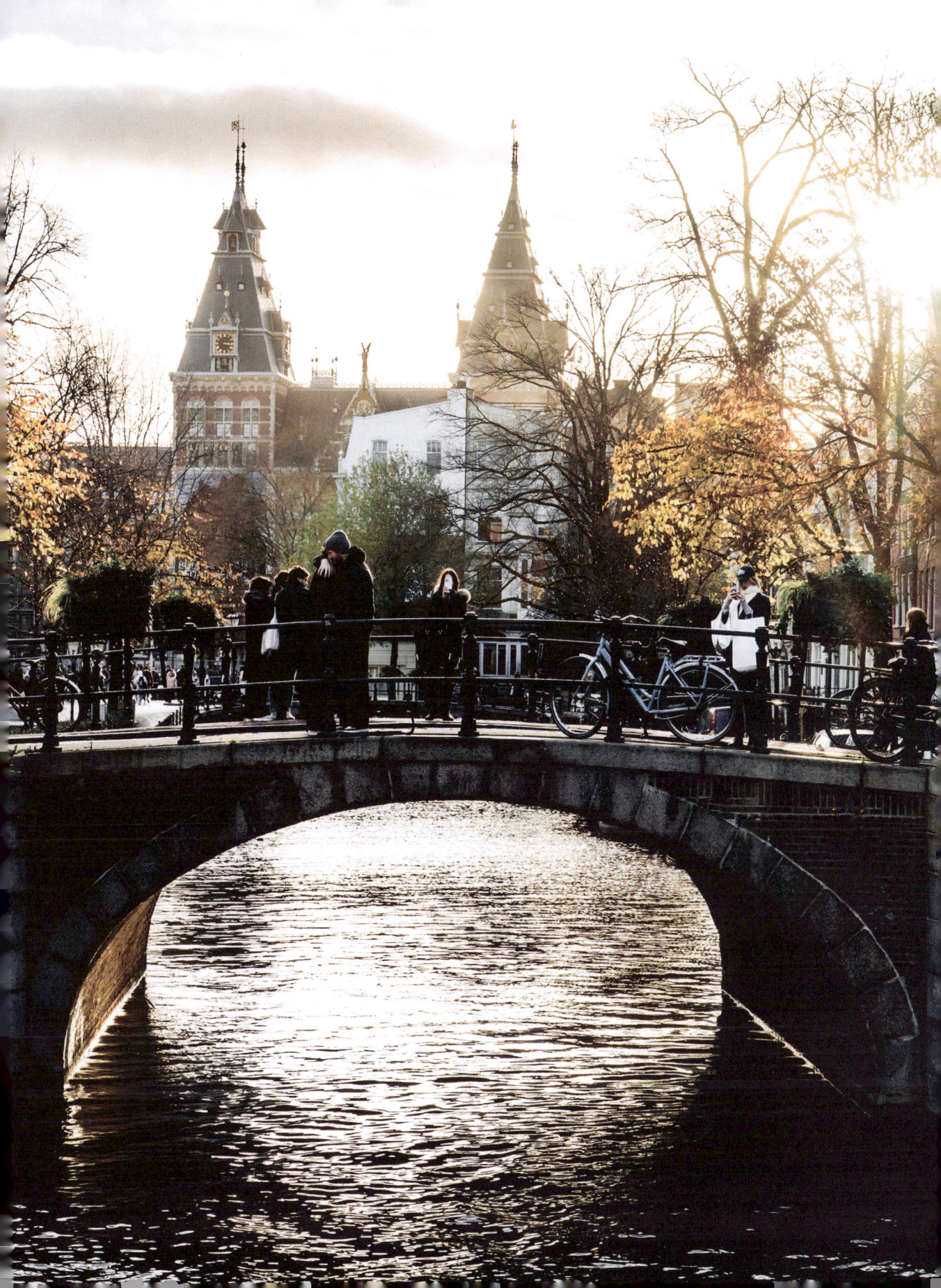

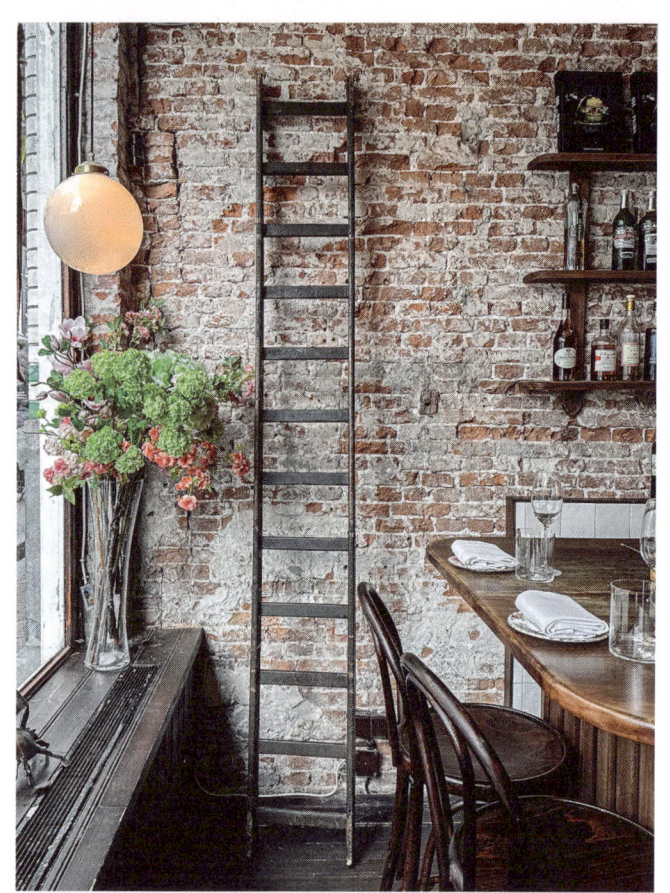
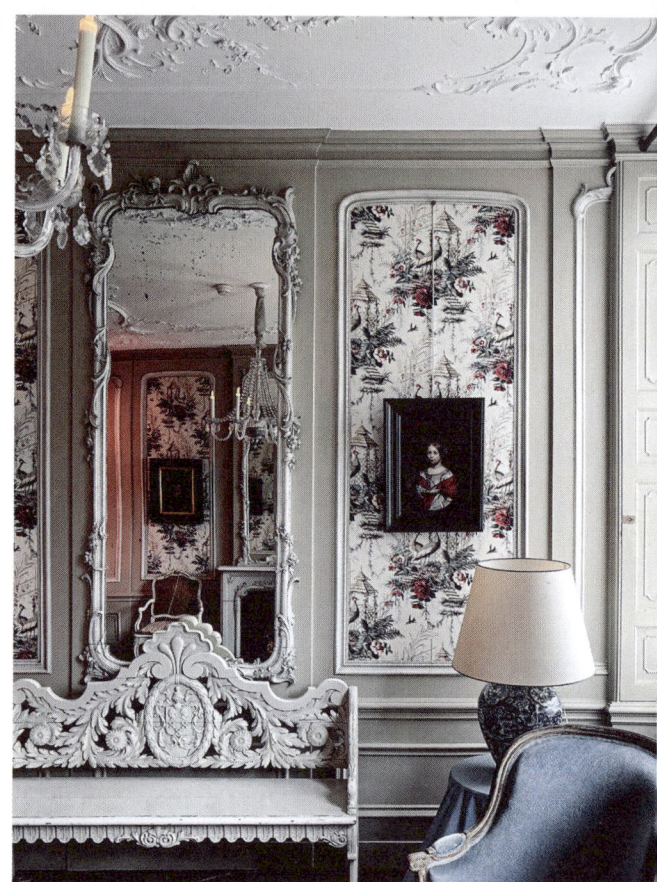
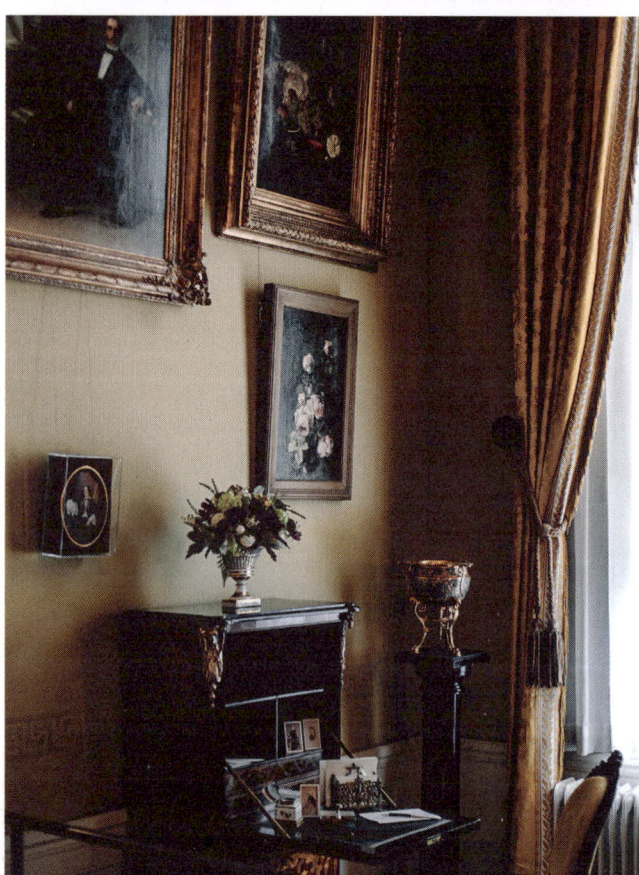
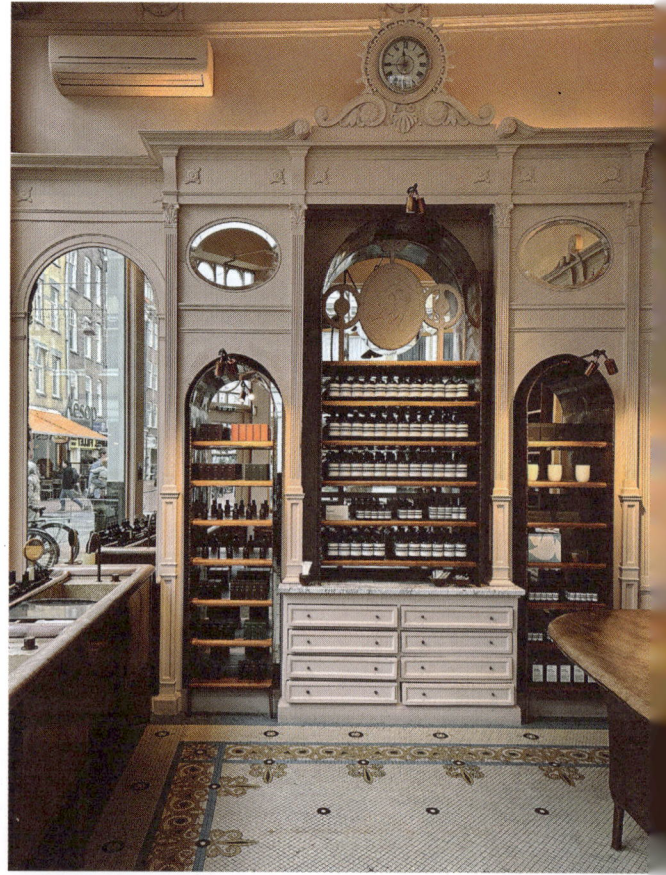

houses have been converted into apartments, museums or are used as offices. Three of the mansions are home to museums. If you have time, I would recommend stopping at *Museum Van Loon*.

As you stroll along Keizersgracht, take a slight left turn onto Reguliersgracht. Named after an order of monks whose monastery was located nearby, this iconic canal is known for its seven bridges, though if you stand where it intersects Herengracht, you can count fifteen bridges in all directions. Look to where the stork statue guards the crossing between Prinsengracht and Reguliersgracht – apparently, the house once belonged to a midwife. Take your time here at Reguliersgracht. For me, this is Amsterdam at its finest: enjoy the serenity of the canal and take some memorable photos. You may want to return a few times more, particularly at night when the little bridges are illuminated.

Finally, continue on Reguliersgracht until you reach Spiegelgracht. This street is renowned for its antique shops, art galleries and unique curiosity stores under the shadow of the Rijksmuseum. Explore the various shops and find a special treasure to take home. Take a leisurely stroll down Nieuwe Spiegelstraat and the district known as Spiegelkwartier to admire the art and browse some specialist shops. Here, you will find nearly 100 art and antique dealers offering an impressive range of items from a remarkable selection of specialist dealers. The quarter's origins date back to the Golden Age when many dealers set up shop along the stretch of road that led up to the Rijksmuseum. Thankfully, it has a very accessible air, and if it's not antiques you are after, there is much more to see and do.

Here are some of my favourite finds on Nieuwe Spiegelstraat and Kerkstraat:

ADDRESSES OF NOTE

A.P. Bloem, **Kerkstraat 151a**
An independently owned florist, established by renowned florists Alexander Posthuma and Melissa Whelan. Their elegant floral boutique displays,

their striking bouquets and their signature style draws inspiration from the beauty of nature, wild fields and the Golden Age.

Staetshuys Antiquairs, **Nieuwe Spiegelstraat 45A**
If you fancy a browse through a fine collection of barometers, planetariums, telescopes, globes and scientific instruments of every kind, you should step inside Staetshuys Antiquairs.

Kunsthandel Inez Stodel, **Nieuwe Spiegelstraat 65**
Inez Stodel, renowned for her extraordinary eye and taste, has specialised in jewels and miniature works of art for over fifty years. She has been joined in the business by her daughter, Leonore van der Waals. In their shop, you will find a broad collection of elegant and original jewels from antiquity to the 1970s, including signed jewels made by grand houses such as Cartier, Tiffany & Co., Marcus & Co. and Van Cleef & Arpels.

Stefs Bakery, **Nieuwe Spiegelstraat 62b**
The constant queue, especially in the morning, informs its popularity. You can't miss the bakery sign or the smell of freshly baked goods wafting out the door. It is the perfect coffee spot before heading to the museums.

Only leave this stretch after lingering a while at Spiegelgracht. It is one of the prettiest little canals in the city, thanks to its year-round lights and views over to the Rijksmuseum.
    Standing in front of *Kramer Kunst & Antiek*, at the intersection with Prinsengracht, will afford you stunning views of arched bridges and the towering Rijksmuseum, or cross over the road and stand on one of the lovely bridges in the heart of the Spiegelgracht. You will have a 360-degree feast for the eyes.
    You can finish your walk here or walk over to *Buffet van Odette* for one of the best meals in Amsterdam. Enjoy a healthy and delicious lunch or supper inside or outside this local restaurant. Opened in 1994 by Odette Rigterink and loved since then, it is best to book so you can guarantee a sampling of their excellent offering, which includes signature dishes like truffle-cheese omelettes and fresh ravioli as well as changing seasonal dishes, all sourced locally.

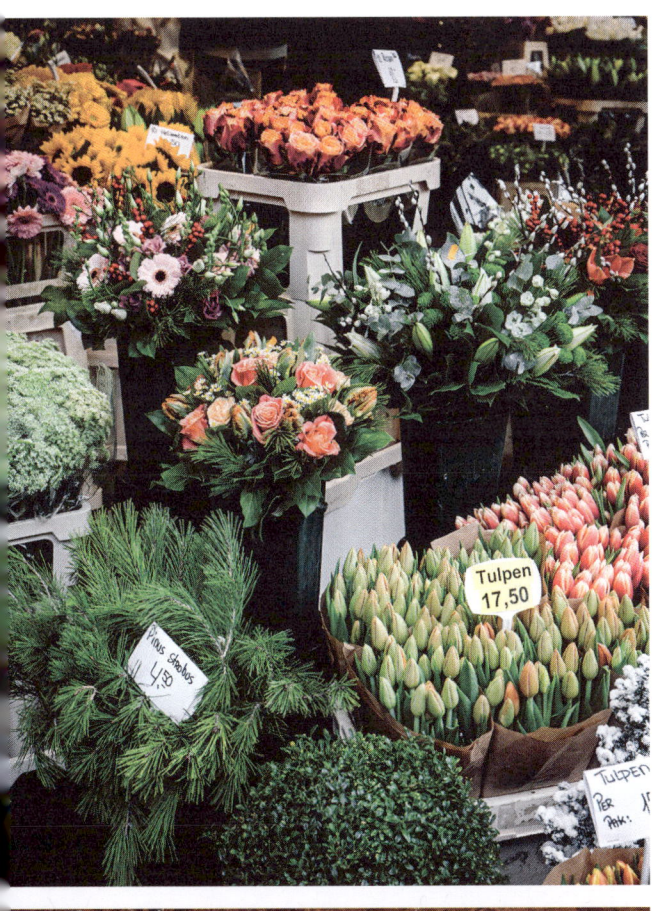
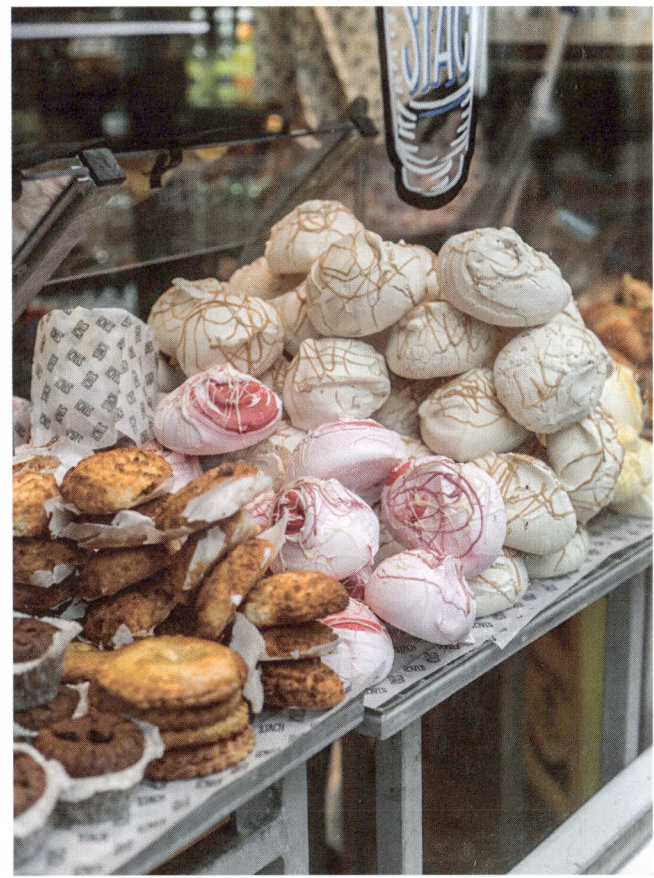
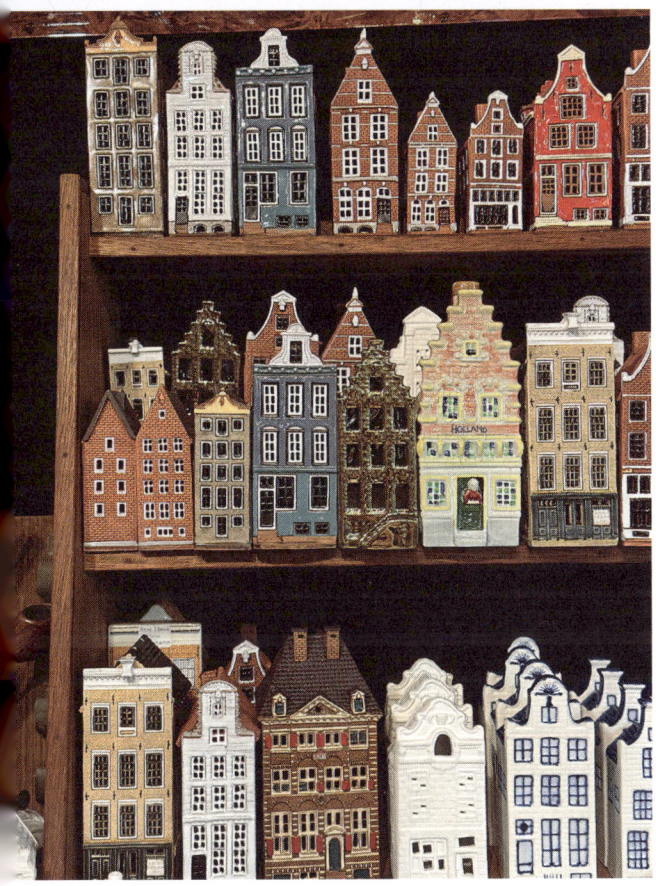
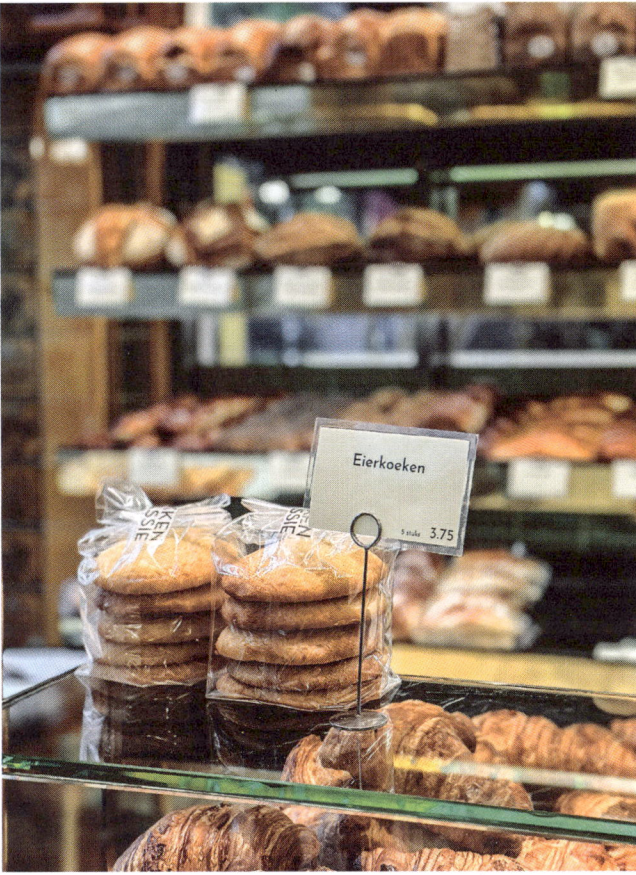

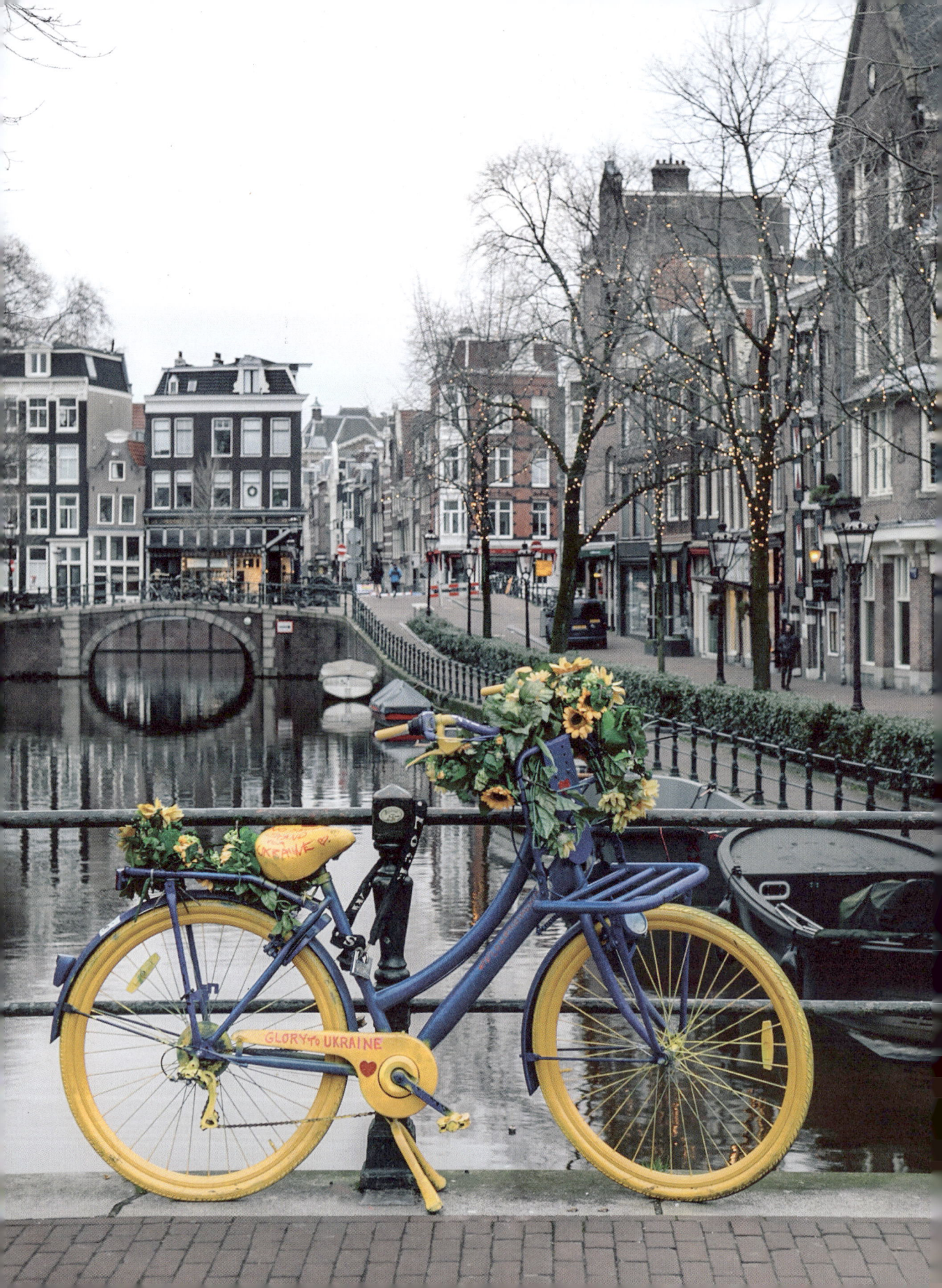

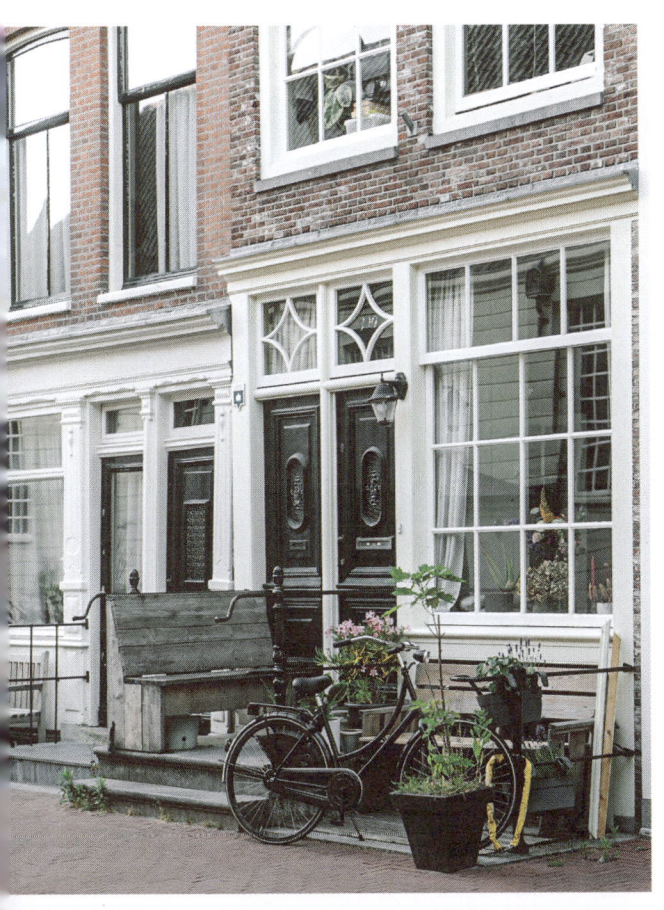
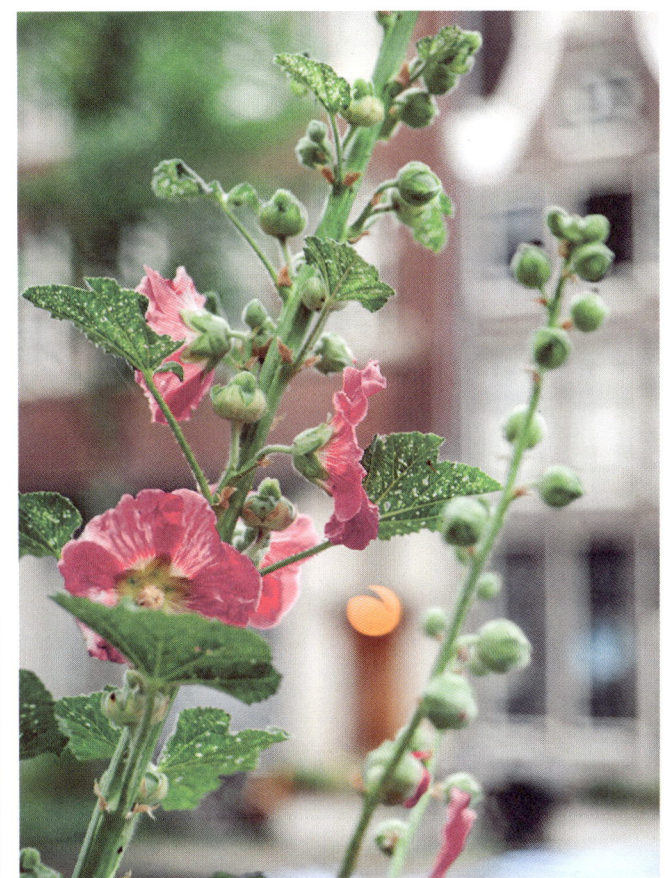
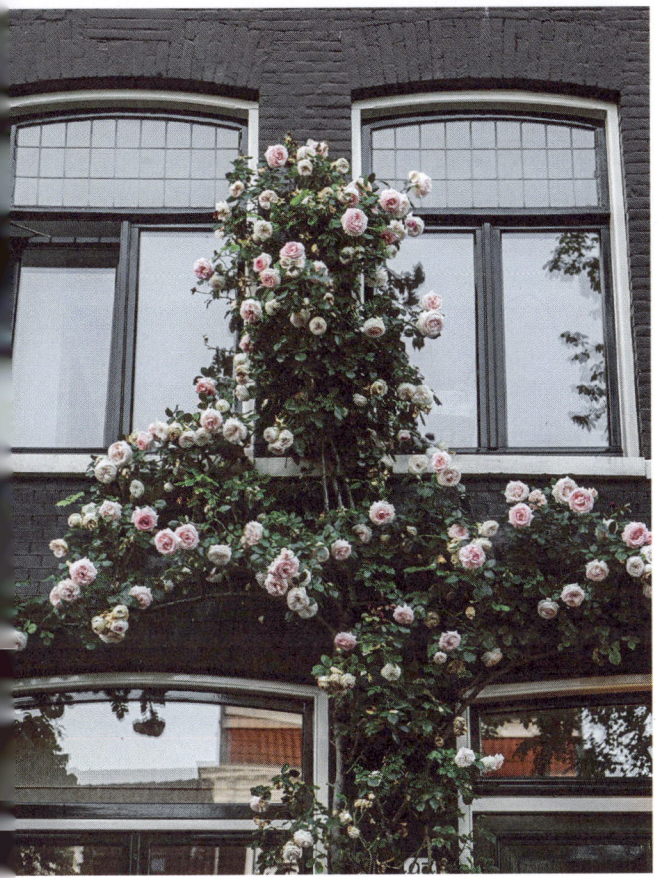
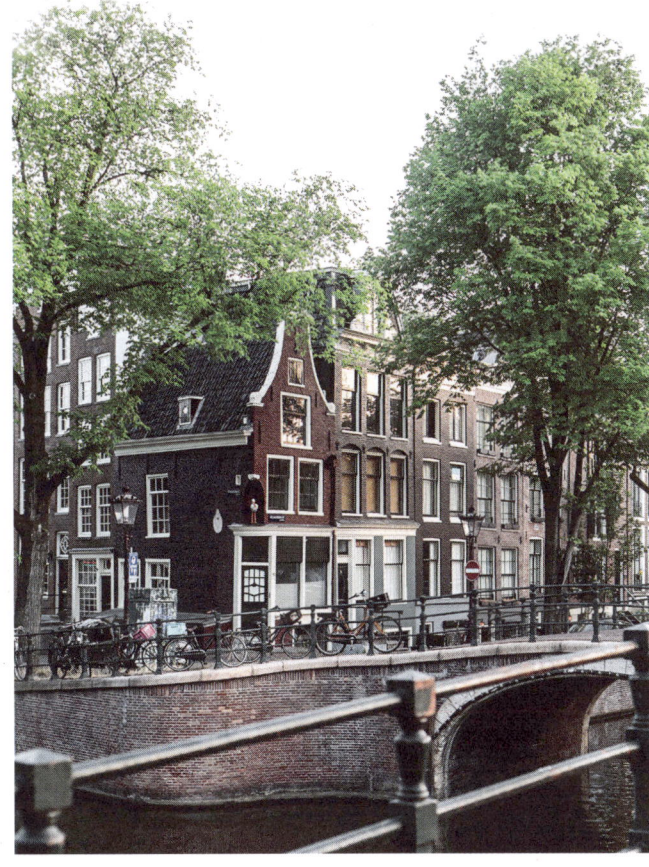

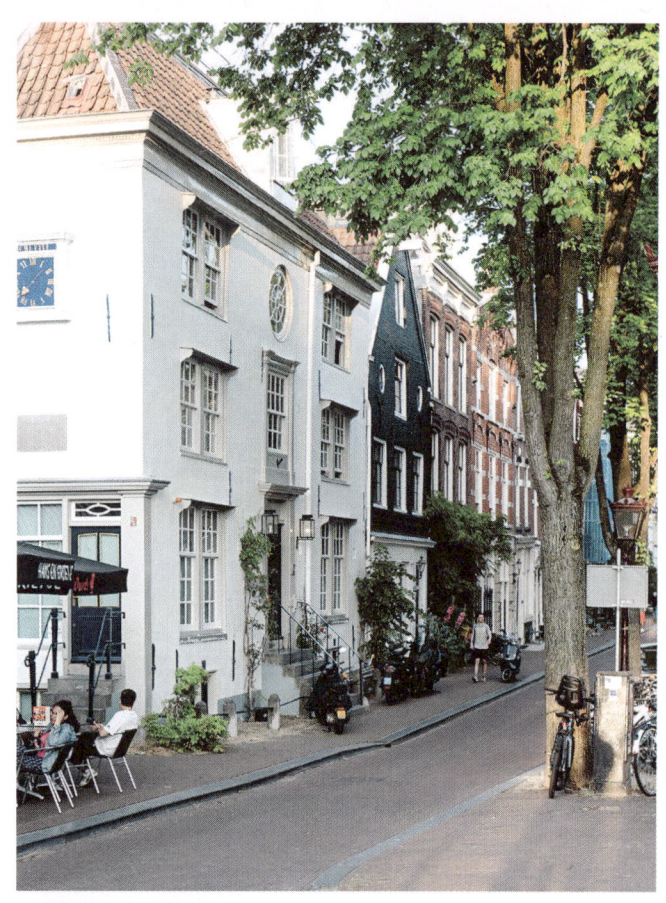
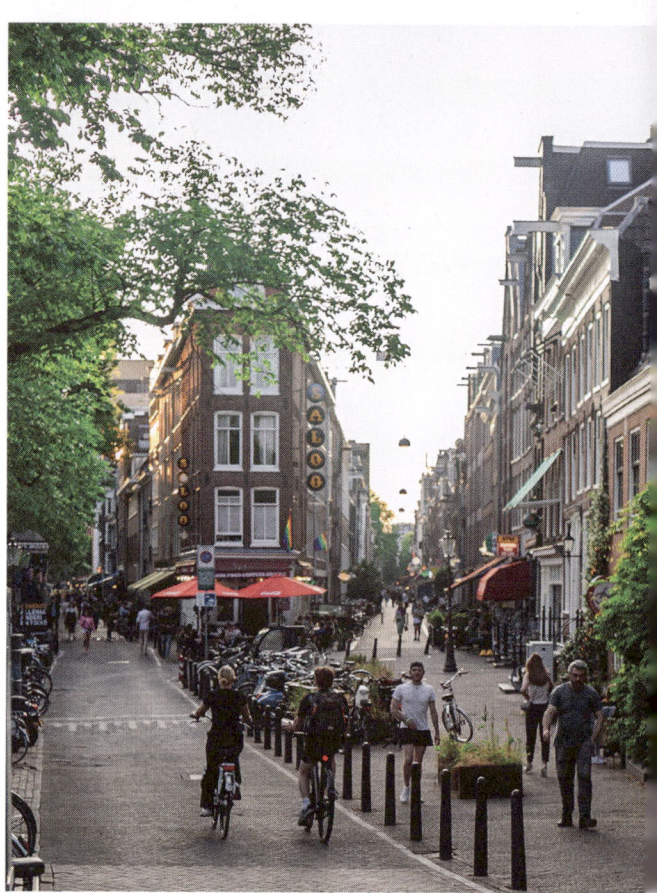

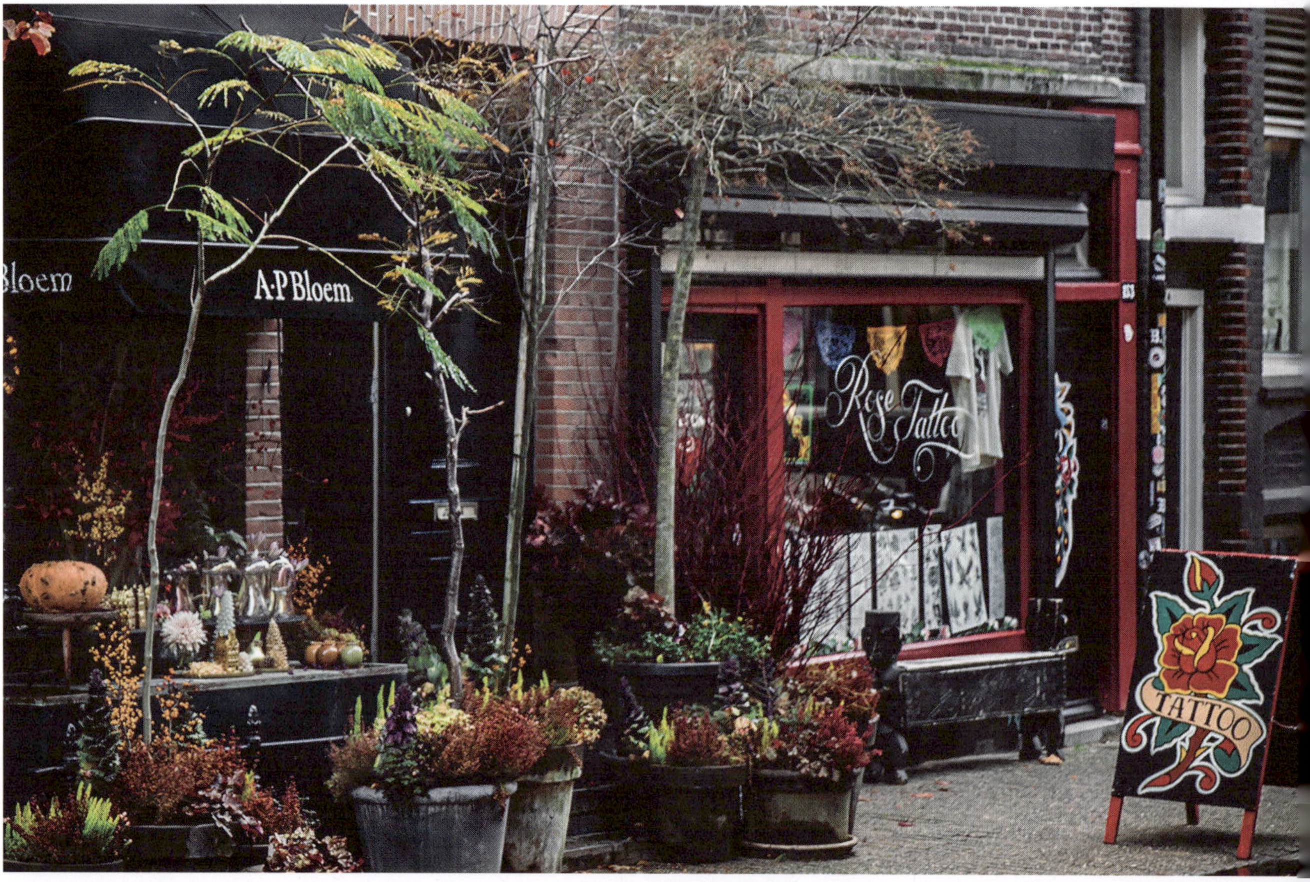

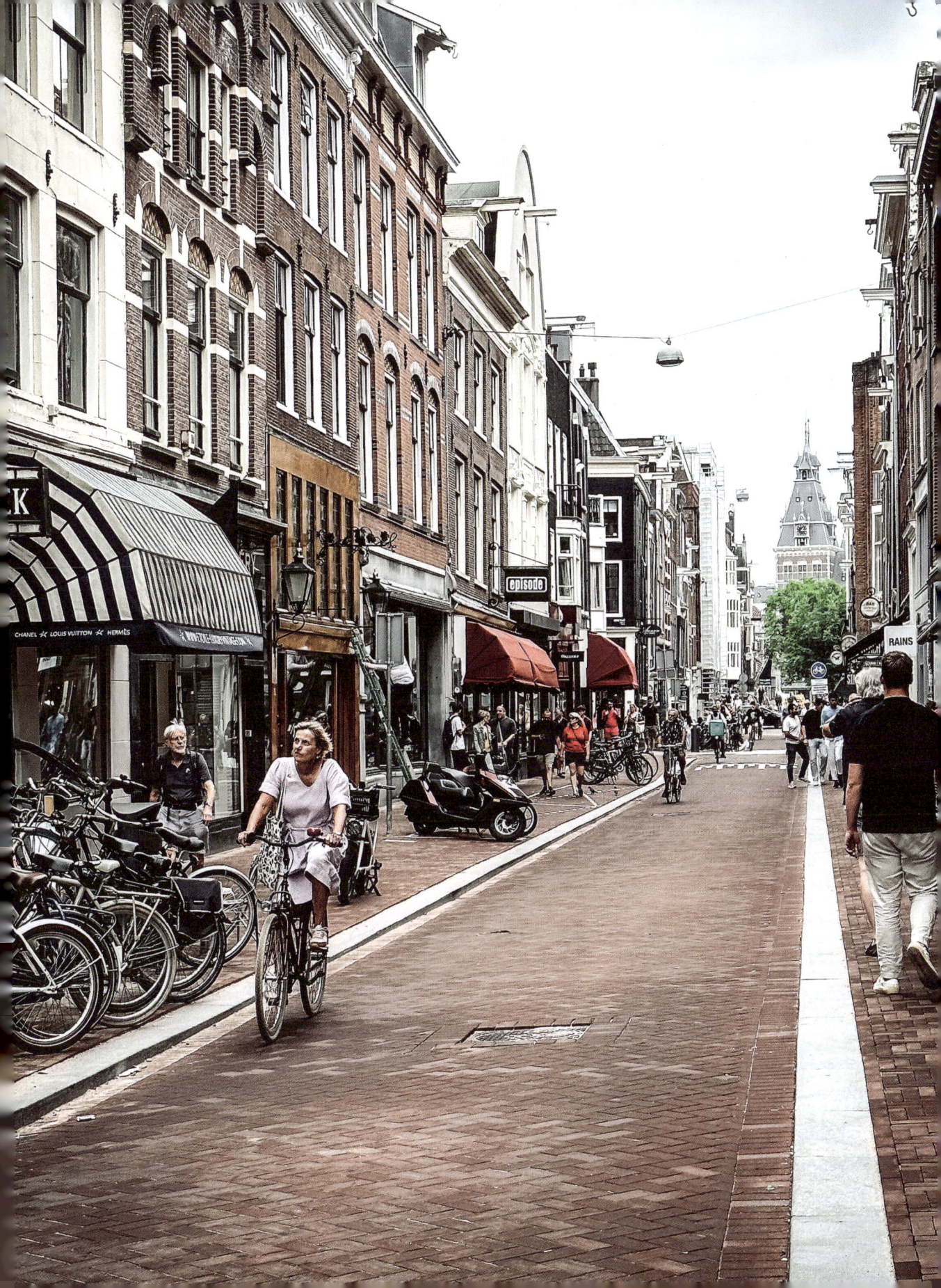

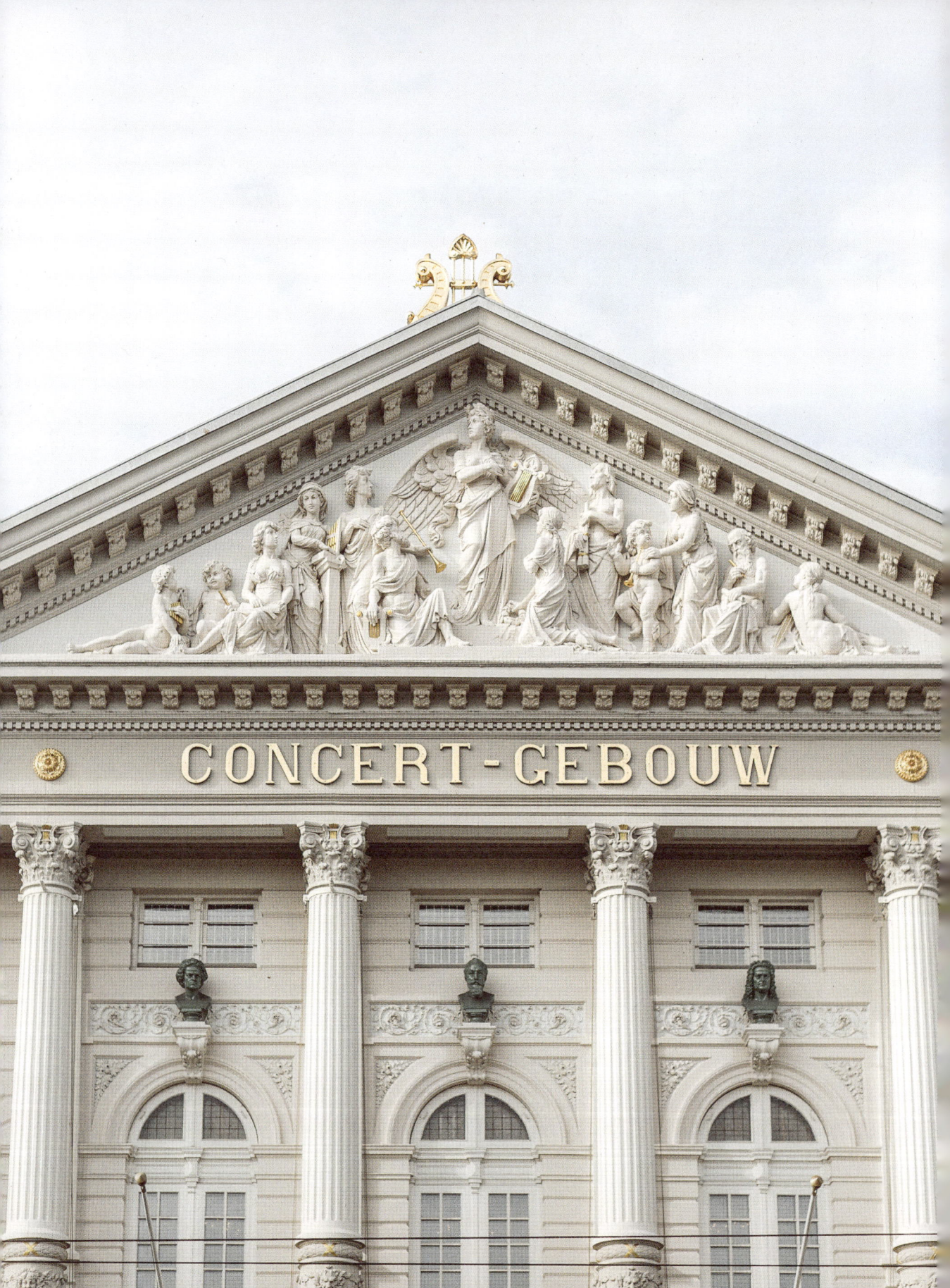

ROUTE TWO

An alternative walk will incorporate a visit to one or two world-class museums in the area.

Head for Weteringstraat 48 and start your day with a speciality coffee, and perhaps receive a visit from the resident ginger cat in this most homely settings: *Back to Black*. After your coffee fix, cross the canal and you will find yourself at the *Rijksmuseum*; stop at the bridge for a little while to take in one of the most beautiful views in the city. The Rijksmuseum is Amsterdam's most visited museum, so booking is essential, and it might be worth trying to go as close to the 9 a.m. opening time as possible to avoid the crowds. Once inside, you can peruse 800 years of Dutch history with great Dutch masters such as Rembrandt, Vermeer and Van Gogh. The museum is spread over four floors and, like the Louvre in Paris, it would be difficult to take it all in in just one visit. Established by King Louis Napolean in 1808 in the Royal Palace on Dam Square, it moved to its present site in 1885. Golden Age paintings are the main draw, peppered through the Long Gallery of Honor, ending with Rembrandt's epic 'The Night Watch' (1642), restored to its former glory in 2022. There are 8,000 masterpieces, which occupy 1.5km of gallery space. Alongside several beautiful works by Rembrandt, you will find Vermeer's 'The Milkmaid' (1660) and 'Woman in Blue Reading a Letter' (1663), works by Van Gogh, and the famous dollhouses and delftware from the Golden Age. It really is the most incredible museum. Take a break now and then with a browse through the shop or a coffee from the cafe, and don't leave without seeing the library. It is only open to art history researchers, but you can view its impressive book collection and features from the viewing platform.

Beyond the Rijksmuseum, there's a large expanse of the park, Museumplein, which features the *Van Gogh Museum* (housing the world's most extensive Van Gogh collection), the *Stedelijk Museum* and the lesser known *Moco Museum*. When you have had your feast of culture, you can retrace your steps back over to Weteringstraat before heading east towards Lijnbaansgracht. Turn right onto Vizelgracht, a charming canal street lined with lovely shops, cafes and restaurants. Make a beeline for *Patisserie Holtkamp*, where you will find savoury croquettes (prawn, cheese and veal) good enough for the Dutch royal family (that's the truth, as apparently Patisserie Holtkamp has been supplying them with these savoury delights for many a year). Of course, if you fancy something sweeter, there's plenty to entice.

Continue walking along Vizelgracht until you reach Prinsengracht. Turn left on to Prinsengracht and keep walking until you get to Utrechtsestraat. Discovering this quaint street has been one of the many highlights of researching this book for me. Packed with so many specialist shops, restaurants and cafes, it's a true gem. Renowned skincare brand *Aesop* has recently found a new home at number 93 in the former home of much-loved candy brand Jamin. The beautiful details of this historic shop have mainly been preserved or reproduced: arched cabinets, wood panelling, antique clocks and copper accents come together to deliver the most beautiful backdrop for Aesop's products. *De Koffie Salon*, at number 130, offers a fine selection of cakes, sandwiches and a great cup of coffee; another option is *Zuivere Koffie* at number 39. For an exceptional treat, visit one-Michelin Star restaurant *Bistro de la Mer* at number 57 or its sister *De Juwelier* at number 51, both owned by Richard van Oostenbrugge.

Once you are done on Utrechtsestraat, head back to the junction of Kerkstraat; continue until you reach Kerkstraat, turn left and continue to the famous and fabulous *Koninklijk Theater Tuschinski* cinema on your right-hand side. This cinema is most likely one of the most beautiful art nouveau cinemas in the world. Its construction was commissioned by Abraham Tuschinski in the early twentieth century, who put his heart and soul into this building. He was not interested in another ordinary theatre; he wanted to build an astonishingly beautiful cinema. He succeeded, and in 1921 the Tuschinski Theatre – rightfully referred to as a 'movie palace' by Abraham – opened its doors.

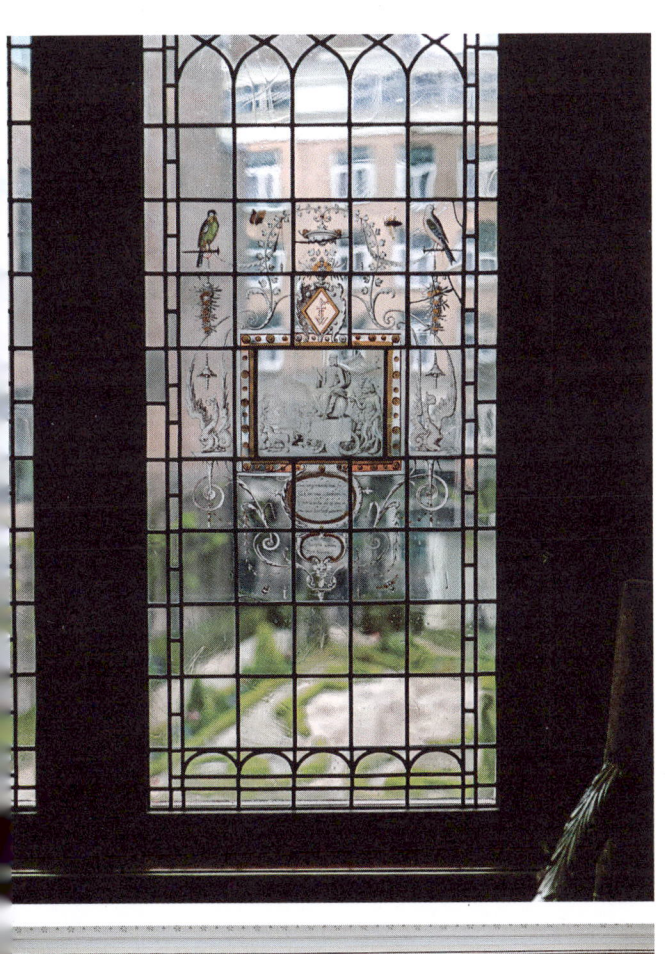
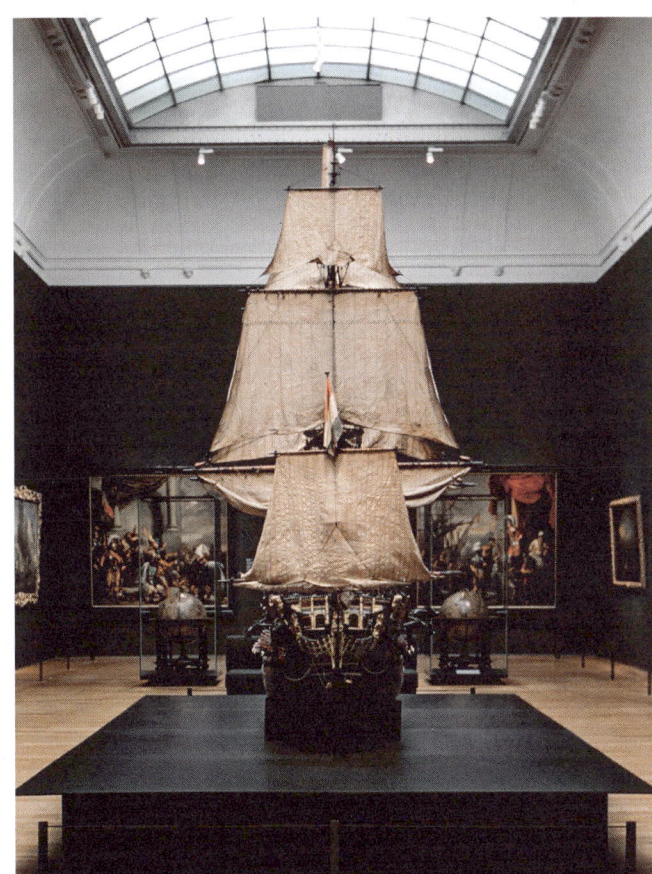
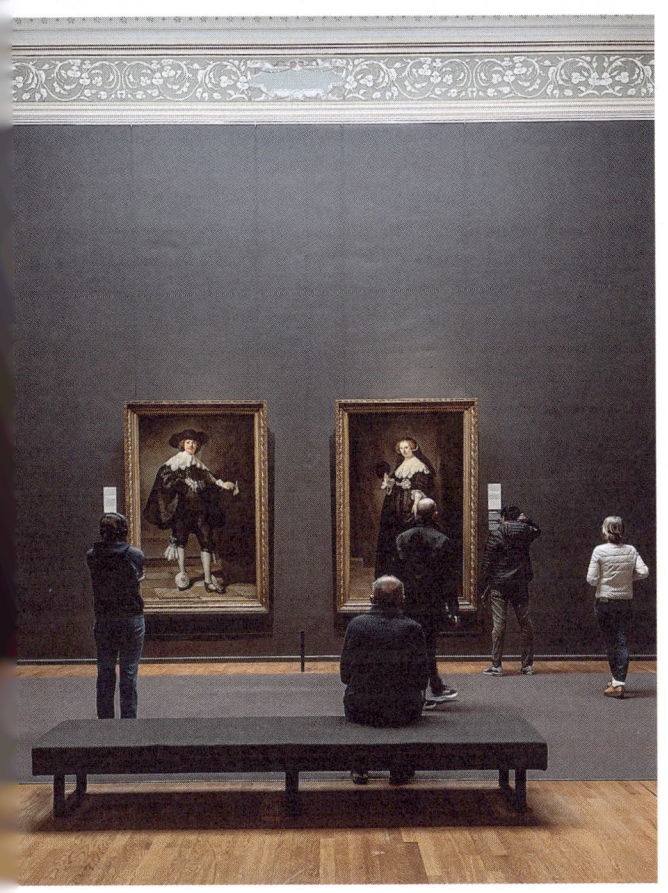
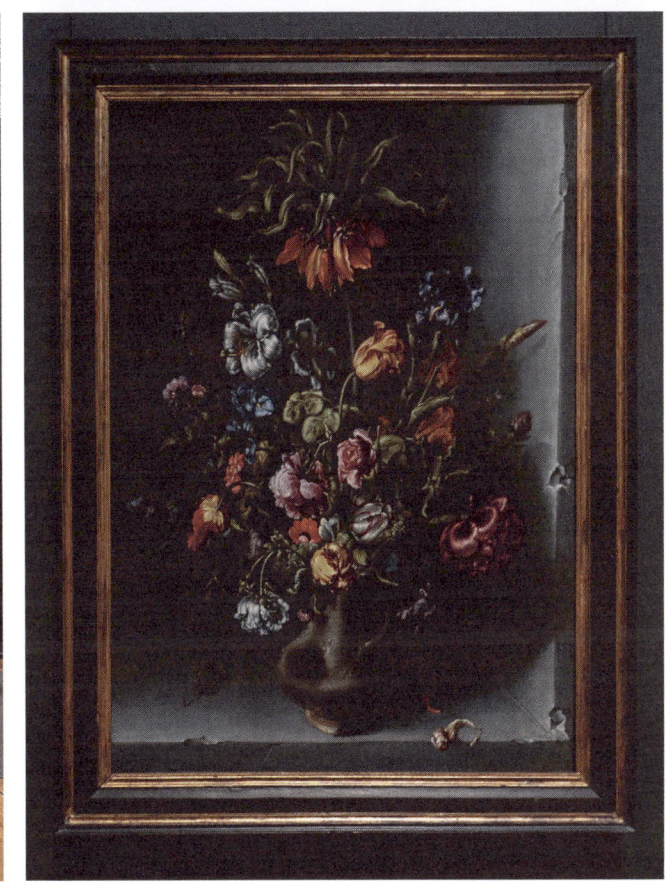

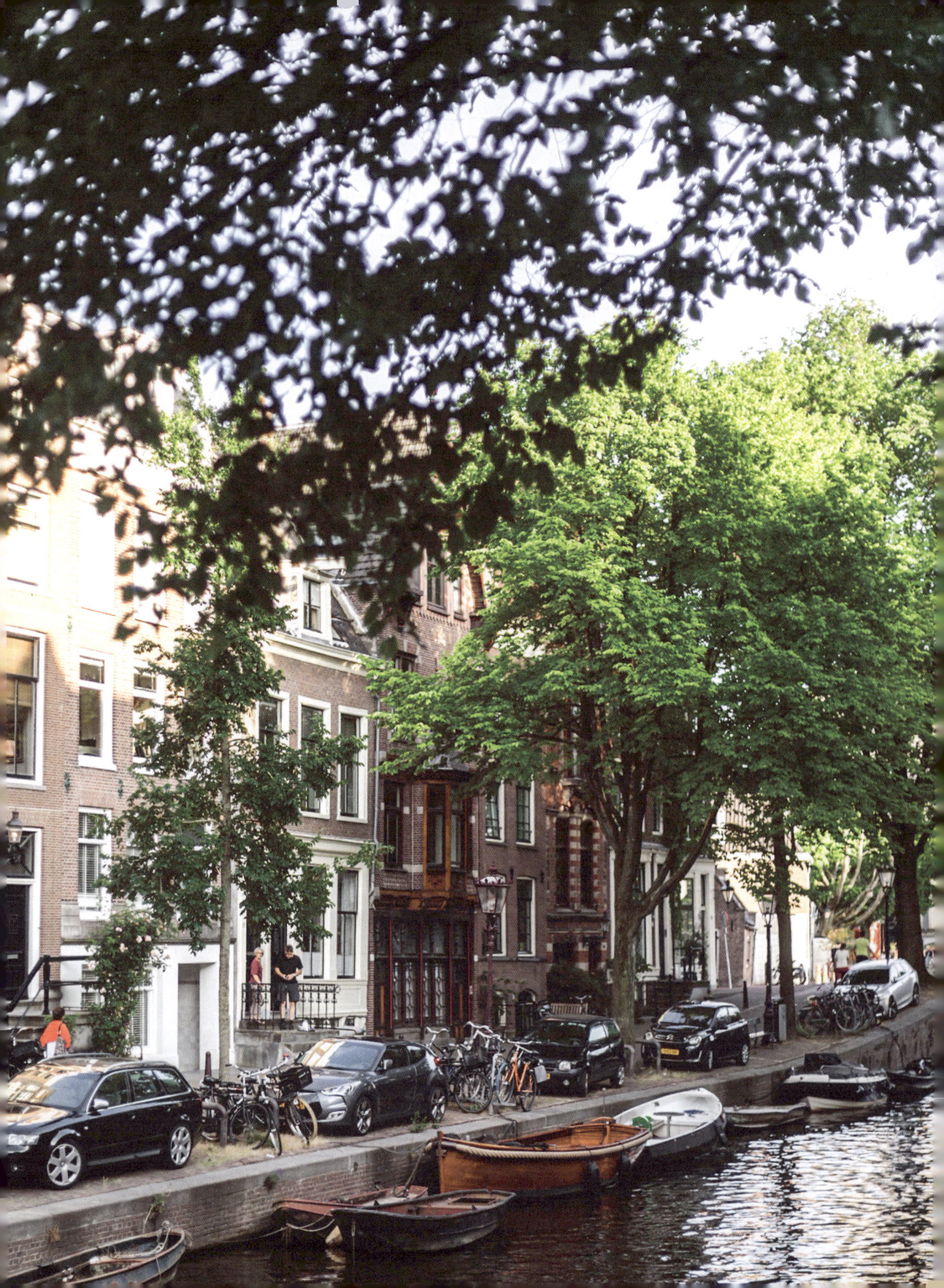

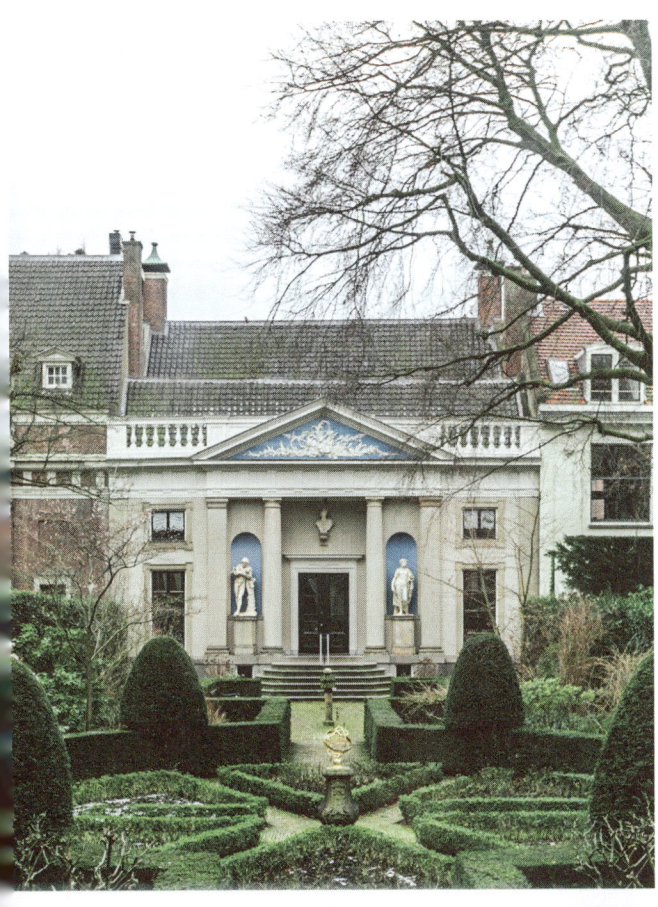
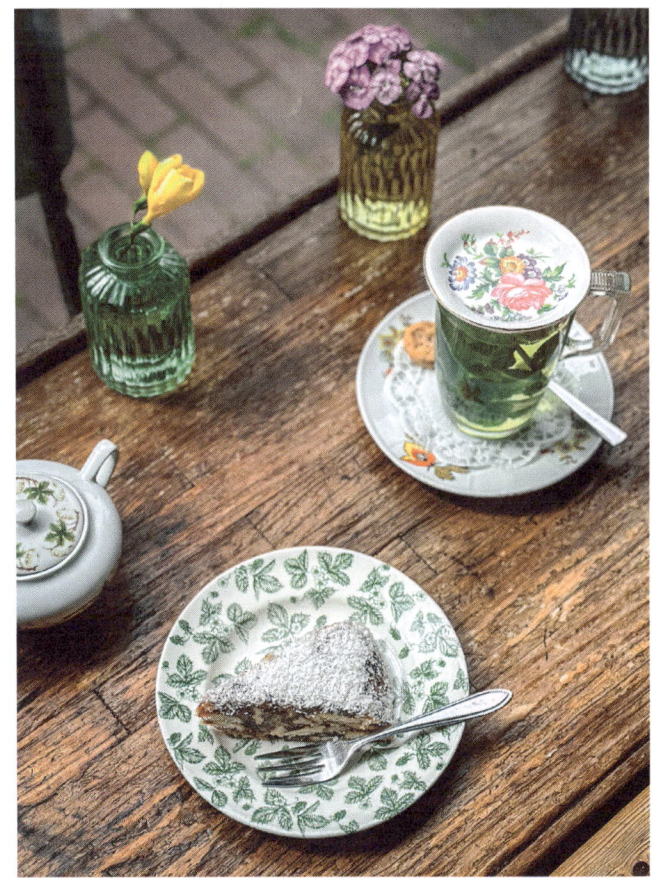
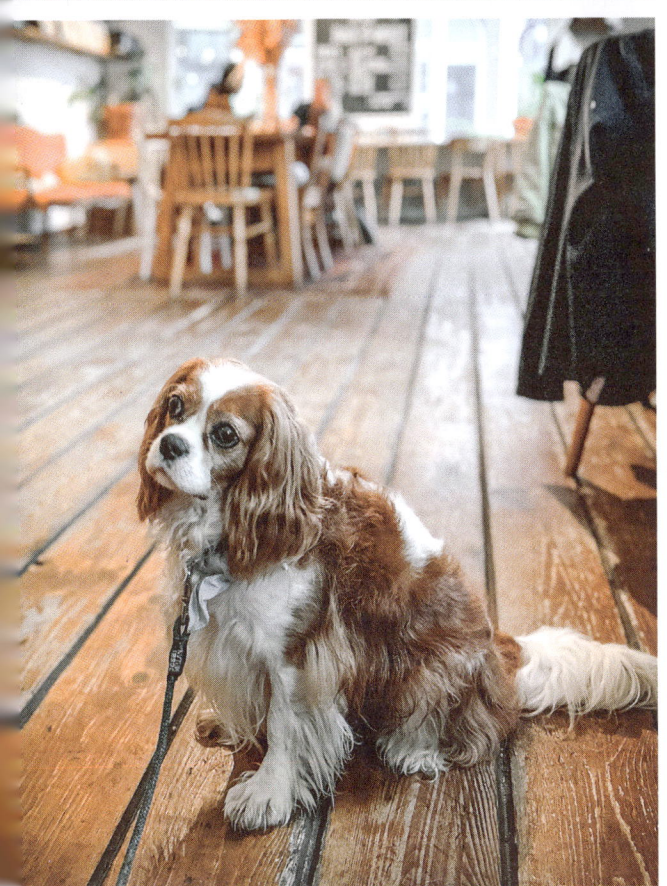
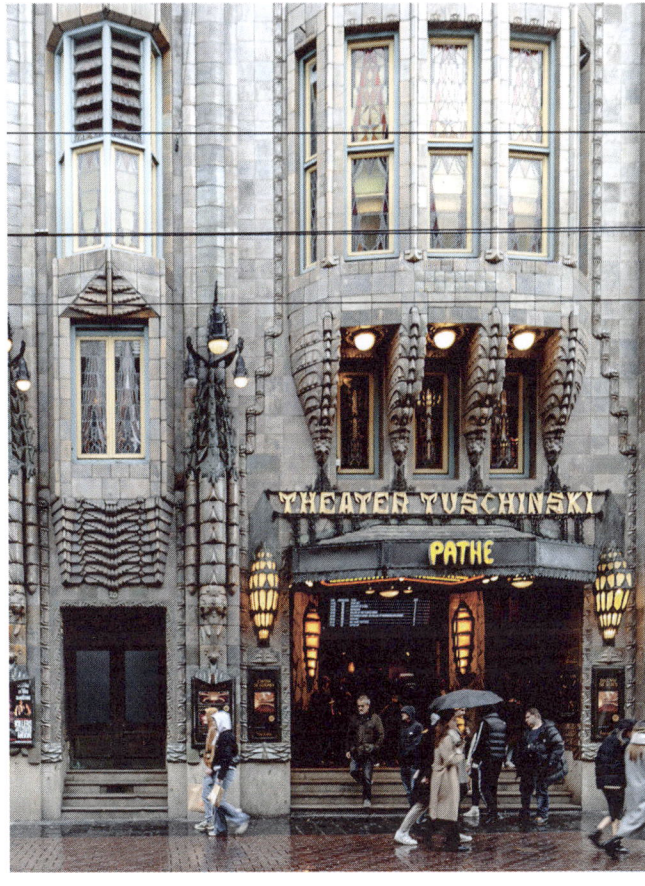

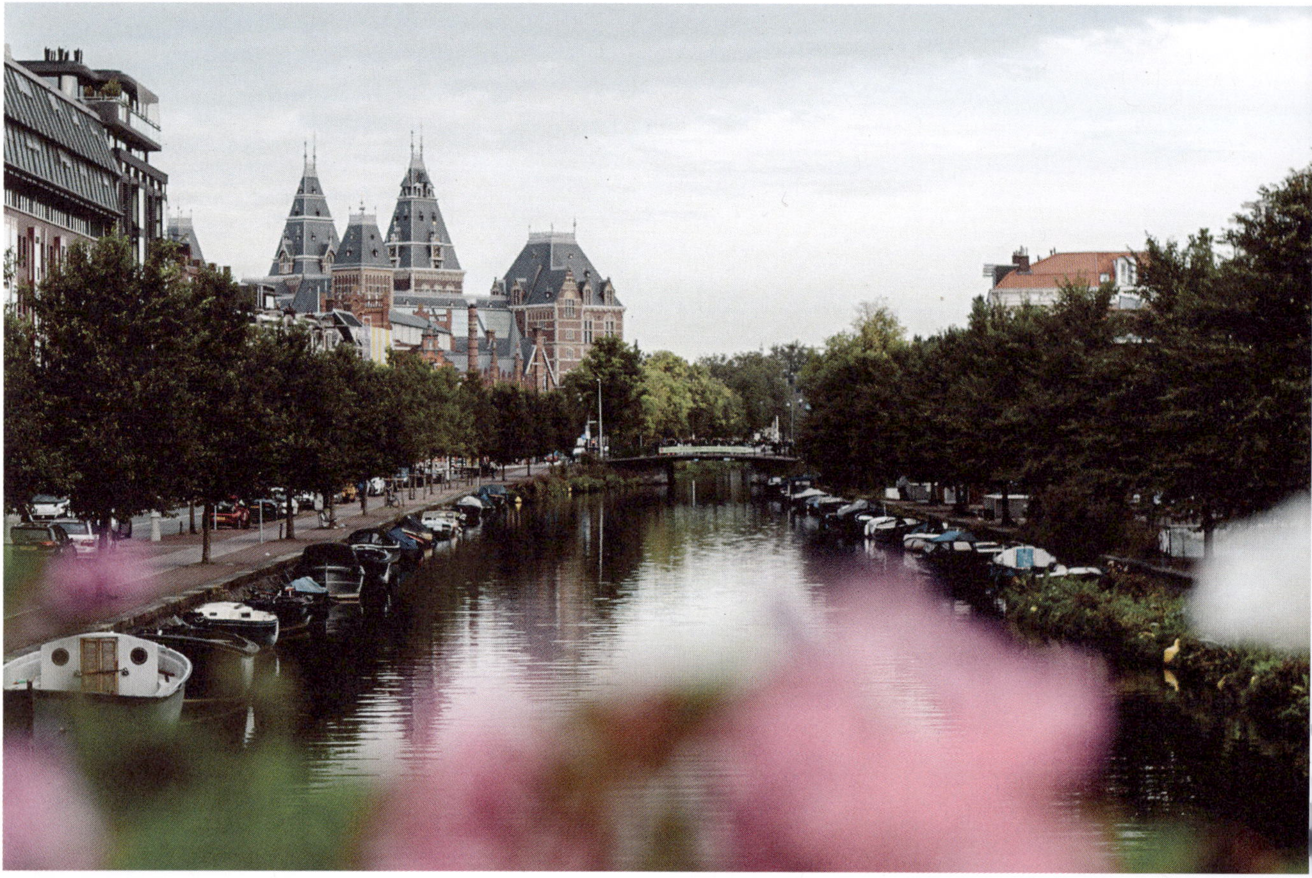

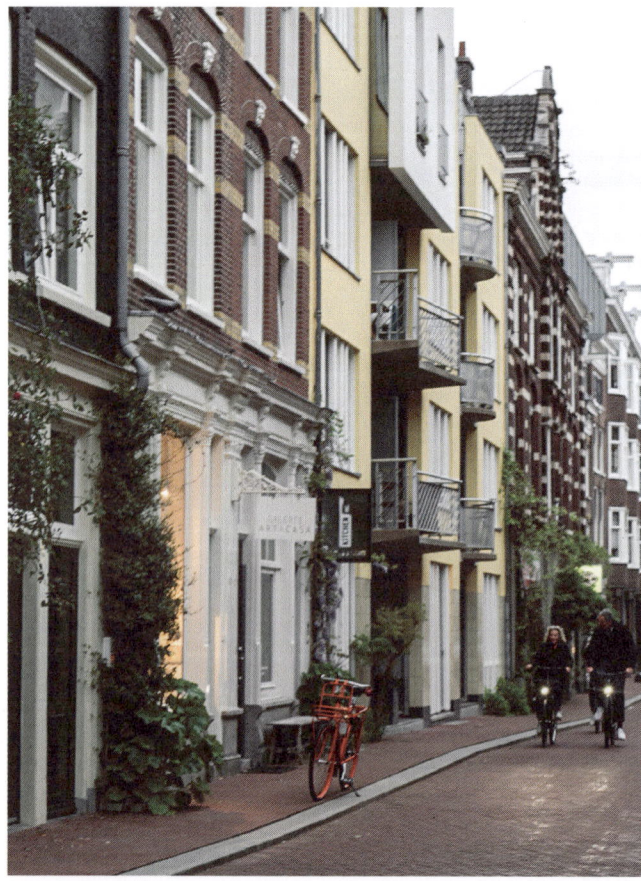
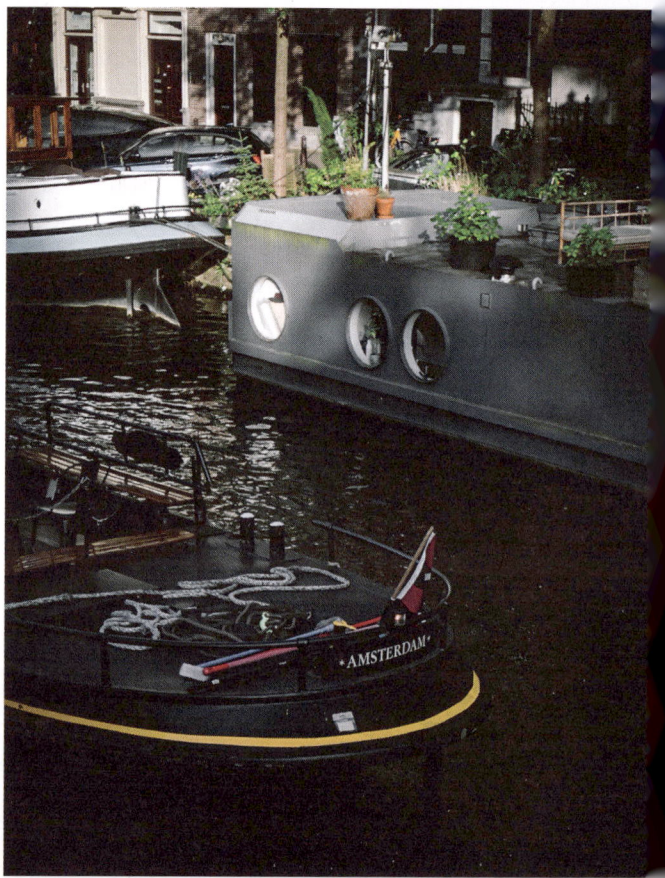

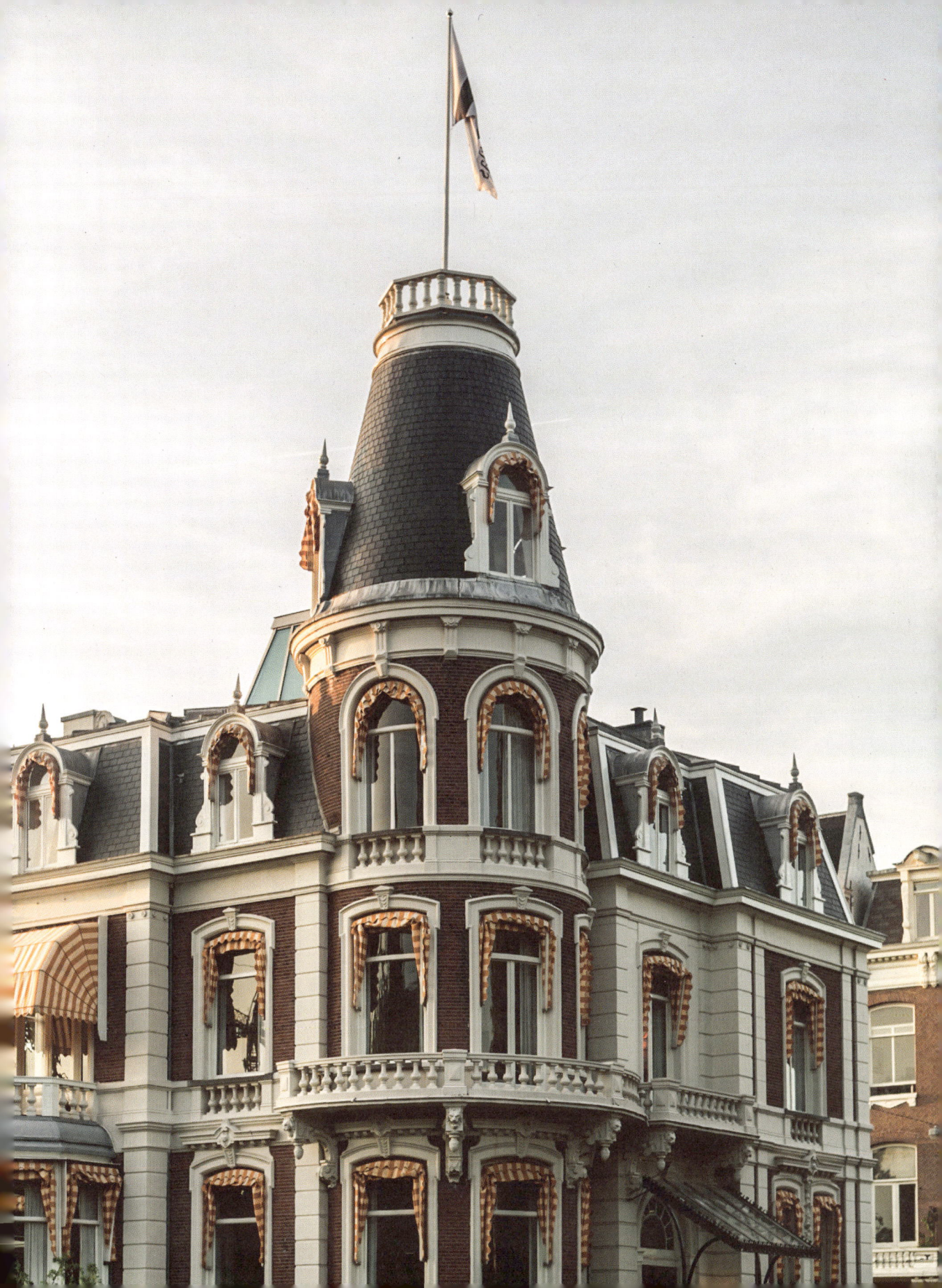

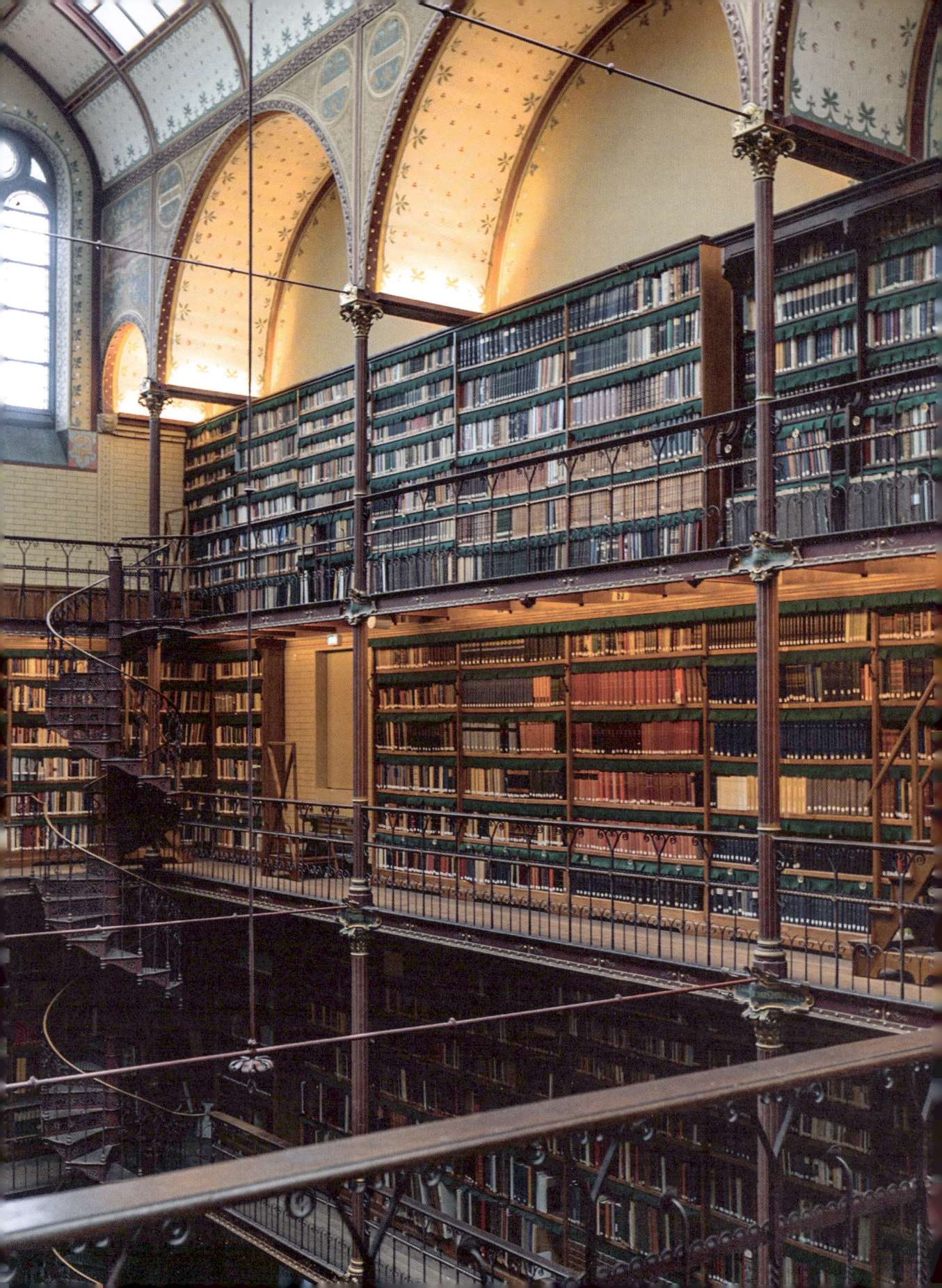

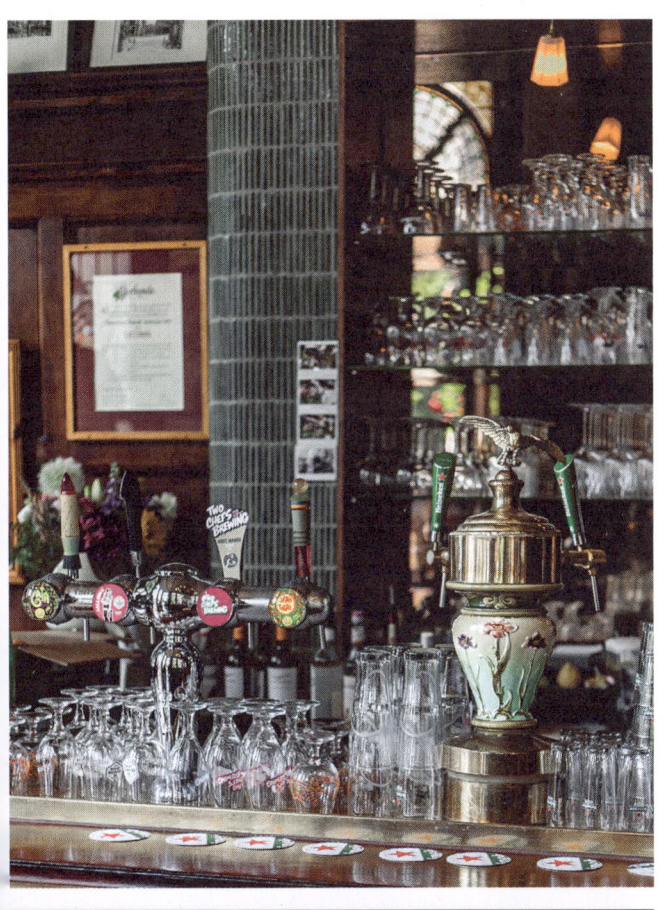
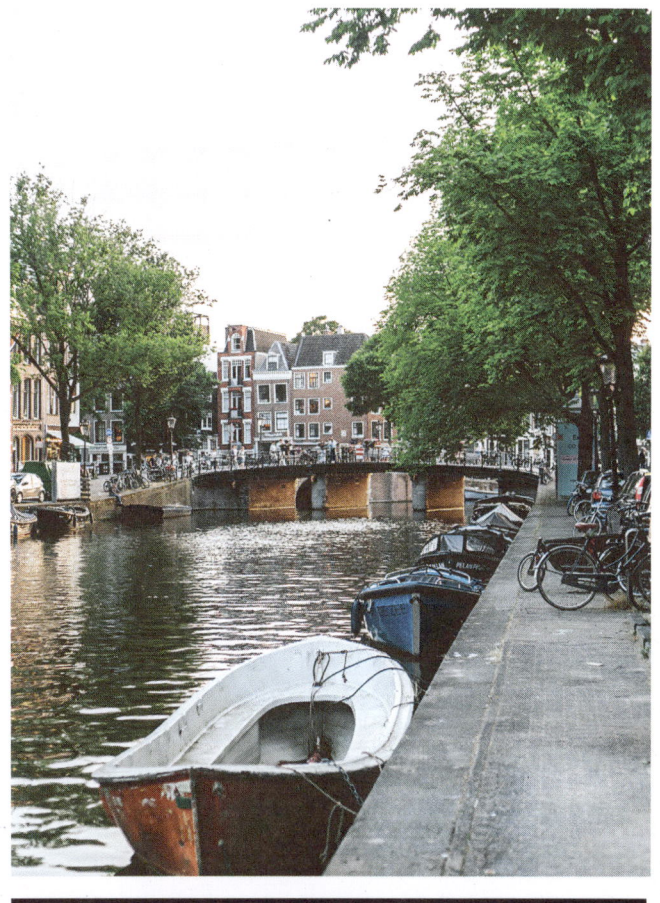
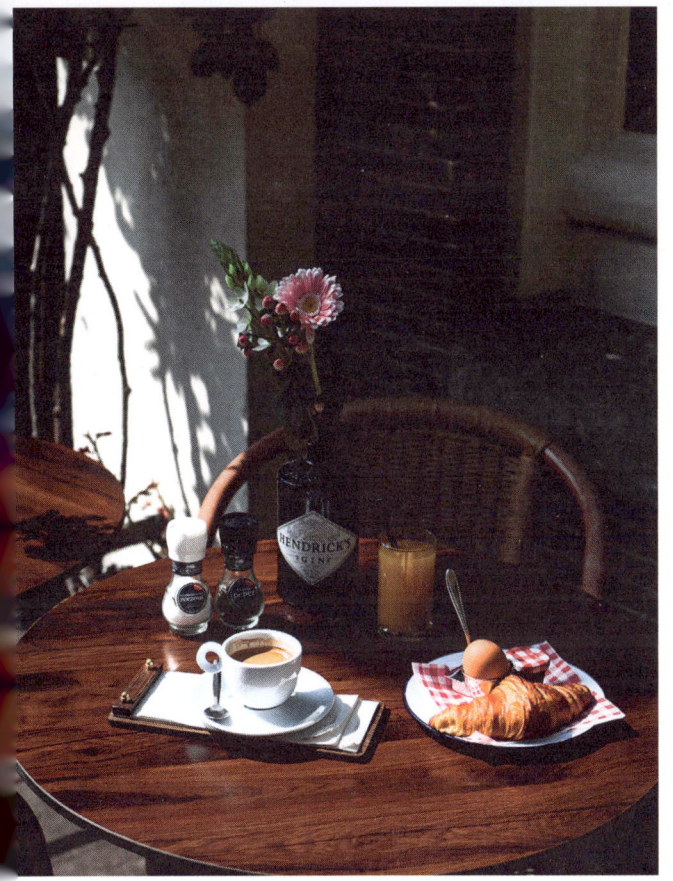

Bieren v/d tap				Bieren v/d Fles	
Jupiler pilsener	5.2%	25cl	3.40	Galipette cidre brut	6.00
Hertog Jan pilsener	5.1%	25cl	3.50	De Koninck	4.70
Leffe blonde	6.6%	25cl	4.80	Corona cerveza	5.60
Hertog Jan Bock	6.5%	25cl	5.20	Boon Kriek	5.20
Tripel karmeliet	8.4%	25cl	5.20	Jopen chapter	6.00
Mooie Nel IPA	6.5%	25cl	5.20	Texels Skuumkoppe	5.00
Franziskamer	5.0%	30cl	5.00	Westmalle trappist - dubbel - trippel	6.00
Hoegaarden wit	4.9%	25cl	4.40	La Chouffe	5.60

Wijn wit

Hoja airen sauvignon Bio	4.60/21.-	
Pinot Grigio Terre di Rai	5.75/27.75	
Rioja blanco real de A8	6.75/32.50	
Chardonnay La côte barrique	7.50/36.50	

rood

Cab. sav. Croix d'Or	4.60/21.-	
Tempranillo Boka Radio	5.75/27.75	
Malbec Pirlet Languedoc	6.75/32.50	
Sangiovese - Lornano - Toscane	7.50/36.50	

CAVA

Savia Viva cava brut	6.00/30.-
Creador traditionelle cava brut	7.50/36.50

Champagne Brut 100% Chardonnay

Blanc de Blanc Lenique 75,-

Rosé Blush - Rosato 5.75/27.75

Duvel 5.60
Zeezuiper tripel 6.00
Orval trappist ale 6.00
Brouwerij t ij ijwit 6.00
Pauwel kwak 6.00

Alcoholvrij /arm & cider

Warsteiner:
 pilsener 0.5% 3.50
 radler 2.5% 4.30
Leffe blond 0.0% 5.9
Jopen nonnetje IPA 0.3% 5.9
Franziskamer weizen a 4.4
Cider 6.0

JORDAAN

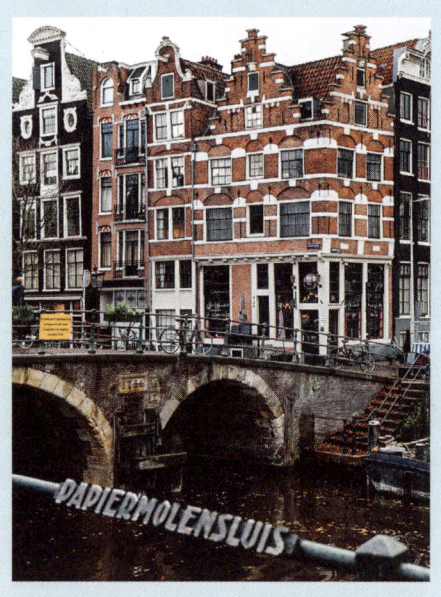

COMMUNITY SPIRIT AND CHARM IN ABUNDANCE:
NARROW STREETS, PICTURESQUE CANALS AND
HISTORIC BUILDINGS; HOME TO NOORDERMARKT

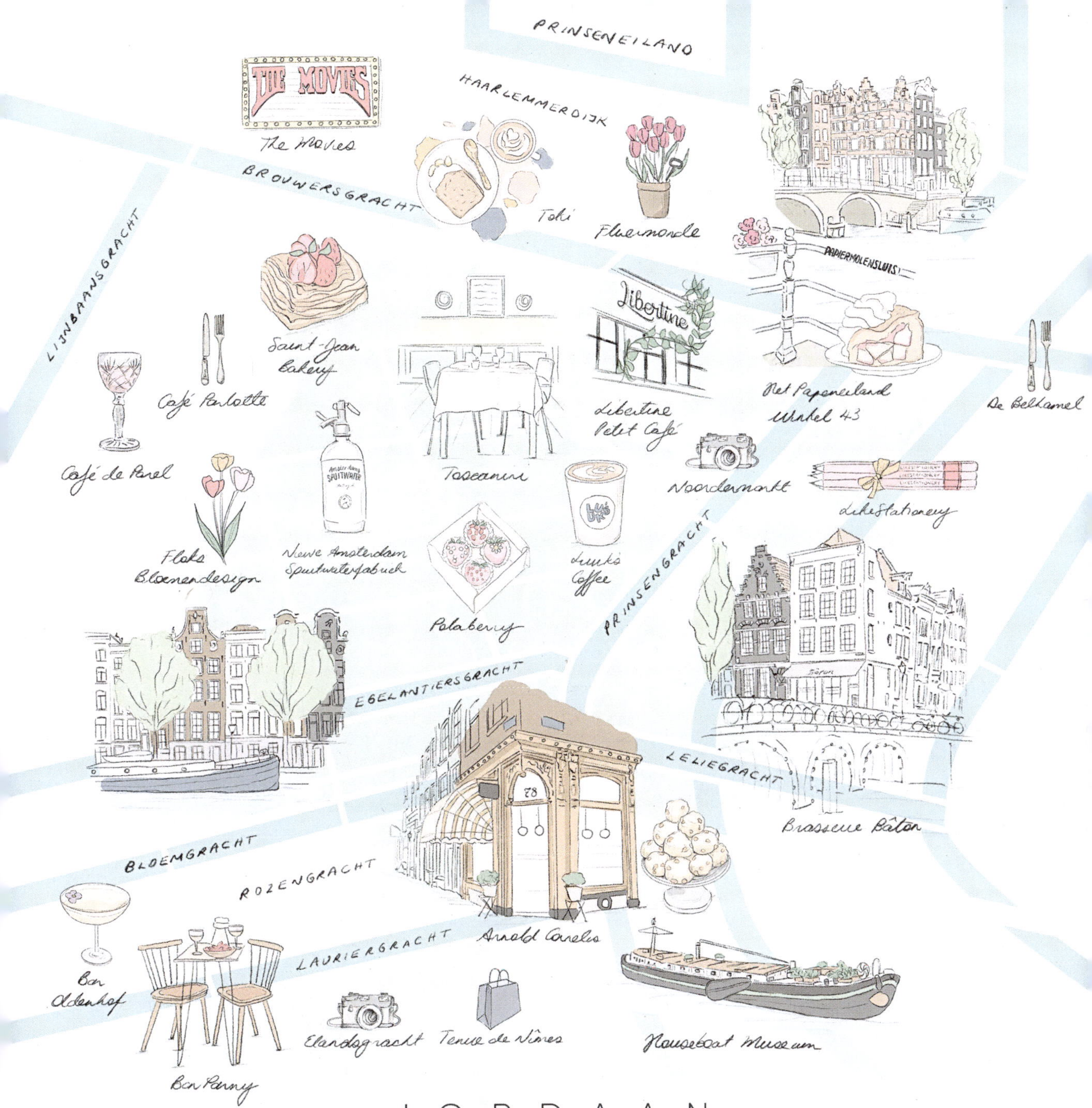

JORDAAN

#prettycityamsterdam

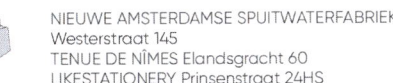 NIEUWE AMSTERDAMSE SPUITWATERFABRIEK Westerstraat 145
TENUE DE NÎMES Elandsgracht 60
LIKESTATIONERY Prinsenstraat 24HS

TOSCANINI Lindengracht 75
LIBERTINE PETIT CAFÉ Noordermarkt 4
CAFÉ DE PAREL Westerstraat 266
CAFÉ PARLOTTE Westerstraat 182
BRASSERIE BÂTON Herengracht 82
DE BELHAMEL Brouwersgracht 60

FLOKS BLOEMENDESIGN MJ, Westerstraat 141
FLEURMONDE Haarlemmerdijk 49

 Egelantiersgracht, Elandsgracht, Noordermarkt, Brouwersgracht
THE MOVIES Haarlemmerdijk 159-163
HOUSEBOAT MUSEUM Prinsengracht 296K

BAR PARRY Eerste Looiersdwarsstraat 15
BAR OLDENHOF Elandsgracht 84H

 TOKI Binnen Dommersstraat 15
POLABERRY Prinsengracht 232H
LUUK'S COFFEE Westerstraat 3

 WINKEL 43 Noordermarkt 43
SAINT-JEAN BAKERY Lindengracht 158H
ARNOLD CORNELIS Elandsgracht 78
HET PAPENEILAND Prinsengracht 2

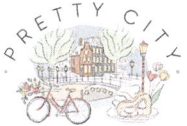
PRETTY CITY
AMSTERDAM

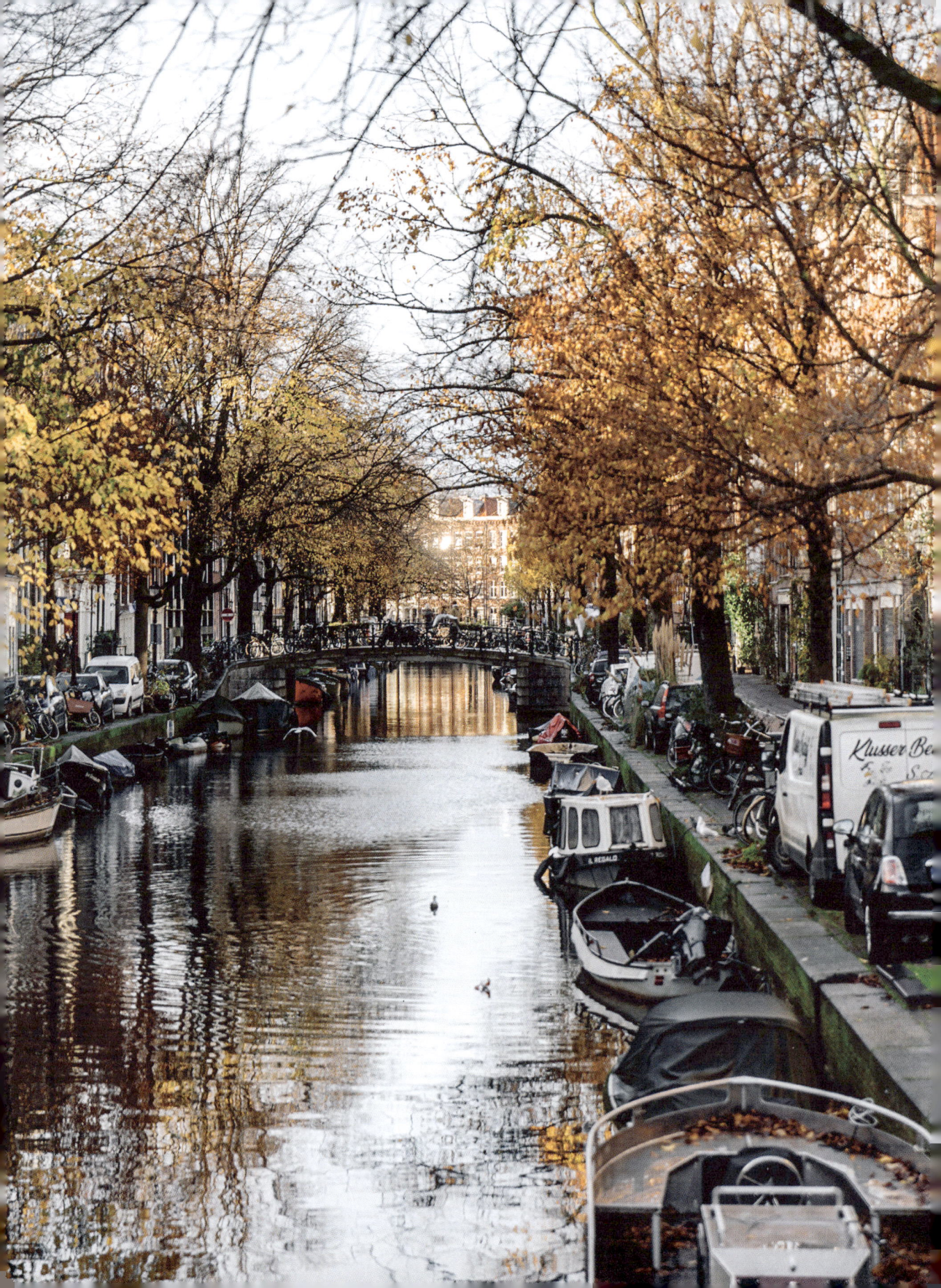

Jordaan, once a place of squalor and poverty on boggy meadowland, is one of the town's most beautiful and sought-after districts. As you wander the quaint streets today, imagining it was once a squalid neighbourhood is impossible. Dating back to the city's first expansion and its canals in the early seventeenth century, the canal belt was developed as a luxury district for traders in the Dutch Golden Age; Jordaan was needed for the working classes whose industries were banned from the town centre. People fleeing religious persecution also made their new homes there. It is renowned for its tight-knit communities, which likely contributed to its gentrification, which began in the 1970s and continued over several decades.

Its boundaries consist of Prinsengracht to the east, Lijnbaansgracht to the west, Brouwersgracht to the north and Leidsegracht to the south. Haarlemmerdijk is, strictly speaking, just beyond the northern boundaries, but it felt right to include it here. It is a labyrinth of narrow streets and canals that follow the course of old paths and ditches, with many of its original canals filled in, so it looks very different to the city centre. Warehouses and small-scale factories were constructed along the broader canals. Today, the district is the beating heart of the city and much loved by locals and visitors alike for its romantic air, smaller canals, many bucolic streets, tiny alleys, art galleries, brilliant shops, top-notch restaurants, outdoor markets and old-world brown bars. It is also the home of the famous *Westerkerk* and the possibly more famous *Anne Frank House*. You can easily be led astray in this romantic pocket for the entire day (or two). While you wander this neighbourhood, be sure to cast your eyes up to the historic gabled stones, intricately carved, that mark the entrances to buildings, and watch out for some *hofjes* (courtyards) that remain open to the public. You can also browse the lovely, bustling markets regularly held at *Noordermarkt*, the Westerstraat and Lindengracht. Experience a Dutch apple pie with whipped cream like no other in *Winkel 43* or *Café 't Papeneiland*. Watch the sun go down at Papiermolensluis and dine your way through Little Italy.

You could start your walk at Brouwersgracht, one of my favourite stretches of canal in Amsterdam, lined with beautiful, preserved seventeenth-century merchant houses. Take some time to admire this

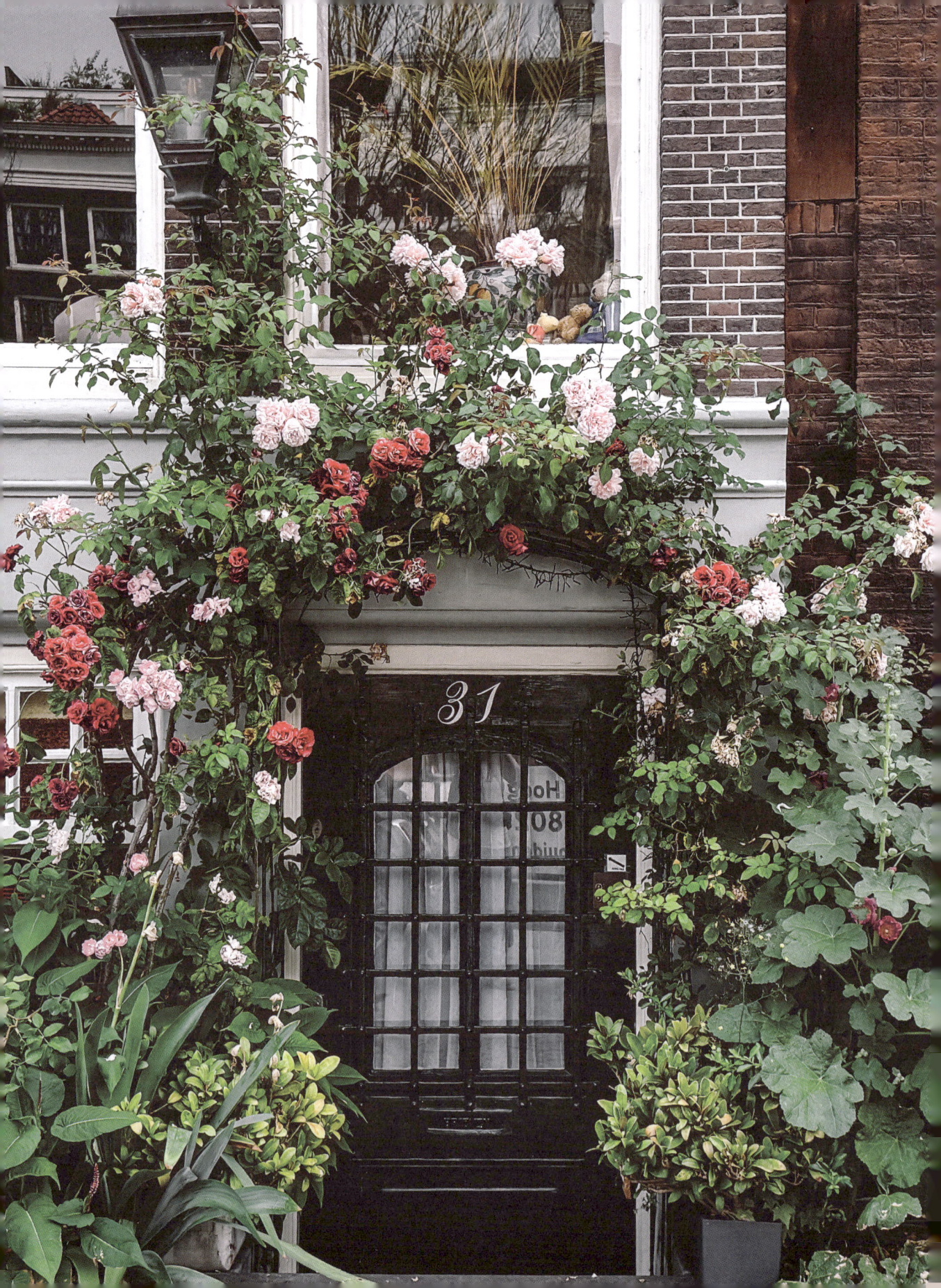

pocket's architecture and charming mercantile heritage. It is a gorgeous walk, especially at dawn, and is as lovely in summer as in winter but extra special in autumn. Whilst the area is mainly residential, you will find one of the most beautiful restaurants, *Restaurant de Belhamel*, at number 60. Inside, its preserved belle époque interior with original art nouveau details mesmerises; its waterside tables perched on the canal are perfect for a sunny lunch during the warmer months. It serves a French Italian menu and is open for lunch and dinner.

From Brouwersgracht, head east towards Haarlemmerdijk and Haarlemmerstraat. Both streets are considered to be one shopping district and are peppered with enough unique vintage shops, concept stores, delis, cosy cafes and local boutiques to keep you busy for an entire day.

Take a stroll and savour the area's lively local ambience, and be sure to note these addresses:

ADDRESSES OF NOTE

The Movies, **Haarlemmerdijk 159–163**
You may not have time for the cinema, but it's worth a visit to this beautiful old-school cinema on this lively strip. Founded in 1912, you can't miss it with its atmospheric facade; it boasts art deco interiors across four rooms. Open daily, you can buy tickets on site.

Fleurmonde, **Haarlemmerdijk 49**
An enchanting local florist that has resided here for many years will catch your eye with its beautiful blooms that spill on to the street.

Six and Sons, **Haarlemmerstraat 41**
A concept store and coffee bar opened by art director Alexander Six in 2019. Step inside to find a wonderful curated space specialising in menswear and unique homeware products, including Campfire Cologne from Portland, Oregon; Tokyo-based Postalco stationery; and Swedish porcelain from Mutti.

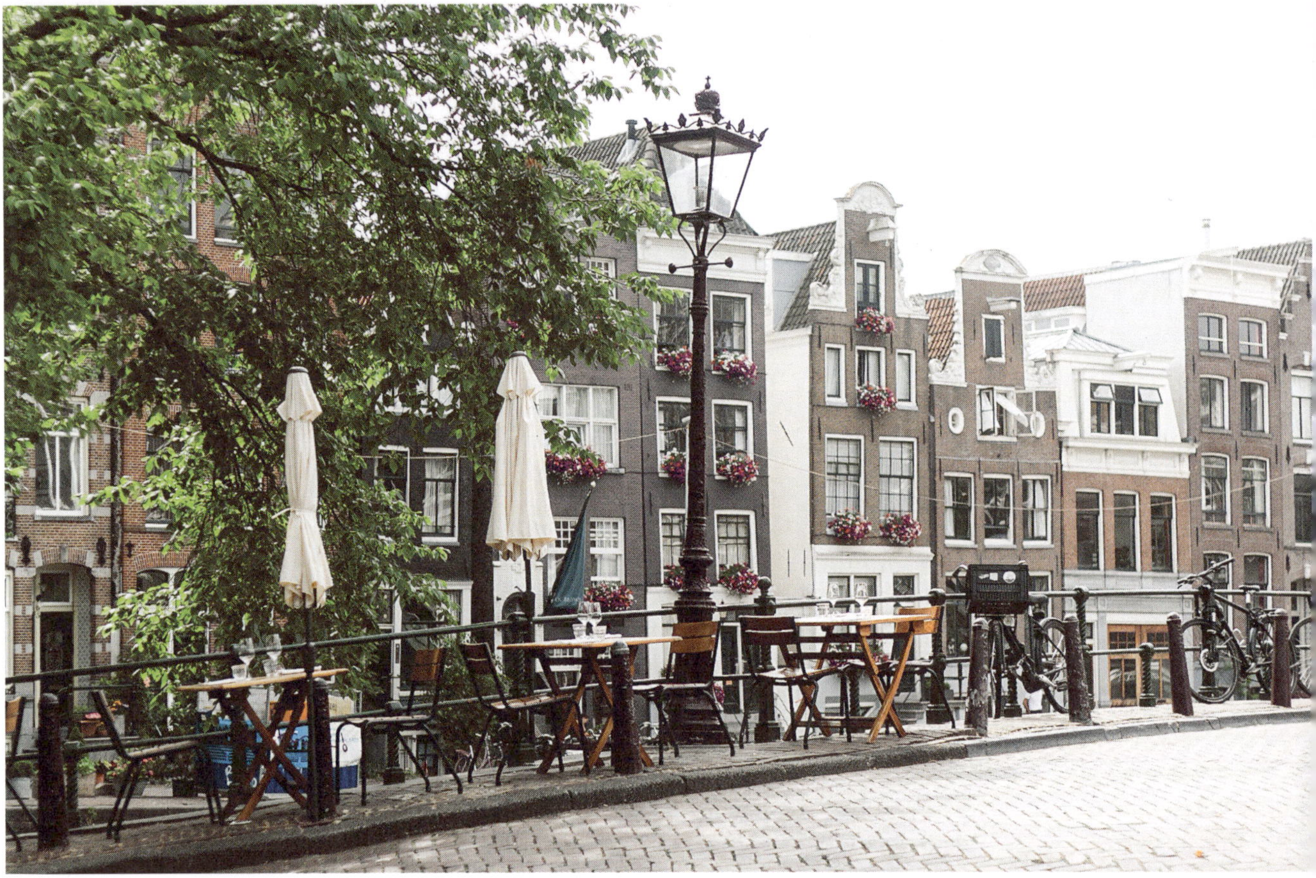

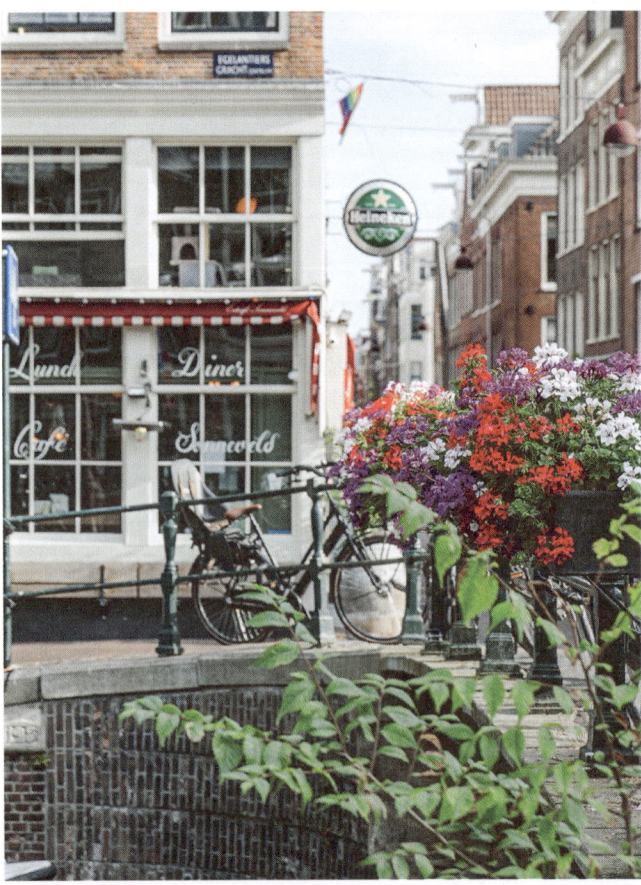
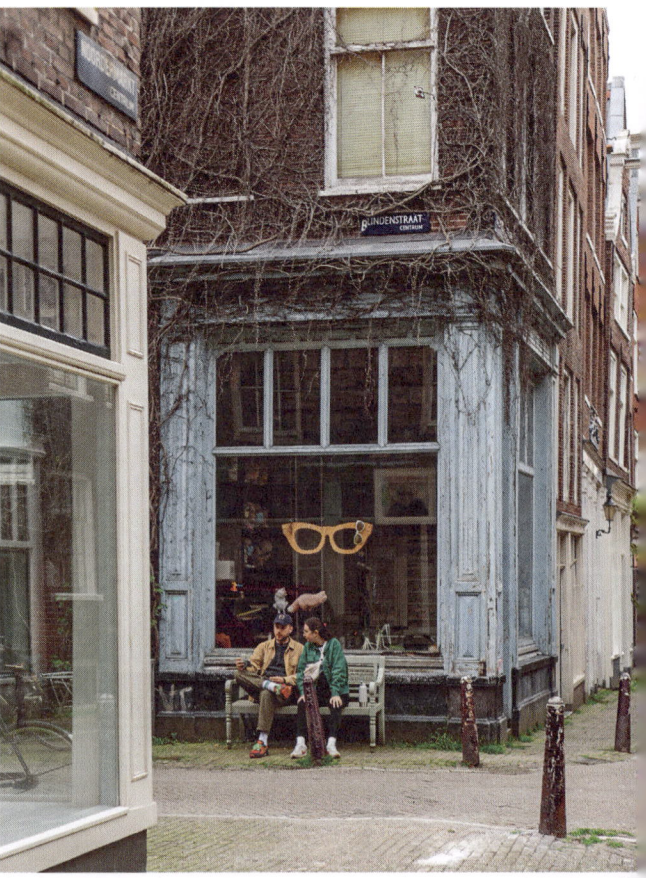

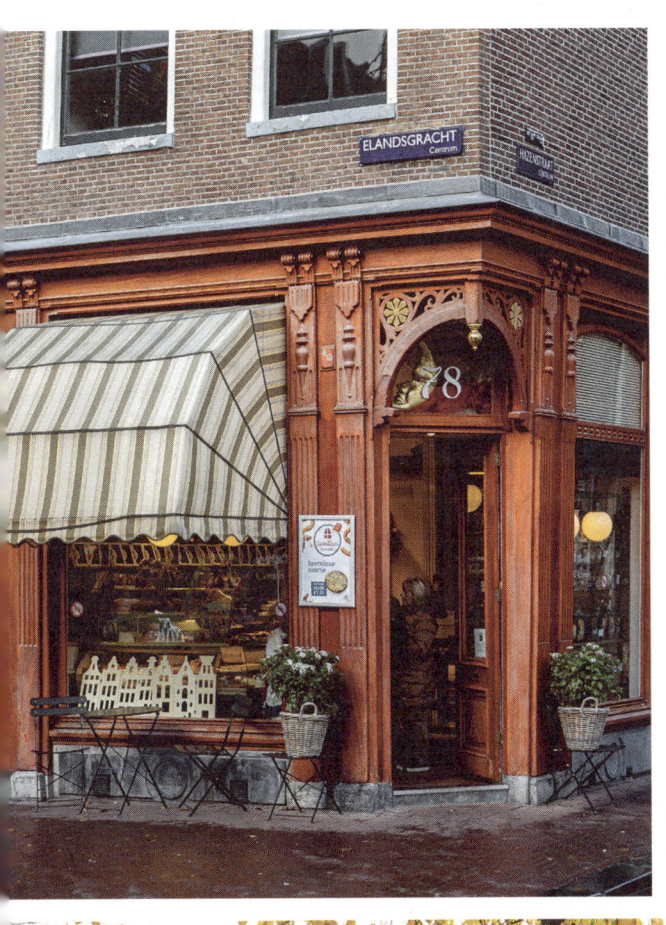
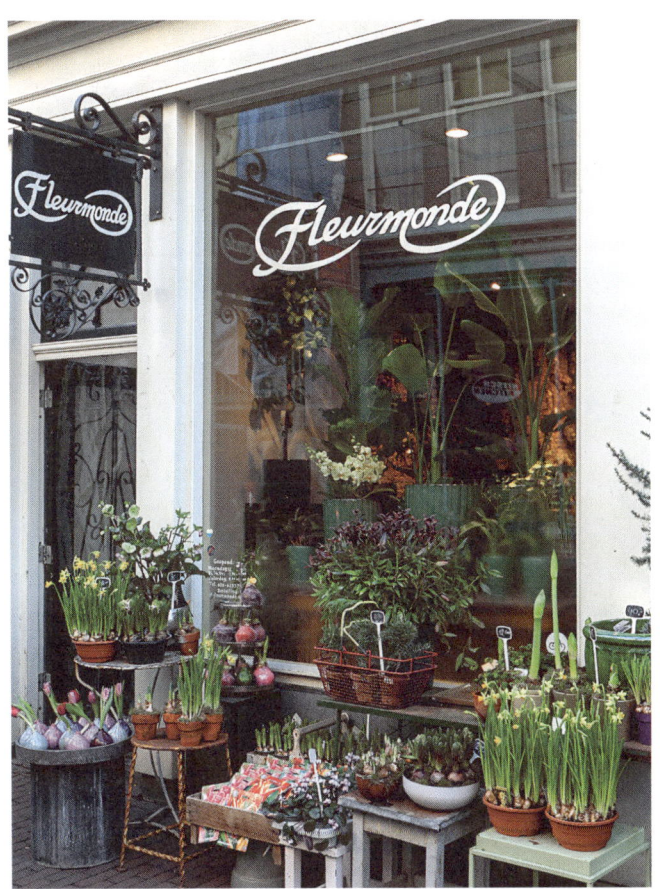

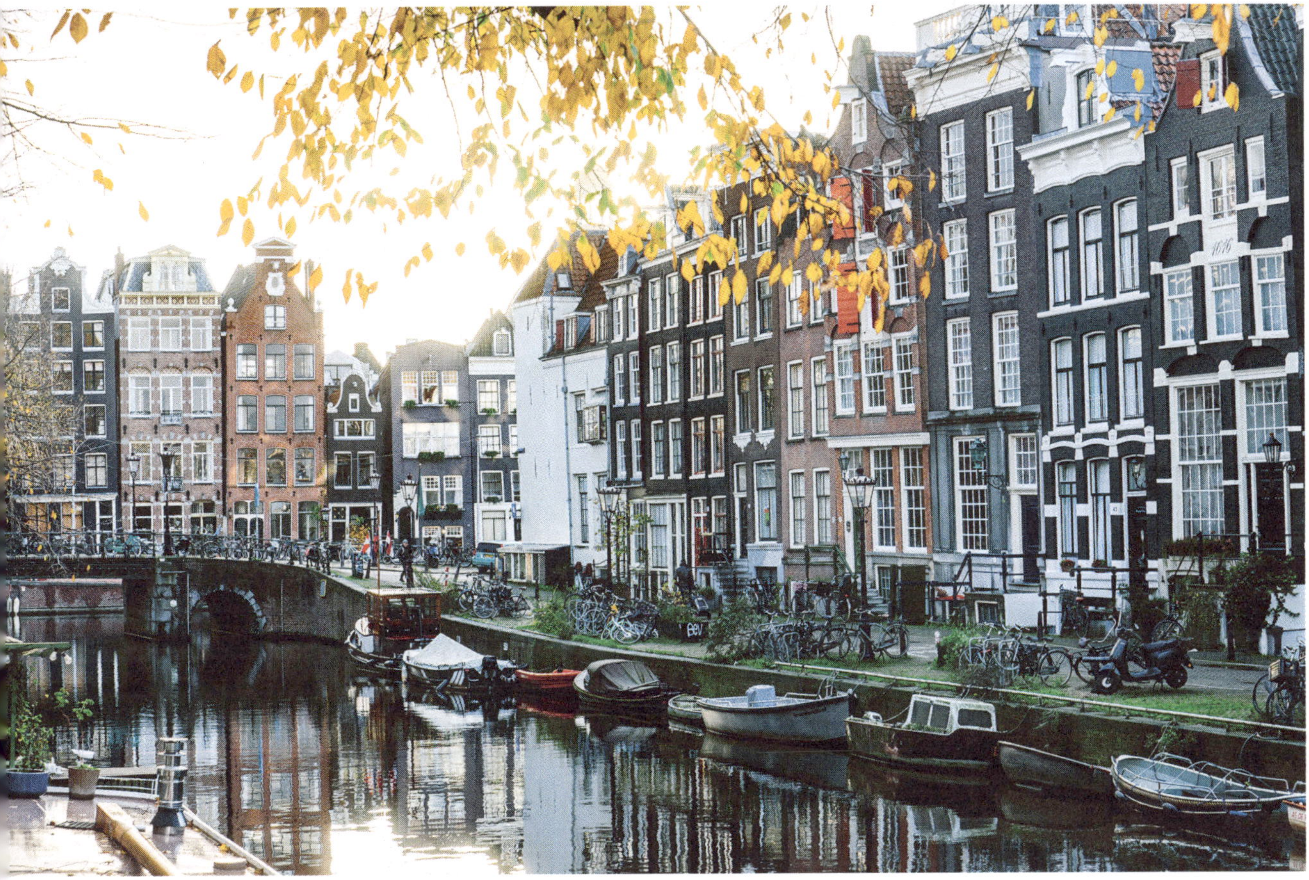

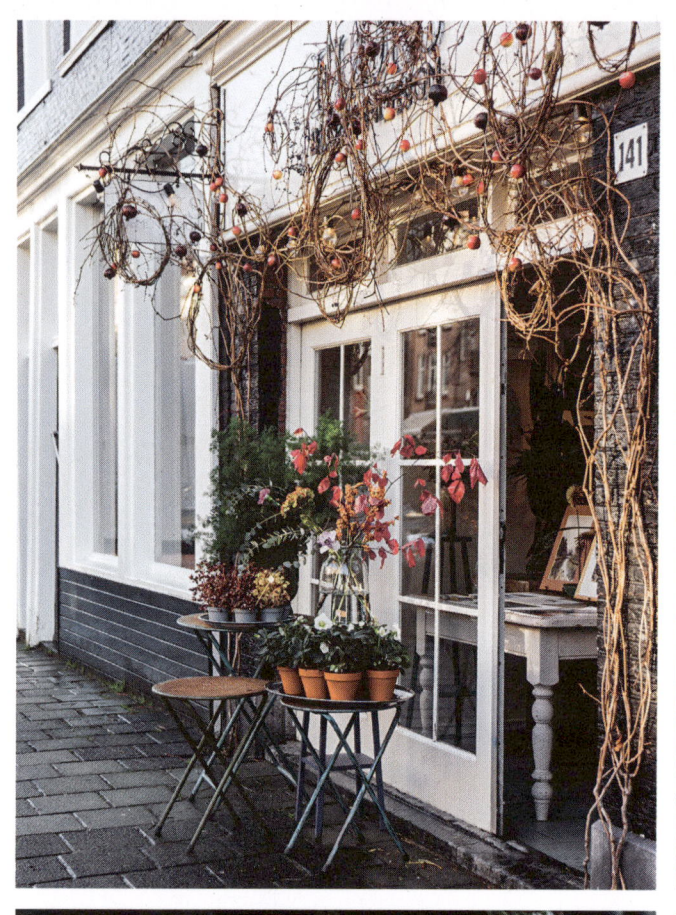
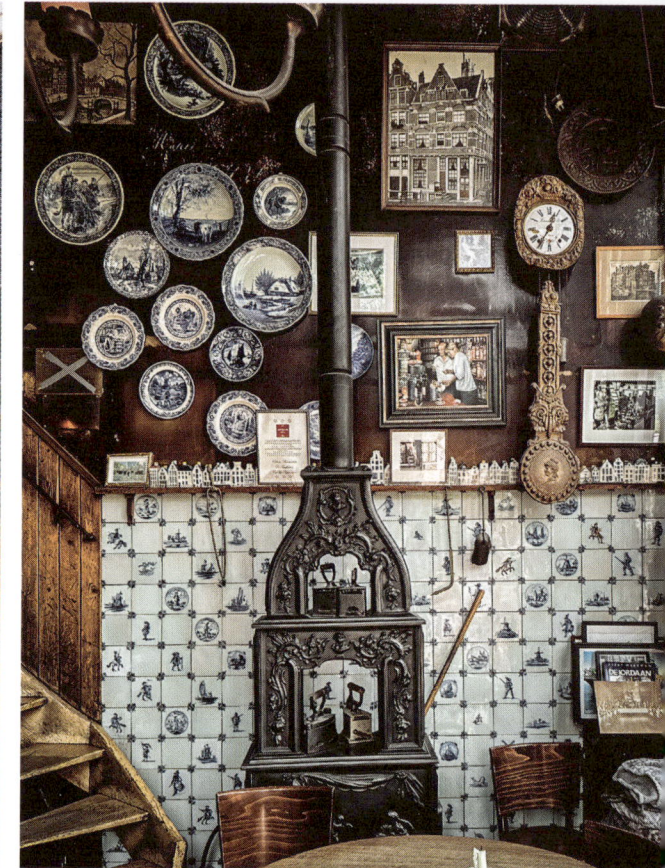
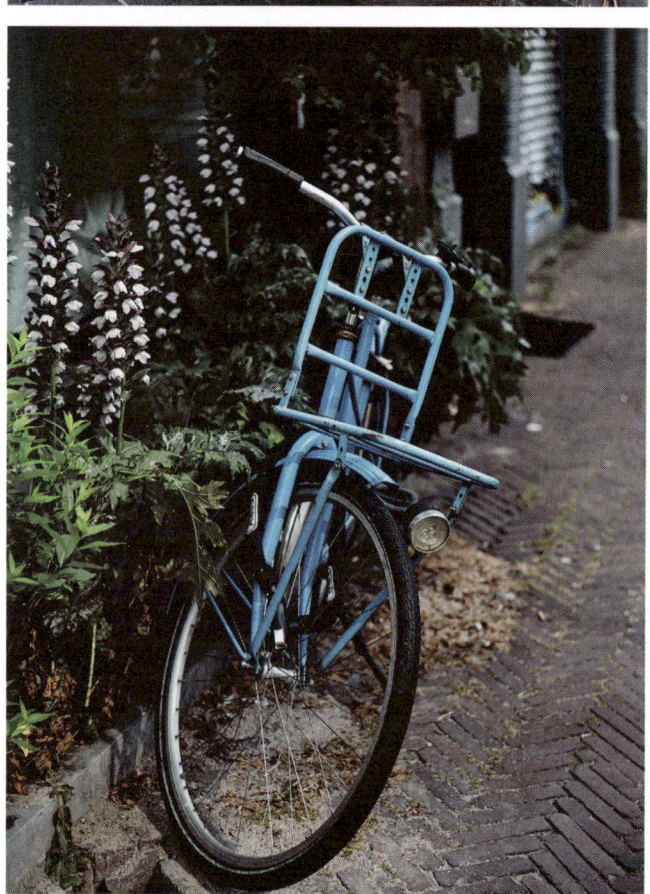
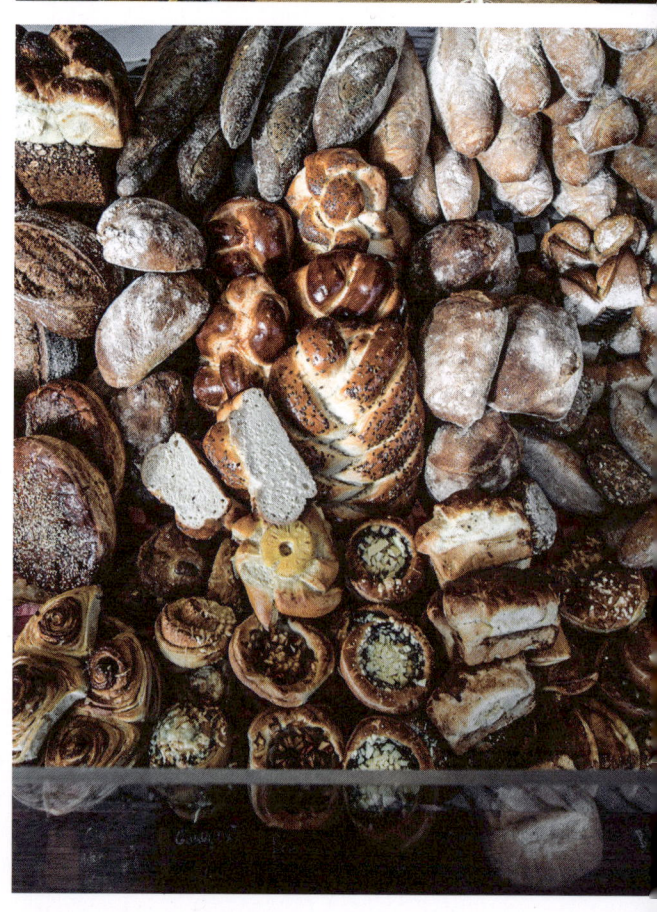

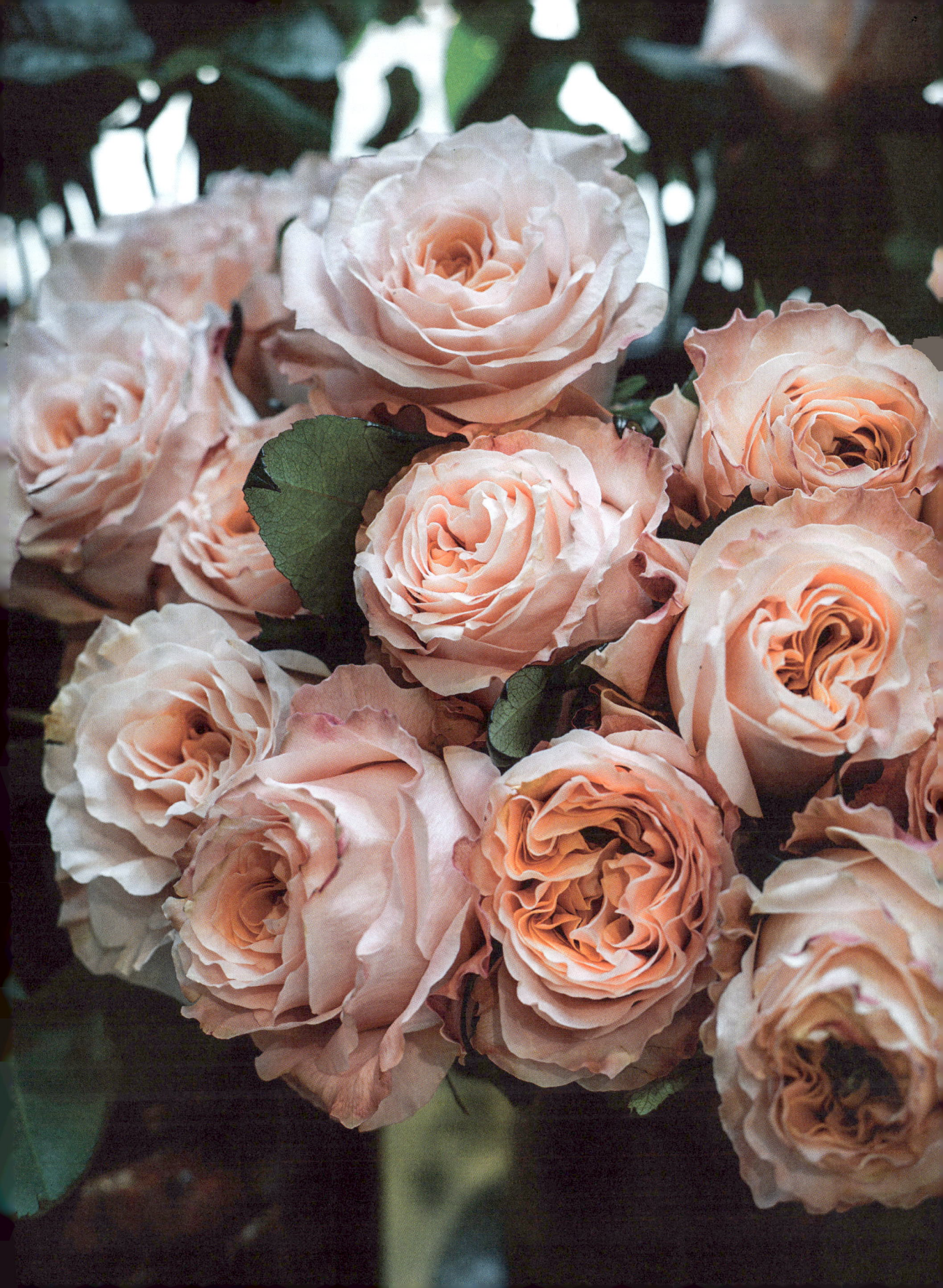

If hunger hits, you have plenty more options along this strip: *Mr Mokum* at Haarlemmerstraat 46, a one-stop shop for great coffee, is perhaps best known for its iconic egg bun and tattoo parlour upstairs. Pop into *Zonnetje Koffie thee en Kruiden* at Haarlemmerdijk 45 for a tremendous takeaway tea and coffee selection from the most beautiful old worldly shop. A short stroll off Haarlemmerdijk and over to a quiet corner of Binnen Dommersstraat, you will find *Toki*, a Japanese-meets-Scandinavian speciality coffee house with beautiful interiors to match its coffee offering. Catch your breath and spend a while here. As well as brilliant coffee, they serve pastries from local bakery Petit Gateau, teas from Brooklyn's Bellocq Tea Atelier, and beers from London's Crate Brewery.

With apple pie in mind, meander over to Café 't Papeneiland. Located on the corner of Prinsengracht and Brouwersgracht, it has a remarkable history dating back to 1642 and a well-deserved reputation for the best apple pie in Amsterdam. If you still have room for something sweet after all your earlier wanders, you can pile into one of the cosy tables inside or sit outside to soak up the atmosphere of the canal. When you are done, cross over the Papiermolensluis (Bridge 57), an iconic stone bridge which dates back to 1781 and boasts one of the most beautiful views in Amsterdam. The name comes from a sign that once hung on the corner house on the Brouwergracht: a paper merchant who kept his trade there was known as 'de Papiermolen'.

Retrace your steps back over the bridge and continue south along Prinsengracht, where you will find *Pompon*, one of the loveliest florists in Amsterdam, which spills over two stores: one for fresh flowers and one for faux. Challenge yourself to see which is which. The fakes are so good that I struggled at first!

Continue south until you find yourself at the chirpy *Noordermarkt*, another centuries-old bustling market. This historic square below the *Noordkerk* dates back to 1623. Cafes and shops surround it and it hosts a farmers' market on Saturdays and an antique market on Mondays. If you visit on these days, take some time to browse the stalls and enjoy the lively ambience of the market. In between browsing, seek out the beautiful *De Weldaad Authentic Interior*, at Noodermarkt 35, for the best in antique and vintage furniture and homewares. Founded in 2002 by former

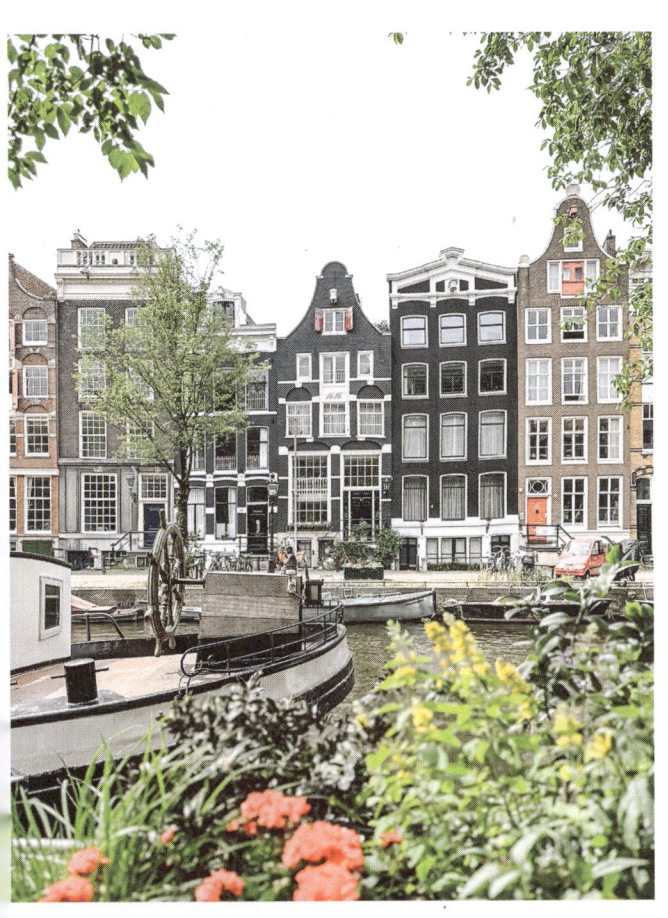
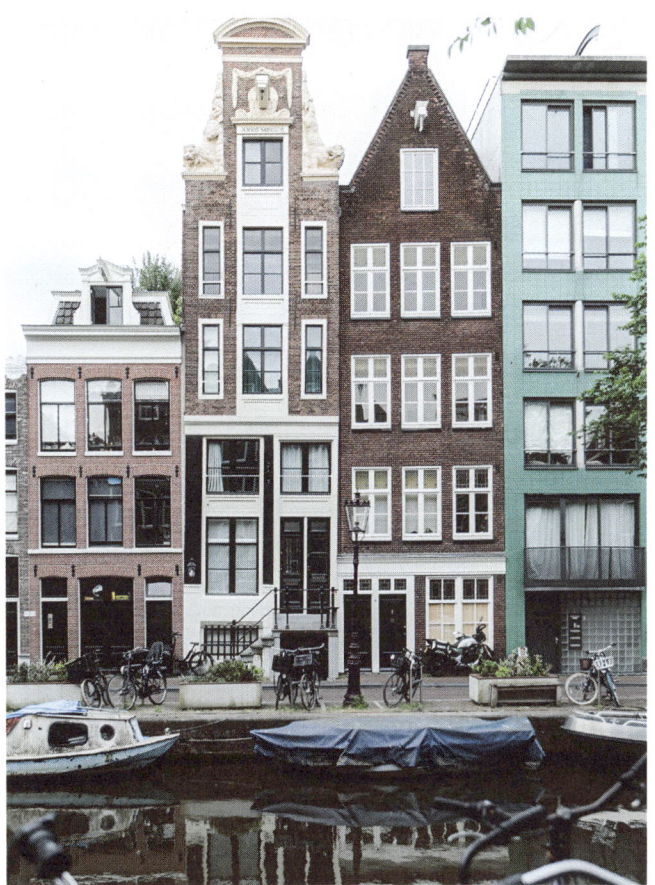
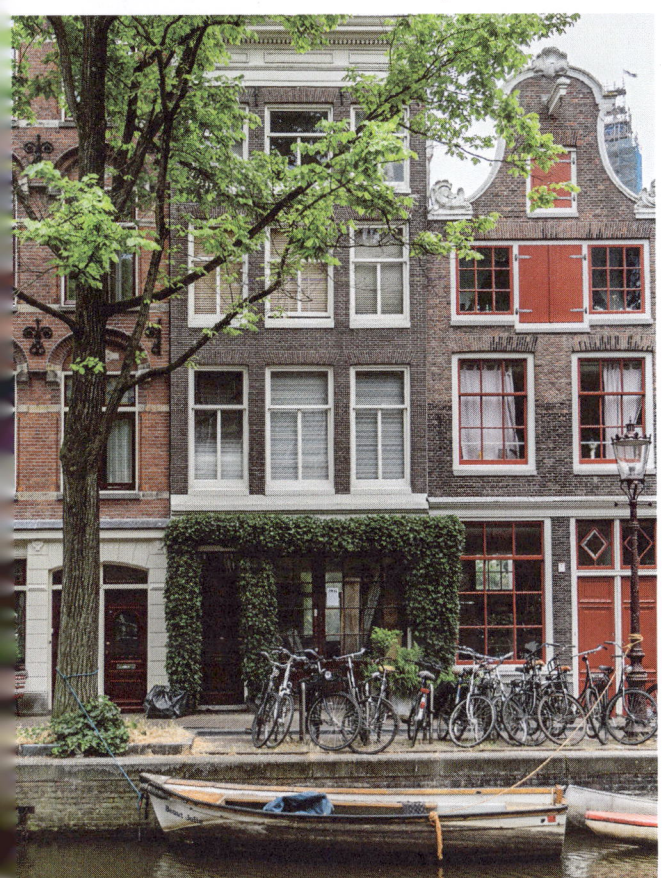
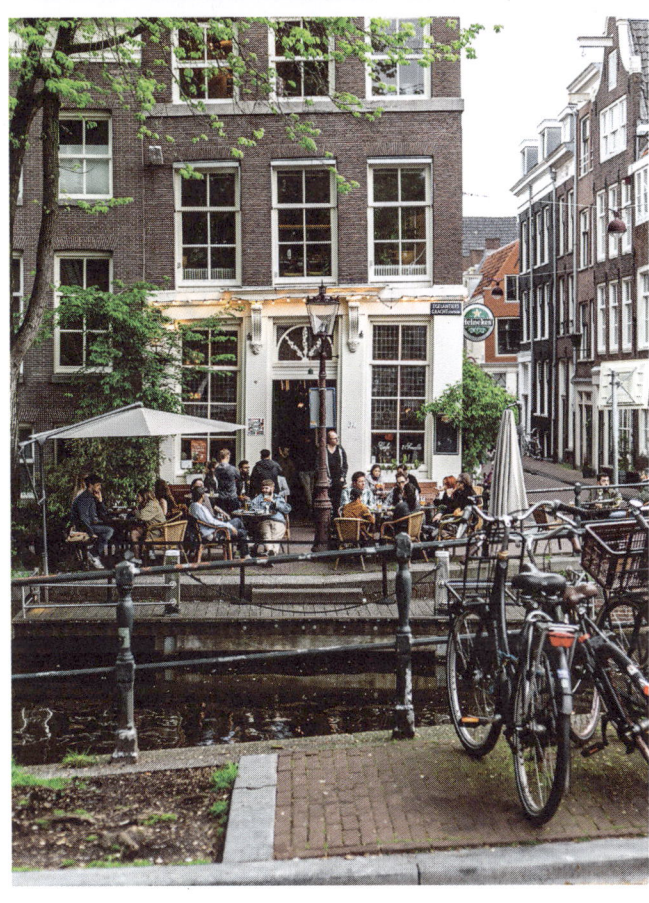

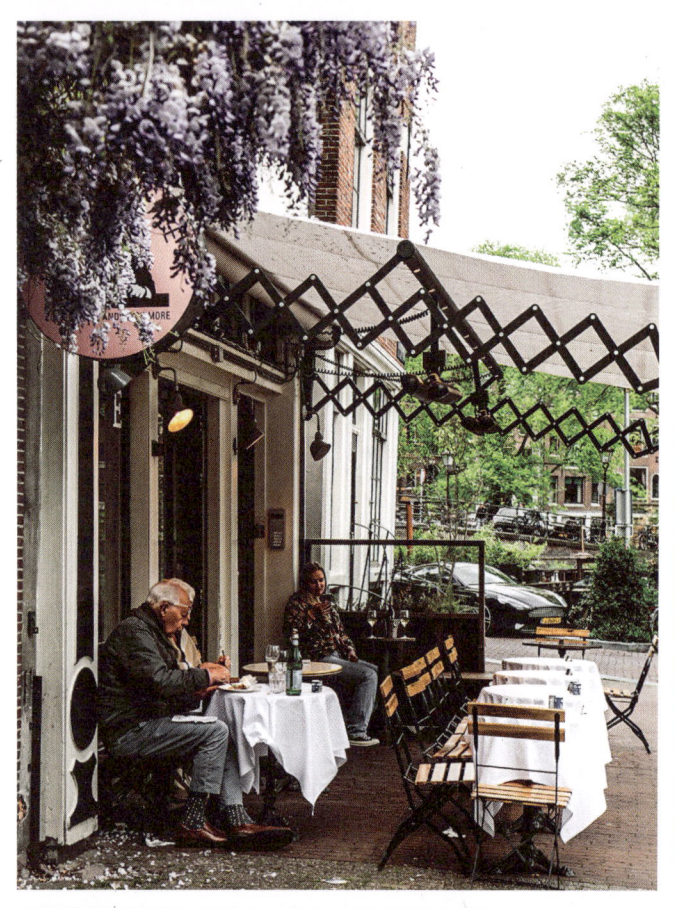
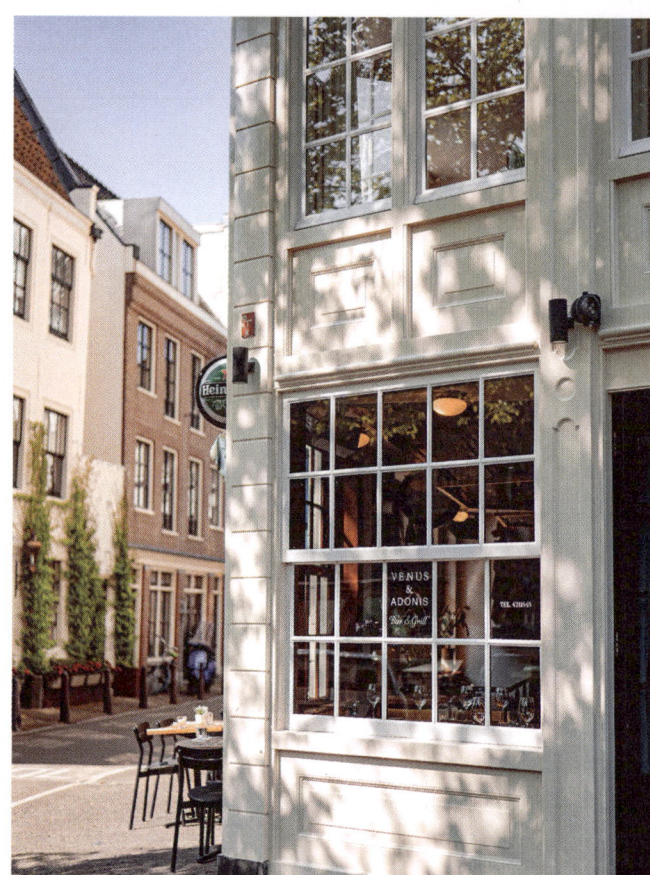
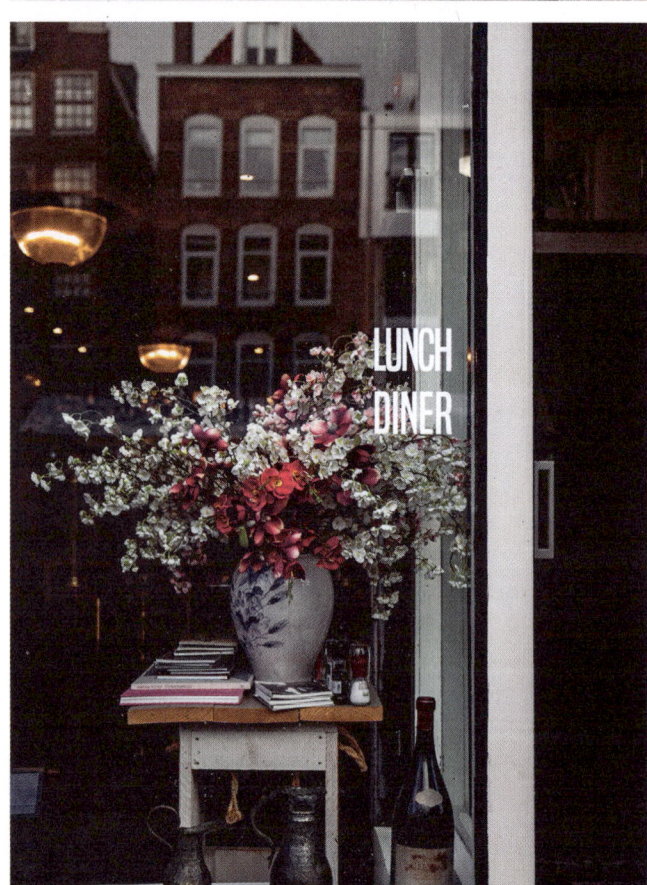
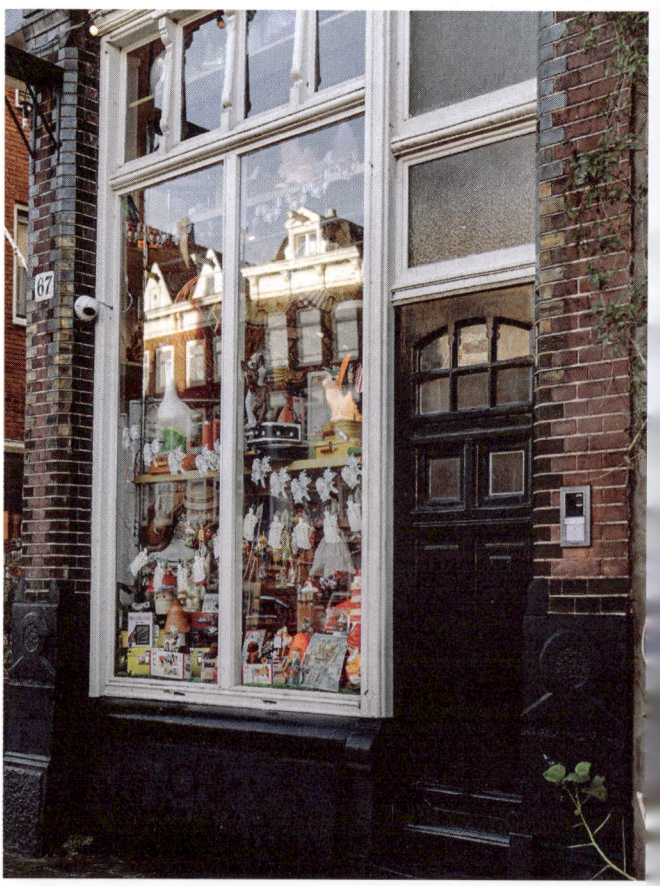

florist Mirjam Verheijke, it is no surprise that its name means 'pleasant atmosphere', as it is one of the most pleasant shops in Amsterdam.

After your mooch, head back out to the square, and from here you can pick up the aroma of wonderful apple pie wafting from *Winkel 43*, which you will find at the corner of Westerstraat, overlooking the Noordermarkt. Expect a queue, but it's worth the wait. You can soak up the charming atmosphere inside or grab a terrace table and enjoy it from there. Of course, it also boasts a delightful lunch menu that changes monthly, ensuring various delicious options. In the evenings, you can unwind with a drink or indulge in their daily changing evening menu, featuring tasty and reasonably priced dishes.

From here, walk south along Noorderkerkstraat (a leafy stretch flanked by the charming and ivy-clad sunglasses shop *Het Brillenpaleis*) towards Lindengracht, a former canal filled in at the end of the nineteenth century. For more than 120 years now, this bustling street has been home to a famous open-air market on Saturdays, offering various goods, including fresh produce, flowers and antiques across its 200-plus stalls. If your visit coincides with the market, join the locals, explore the market and soak in the vibrant atmosphere. It's not unusual to find live music entertaining the crowds. Don't worry if your visit doesn't coincide with the market day, as it's worth a wander over for a coffee and some baked goods (sweet and savoury) at the brilliant *SAINT-JEAN*. Their bakery is open daily and serves speciality coffee and plant-based goodies. Also, along this stretch you will find the Italian gem *Toscanini* (number 75). Chances are that if you haven't booked, you will struggle to get a table, so note its next-door deli, where you can stop in and enjoy a pastry, focaccia or something more substantial. Grab a lovely outside table or take it away and enjoy it by one of the nearby canals. If you only fancy a drink, you could head for a beer at *Café Thijssen*, named after famed Jordaan resident and writer Theo Thijssen.

Alternatively, you can continue along Westerstraat, where you can spend another hour or two away exploring this local gem. This charming street is also brimming with trendy shops, cosy cafes and local bars. Take a stroll and soak in the laid-back vibe of this area.

I recommend browsing the old-fashioned wooden games, masks and costumes in nostalgia-packed toyshop *Mechanisch Speelgoed*

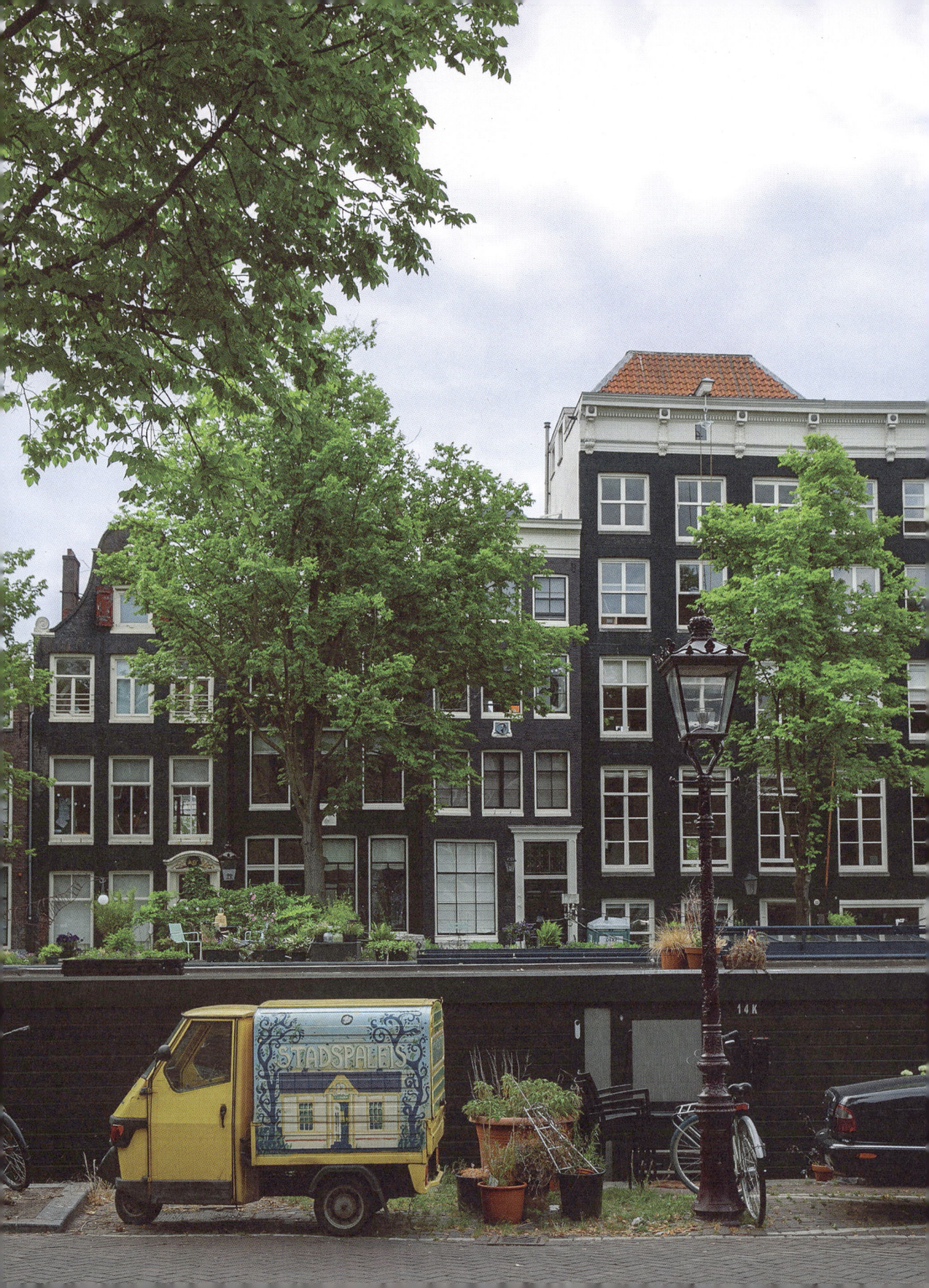

at Westerstraat 67; second-hand vintage shop *Spuitwaterfabriek* at number 145; and you can pick up some beautiful blooms further along at Floks Bloemendesign (number 141). Number 153 is home to a charming interior-design boutique, *Mar Decor*. If thirst or hunger strikes, cross over the road to *Café Parlotte* (number 182). It opens at around 4 p.m., and whether you choose a glass of wine with some cheese or book in for dinner, I'm sure you won't be disappointed. An alternative and equally great option for dinner can be found in *Café de Parel* at number 266. This cosy neighbourhood gem in a former brown bar offers a beautiful fish-centric set menu with three to five seasonal ingredients and an impressive menu of natural wines.

Finish your walk by making your way to Tweede Tuindwarsstraat. This quaint street is known locally as Little Italy and is loved for its unique shops, cosy restaurants and miniature art galleries. Take some time to explore the local businesses and appreciate the artistic flair of this neighbourhood. It's not just Italian fare on offer but do note *La Perla Pizza* at number 53 for the best in wood-fired pizzas and pasta, *Monte Pelmo* (number 17) for your ice-cream dessert, *Café de Tuin* (number 13) for some great bitterballen and, of course, *Het Oud-Hollandsch Snoepwinkeltje* (number 2) for the best liquorice in town.

You can expect a warm welcome, a brown interior and lots of cosiness in *Café Sonneveld* on the corner of Egelantiersgracht and Tweede Egelantiersdwarsstraat. Sit outside under the red and white awning for the beautiful views of the canals and nearby *Westerkerk*, but stay for the lovely atmosphere and traditional Dutch dishes. Catch your breath and relax before continuing your tour along Egelantiersgracht. Many of the Jordaan canals were filled in during the nineteenth century, but, thankfully, this beautiful stretch maintained its open-water connection between Prinsengracht and Lijnbaansgracht. Like much of the Jordaan area, the houses along here were built for artisans, so they were constructed on a much smaller scale than the grand mansions of Prinsengracht, Herengracht and Keizersgracht. As a result, they are in great demand as residences. A walk around here will reveal some of the most picturesque homes in Amsterdam. A stroll to its junction with Prinsengracht will lead you to the famous *Café 't Smalle*, with roots back to the 1700s when it served as a distillery. It gets its name from the small, narrow building it occupies.

Inside, you'll find beautiful vintage interiors, wooden panelling, floors and a mezzanine snug, but the outside seating impresses. Its canal-side terrace is perfect for enjoying a sunny drink and watching the boats pass.

Take in some more of Prinsengracht with a walk further south. The *Amsterdam Tulip Museum and Shop*, housed in a beautiful canal house, educates all on the vivid history of the much-loved flower. *Raïnaraï Deli* (252 Prinsengracht) offers goods from the nomadic kitchen of Algeria. The display cases under the front window overflow with fresh fruit and vegetables and are enough to draw you in. Grab some wholesome supplies and stretch your legs further south along Prinsengracht. The striking 360-degree views of the merchants' houses and canals here are beautiful to behold. *Venus & Adonis* is a local favourite, serving delicious plant-based dishes, succulent steaks and ribs and locally caught fish alongside an extensive natural wine selection, Dutch beers and expertly crafted cocktails. Its interiors are stunning, as are its delicious canal-side views.

A few doors away, the *Tertius Collection* on Prinsengracht is a unique gallery and interior-design shop offering a fascinating mix of old masters and modern art and design. In the tastefully decorated store, you will find special objects from the world's most famous artists and designers.

Finish your walk around Jordaan with a stroll down Elandsgracht, another bite-sized shopping street flanked by a statue of a local legend, the folk singer Johnny Jordaan. Every shop along this street has just the perfect bit of sparkle: from gorgeous concept store *Tenue de Nîmes* to *Arnold Cornelis* sweets; from restaurants like *Balthazar's Keuken* to home-roast coffee house *Rum Baba*. End your visit with a look through the antiques, art and bric-a-brac at *Antiekcentrum*.

ADDRESSES OF NOTE

Fleuremonde, **Haarlemmerdijk 159–163**
There is just something utterly charming about this sprawling local florist flooded with natural light. Everywhere you look there is a mix of colourful blooms, plants and ceramics that creates an aesthetic that looks like it has

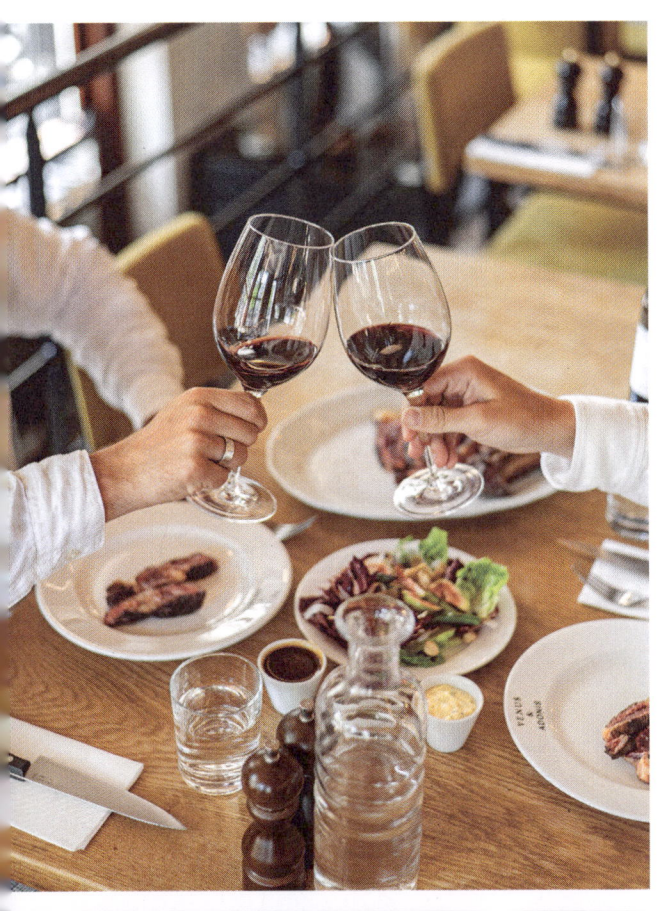
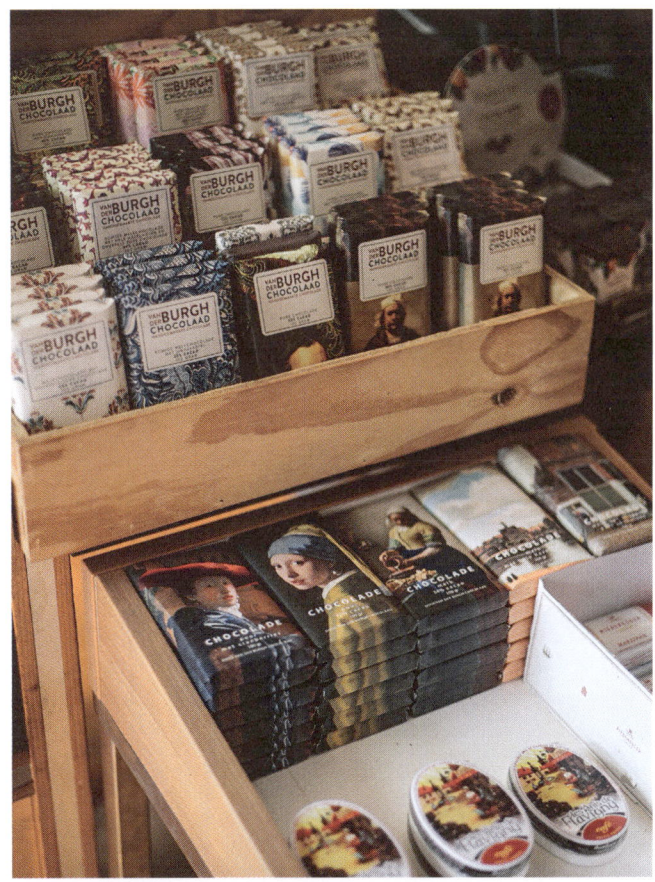
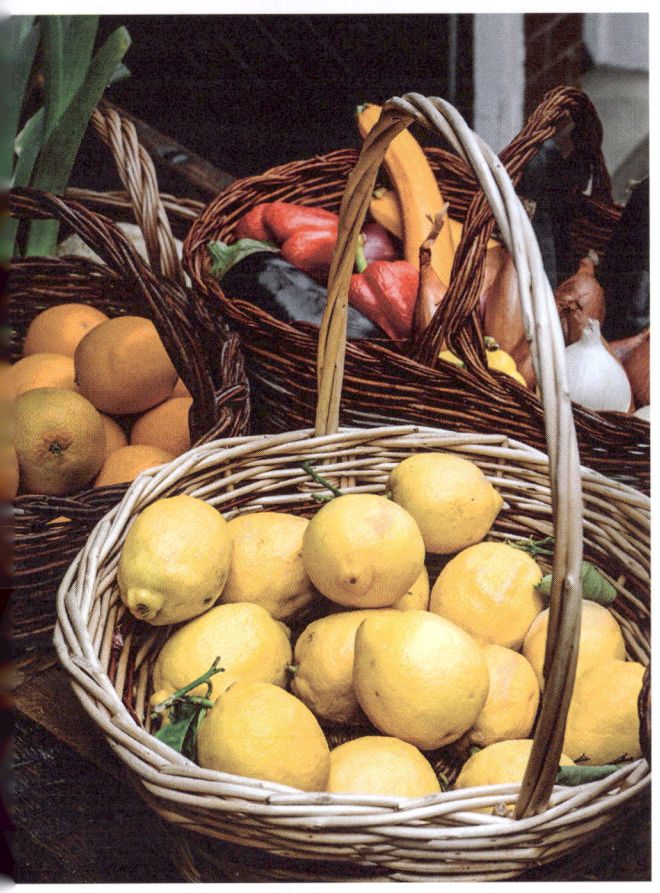
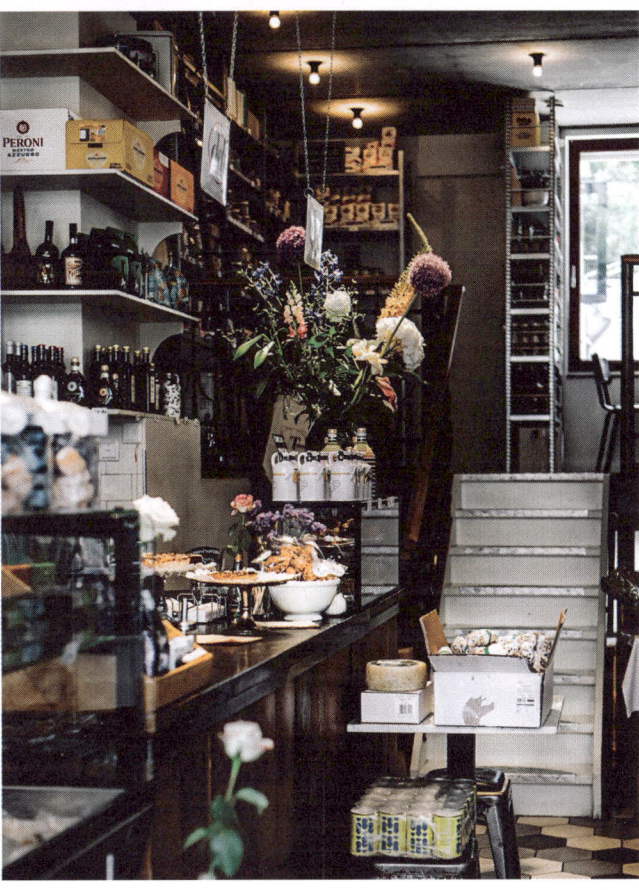

been put together with much love. If you are not in the market for flowers then a stop to admire its striking facade should suffice.

Toki, **Binnen Dommersstraat 15**
A light-filled cafe occupying a stunning corner spot in a lovely pocket of Amsterdam. As well as craft beers and speciality coffee, Toki offers an excellent choice of specialty tea from Brooklyn-based tea emporium Bellocq. Owner Jeff Flink places a meticulous blend of Scandinavian and Japanese interior elements front and centre and succeeds in creating a lovely laid-back space.

Café 't Papeneiland, **Prinsengracht 2**
A much-loved canal-side brown bar with cosy interiors and a small but lovely terrace serving one of the tastiest apple pies in Amsterdam. You can also sample other Dutch cafe classics like smoked raw sausage (ossenworst) and Dutch meatballs (bitterballen).

Papiermolensluis (Bridge 57)
An iconic stone bridge dating back to 1781.

Pompon Flowershop and Pompon Forever Flowers, **Prinsengracht 8–10 & 12**
Best known for its beautiful bouquets, Pompon has been a household name in Amsterdam for over forty years. Bright whitewashed floors and walls provide the perfect backdrop for the beautiful bunches.

Noordermarkt
A bustling square, especially during the Saturday boerenmarkt (organic farmers' market) and the Monday flea market.

Winkel 43, **Noordermarkt 43**
Cosy interiors marry with a sprawling outdoor terrace. You can expect a very long queue on market days, but it's worth the wait. Popular for its famed apple pie and small dishes.

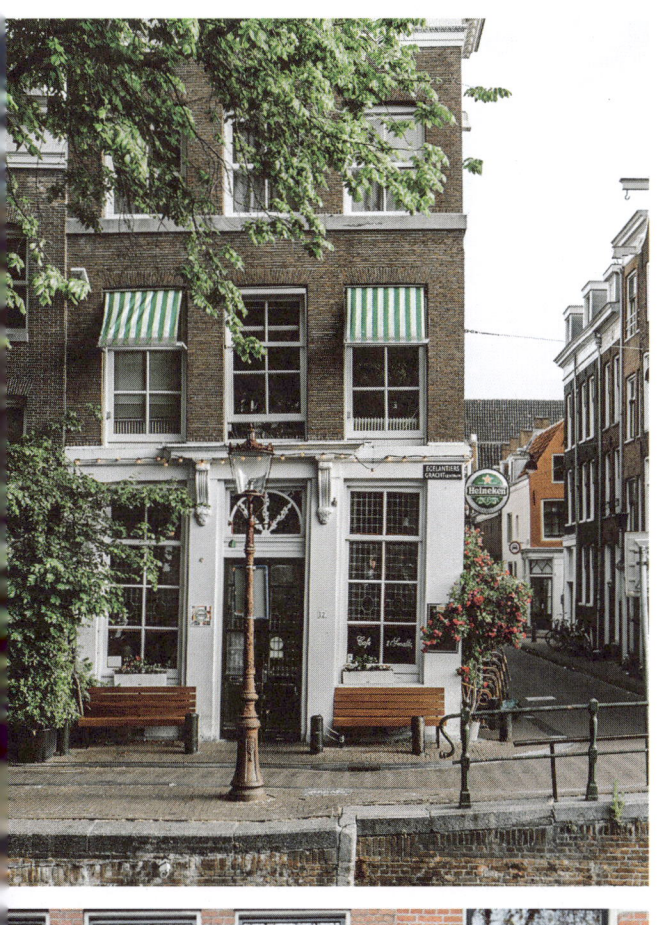
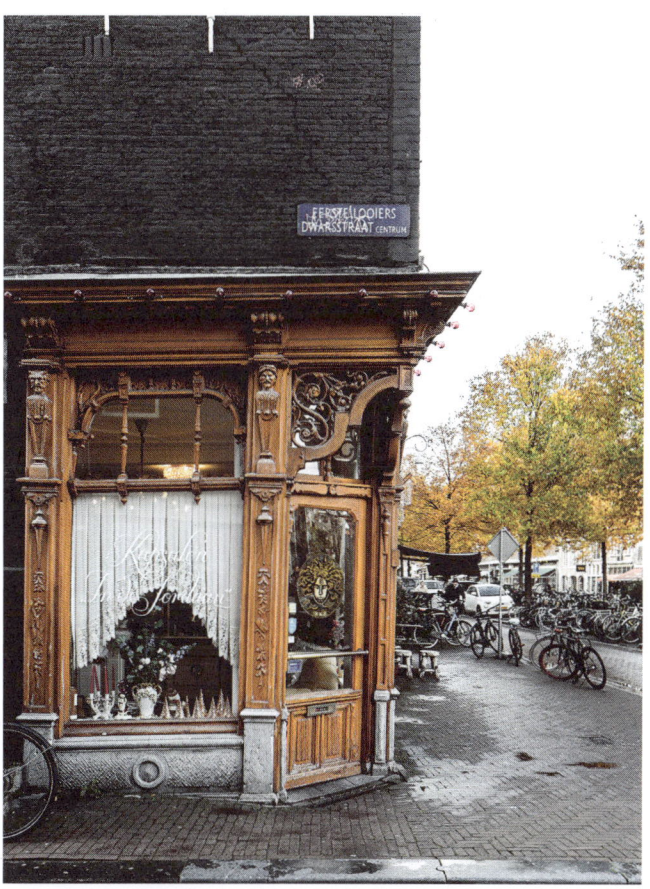
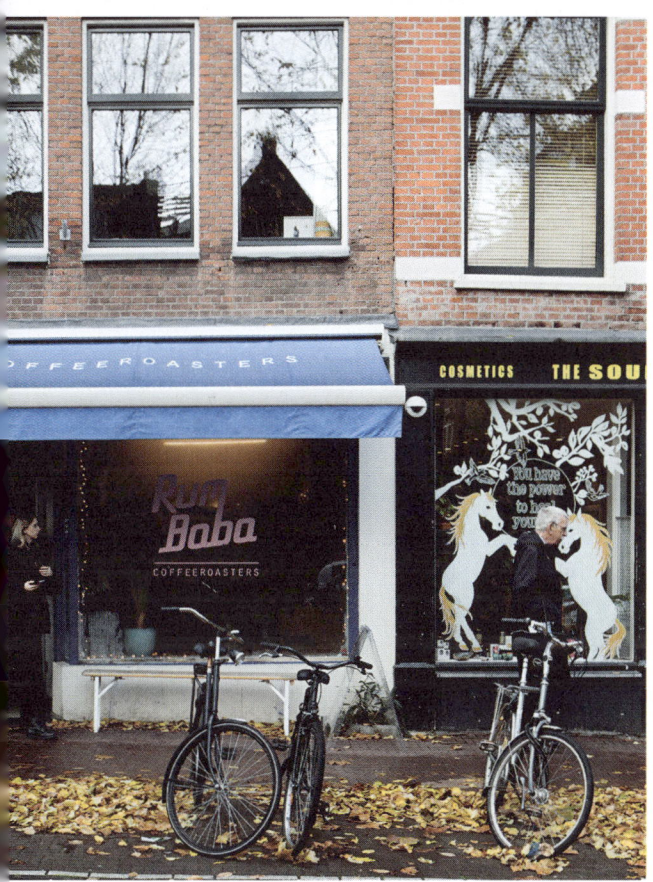
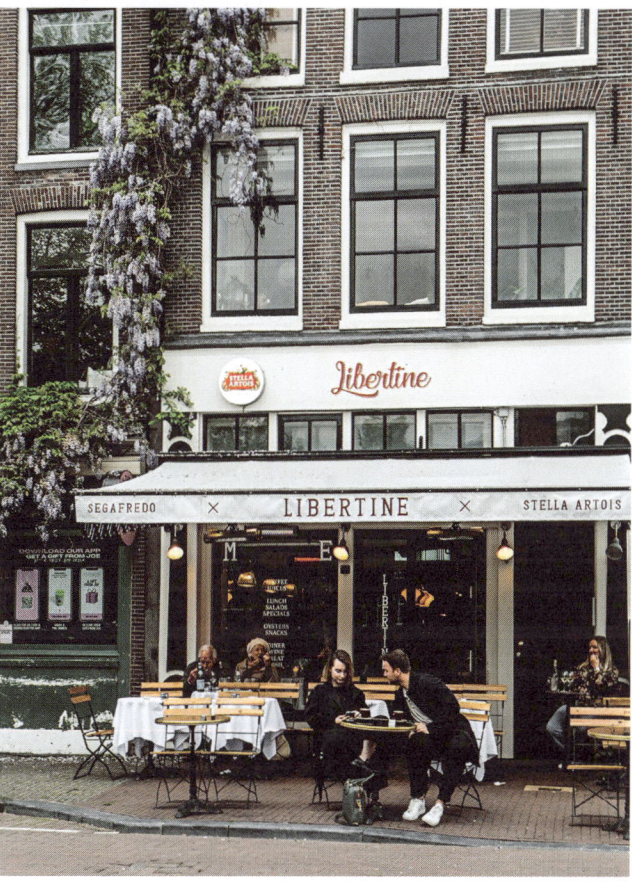

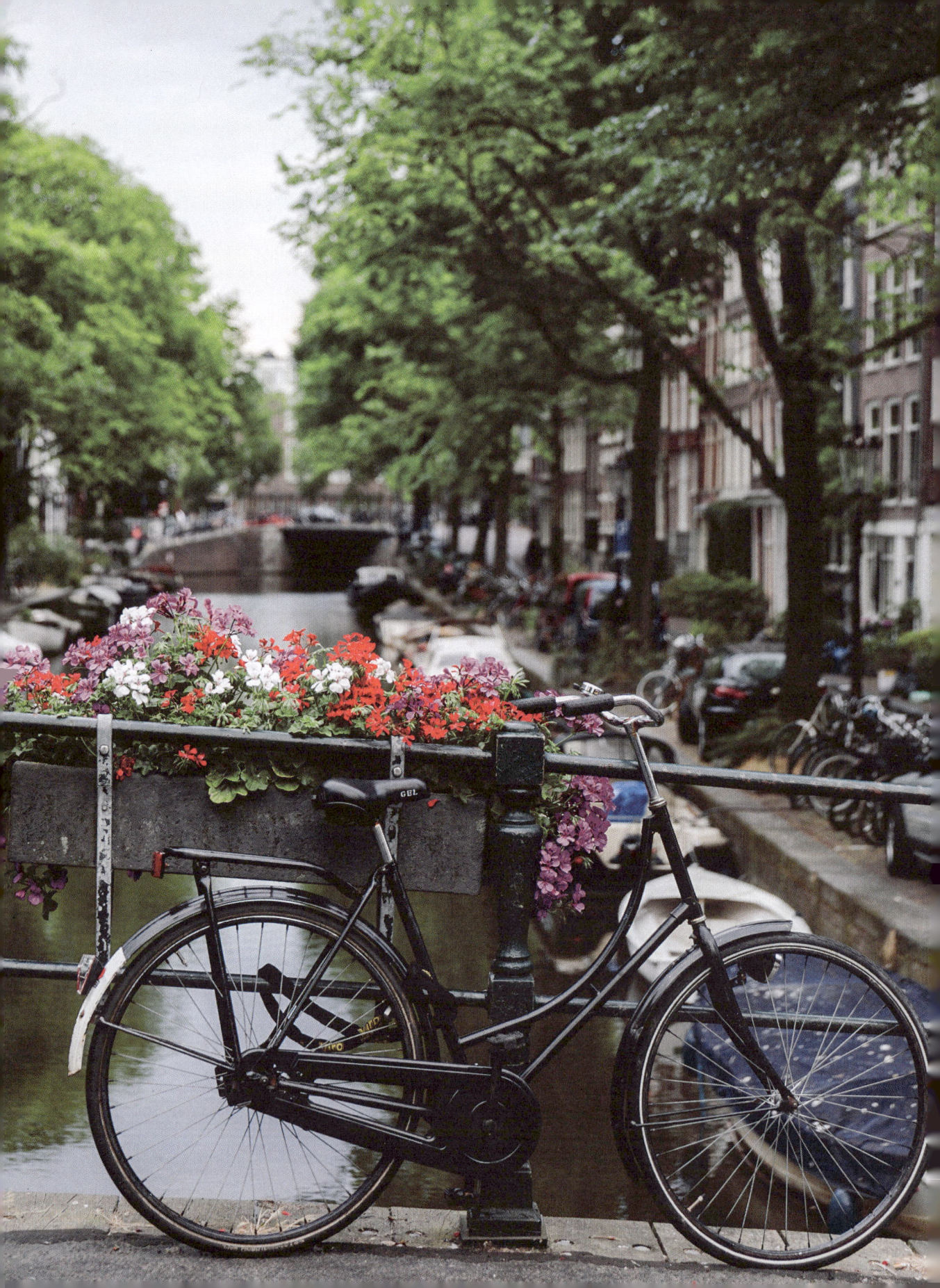

De Weldaad, **Noordermarkt 35**
An oasis of colour and charm is the unexpected treasure to be found hidden behind the unassuming facade of De Weldaad. An interior emporium housed in a former garage in the heart of the market square, selling a beautiful selection of vintage and artisan pieces.

Libertine Petit Café, **Noordermarkt 4**
A relaxed, all-day dining restaurant serving an incredible selection of French classics. A simple meal on the terrace is a must. Located moments from the bustle of the market square, its a place to see and be seen.

Het Brillenpaleis, **Noorderkerkstraat 18**
Situated on the quaint corner of Lindenstraat and Norderkerkstraat, Brillenpaleis is a charming eyeglasses store with the prettiest ivy-clad facade.

SAINT-JEAN, **Lindengracht 158**
A wonderful plant-based bakery and cafe serving the most delicious baked goods and pastries, and speciality coffee from acclaimed roasters Bocca and Mota. I can tell you I had no idea its pistachio cruffin was plant-based until I read about it after my visit.

Toscanini, **Lindengracht 75**
Amsterdam has its fair share of great Italian restaurants, but Toscanini has long been regarded as one of the best. It is much loved for its simple but delicious Italian cuisine, superb wine list, open kitchen, and modern, rustic interiors.

Toscanini Deli, **Lindengracht 79**
Toscanini's popularity means it can sometimes be a struggle to reserve a table, but its next-door deli allows everyone to sample its dishes – a bijoux deli offering a vast selection of Italian produce. Enjoy a tasty coffee with a focaccia or cinnamon brioche on their terrace, or take away some freshly made dishes.

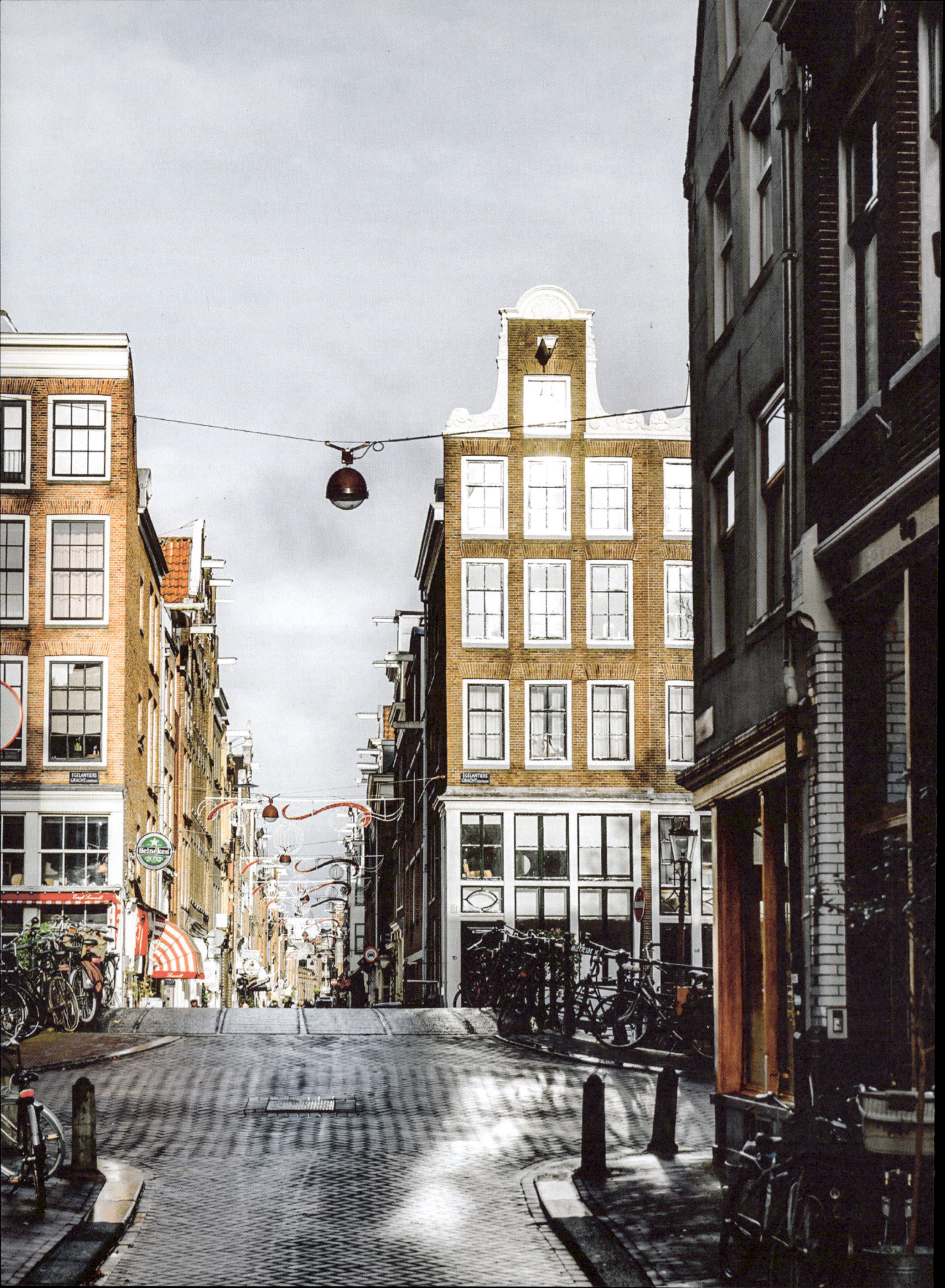

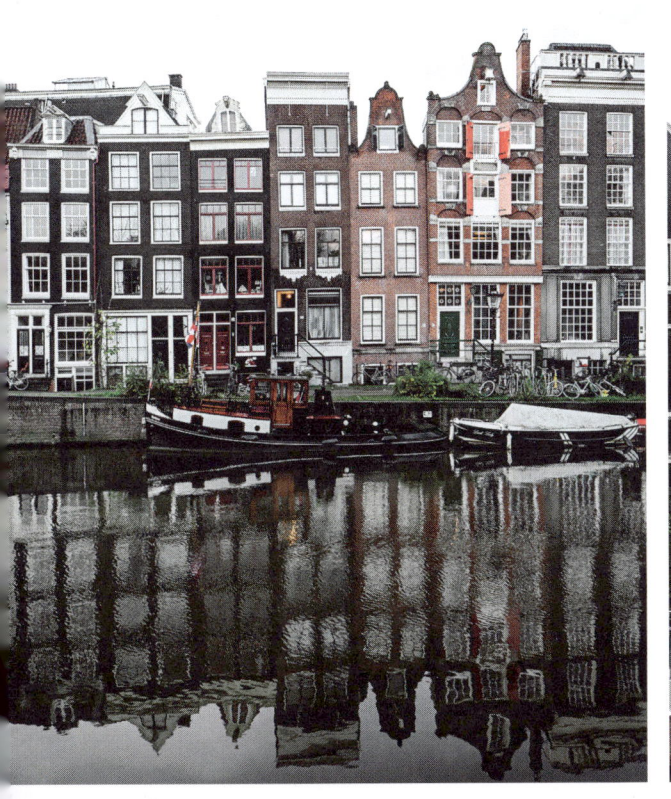
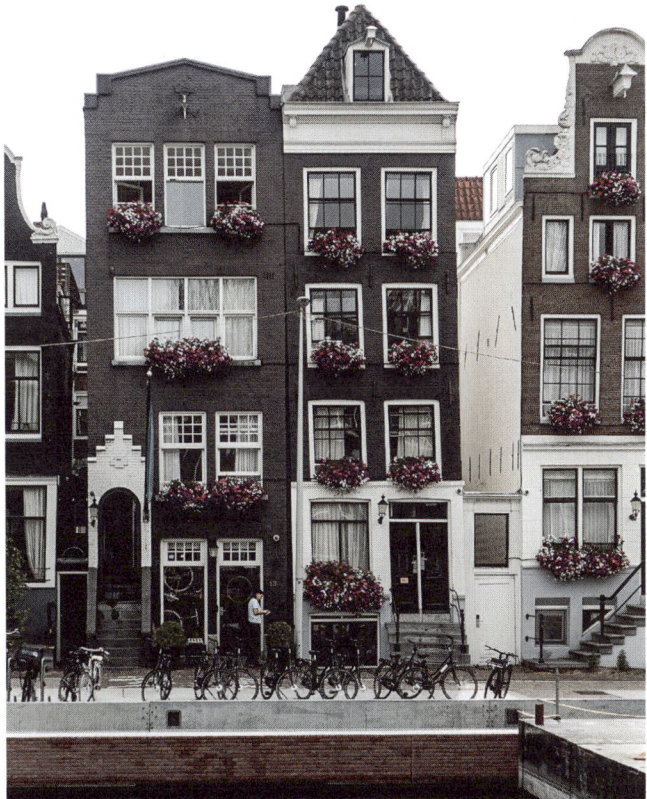
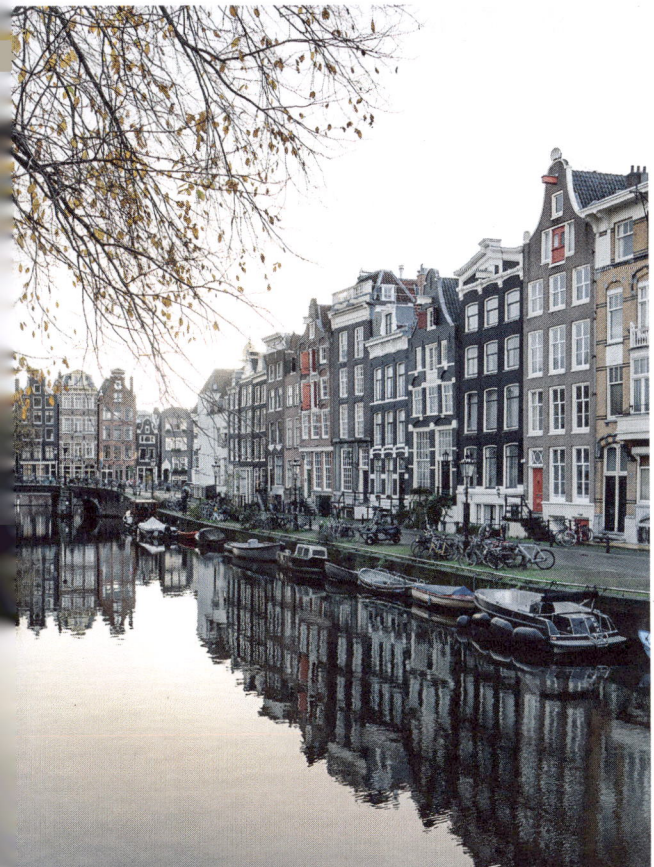
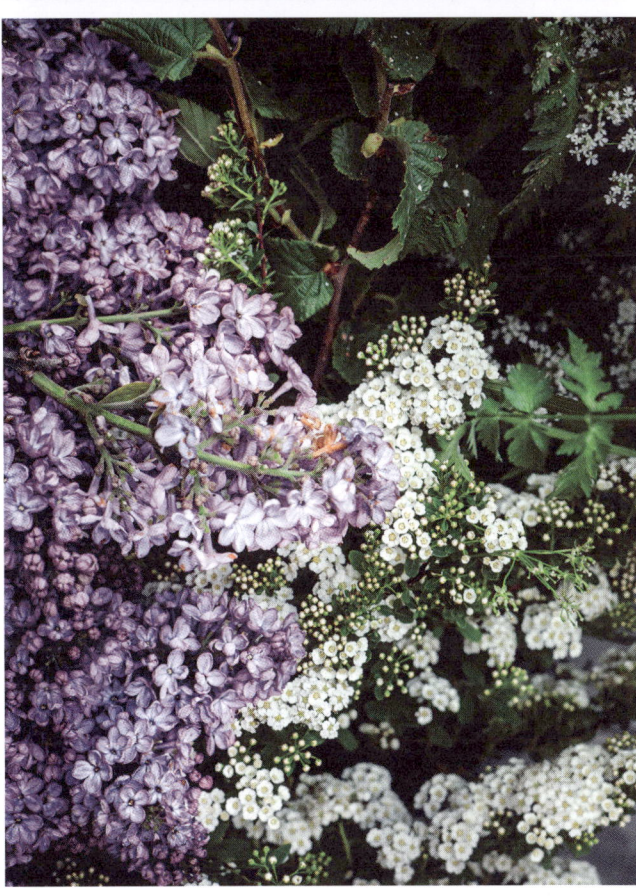

Mechanisch Speelgoed, **Westerstraat 67**
A tiny store with a rich collection of retro mechanical toys. Not just confined to inside the shop, nostalgic toys hang from the beautiful windows and out onto the little street.

Floks Bloemendesign, **Westerstraat 141**
A small, quaint florist selling flowers for every occasion. Colour and texture are woven through the elegant displays.

Nieuwe Amsterdamse Spuitwaterfabriek, **Westerstraat 145**
If your visit coincides with the Noordermarkt Monday flea market, you are in for a special treat. However, if it doesn't you could browse this second-hand thrift store instead.

Luuk's Coffee, **Westerstraat 3**
This welcoming cafe is the perfect spot to grab an espresso or flat white and enjoy it along the canal or browsing the farmers market on Noordermarkt.

Mar Décor, **Westerstraat 153**
This beautiful interior store brings some extra magic to Westerstraat. Pop in to browse its highly curated selection of ceramics, glassware and tableware.

Café Parlotte, **Westerstraat 182**
Café Parlotte is the sweet little bistro every neighbourhood needs. Its interiors are eclectic and romantic: the perfect backdrop for its delicious oysters, charcuterie, organic wines, and beer.

Café de Parel, **Westerstraat 266**
De Parel is yet another great reason to visit Westerstraat. This former brown bar turned bistro entices with its ever-changing seasonal menu, excellent wine list and cosy atmosphere. Its traditional stained-glass windows and tile tableaus create the perfect setting.

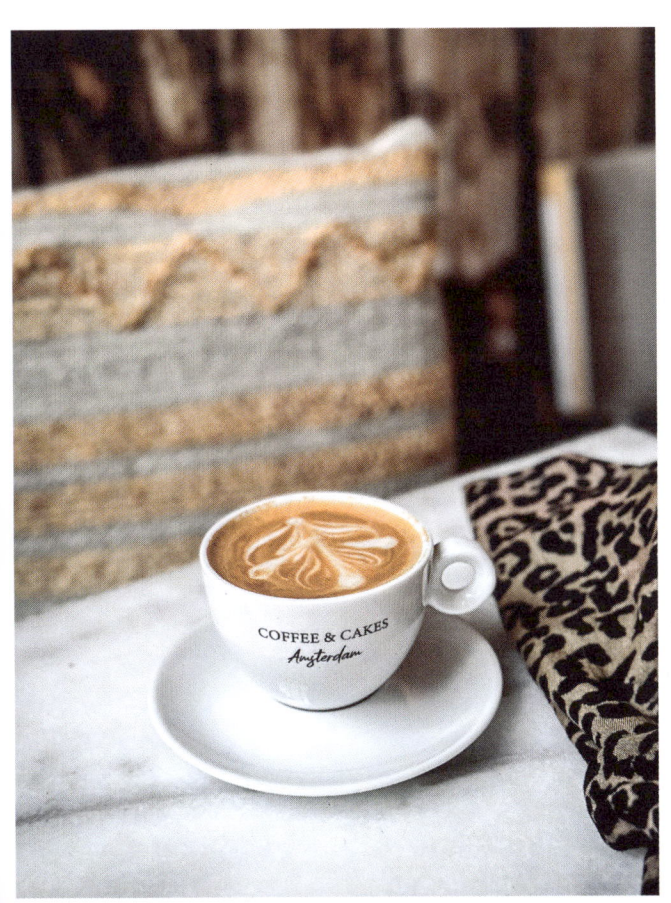
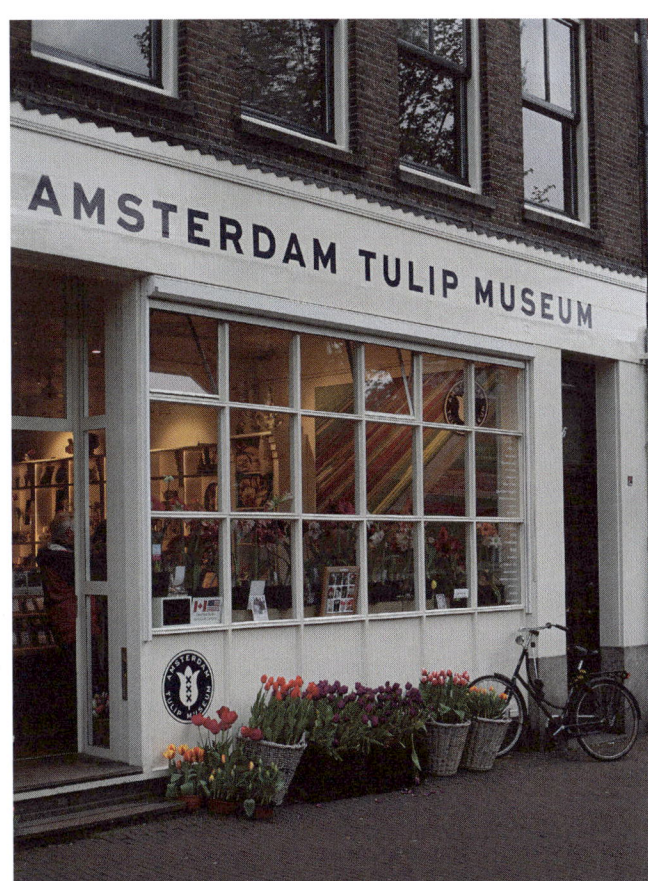
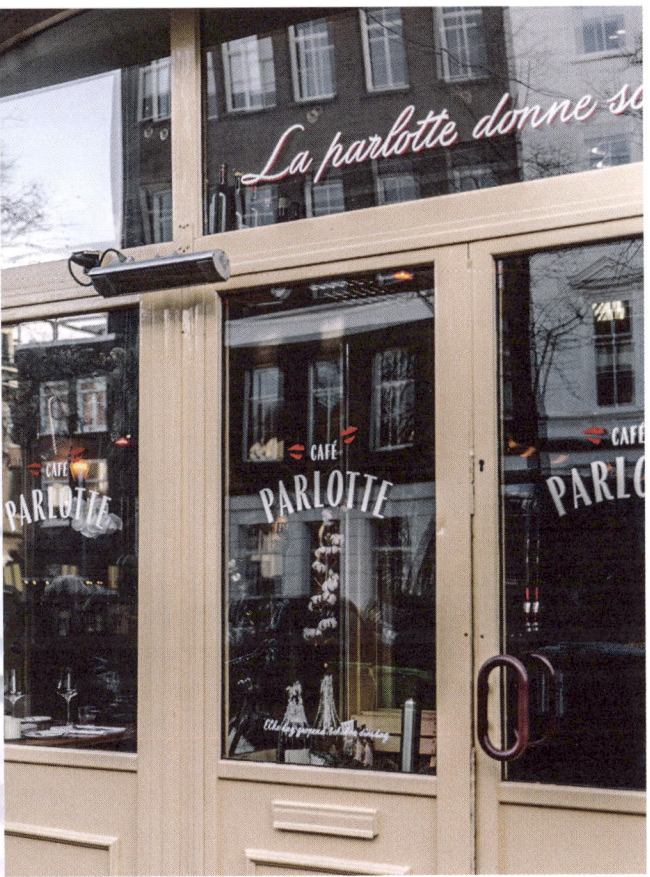
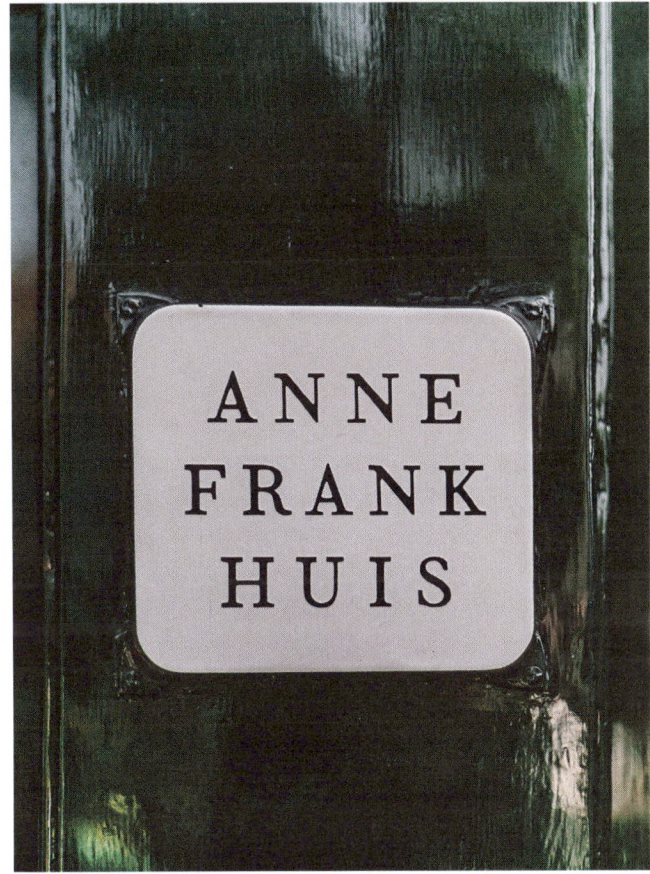

Café de Tuin, **Tweede Tuindwarsstraat 13**
This laid-back brown bar is the perfect spot to head for '*gezellig*', that cosy atmosphere so prominent in Amsterdam. Café de Tuin is loved by locals and visitors alike for its hospitable ambience, selection of great beers, and bitterballen.

Monte Pelmo, **Tweede Tuindwarsstraat 13**
Dating back to 1957, Monte Pelmo is the perfect place to enjoy Italian-style gelato after lunch or dinner.

La Perla Pizza, **Tweede Tuindwarsstraat 53**
A no-frills restaurant serving what many locals call the best pizza in Amsterdam. Pizzas and pasta here are just that little bit more delicious thanks to the fact that many of their ingredients are imported weekly from Italy. If you don't secure a table here, you can enjoy a takeaway from its offering across the street.

Het Oud-Hollandsch, **Tweede Egelantiersdwarsstraat 2**
Across the street from La Perla Pizza you will find a unique old-school candy store that displays its incredible selection of liquorice, caramels and polka pastilles in glass jars.

Café Sonnenveld, **Egelantiersgracht 72–74**
After spending a day exploring Jordaan, there is no better place to stop for a drink or light bite than at the foot of quaint Hilletjesburg. With stunning views of Westerkerk and a romantic ambience, a stop at Café Sonnenveld shouldn't be missed.

Café 't Smalle, **Egelantiersgracht 12**
Café 't Smalle's brown wood panelling and beautiful brass fittings echo its eighteenth-century roots when it was a liquor distillery under Pieter Hoppe. There is a romance to sipping a cold beer on its stunning canal-side terrace that's hard to beat. The dark-panelled walls and mezzanine-level seating area inside help to make its interiors a little extra inviting.

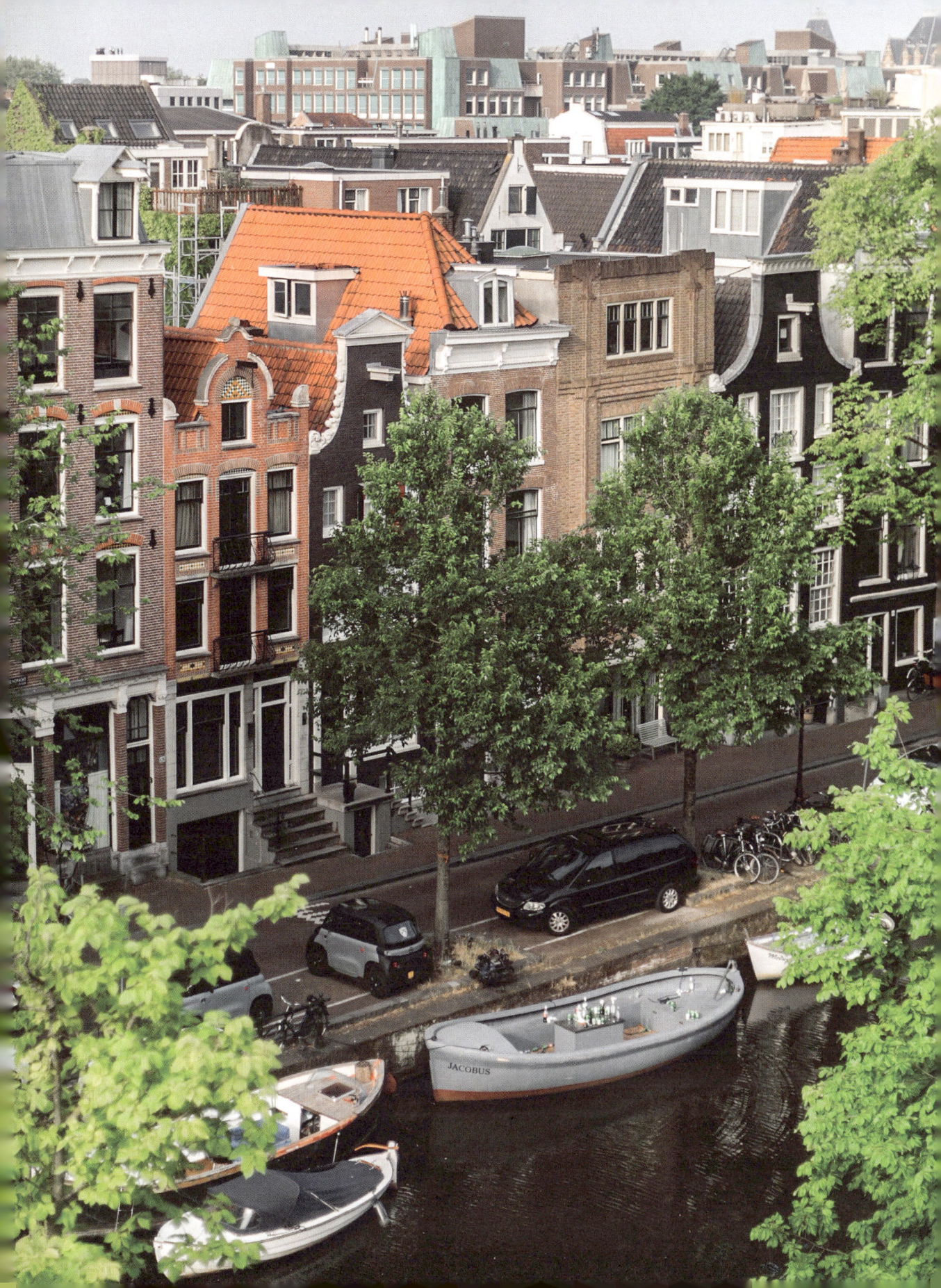

DE PIJP

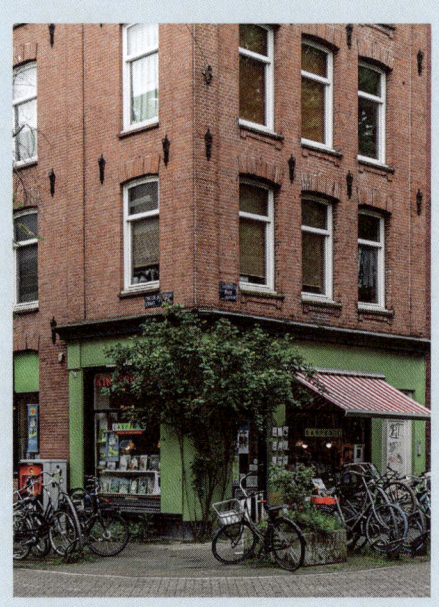

LOCAL AND VIBRANT ATMOSPHERE WITH AN
ECLECTIC MIX OF CULTURES, TRENDY BARS,
ONE-OFF SHOPS AND HOME TO THE FAMOUS
ALBERT CUYP MARKT

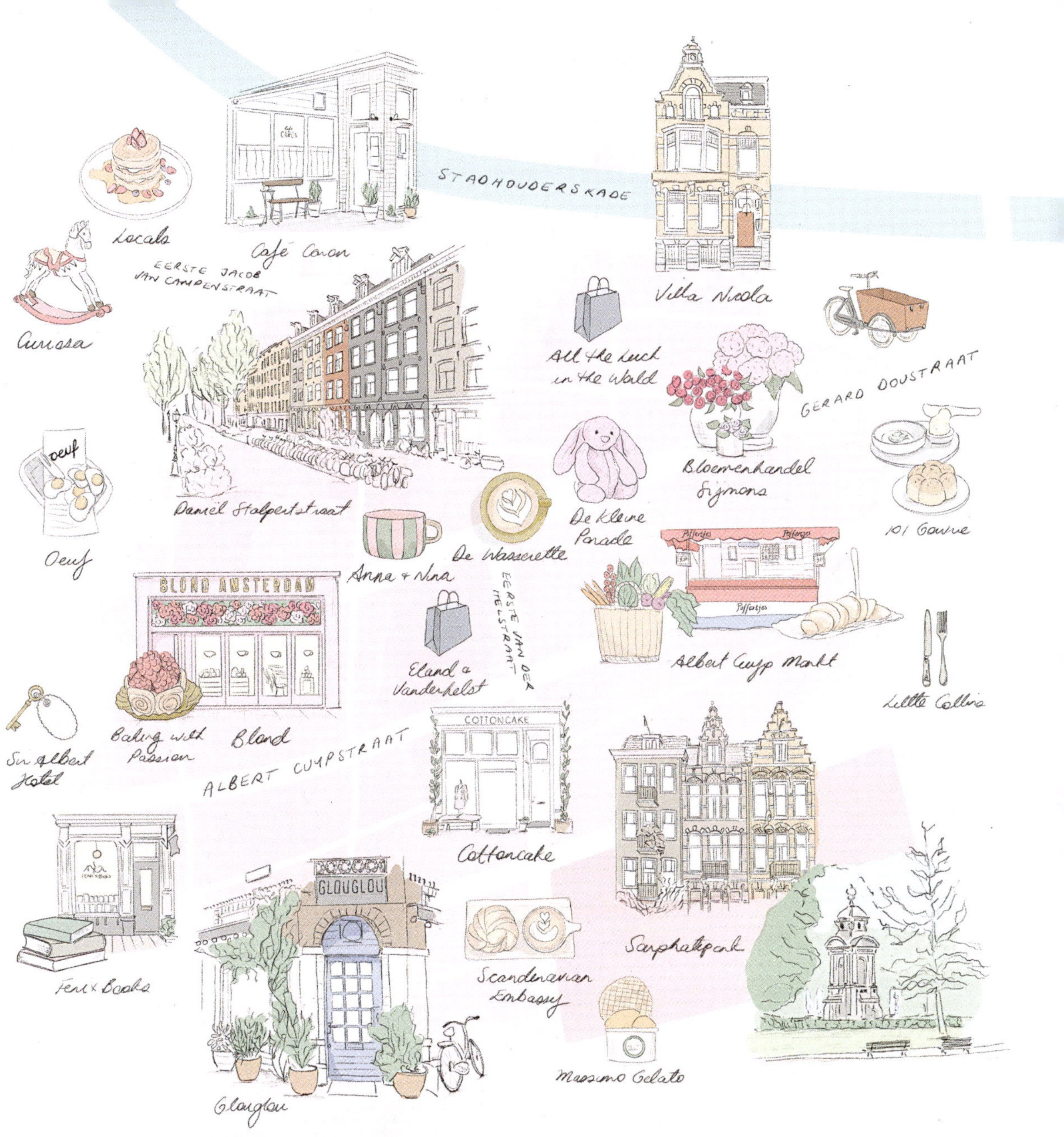

DE PIJP

#prettycityamsterdam

 COTTONCAKE Eerste van der Helststraat 76HS
ELAND & VANDERHELST Eerste van der Helststraat 62
CURIOSA Eerste Jacob van Campenstraat 1
BLOND AMSTERDAM Ferdinand Bolstraat 44H
ALL THE LUCK IN THE WORLD Gerard Doustraat 86HS
DE KLEINE PARADE Gerard Doustraat 144
ANNA + NINA Gerard Doustraat 94

 BLOEMENHANDEL SIJMONS Gerard Doustraat 158

 SCANDINAVIAN EMBASSY Sarphatipark 34
DE WASSERETTE Eerste van der Helststraat 27

 BAKING WITH PASSION Albert Cuypstraat 53
MASSIMO GELATO Van Ostadestraat 147H

 Albert Cuyp Markt, Eerste Jacob van Campenstraat, Sarphatipark, Daniël Stalpertstraat, Gerard Doustraat, Eerste van der Helststraat

 SIR ALBERT HOTEL Albert Cuypstraat 2-6
VILLA NICOLA Nicolaas Witsenkade 21

 GLOUGLOU Tweede van der Helststraat 3

LOCALS Eerste Jacob van Campenstraat 27H
CAFÉ CARON Frans Halsstraat 28
101 GOWRIE Govert Flinckstraat 326HS
LITTLE COLLINS Eerste Sweelinckstraat 19F
OEUF AMSTERDAM Daniël Stalpertstraat 36

 FENIX BOOKS Frans Halsstraat 88

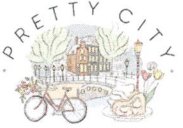

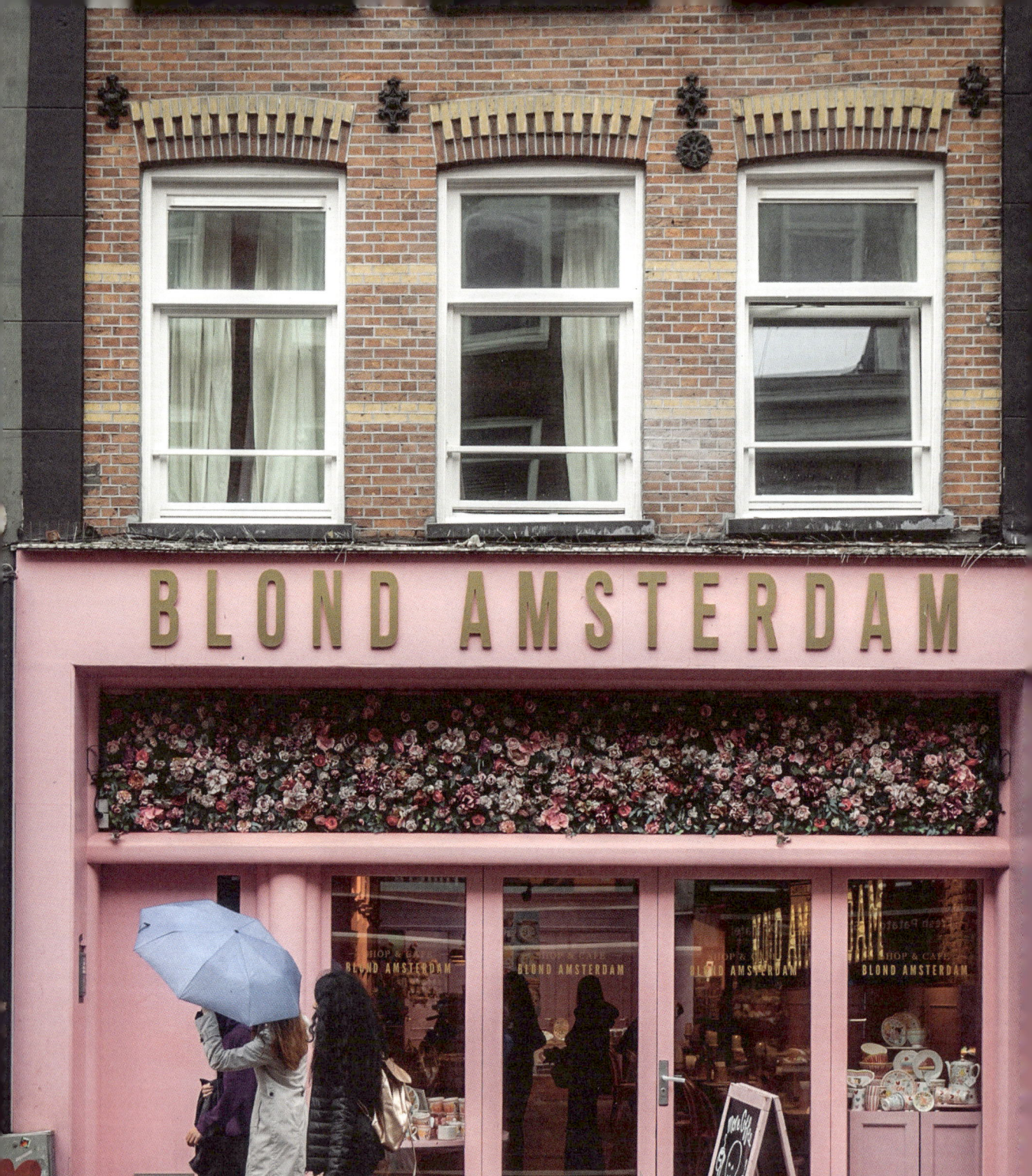

De Pijp, in the south of the city, oozes bohemian neighbourhood charm and vibrant and diverse pockets with a rich history. It was developed in the late nineteenth century to alleviate overcrowding in the city centre. It was initially a working-class area, but over time it has transformed into a trendy and multicultural district known for its lively atmosphere, diverse food scene and bustling street markets.

The neighbourhood is named after the narrow streets that resemble smoking pipes (*pijp* in Dutch). One of its most famous landmarks is the *Albert Cuyp Markt*, which has been operating since 1905 and is a great place to experience the local culture and cuisine. De Pijp is also known for its architecture, with many buildings constructed in the distinctive Amsterdam School style. At the beginning of the twentieth century, it became a popular area for writers, artists and students, transforming it into the Latin Quarter it is today, with a distinct creative energy. The early twentieth-century Haussmann-style urban planning for De Pijp, characterised by wide boulevards and uniform building heights, never materialised. Instead, the area underwent more organic and diverse development, resulting in its unique and vibrant character today. Head to one of the umpteen gorgeous local cafes for a slice of the unique ambience and food; shop till you drop along Gerard Doustraat; enjoy a late-night cocktail or natural wine in *Mokum* or *Glouglou*; and smell the best of Dutch flowers at *Bloemenhandel Sijmons*.

Starting at the north end of Ruysdaelkade (apparently the south end is home to a mini red-light district, but you will have no sense of that if you begin your walk along this beautiful stretch), admire the beautiful architecture before you get to Eerste Jacob van Campenstraat, also known for its charming architecture and local atmosphere. Antiques shop *Curiosa by Marjan Tiller* at number 1 and organic food store *De Aanzet*, across the road at number 10, are lovely introductions to the village-like enclave. From there, you can continue to Daniël Stalpertstraat, which offers a mix of residential buildings and local businesses, providing another lovely glimpse into everyday life in De Pijp.

At the corner of Frans Halsstraat, you will find French bistro-style *Café Caron*, where Chef Alain Caron and his sons offer French classics. Continue along this charming street by browsing the books on sale at *Felix Books*, or enjoy an egg-centric dish (soldiers, omelettes, benedicts and florentines) on the terrace under the awning at the gorgeous restaurant *Oeuf*. A table inside will reveal the quaint little interior: wooden cabinets, dripping candles and marble tables galore.

From here, head for Gerard Doustraat, the very definition of a local gem, best known for its one-off shops, cafes and bars; it's flooded with the most beautiful boutiques. If you have time, relax and browse them one by one; if not, head straight for concept store *Anna + Nina* at number 94, a treasure trove of beautiful items inspired by the distant travels of the two owners, Anna de Lanoy Meijer and Nina Poot. Here, you will find the best in colourful glassware, artisan goods, beautiful jewellery and clothing from their brand.

Then go to the famous *Albert Cuyp Markt*, one of Amsterdam's largest and most popular outdoor markets. Here, you can experience the bustling market atmosphere and sample a variety of local delicacies: everything from raw herring to farm-fresh fruit and more than thirty types of liquorice. Snack on free samples, but leave room for poffertjes – fluffy mini pancakes dusted with sugar.

After visiting the market, stroll through *Sarphatipark*, a beautiful green space in the heart of the neighbourhood, perfect for relaxing and enjoying nature. It was designed in the English Garden style and named after the Jewish doctor and philanthropist Samuel Sarphati (1813–66), whose marvellous nineteenth-century monument dominates the park. If you need a coffee fix, pop into the *Scandinavian Embassy*, a much-loved cafe that overlooks the park and offers an array of regularly changing Nordic roasted coffees alongside Swedish-inspired dishes and some to-die-for cinnamon buns. It was founded by Nicolas Castagno and Rikard Andersson in 2013 and is highly regarded in the city.

The pedestrian-only Eerste van der Helststraat is another street worth mentioning for its unique charm and architecture. When it's time for a little more shopping, *COTTONCAKE* at number 76, for healthy lunches and organic coffee alongside a stunning edit of fashion labels, or *Eland & Vanderhelst* at number 62, for a unique selection of homewares, are amongst its finest highlights. End your visit to De Pijp with a glass or two at *Glouglou*.

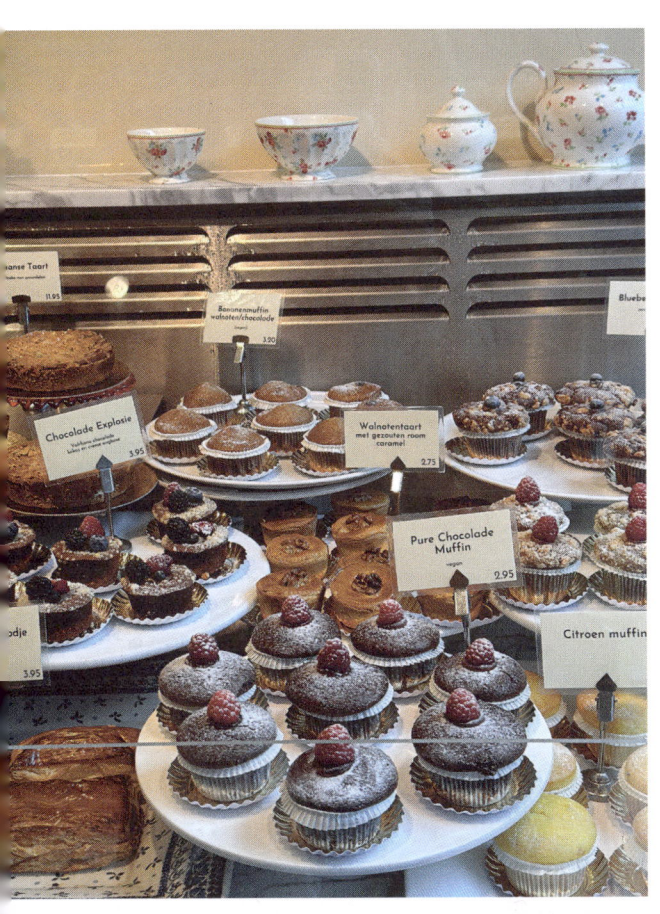
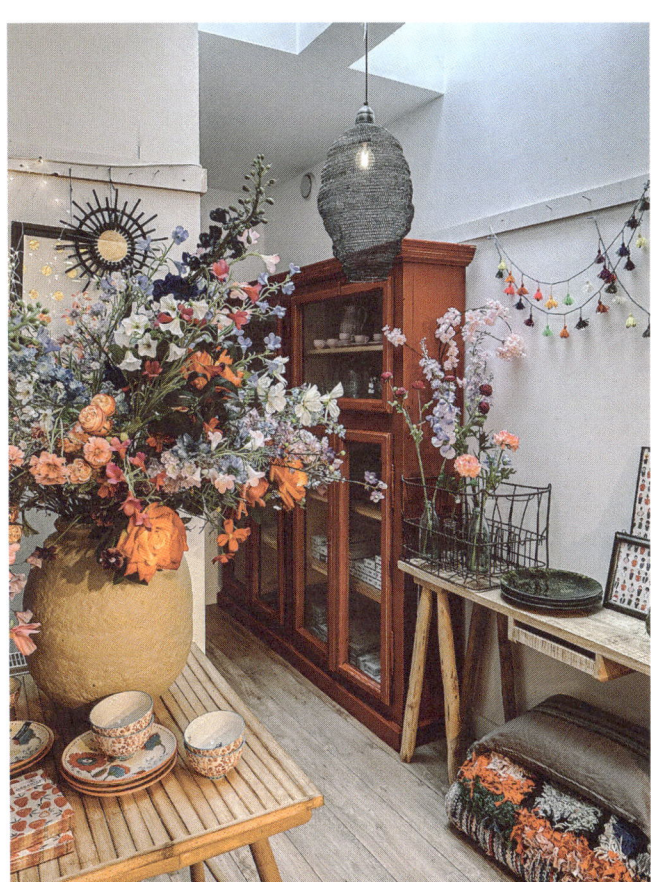
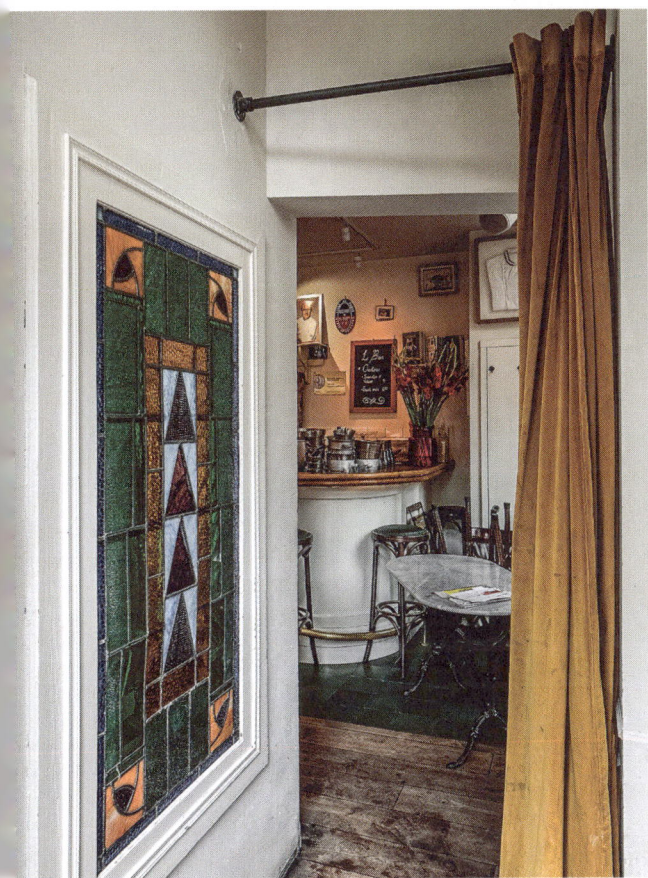
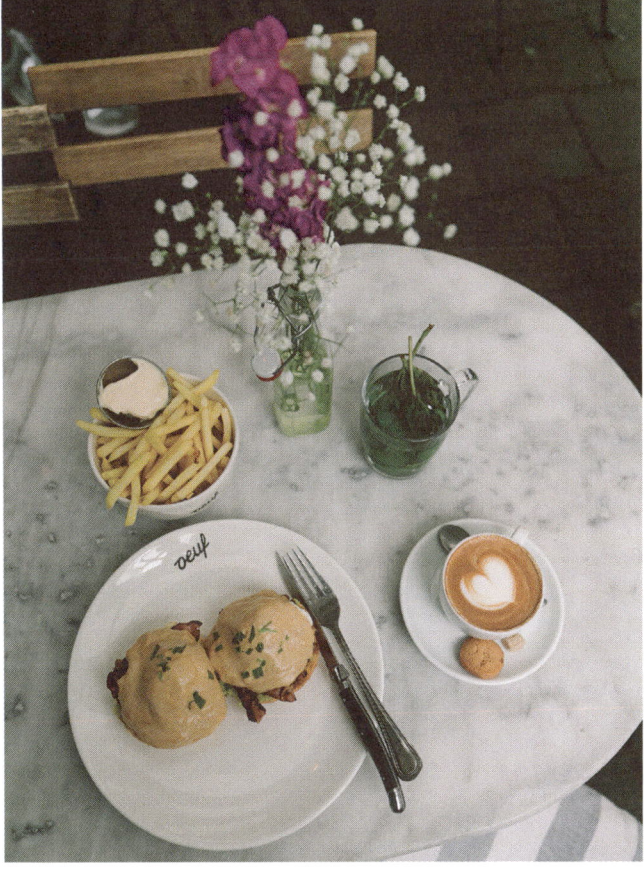

ADDRESSES OF NOTE

Albert Cuyp Markt
The chances are if you know Amsterdam you know the Albert Cuyp Market. The market began life in 1904 and now the 300 stalls which line the long stretch of Albert Cuypstraat are among the most emblematic symbols of the city. Open every day except Sunday, it is a delightful place to embrace the richness of culture and cuisine.

Sir Albert, **Albert Cuypstraat 2–6**
Set behind a beautiful redbrick facade of a former nineteenth-century diamond factory, this hotel proudly provides a sense of style and sophistication for the culturally curious. On the ground floor the Izakaya Asian Kitchen and Bar serves Japanese-influenced cuisine.

Ouef, **Daniel Stalpertstraat 36**
Ouef's popularity is attributed to its simple menu offering and romantic décor. The carefully selected menu is dedicated to eggs in all their forms and inspired by the worldwide travels of its owners. The Oeuf Truffle Special, French toast, omelettes and shakshuka are amongst the favourites served here.

Little Collins, **Sweelinckstraat 19**
Brunch lovers flock to Little Collins to enjoy its delicious dishes and speciality coffee. This local favourite does not take reservations so, to increase your chances of a spot at its communal table or sunny terrace, arrive outside regular dining hours.

Cotton Cake, **Eerste van der Helststraat 76**
Cotton Cake mingles a great little cafe with a stunning little concept store. The stark white interior acts as an ideal backdrop to display the meticulously selected clothing and vintage pieces.

Eland & VanderHelst, **Eerste van der Helststraat 62**
An elegant store for a beautifully curated selection of homewares and gifts.

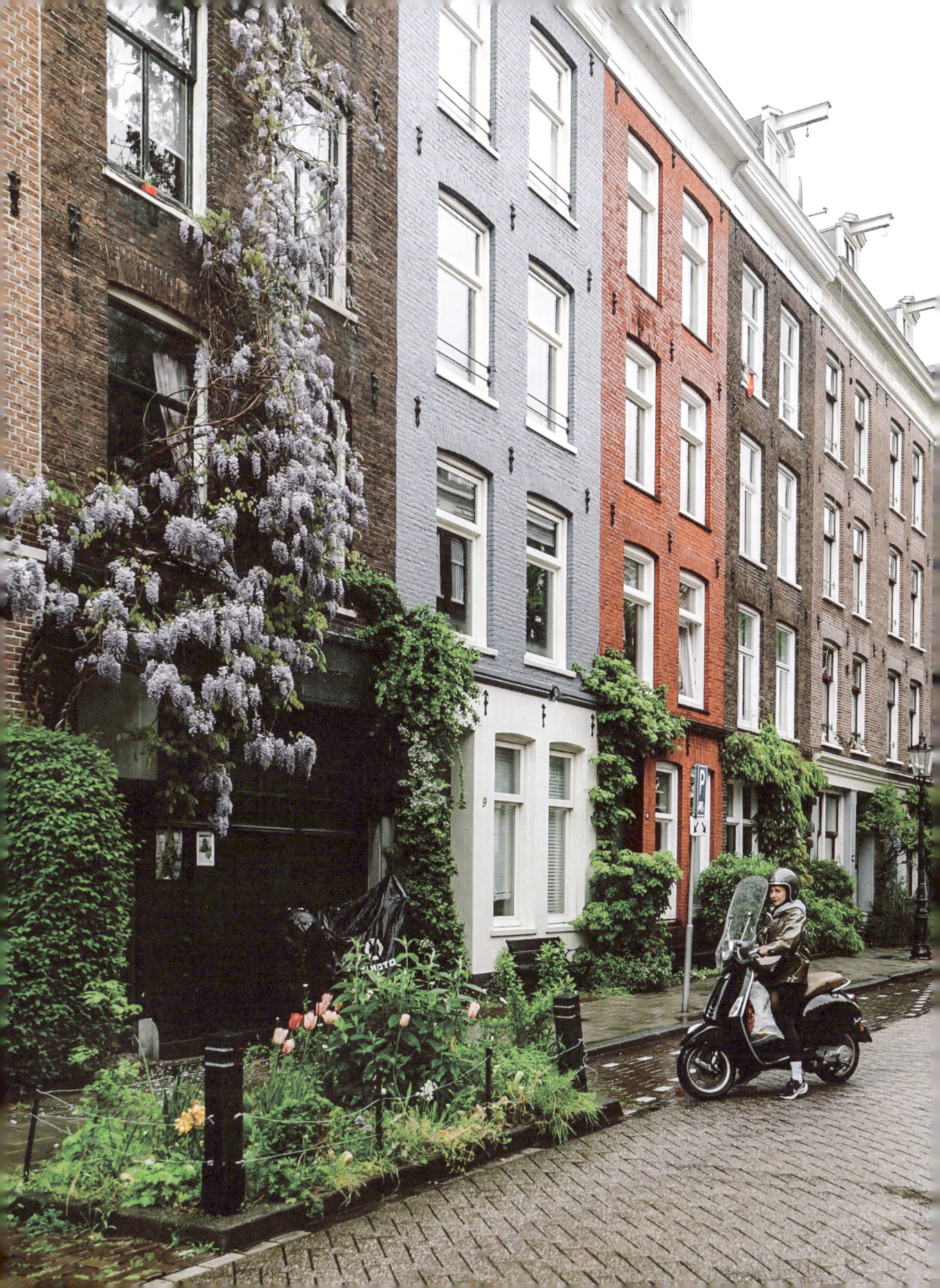

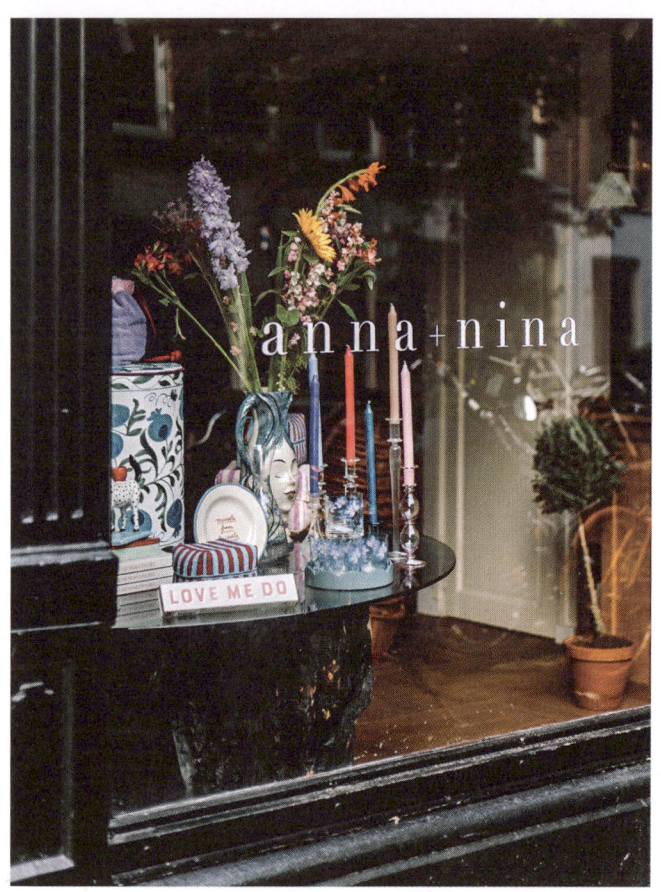
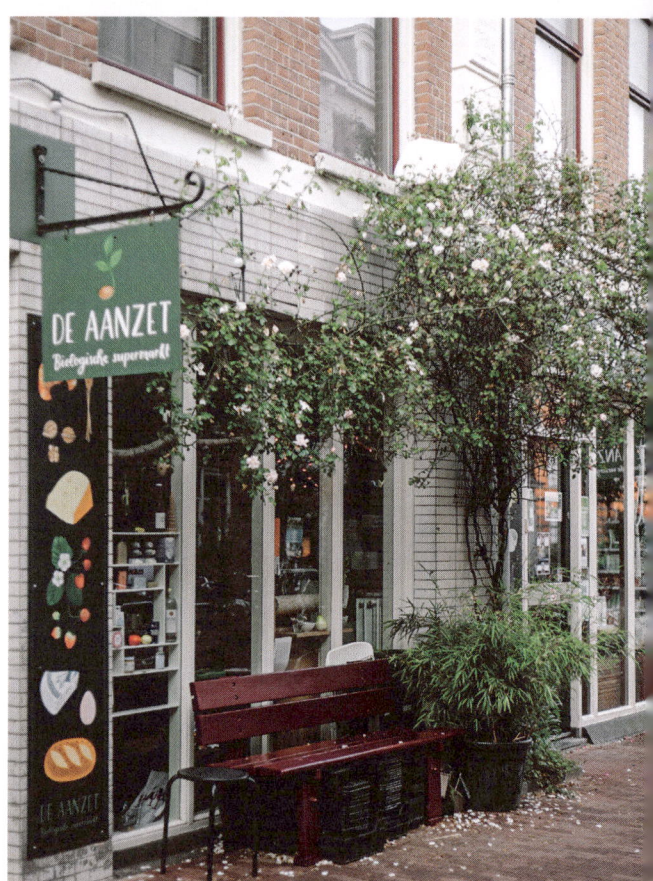
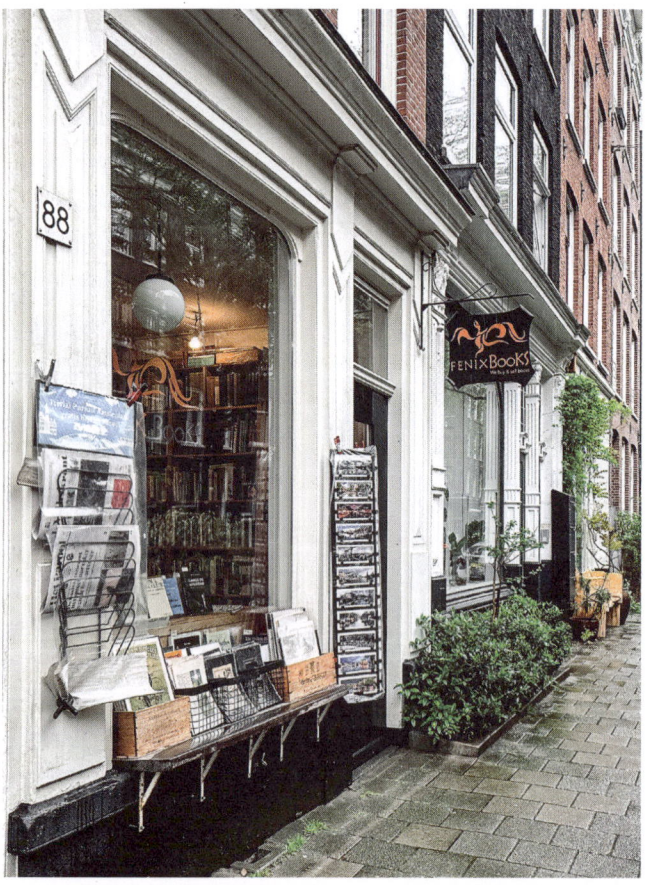
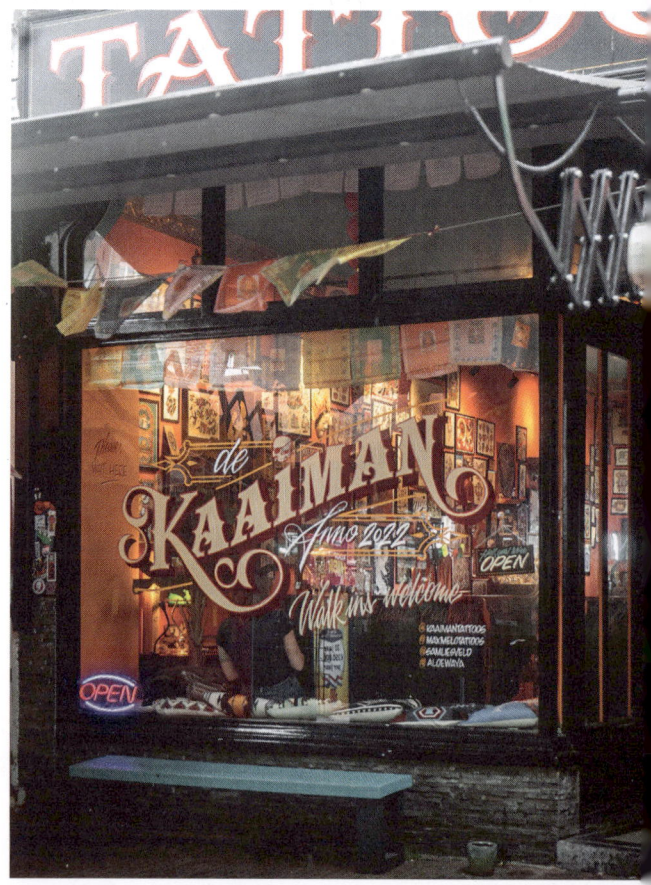

Locals All Day Brunch, **Eerste Jacob van Campenstraat 27**
Another great option for breakfast, brunch or lunch in the area. Enjoy classics like eggs benedict and avocado toast.

Café Caron, **Frans Halsstraat 28**
This cosy bistro is run by well-known TV personality Alain Caron and his family. Café Caron has satisfied a continual clientele since 2016. Escargots and characturie are among the French classics available here. The interior design is simple yet elegant, with rustic tables and chairs and ambient lighting adding to the romantic atmosphere.

Glouglou, **Tweede van der Helststraat 3**
In addition to an impressive list of natural wines, this charming bar serves small plates. Embrace the unique atmosphere inside or out.

All the Luck in the World, **Gerard Doustraat 86**
There are many great independent boutiques to celebrate in Amsterdam but this jewellery and vintage store is particularly distinctive. This is one of three of their boutiques in Amsterdam. All jewellery pieces are made with the best of materials sourced locally and they line the boutique's shelves alongside a lovely collection of stationery, vintage furniture and homewares. A visit is a must.

Anna + Nina, **Gerard Doustraat 94**
A treasure trove of beautiful things, inspired by the global travels of founders Anna de Lanoy Meijer and Nina Poot. Established in 2012 and originally focused on charm-like jewellery and fashion accessories, they now stock a beautiful homeware collection, which is inspired by their travels through Thailand, Bali and India. They focus on sensory designs that embrace life's magical moments.

Bloemenhandel Sijmons, **Gerard Doustraat 158**
Bloemenhandel Sijmons is crammed with the freshest selection of seasonal blooms and unique arrangements. Visit for all your floral needs.

Sarphatipark
A little green oasis in the heart of the village; the perfect spot to relax for a while or to simply meander through.

Scandinavian Embassy, **Sarphatipark 34**
Coffee lovers should head straight for this brilliant ambassador for Scandinavian roasted coffee. Various independent coffee roasters from Denmark, Norway and Sweden are offered here; coffees from Koppi, Drop Coffee and the Coffee Collective can be enjoyed alongside a delicious selection of pastries and buns.

Massimo Gelato, **Van Ostadestraat 147**
Satisfy any gelato cravings with a scoop or two at Massimo Gelato, a renowned Italian ice-cream parlour and cafe. Offering a great range of flavours, from classics to the more exciting. They also serve great coffee and pastries.

Fenix Books, **Frans Halsstraat 88**
The super-cosy bookstore that every local neighbourhood needs, sourcing, selling and buying antiquarian tomes since 1994.

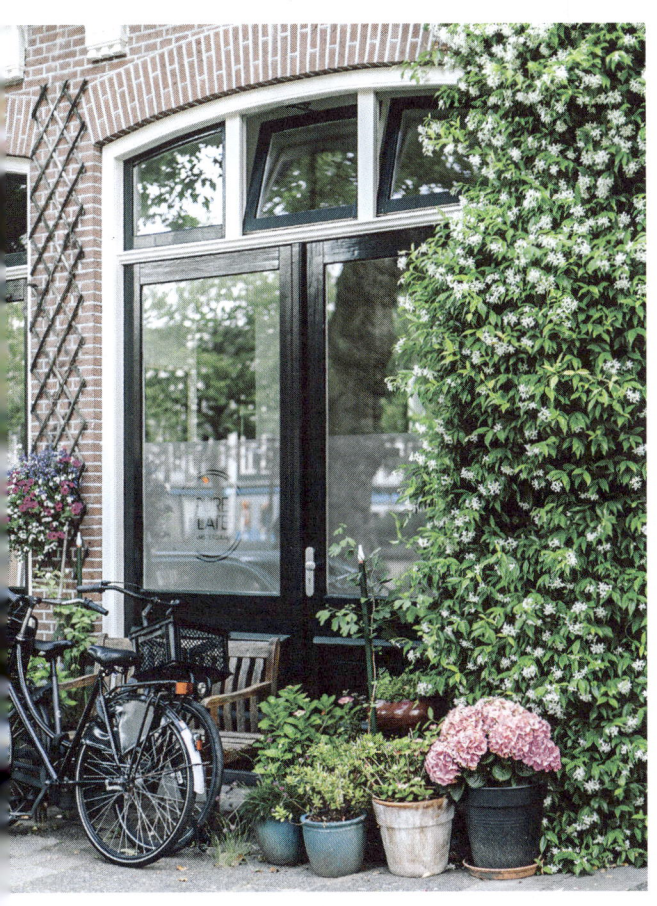
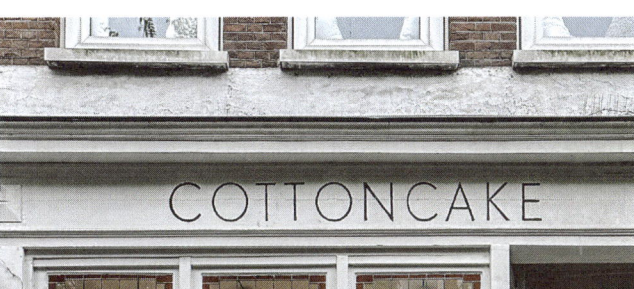
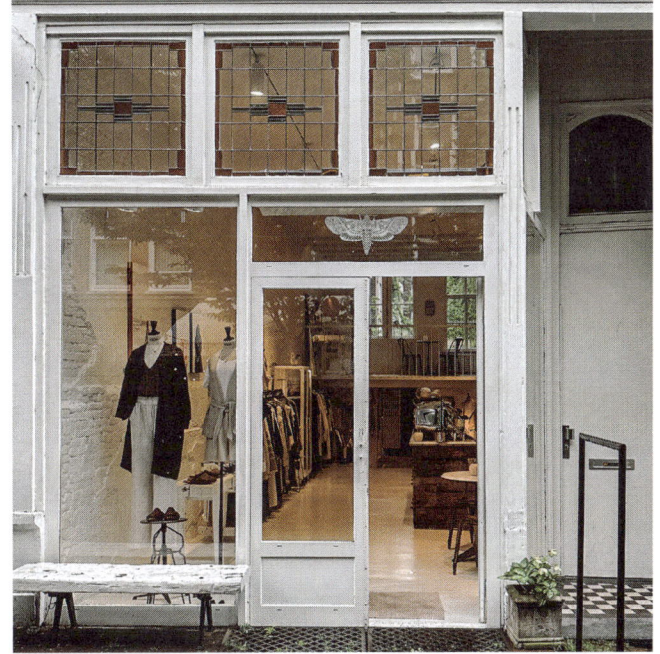
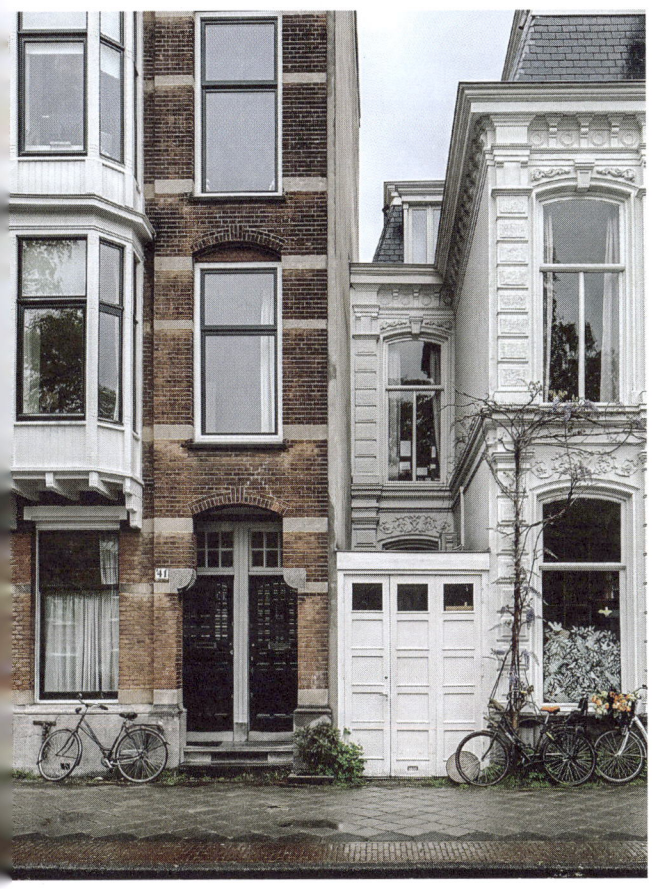
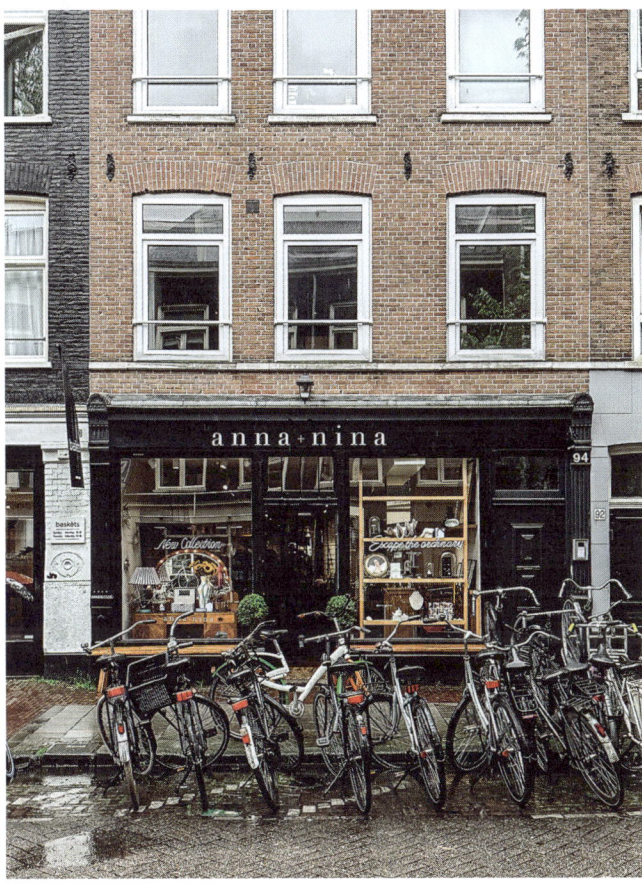

OUD-WEST

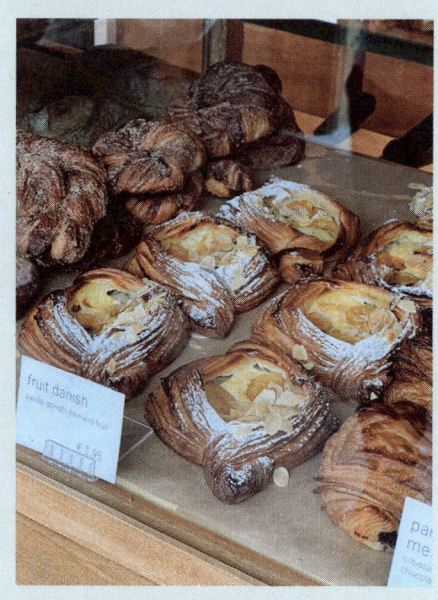

A LAID-BACK ATMOSPHERE ENHANCED WITH
PLENTY OF LOCAL BAKERIES, VINTAGE SHOPS AND
TOP-NOTCH RESTAURANTS

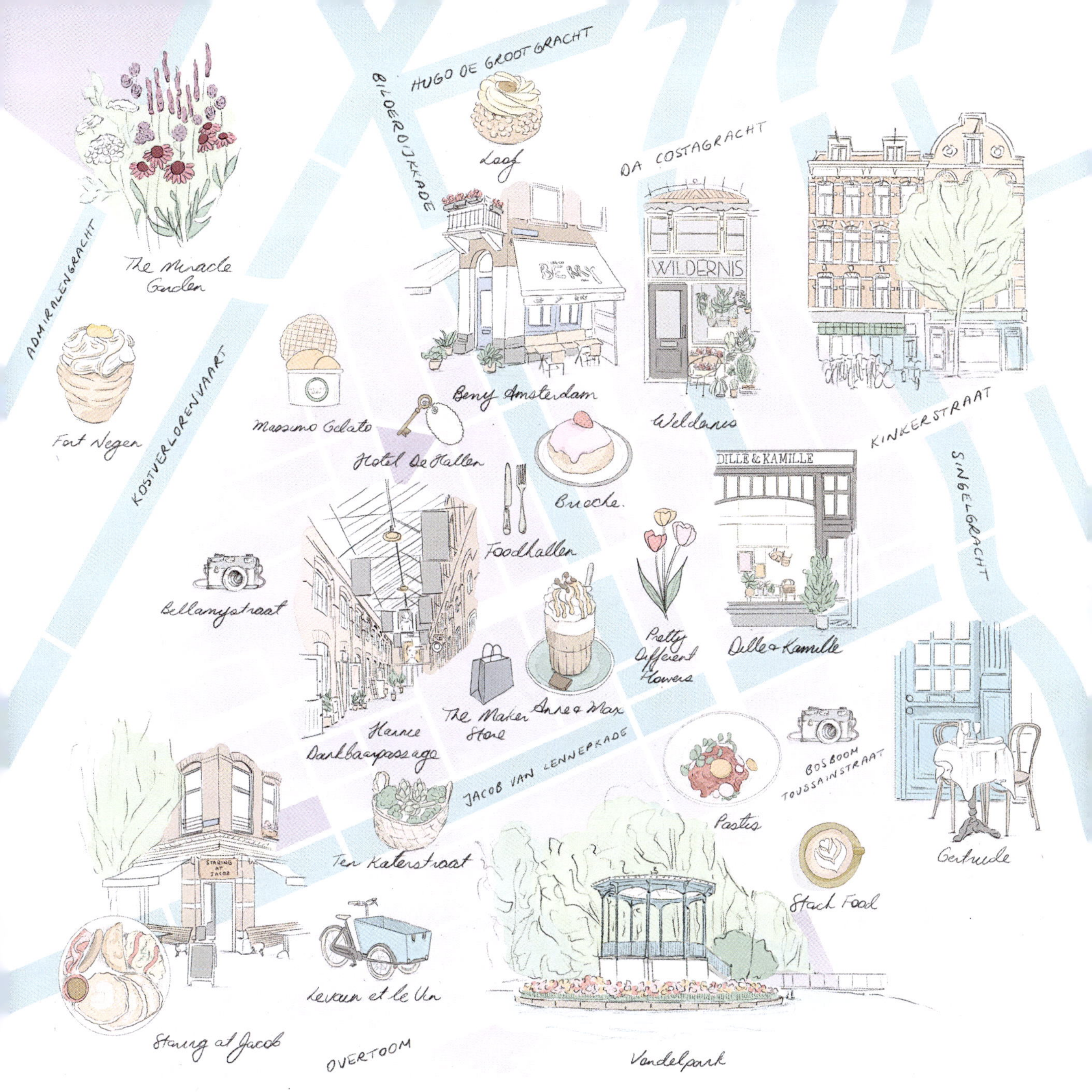

OUD-WEST

#prettycityamsterdam

 DILLE & KAMILLE Bilderdijkstraat 187–189
THE MAKER STORE Hannie Dankbaarpassage 39

 BERRY AMSTERDAM Bilderdijkkade 27
STACH FOOD Overtoom 112

 LOOF Bilderdijkstraat 38
BRIOCHE. Bilderdijkstraat 164H
MASSIMO GELATO Jan Hanzenstraat 15
FORT NEGEN Jan Evertsenstraat 31

 HOTEL DE HALLEN Bellamyplein 47

 Vondelpark, Bellamystraat, Ten Katestraat, Bosboom Toussaintstraat, The Miracle Garden, Hannie Dankbaarpassage

 WILDERNIS Bilderdijkstraat 165F
PRETTY DIFFERENT FLOWERS Bilderdijkstraat 196Hs

 GERTRUDE Bosboom Toussaintstraat 28H
STARING AT JACOB Jacob Van Lennepkade 215
LEVAIN ET LE VIN Jan Pieter Heijestraat 168
FOODHALLEN Hannie Dankbaarpassage 16
PASTIS Eerste Constantijn Huygensstraat 15
ANNE&MAX Tollensstraat 57Y

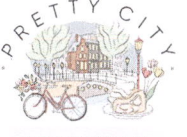

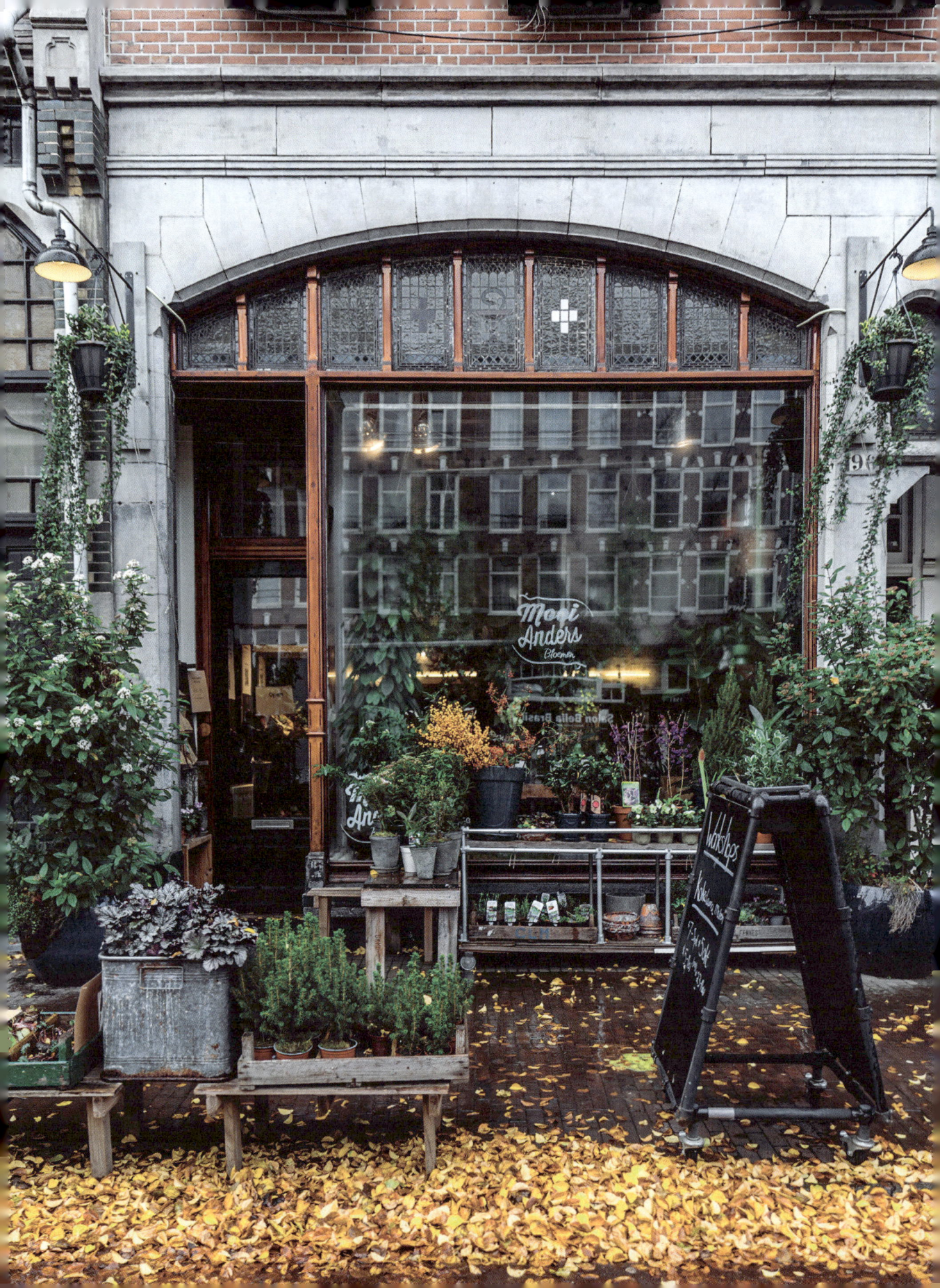

Oud-West is a vibrant and diverse neighbourhood known for its mix of cultures, trendy shops and cosy cafes. While it isn't home to many museums or iconic monuments, it's a great place to explore local markets, enjoy multicultural cuisine and soak up the area's unique atmosphere. Whether interested in art or food or simply strolling through charming streets, Oud-West has something for everyone. It is bordered by the stately Vondelpark and Kostverlorenvaart to the north, Singelgracht to the west, Overtoom to the South, and Kinkerstraat to the east. Seek out the flurry of local bakeries, cafes and restaurants, lose an hour or two in *De Hallen* or along the bustling *Ten Katemarkt*, and take note of the street names in the area, with many named after notable national poets – for example, Kinkerstraat, named after Johannes Kinker.

You could start your walk at the exceptional Bilderdijkkade, where an entire morning or afternoon could be whiled away, buzzing in and out of shops and cafes. Begin with a simple coffee or muffin from *Berry* at number 27. A gorgeous laid-back living-room cafe is the perfect introduction to this casual neighbourhood. If you have a little time, stop at *Iouf* (number 38), which is undoubtedly one of the finest bakeries in Amsterdam. Next door, *Café Binnenvisser*, with the same owners, falls somewhere between retro pub and cosy wine bar; *Collins* restaurant, further along at number 140, is equally pleasing. *Wildernis* plant shop at number 165F and *Pretty Different Flowers* florist at number 196Hs shouldn't be missed; neither should fabulous homewares store *Dille & Kamille* at number 187–189.

When you have finished browsing, cross over the canal from here and turn left on Tollensstraat to reach De Hallen. A former tram depot, it is now home to a brilliant indoor food market, a range of independent design shops, a magnificent food hall, a cinema and a boutique hotel. Hannie Dankbaarpassage forms part of the De Hallen cultural centre. This partially covered passage is home to the best in shops, including *Denim City* and *The Maker Store*, which sells art, handcrafted fashion and objects with a story. You'll also find a handy bike repair shop, a kids' photographer, a hairdressing salon and the very popular *Foodhallen* here. Once a month, the shops host a Maker Market, where Amsterdam-based artisans are invited to sell their wares. Discover stands and displays of prints, accessories, clothing, knickknacks and trinkets to take home.

Once you have your fill of browsing, exit Ten Katemarkt, a lively daily market with just over 100 stalls stretching across Jan Hanzenstraat and Borgerstraat, with a bit of spill over on to Kinkerstraat.

As you walk along Bilderdijkstraat and Kinkerstraat, you'll encounter an array of trendy shops, cafes and restaurants. These bustling streets are perfect for soaking up the local atmosphere, but save your appetite for Bosboom Toussaintstraat, an exceptional tree-lined street flooded with brilliant eateries: *De Italiaan* at number 29 or *Gertrude* at number 28-H (probably named after well-known Dutch writer Geertruida Bosboom-Toussaint) are both highlights.

Throughout your walk, watch out for street art, historic buildings and hidden gems that make Oud-West a captivating neighbourhood to explore.

ADDRESSES OF NOTE

Berry Amsterdam, **Bilderdijkkade 27**

Iouf, **Bilderdijkstraat 38**

Wildernis, **Bilderdijkstraat 165F**

Collins, **Bilderdijkstraat 140**

Pretty Different Flowers, **Bilderdijkstraat 196Hs**

brioche, **Bilderdijkstraat 164H**

Dille & Kamille, **Bilderdijkstraat 187–189**

Gertrude, **Bosboom Toussaintstraat 28H**

De Italiaan, **Bosboom Toussaintstraat 29**

Ulmus, **Cabralstraat 7**

Pastis, **Eerste Constantijn Huygensstraat 15**

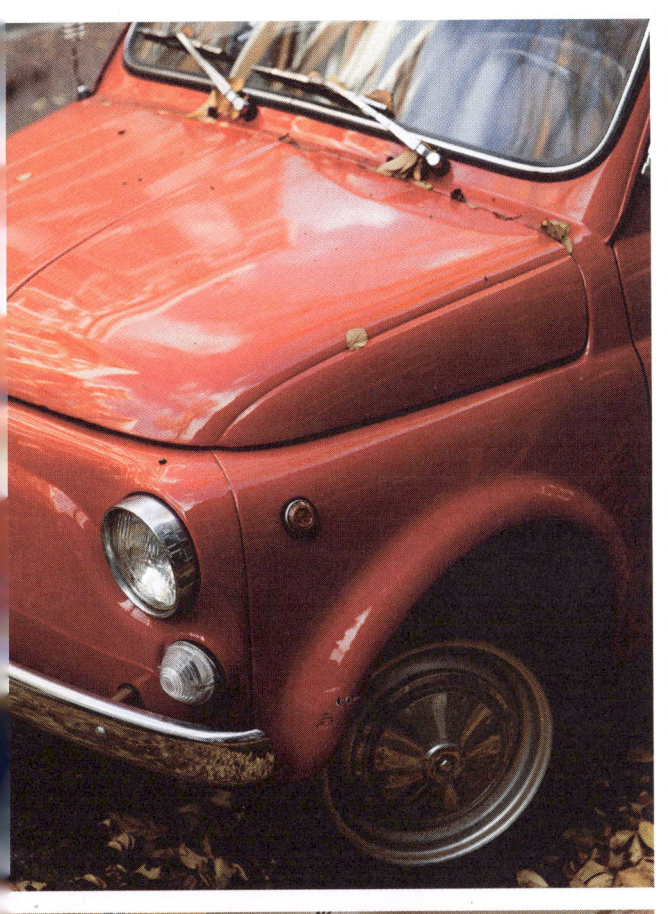
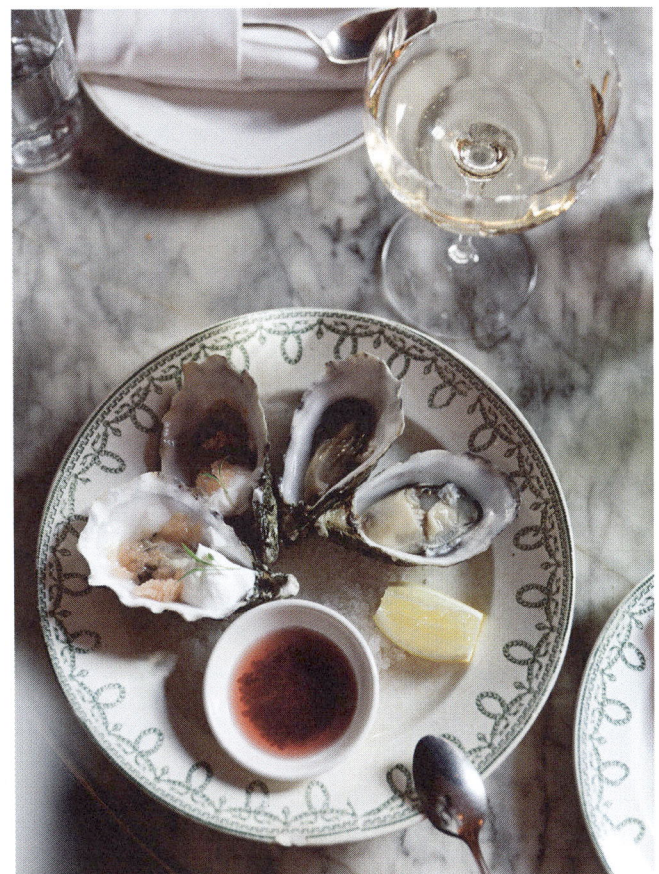
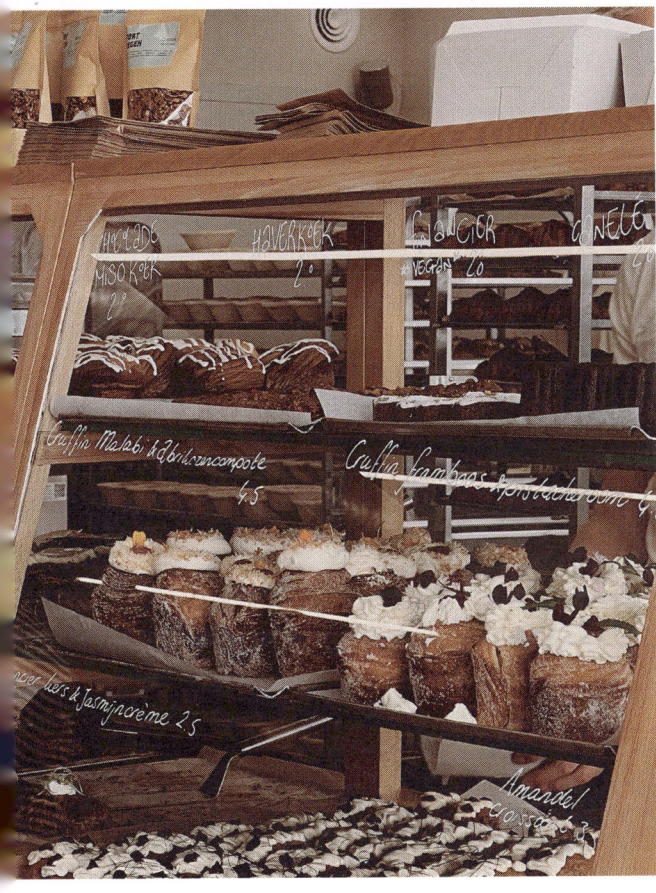
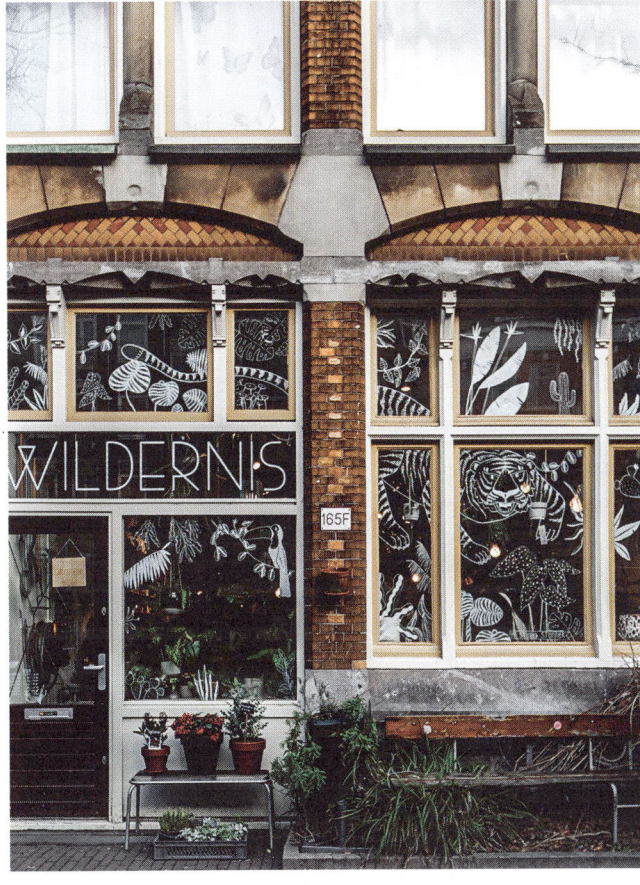

The Miracle Garden, **Erasmuspark**

Foodhallen, **Hannie Dankbaarpassage 16**

The Maker Store, **Hannie Dankbaarpassage 39**

De Hallen, **Hannie Dankbaarpassage 47**

Staring at Jacob, **Jacob van Lennepkade 215**

Fort Negen, **Jan Evertsenstraat 31**

Massimo Gelato, **Jan Hanzenstraat 15**

Levain et le Vin, **Jan Pieter Heijestraat 168**

Stach, **Overtoom 112**

Anne & Max, **Tollensstraat 57Y**

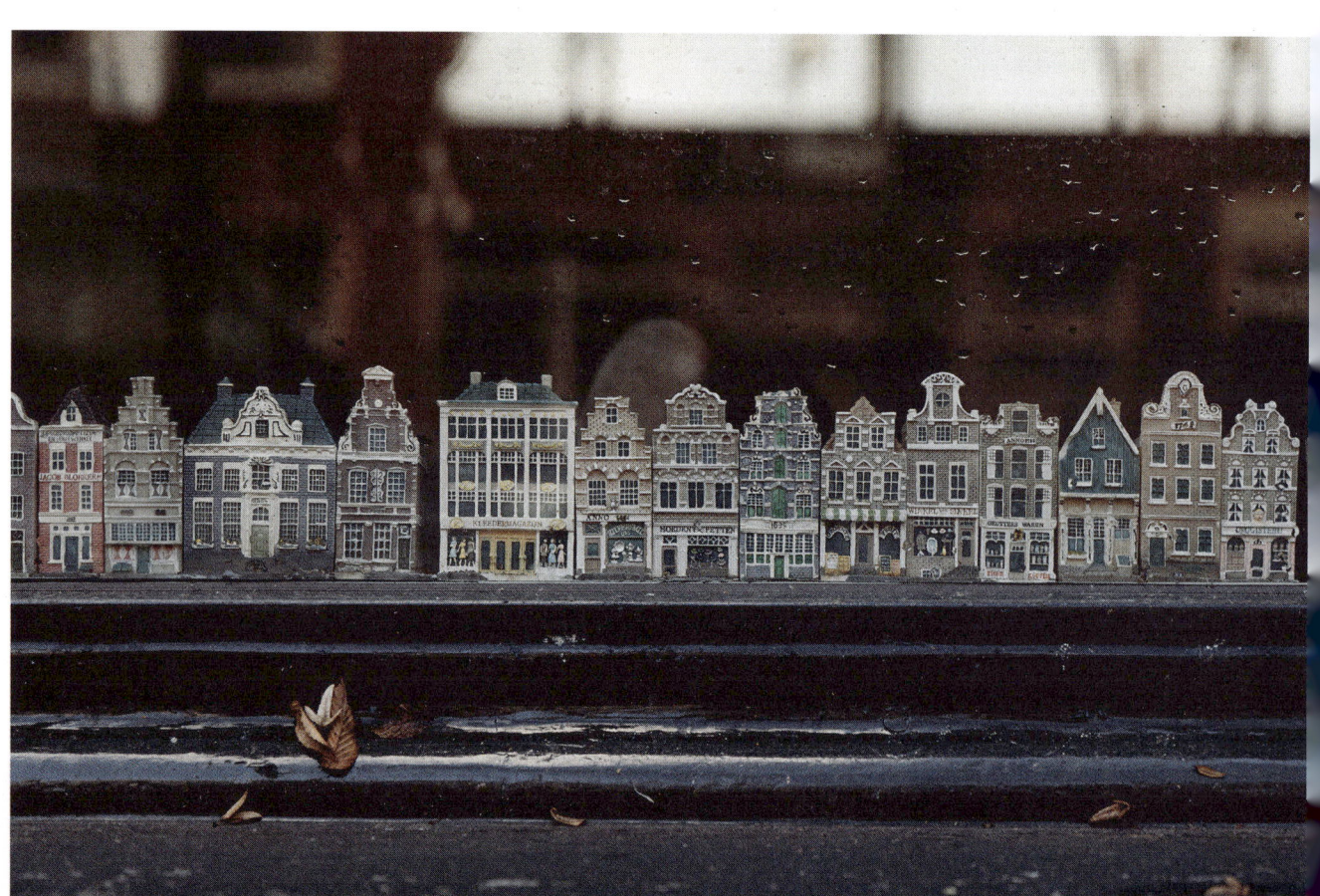

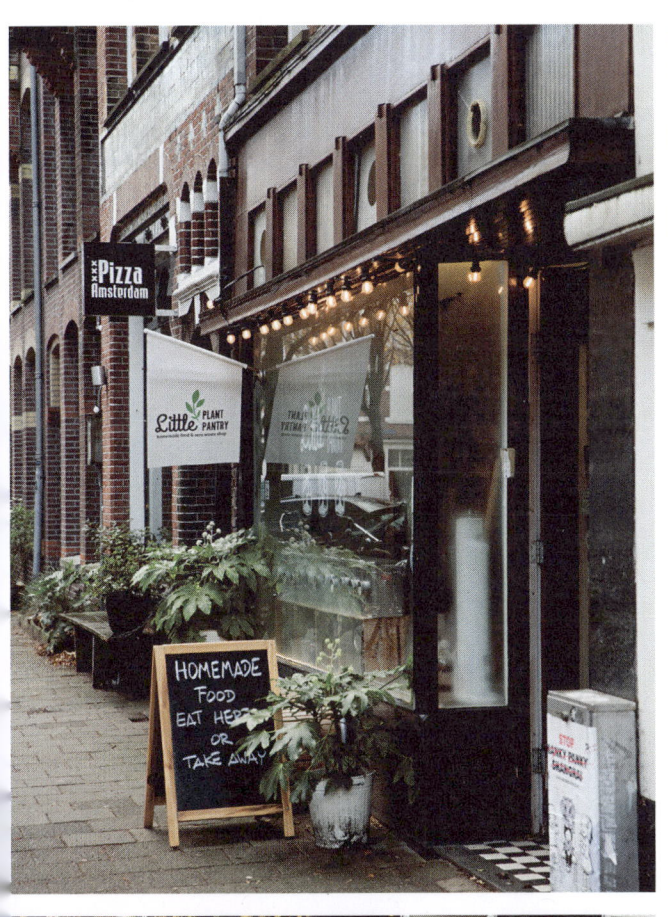
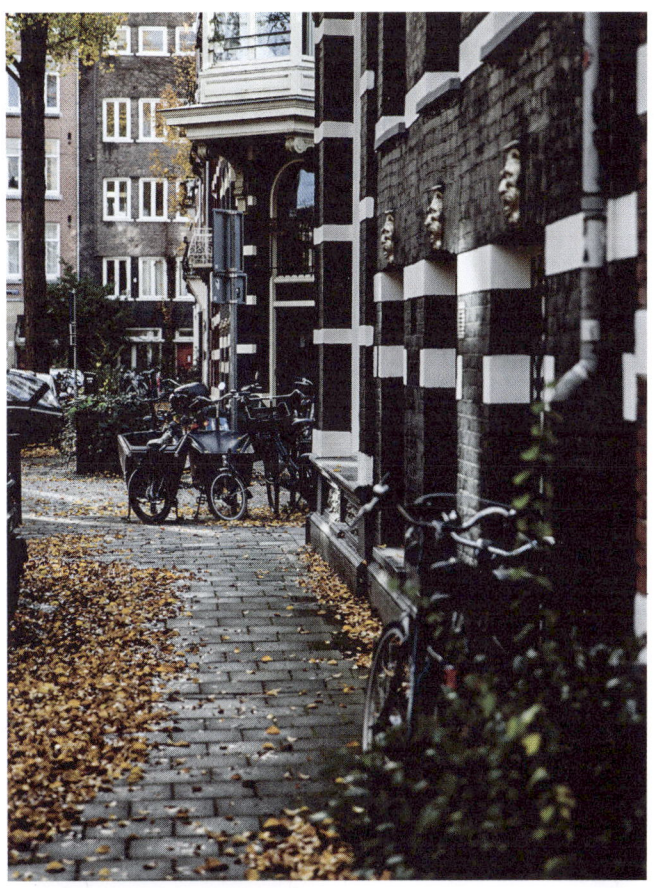
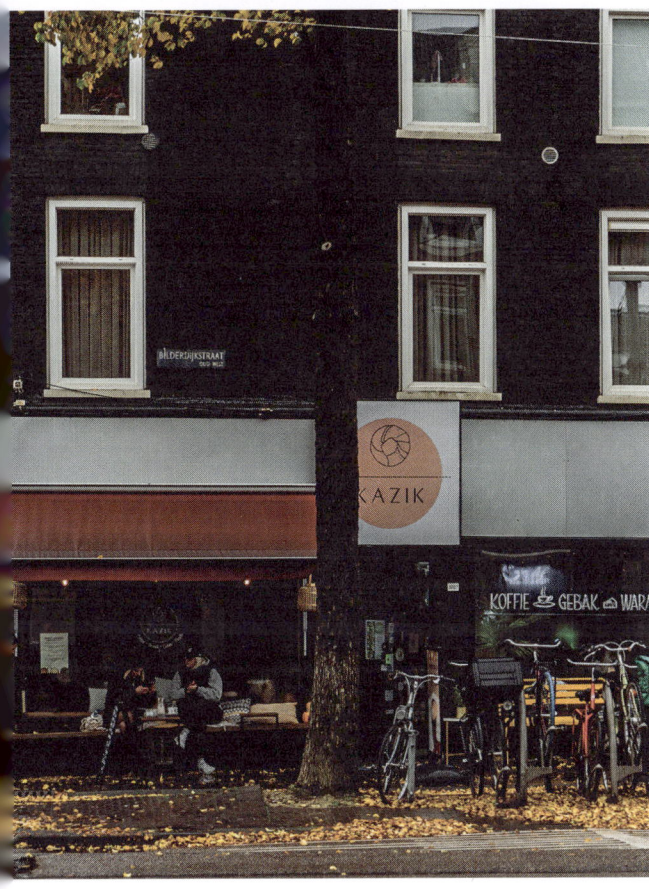
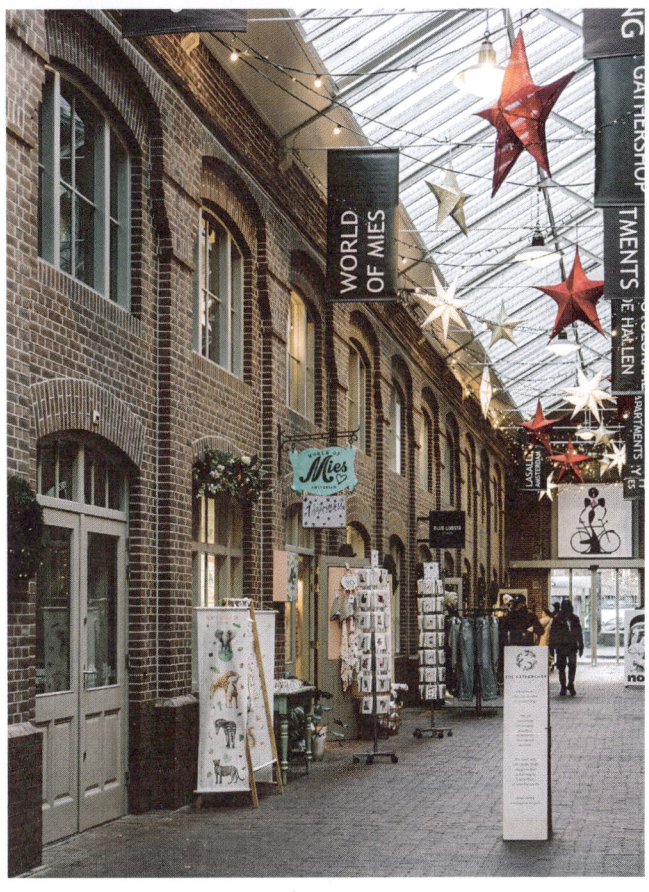

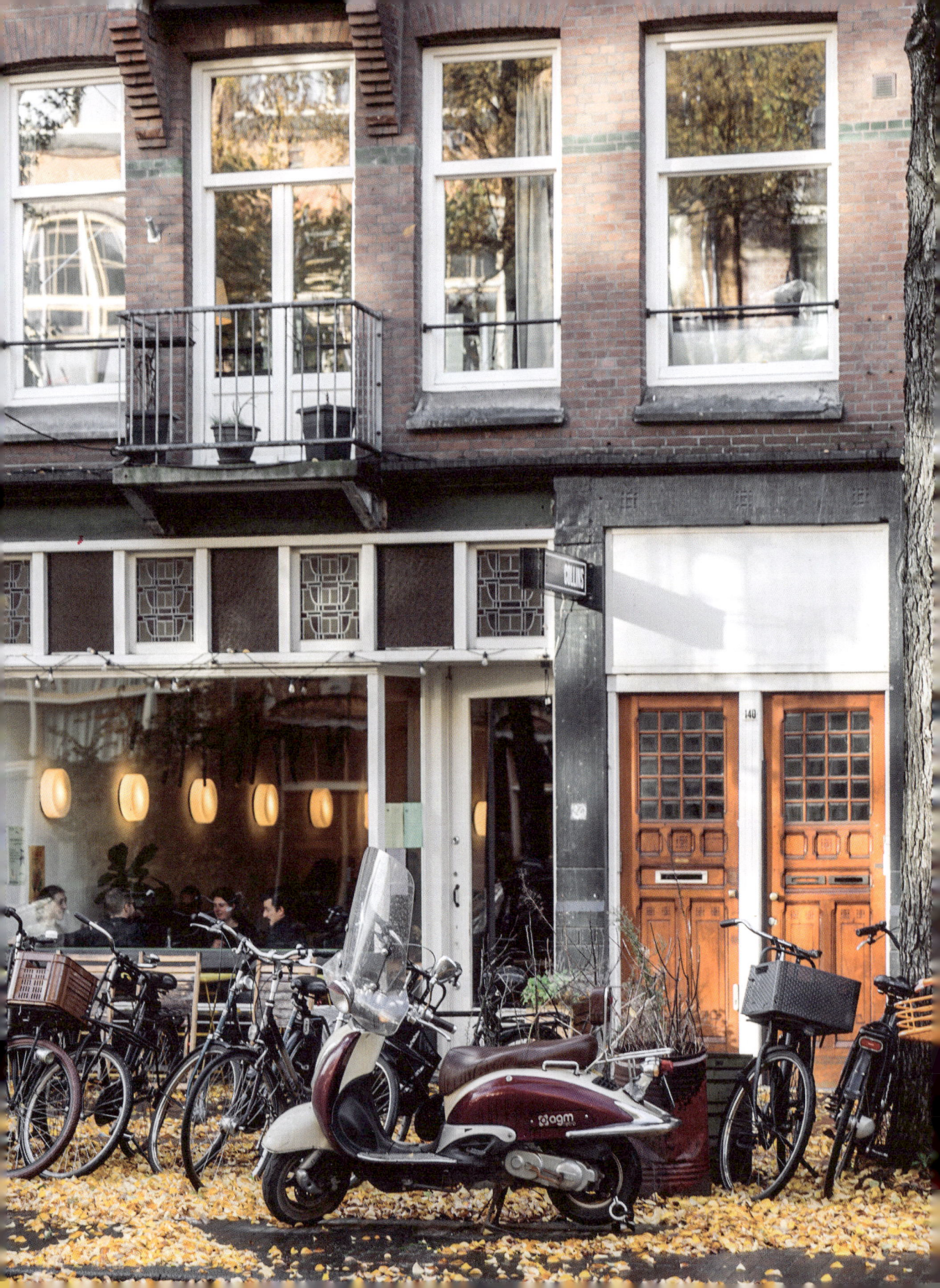

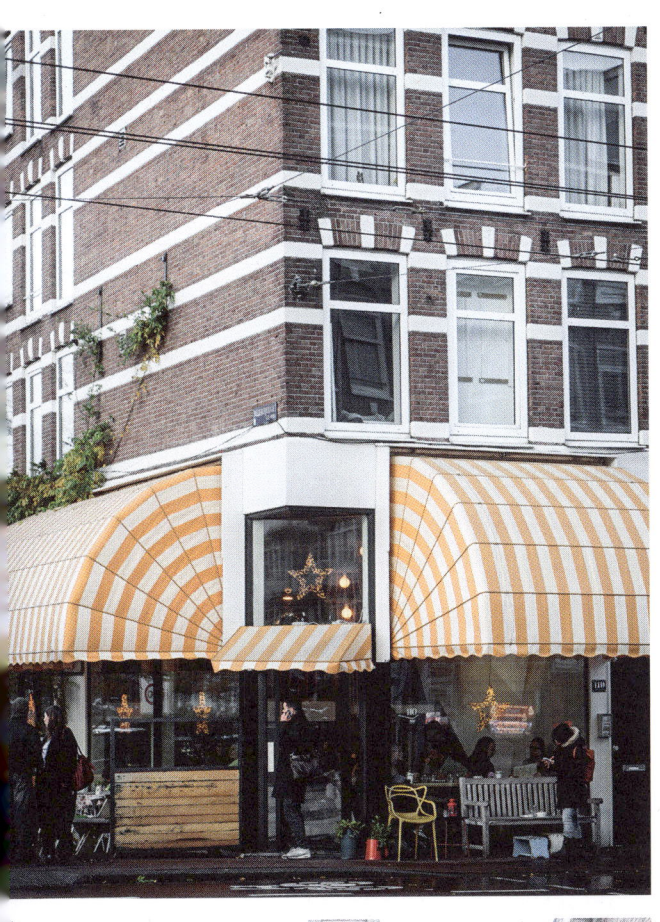
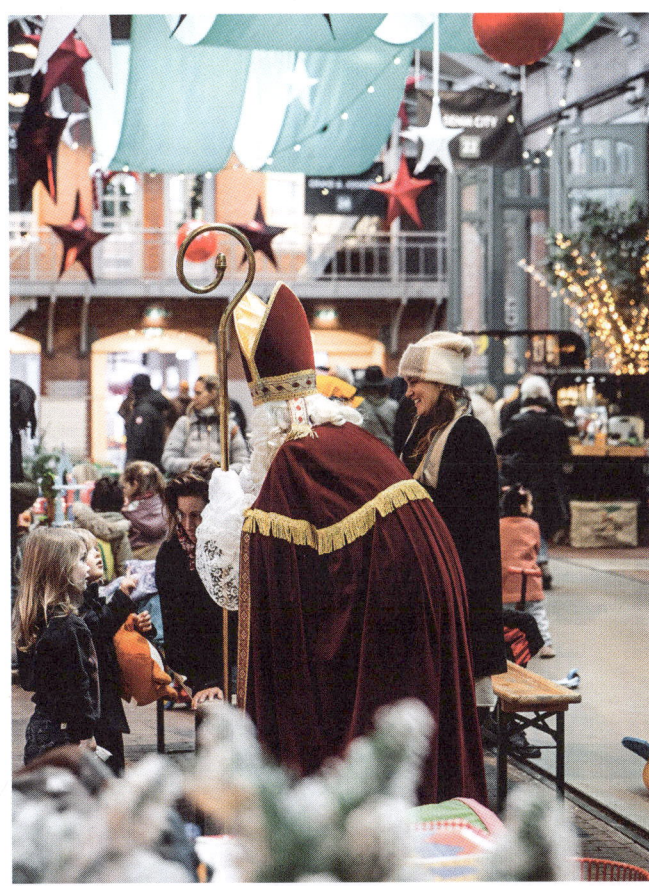
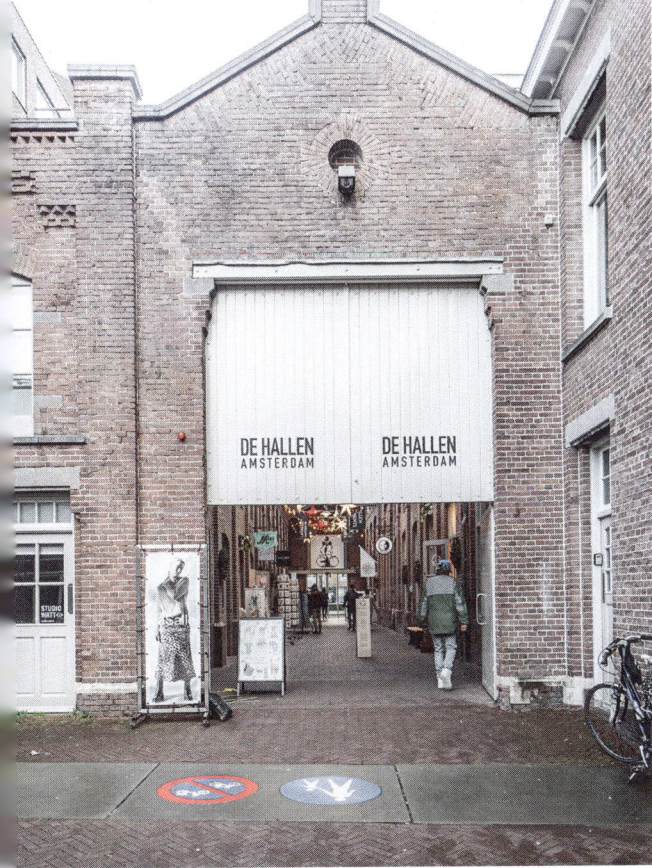
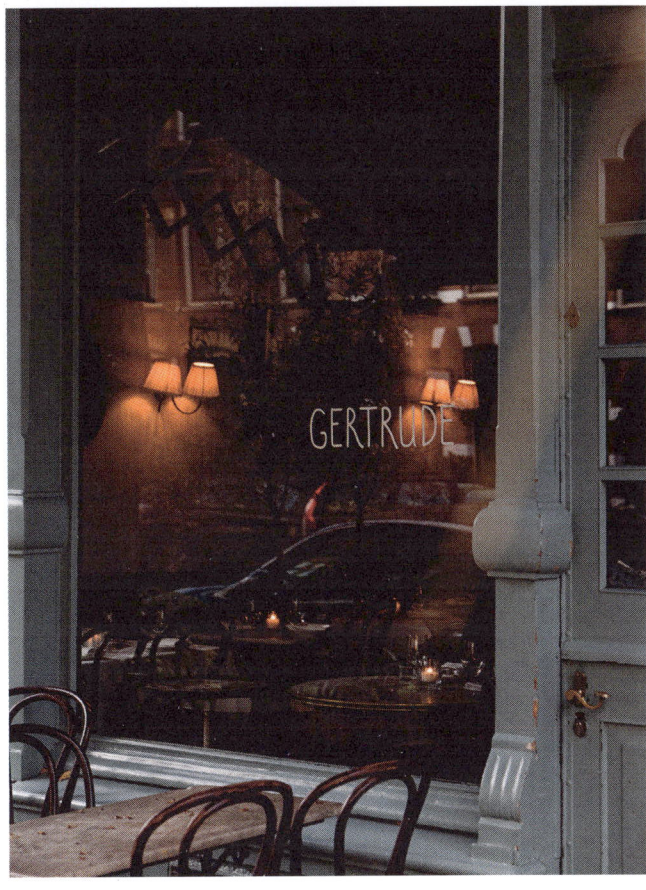

MEDIEVAL CENTRUM, OUDE ZIJDE AND NIEUWE ZIJDE

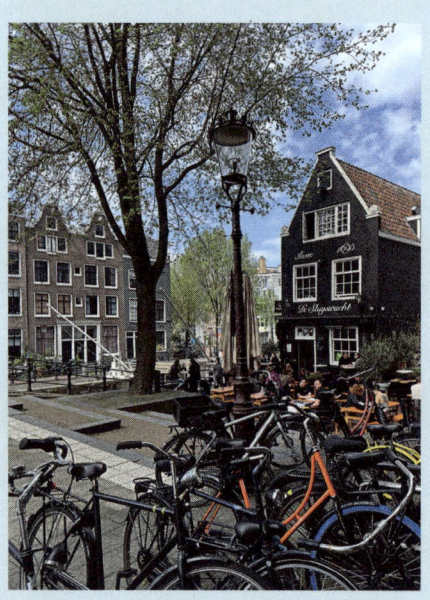

AMSTERDAM'S OLDEST QUARTER; BUSY WITH VISITORS BUT BRIMMING WITH HIDDEN GEMS

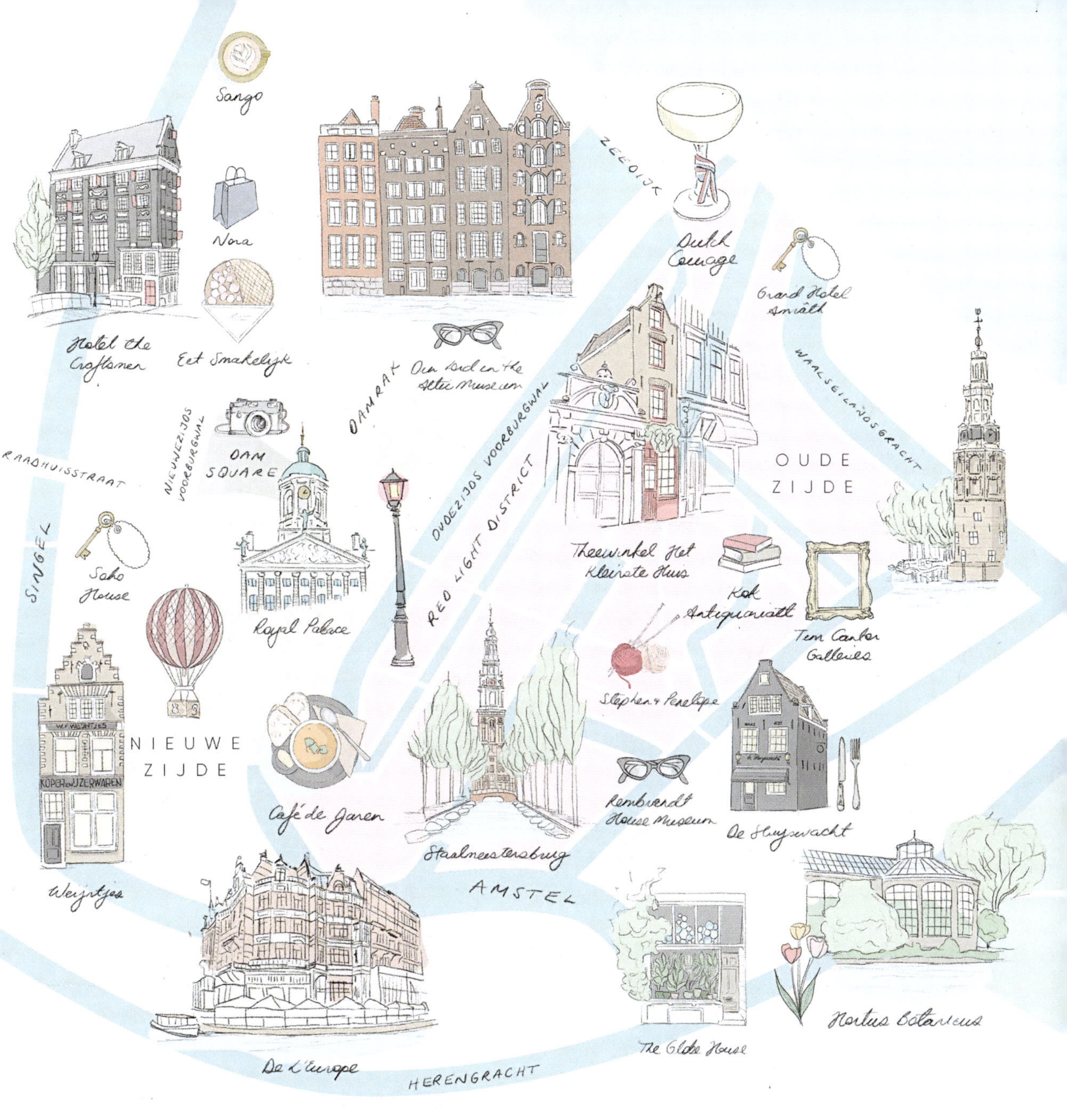

MEDIEVAL CENTRUM

#prettycityamsterdam

 NORA Oude Nieuwstraat 23
THEEWINKEL HET KLEINSTE HUIS Oude Hoogstraat 22
STEPHEN & PENELOPE Nieuwe Hoogstraat 29

 SANGO Stromarkt 15

 EET SMAKELIJK Spuistraat 60

 DUTCH COURAGE Zeedijk 12
IN 'T AEPJEN Zeedijk 1
DE SLUYSWACHT Jodenbreestraat 1

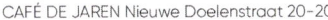 CAFÉ DE JAREN Nieuwe Doelenstraat 20-20

 Staalmeestersbrug, Weijntjes, Damrak, Hortus Botanicus, The Globe House, Royal Palace

 TIM CANTOR GALLERIES Nieuwe Hoogstraat 6H
OUR LORD IN THE ATTIC MUSEUM Oudezijds Voorburgwal 38-40
REMBRANDT HOUSE MUSEUM Jodenbreestraat 4

 KOK ANTIQUARIAAT A Oude Hoogstraat 18

 DE L'EUROPE Nieuwe Doelenstraat 2-14
HOTEL THE CRAFTSMEN Singel 83
GRAND HOTEL AMRÂTH Prins Hendrikkade 108
SOHO HOUSE Spuistraat 210

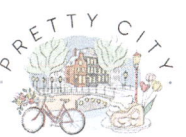

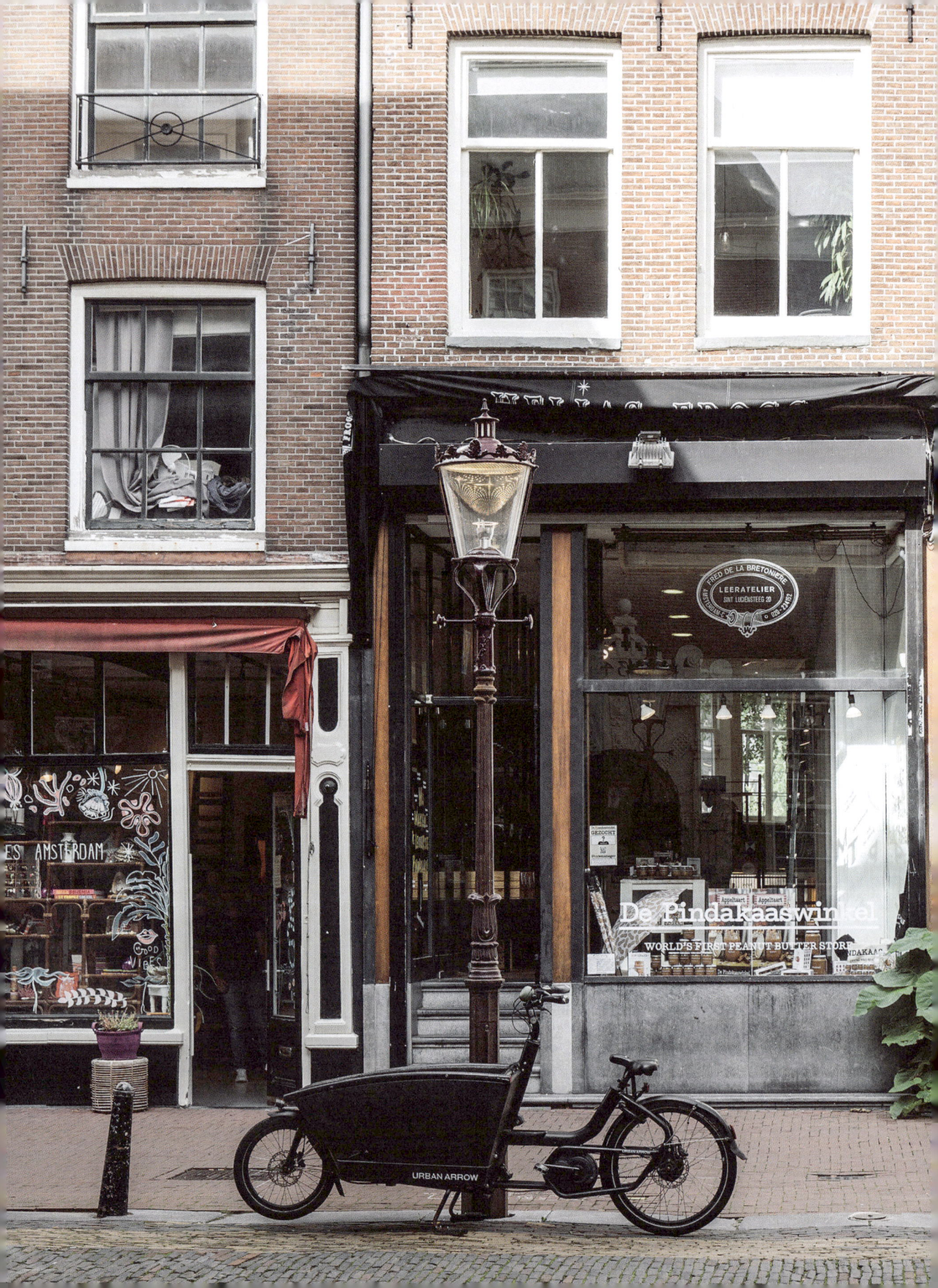

NEIGHBOURHOODS 143

Standing in front of Central Station, one of the most beautiful buildings in Amsterdam, facing Damrak and with your back to Dam Square, one can easily divide the city into two: the old side (Oude Zijde, to the left) and the new side (Nieuwe Zijde, to the right). The earliest maps of Amsterdam, dating back to 1538, suggest the two sides have been separated by Damrak (the street that leads from Central Station to Dam Square) and Rokin (which takes you from Dam Square to Muntplein) since as far back as 1538. This division between Old Side and New Side has always remained, and both have much to offer, but they are busy – very busy – so planning your visit is crucial.

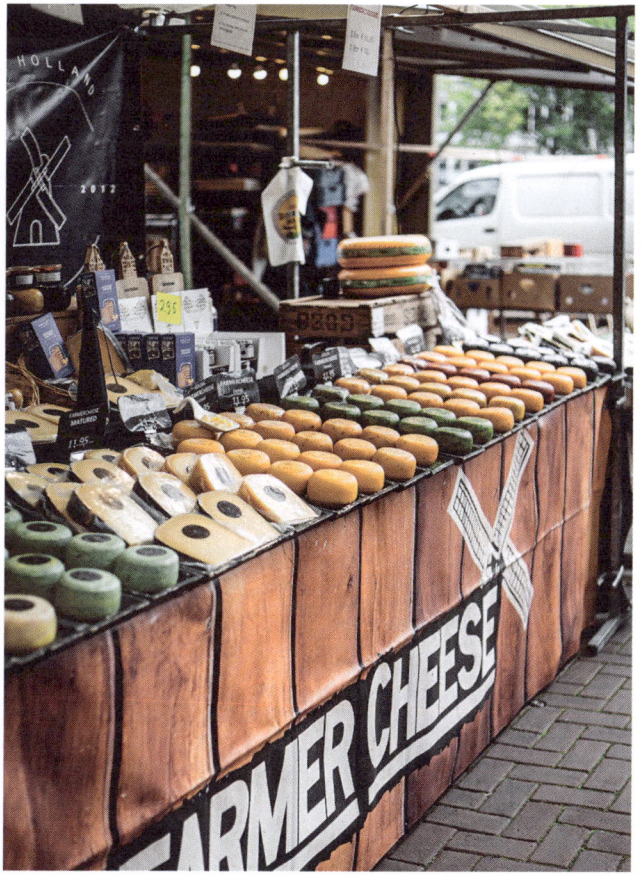
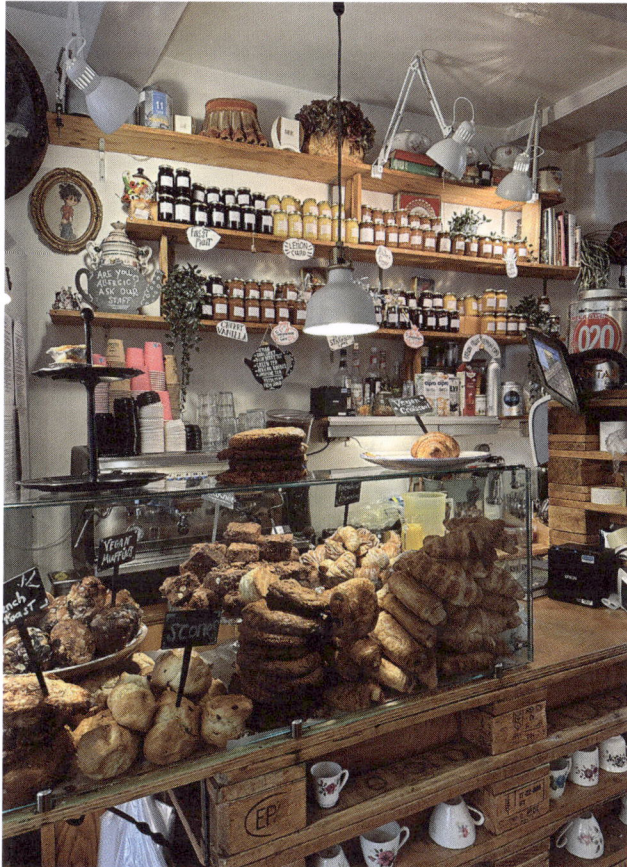

OUDE ZIJDE

Oude Zijde (on the left, with Central Station to your back) is one of the city's oldest parts and has a rich history. It is located on the east bank of the Amstel river. The area is known for its maze of narrow canals, winding streets, historic buildings and the infamous red-light district. The red-light district occupies much of De Wallen and is known the world over for its open displays of sex work, which attract millions of visitors every year.

THE RED-LIGHT DISTRICT/DE WALLEN

De Wallen, as it is known to locals, is one of the oldest districts in Amsterdam; in fact, this is where the city started. Ever since it was built, around 1385, it has been famous and notorious for the women inhabiting its streets. At the beginning of the fifteenth century, the neighbourhood began to expand eastward, fuelled by an influx of Portuguese and Jewish refugees fleeing persecution, many of whom were very skilled merchants who brought prosperity to their new home of Amsterdam. Due to its proximity to the harbour, the district quickly became a hub for prostitution and it has been so ever since. Since 2000, sex work has been a legal profession in the Netherlands, meaning workers can benefit from social programmes, although it remains a subject of debate and intrigue, and it draws millions of visitors annually.

Neon-red lights illuminate the window brothels around a warren of medieval alleyways. The area borders on Lange Niezel and Korte Niezel streets in the north; Zeedijk and Nieuwmarkt in the east; Koestraat and Sint Jansstraat in the south; and Warmoesstraat in the west. The red-light district is not for everyone: it wasn't for me, but I am so glad I explored it and now have a newfound appreciation for its historical legacy and importance to Amsterdam, and a realisation that the history of Oude Zijde is not only about prostitution. Indeed, in terms of size, the red-light area itself measures only 250m x 250m of De Wallen's kilometre square.

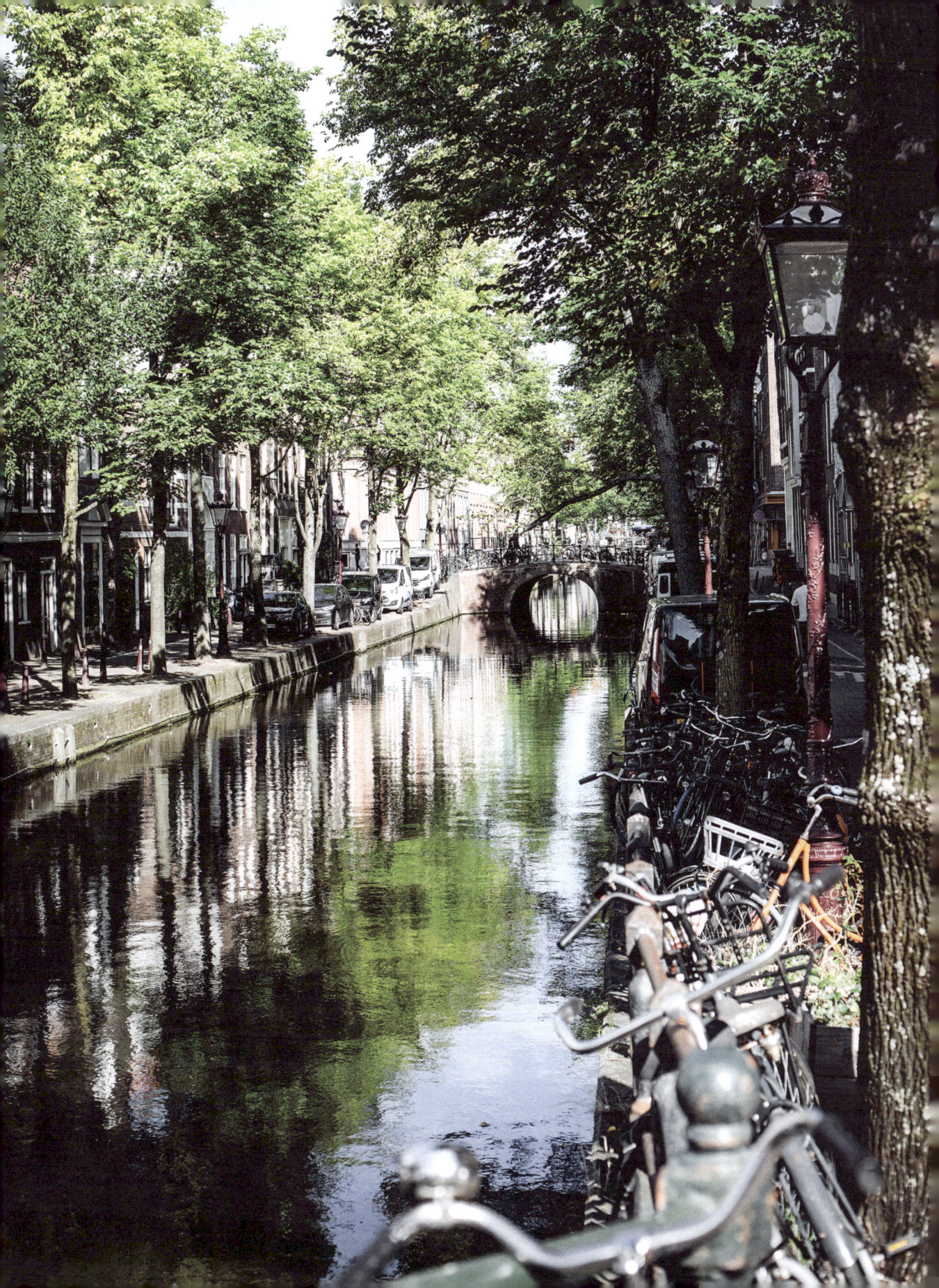

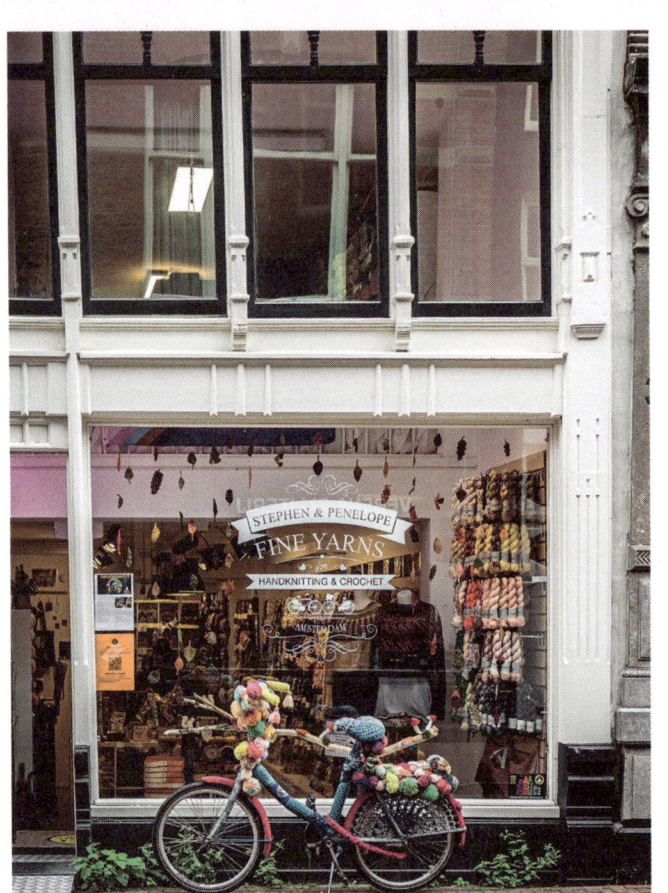
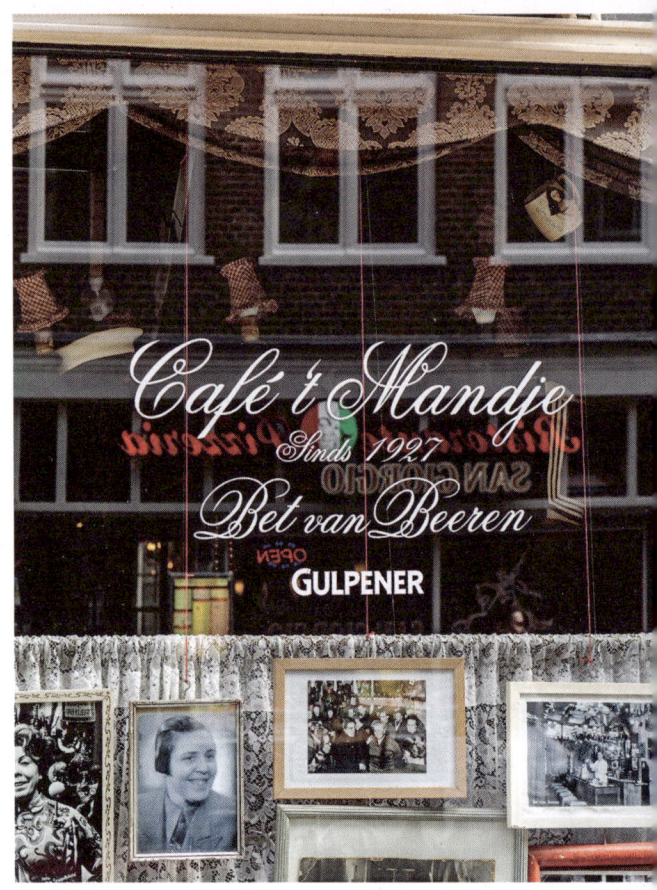
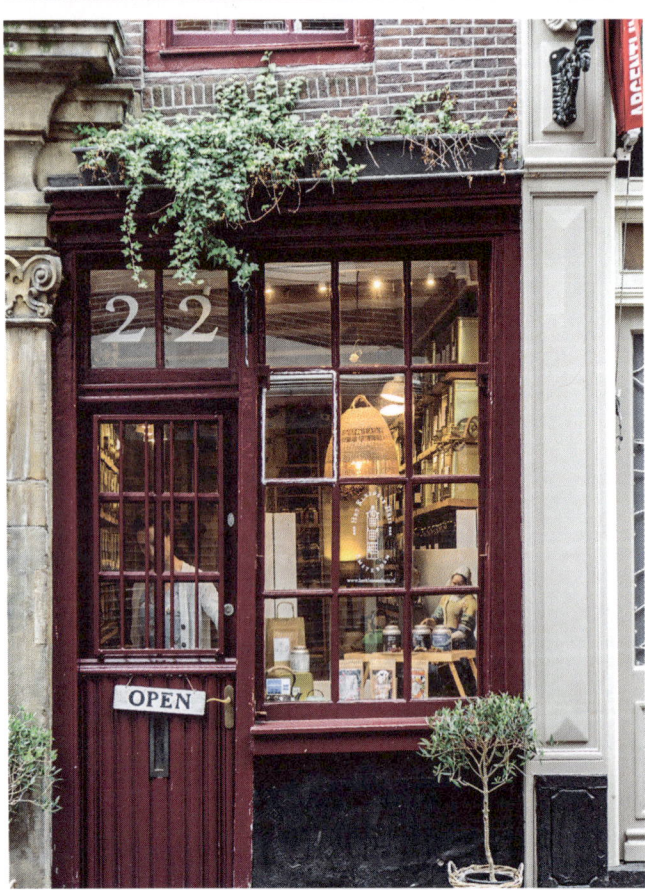
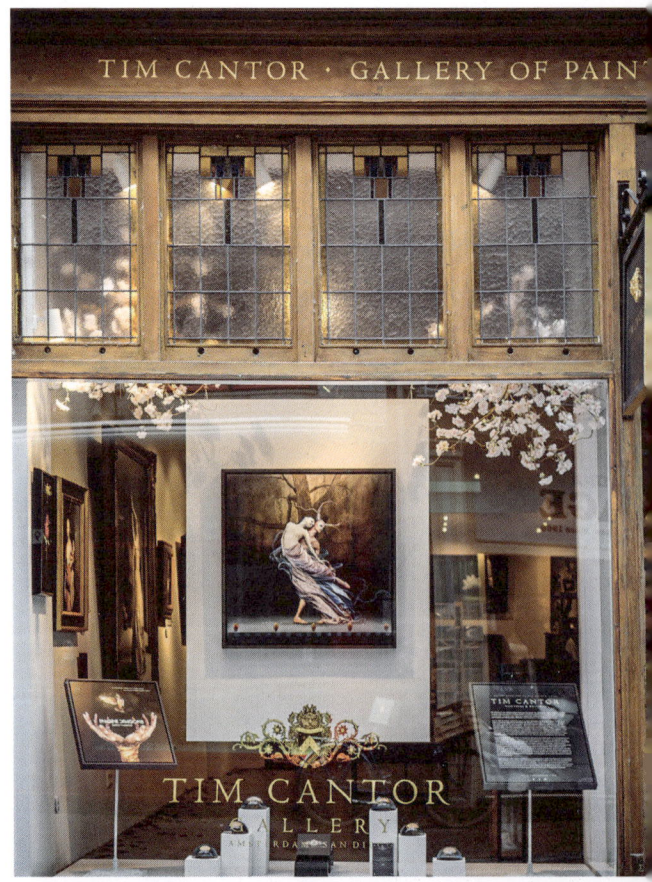

A visit in less busy times, particularly during the day, will unveil a host of beautiful gems and discoveries. Nowhere else is Amsterdam's spirit of tolerance so evident. Its obvious open-mindedness and acceptance of prostitution inspired me to reflect on the value of acceptance and freedom. Despite its age, Amsterdam's oldest district is remarkably well preserved and has a profound connection with religion, evident in its many churches. It was also home to one of Amsterdam's most prolific artists: Rembrandt, the creator of 'The Night Watch' and 300 other works.

Follow my discerning selection to discover the best of this historic district without the red lights.

ZEEDIJK

One of the best-known streets in Oude Zijde is Zeedijk, an important trade route in the Middle Ages. Curving along the red-light district's northern edge, it was initially constructed as a protective dike against the encroaching sea. Nowadays, Zeedijk thrives with its many restaurants, cafes and shops. It is also the location of Amsterdam's famous Chinatown. In the seventeenth century, the buildings in and around the bend of the Zeedijk – roughly between numbers 31 and 44 – were among the most prestigious places to live for wealthy merchants . Despite its chequered past, it still shows signs of its elegant heritage. When they later moved to Herengracht, Zeedijk and its surroundings slowly transformed into a centre for nightlife, entertainment and prostitution. Its decline was at its worst in the 1970s, when it was plagued by drug addicts and pickpockets and deemed unsafe. Thankfully, diligent efforts since the 1980s have transformed it back to glory, and its chequered past doesn't undermine its charm: it's a lovely stretch to wander.

I first meandered to it early and returned a few times to ensure it was worth a mention. Its abundance of lovely old-world pubs, ornate gable stones and historic architecture contribute to a beautiful village feel – a far cry from its seedy past.

ADDRESSES OF NOTE

Int Aepjen, **Zeedijk 1**
Officially Amsterdam's oldest brown bar. Dating from 1475, it's housed in one of the last two wooden buildings in the city. A tavern since the seventeenth century, legend has it that sailors often paid their tabs by donating their pet monkeys from faraway places.

Dutch Courage, **Zeedijk 12**
A cocktail bar that celebrates old Dutch liquors and has an impressive offering of local and speciality jenevers from all over Europe.

De Roode Laars, **Zeedijk 17**
An authentic liquor-tasting room and very cosy bar in a former shoemakers.

Damstraat, Oude Doelenstraat, Nieuwe Hoogstraat and Pijlsteeg (an alley parallel with Damstraat) form one of the city's oldest shopping areas. Although they are mostly packed with tourist traps today, many traces of their incredible historic past can be found along Oude and Nieuwe Hoogstraat.

OUDE HOOGSTRAAT

Oude Hoogstraat was constructed in the fifteenth century and was once one of the richest passages in town. Around that time, the grounds of monasteries, such as the Bethaniënklooster and the Friars Minor Monastery, were also located on and around Oude Hoogstraat. After the Alteration in Amsterdam (the transition to Protestantism) in 1578, these buildings were given new purposes. From 1409, the chapel of Sint-Paulusbroederklooster became the *Walloon Church* (a national heritage site since 1970). A passage was made on the north side of the church with a gate on Oude Hoogstraat. The gate from 1616 is attributed to Hendrick de Keyser and is decorated with skulls, referencing the funeral processions that entered

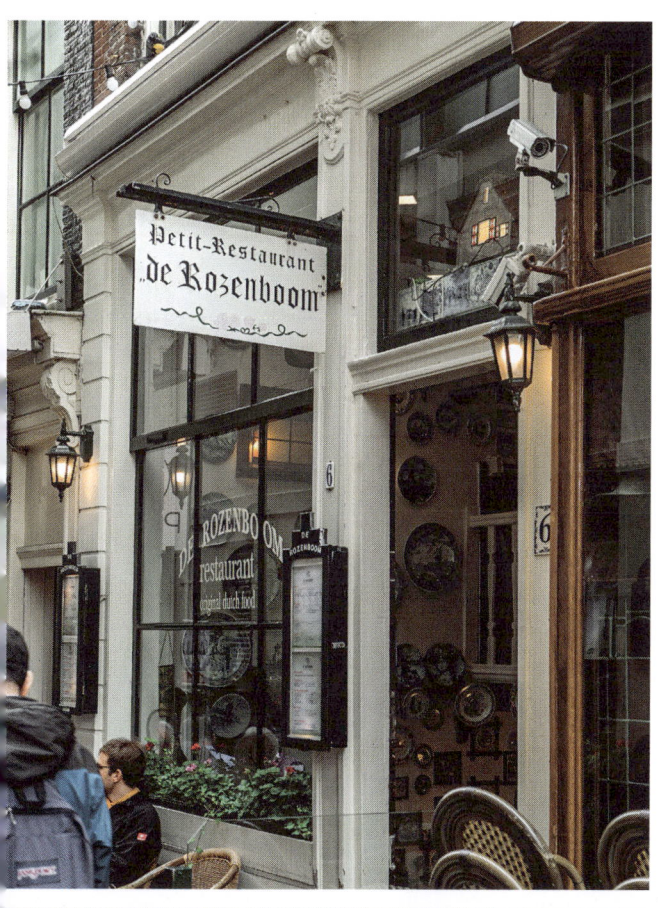
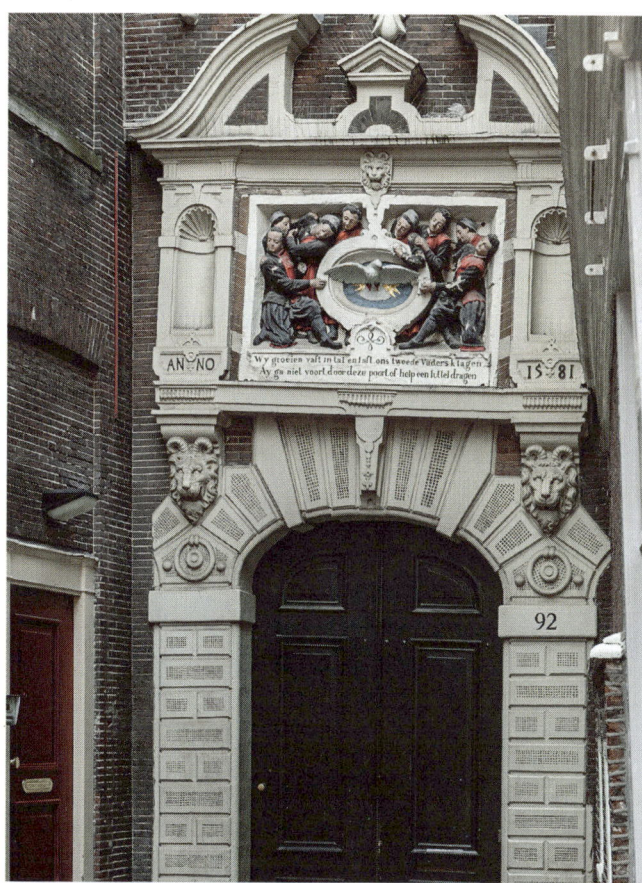
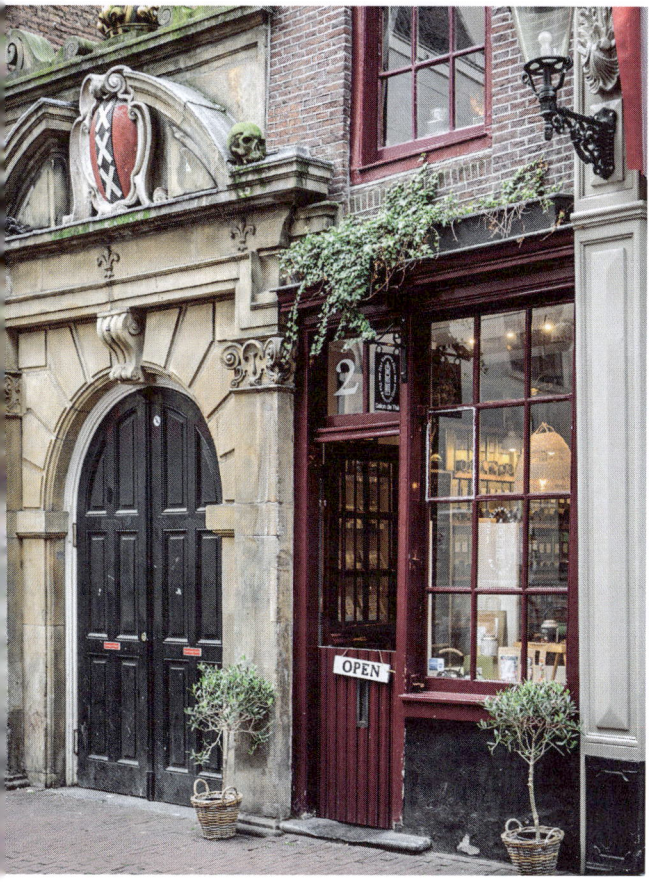
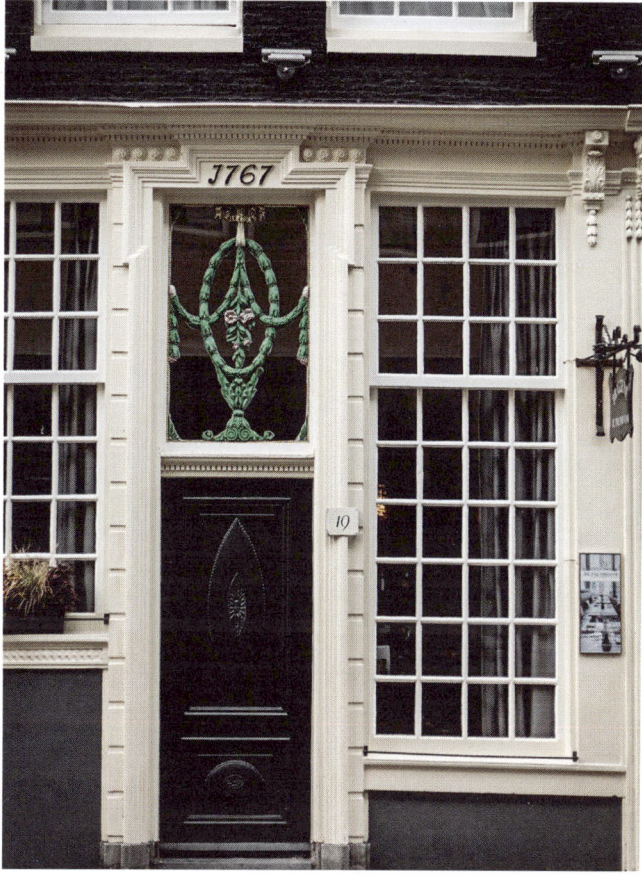

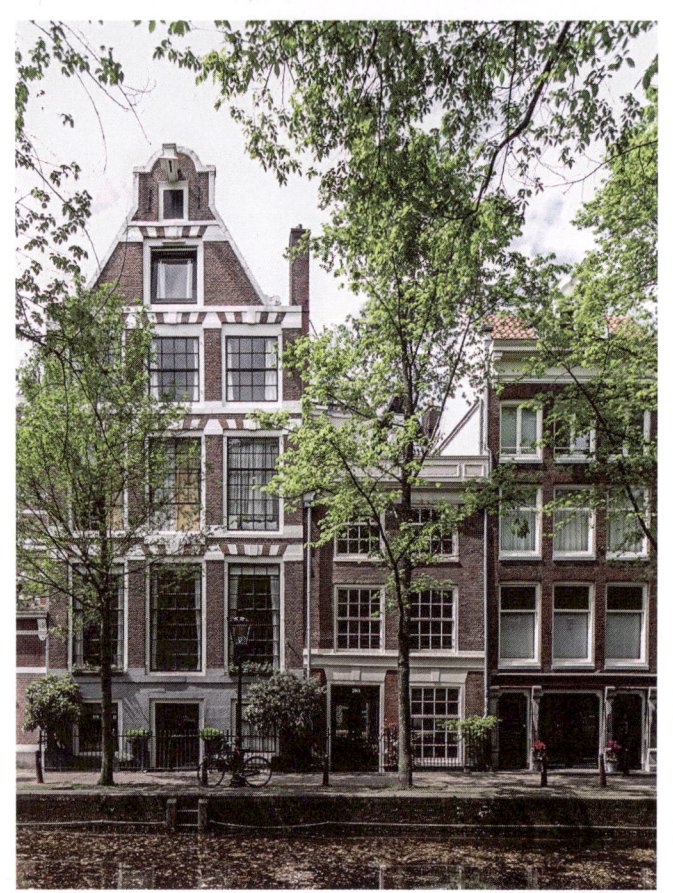
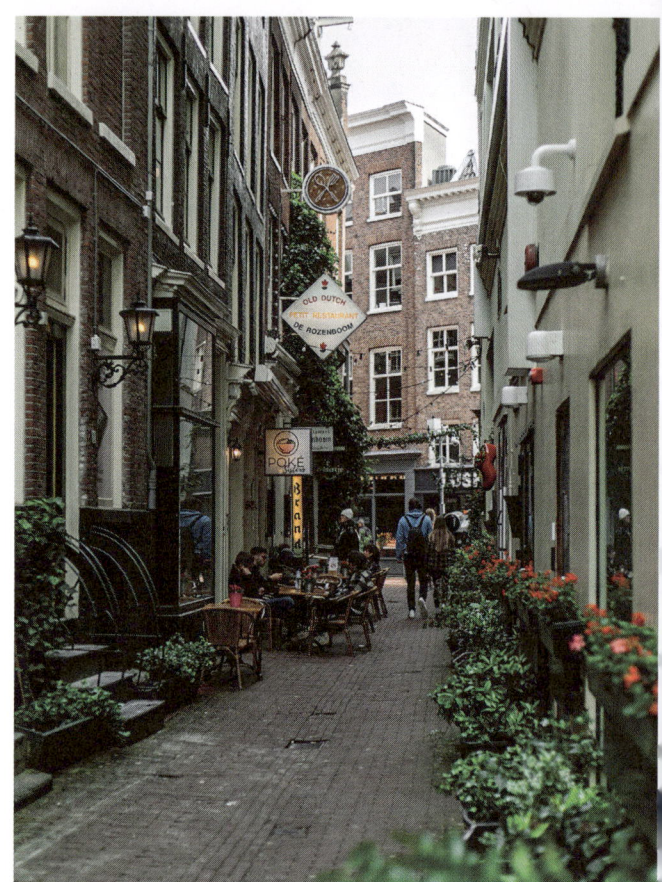
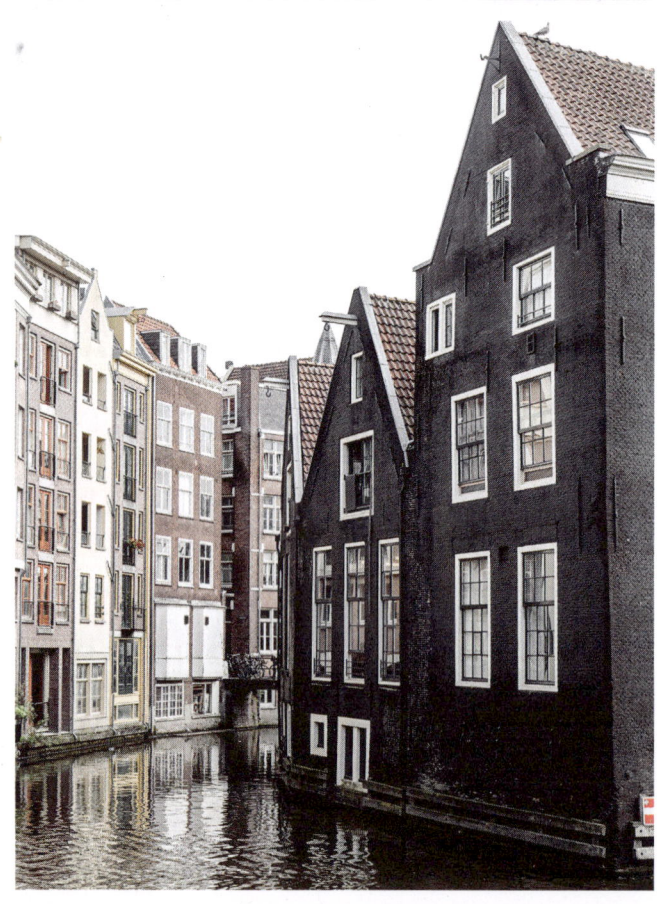
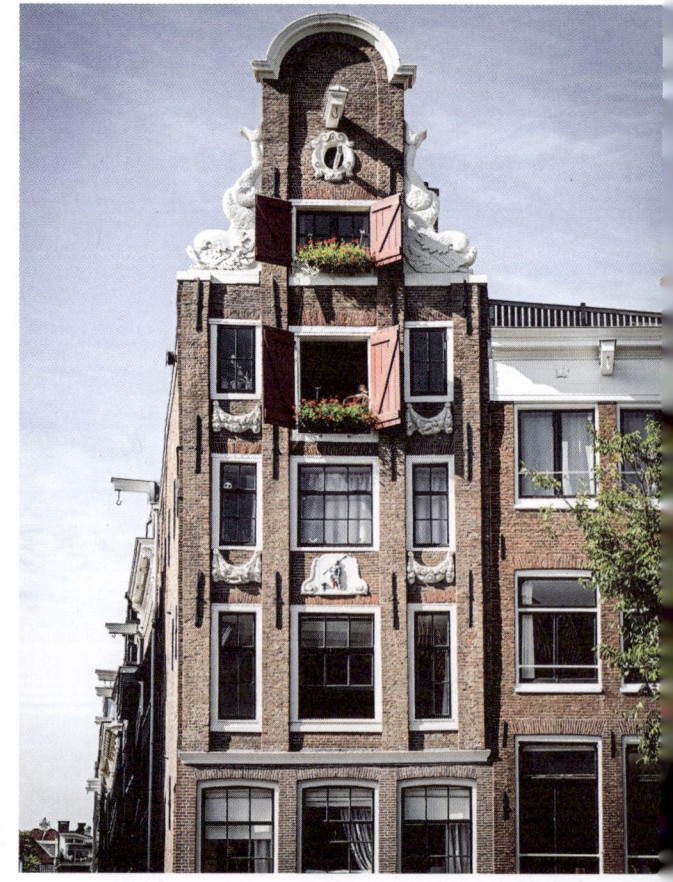

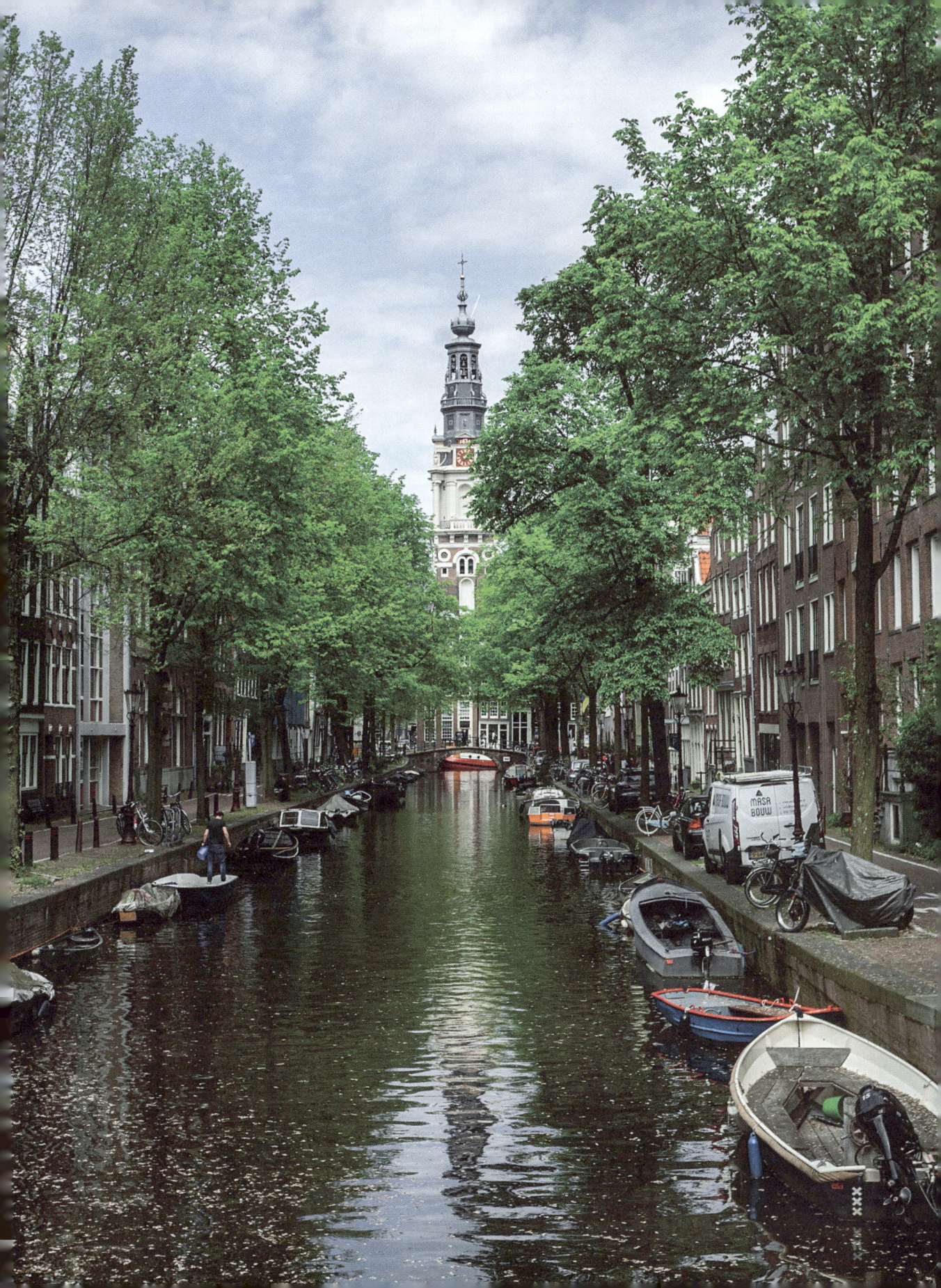

and left the church through this gate. The gate is also adorned with the Amsterdam coat of arms. During the Second World War, the occupying forces set up roadblocks, barbed wire and signs with the inscription '*Joodsche Wijk / Judenviertel*' in the old Amsterdam Jewish Quarter. The Bushuissluis (Bridge 224), located between Oude and Nieuwe Hoogstraat, was also cordoned off with barbed wire.

Oude Hoogstraat is still home to, among other things, the *Oost-Indisch Huis*, the former administrative office of the Amsterdam Chamber of the VOC (Dutch East India Company) and the United East India Company. The building and its beautiful courtyard, built in 1606, were the first constructed especially for the VOC. Ship crews were also recruited from this building, and the VOC's archives and maps were kept here.

Next door, at number 22, you will find *Het Kleinste Huis*, the building that has housed a beautiful tearoom since 2014, just over 2m wide and 5m deep. Step beyond the charming half-door and discover the absolute charm of the little tea shop.

A former department store at numbers 14–18 is today occupied by the most beautiful book shop, *Antiquariaat Kok*. They specialise in classical archaeology, art (before 1800), architecture, biology, the Olympics, applied art, and topographical maps and prints. They have a (very) large stock on most other fields as well.

NIEUWE HOOGSTRAAT

In the late sixteenth century, Nieuwe Hoogstraat was constructed, again explicitly as a shopping street. Together with the previously mentioned streets, Nieuwe Hoogstraat was part of the city's primary east–west axis, which ran from Dam Square to Sint Antoniesdijk, the then eastern border of the city. Located in the shadow of the Zuiderkerk, the Nieuwe Hoogstraat is now a varied and unique shopping street, with artisan and specialised shops very much sought after by vintage enthusiasts. From a colourful yarn store, *Stephen & Penelope*, at number 29, to the enchanting *Tim Cantor Galleries* at number 6, Nieuwe Hoogstraat is worth a visit.

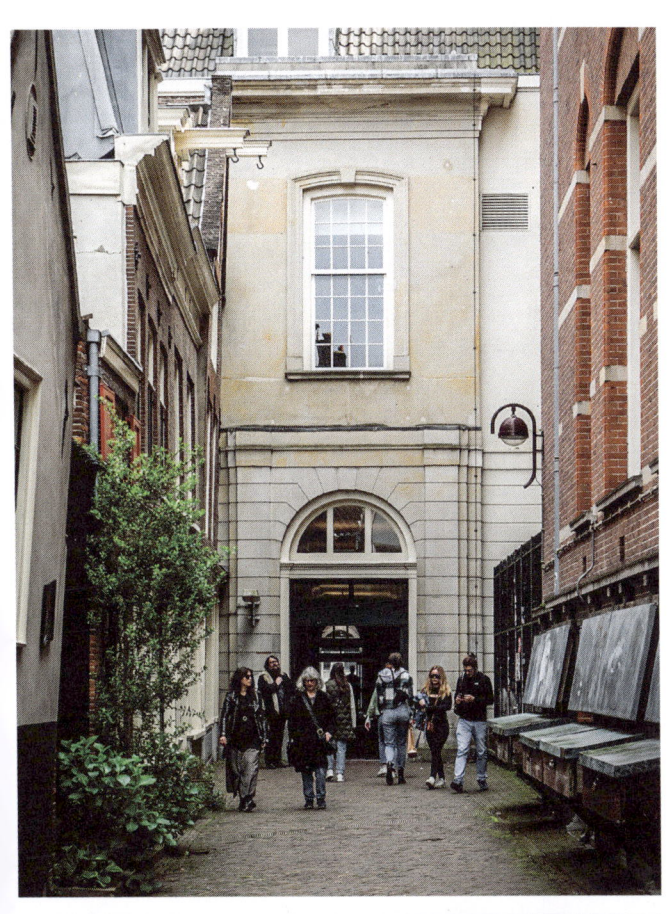
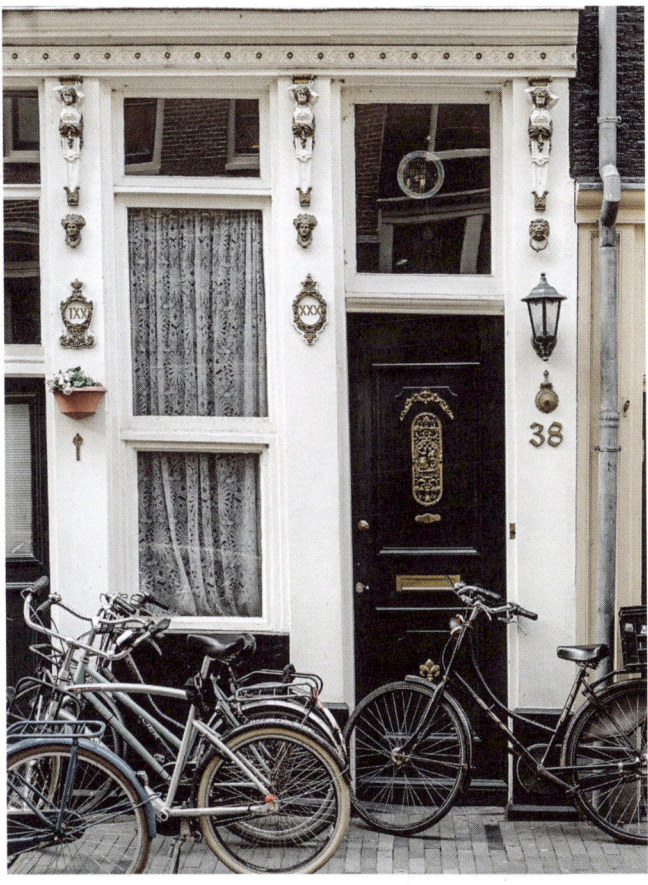
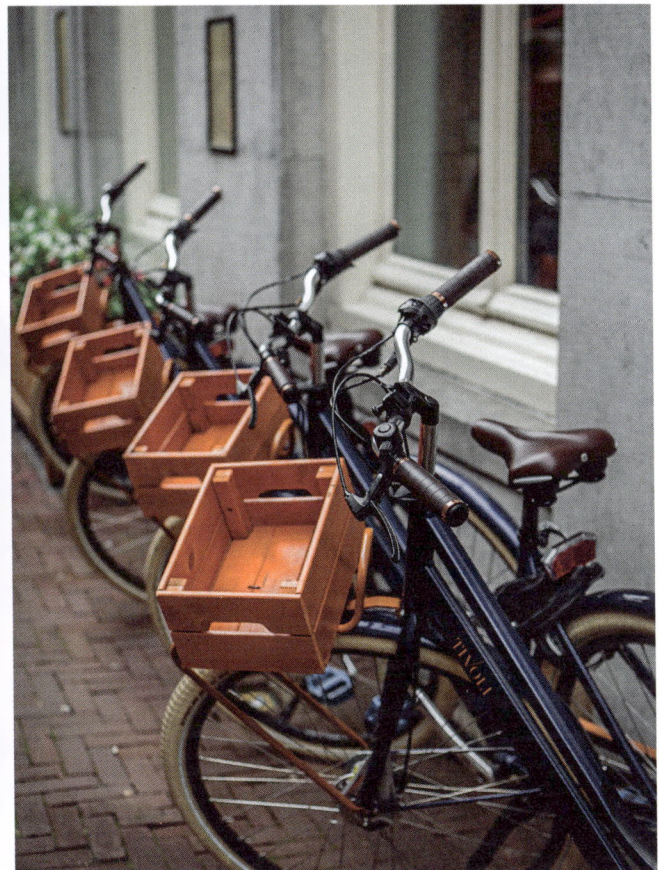
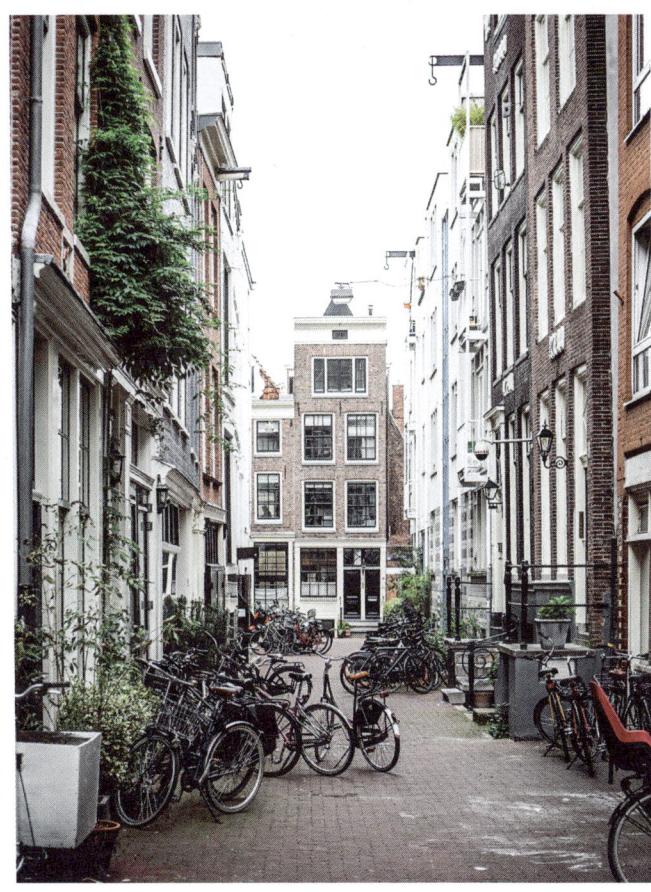

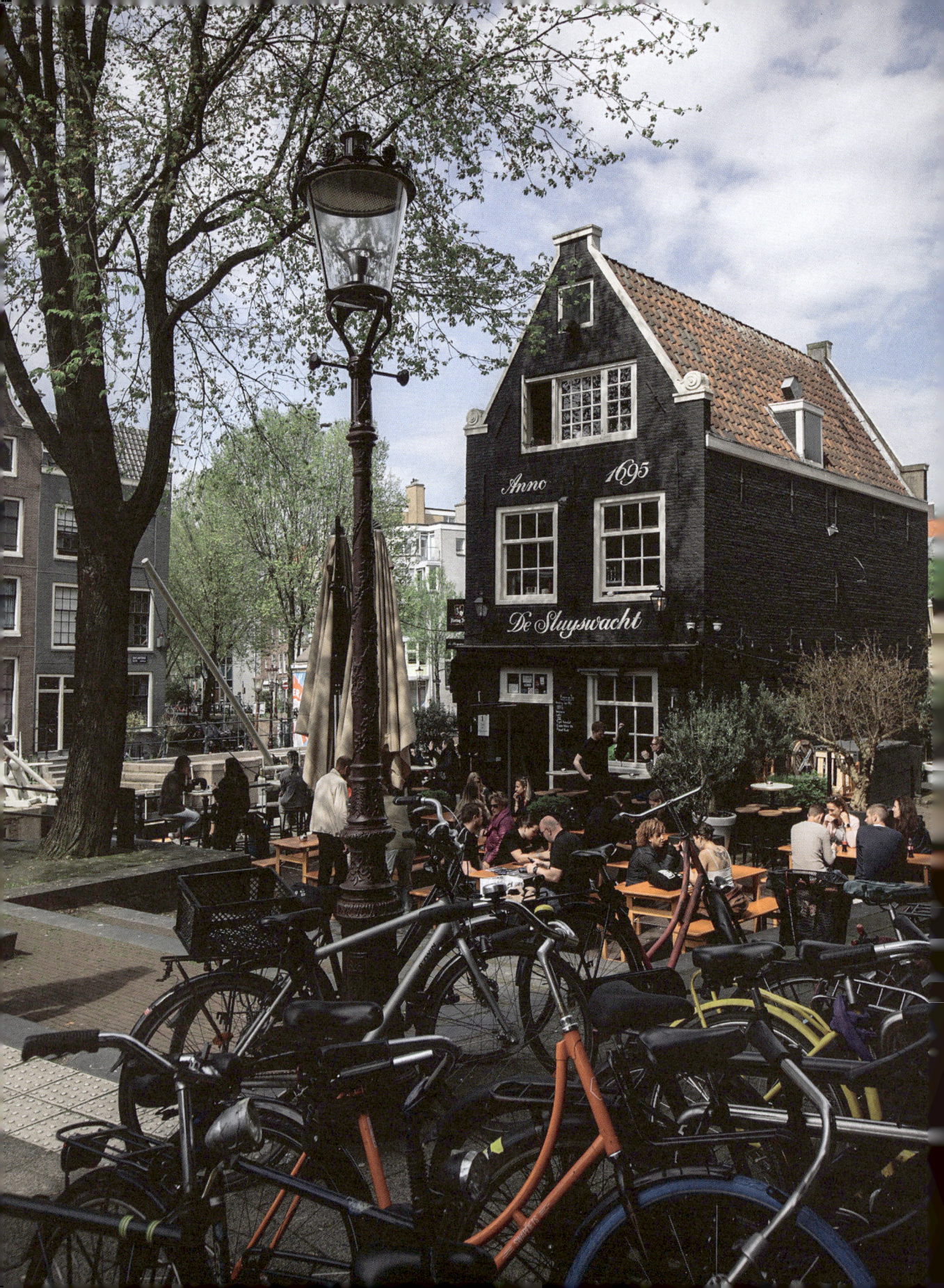

Tim Cantor began painting at age 5 with oil paints left to him by his great-grandfather, the English artist Lloyd Dundas Whiffen (1885–1951). At the age of 15, he won a Bank of America achievement in arts award and was given his first gallery exhibition, where one of his paintings was acquired for the permanent collection of the White House. Inspired by classical masters and his genius imagination, Tim Cantor often works through the night, producing a breathtaking collection of dramatic art, poetry and prose. Step inside his gallery, where you will feel you are walking through a secret garden as you gain an insight into his genius mind – an utterly moving gallery in every way.

NIEUWE DOELENSTRAAT

A beautiful, historic street – best known today for the *De L'Europe* (numbers 2–14), the *Doelen Hotel* (number 26) and the grand *Café de Jaren* (number 20) – Nieuwe Doelenstraat is an extension of Kloveniersburgwal and runs from the corner with Staalstraat in a south-westerly direction to the Oude Turfmarkt, where the Doelensluis is located over the Rokin. The *Kloveniersdoelen*, where 'The Night Watch' hung initially, was also located on this street. Part of the University of Amsterdam (UvA) is also on the street, including the *University Theater*. Nieuwe Doelenstraat forms the south-eastern border of the Binnengasthuis complex, where a large part of the UvA is located, and the first houses along here date from 1631. In 1635, Rembrandt van Rijn and his wife Saskia moved to a rental home in the current Café de Jaren. They continued to live there until 1637, after which they moved to the Jodenbreestraat. During the Second World War, the infamous Jewish Affairs Bureau was located at number 13; this building has since been demolished.

ADDRESSES OF NOTE

Droog, **Staalstraat 7B**

Dutch concept design brand Droog have opened a hotel with only one bedroom in the original home of Amsterdam's textile guild, where guests who venture out from their room can attend lectures, visit exhibitions and shops or relax in a 'fairy-tale garden' without leaving the building. It challenges the notion of a hotel. Its shop on the ground floor sells a wide range of products from iconic Dutch artisans.

Oude Kerk, **Oudekerksplein 23**

Another important attraction in Oude Zijde is the Oude Kerk (Old Church), which dates from the thirteenth century and is one of the oldest buildings in the city. The church has a characteristic leaning tower and is a popular tourist destination. Oude Kerk's initial Catholic interior, which included lavish decorations, statues and paintings, was severely damaged and nearly destroyed during the period in the sixteenth century when Protestants were destroying Catholic churches; thankfully, its ceiling paintings and stained glass were saved. Many notable Amsterdam citizens have been buried here, including Saskia van Uylenburgh. You will find her grave at number 29K in the Weitkopers Kapel. Nowadays, the Oude Kerk hosts many social events, such as exhibits and concerts.

In addition to the Oude Kerk, there are numerous other historic buildings in Oude Zijde, such as the *town hall*, the *Beurs van Berlage* (Stock Exchange) and the *Royal Palace* on Dam Square.

Zuiderkerk, **Zuiderkerkhof 72**

The Renaissance-style Zuiderkerk was constructed between 1603 and 1611 and held the title of the first Protestant church in Amsterdam; the tower with pillars and bulbous spire was completed in 1614 and is a landmark of Amsterdam. Hendrick de Keyser designed the church as a pseudo-basilica with a central nave and two lower side aisles, six bays long, with Tuscan columns, timber barrel vaults and dormers.

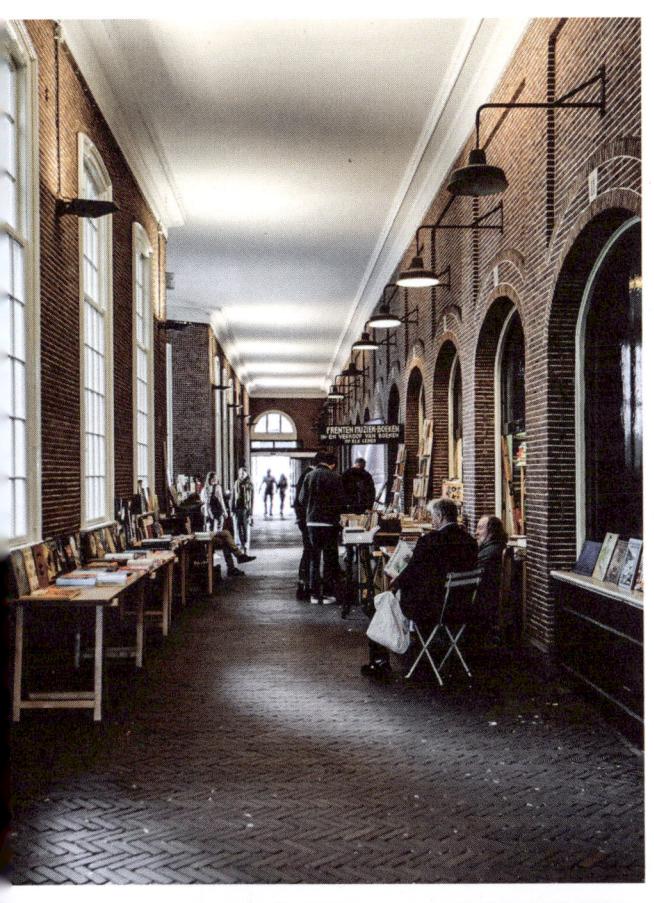
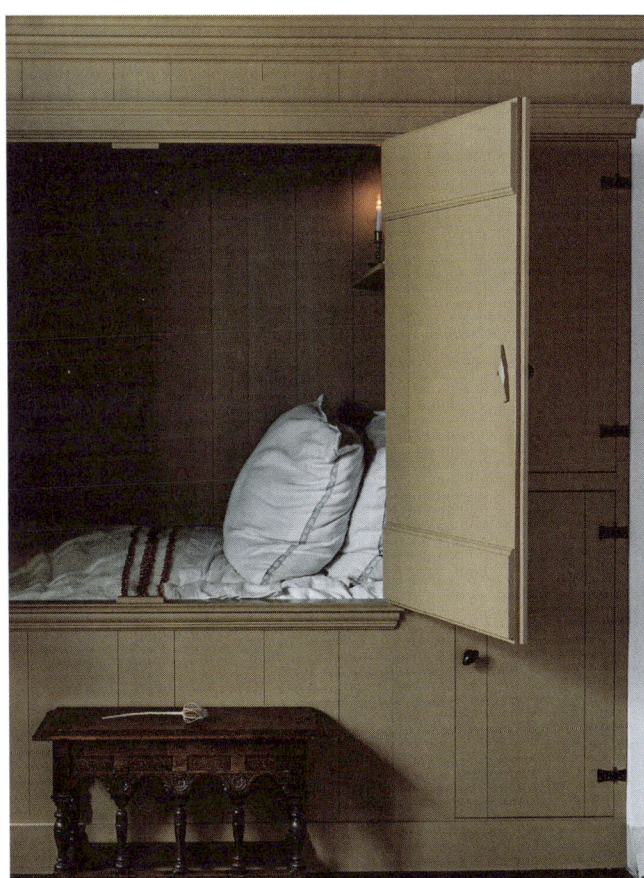
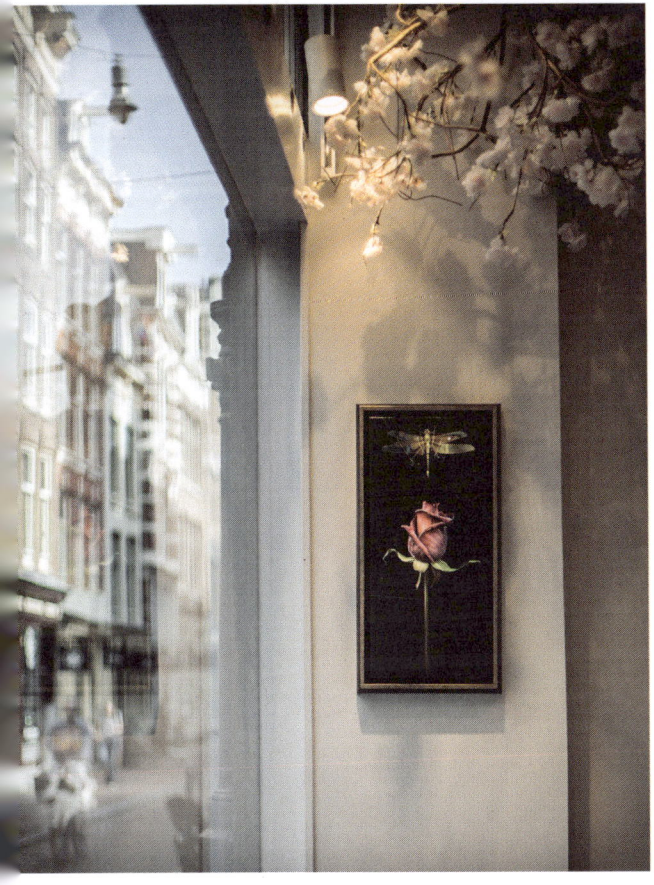
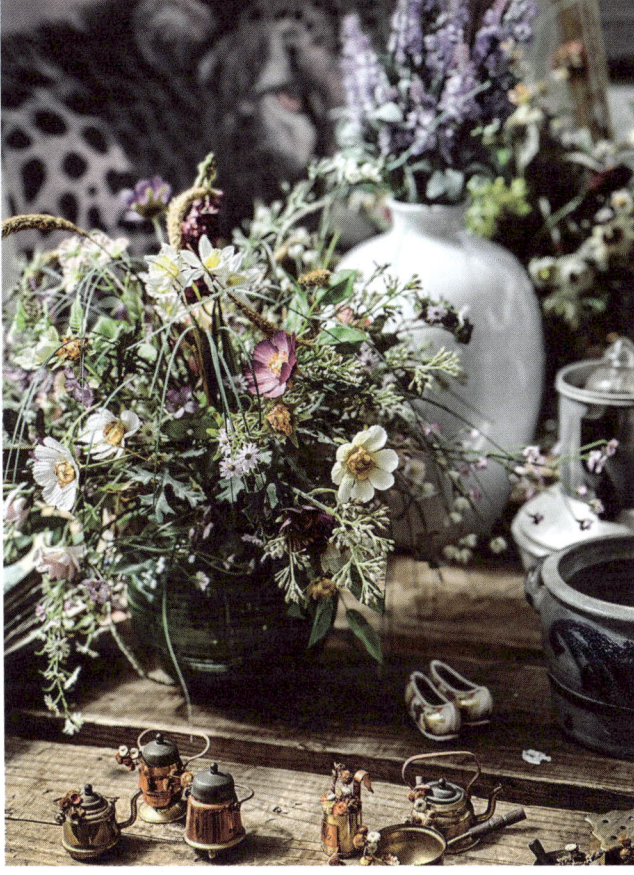

The top gables face north and south are crowned by balustrades reminiscent of the Noorderkerk and the Westerkerk. However, the rectangular shape of the windows is unique to the Zuiderkerk.

Between 12 and 1 o'clock in the afternoon, different pieces of music can be heard from chimes in the tower. French impressionist painter Claude Monet painted the church during a visit to Amsterdam. Today, it serves as an information centre and holds a permanent exhibition on the urban structures of Amsterdam. Three of Rembrandt's children were buried here. Climb to the top for brilliant views.

The view from Staalmeestersbrug bridge is one of the most magnificent views in Amsterdam. Narrow and quaint Staalstraat is flooded with lovely cafes, shops and canal views.

Museum Ons' Lieve Heer op Solder, **Oudezijds Voorburgwal 38–40**
Our Lord in the Attic Museum, also known as Amstelkring Museum, is one of the oldest in Amsterdam. As you enter this uniquely preserved seventeenth-century canal house, you would have no idea what is hidden inside: an exquisitely appointed hidden church, evoking an era when Catholics were forced to worship secretly.

Until the sixteenth century, Amsterdam had been predominantly Roman Catholic, but that changed as the Protestant reformation, the Alteration, seized control of all Catholic churches, chapels and monasteries – effectively banning Catholics from worshipping in public. So, they had to find a way to practise their religion secretly. Hidden churches began springing up in private homes across the city. This is one of the only remaining examples. In the 1660s, a wealthy Catholic merchant named Jan Hartman purchased the gabled townhouse and two others behind it, converting all three contiguous attics into a single chapel, hence its name: Ons' Lieve Heer op Solder (Our Lord in the Attic).

Worshippers entered discreetly from a side street and climbed a narrow, three-storey staircase to reach the clandestine church, which could accommodate about 150 people. The chapel has been remodelled over the centuries but retains its Dutch classical style. It is spread over multiple levels, with two upper galleries and a soaring ceiling decorated with a

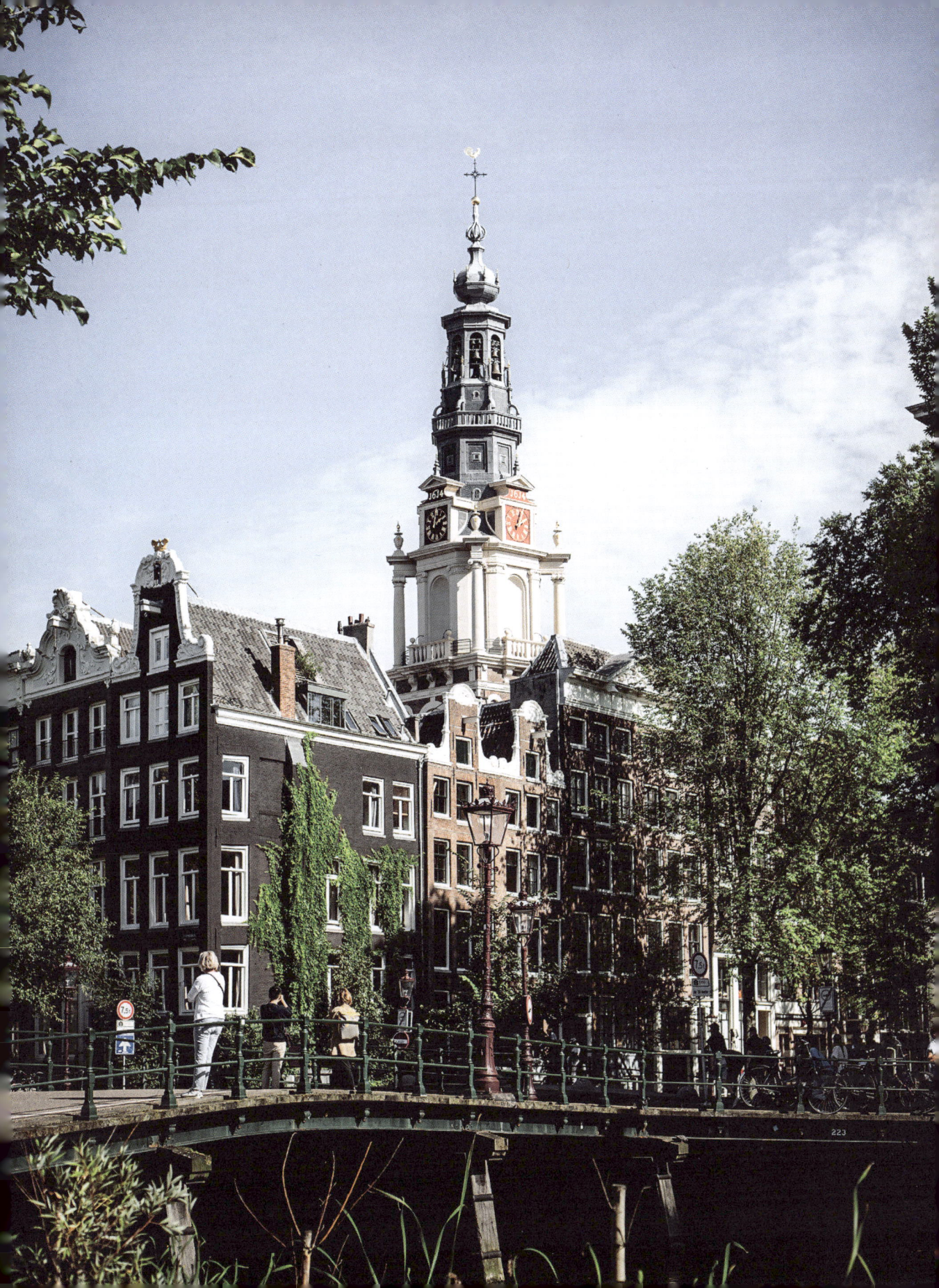

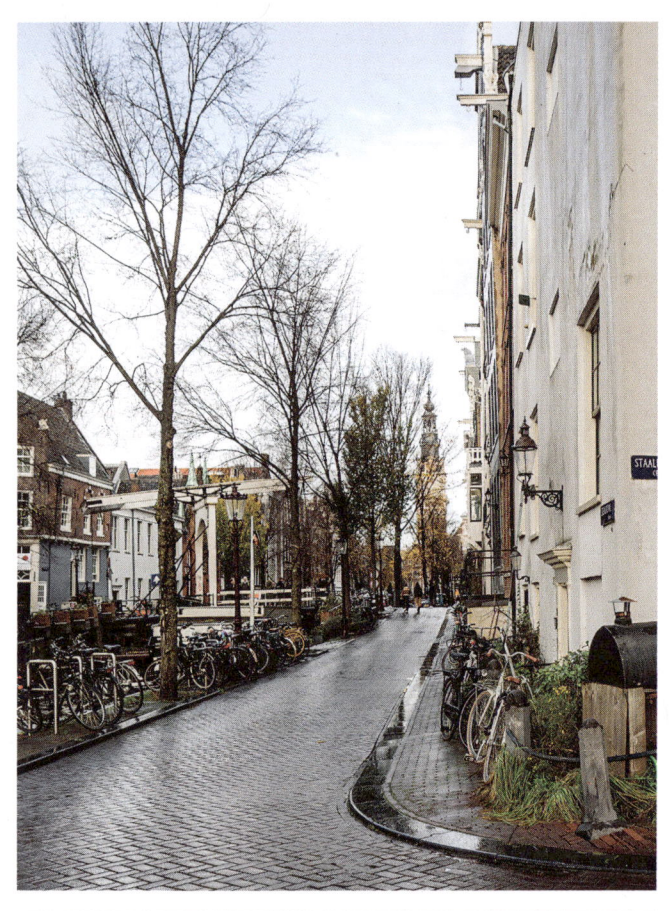
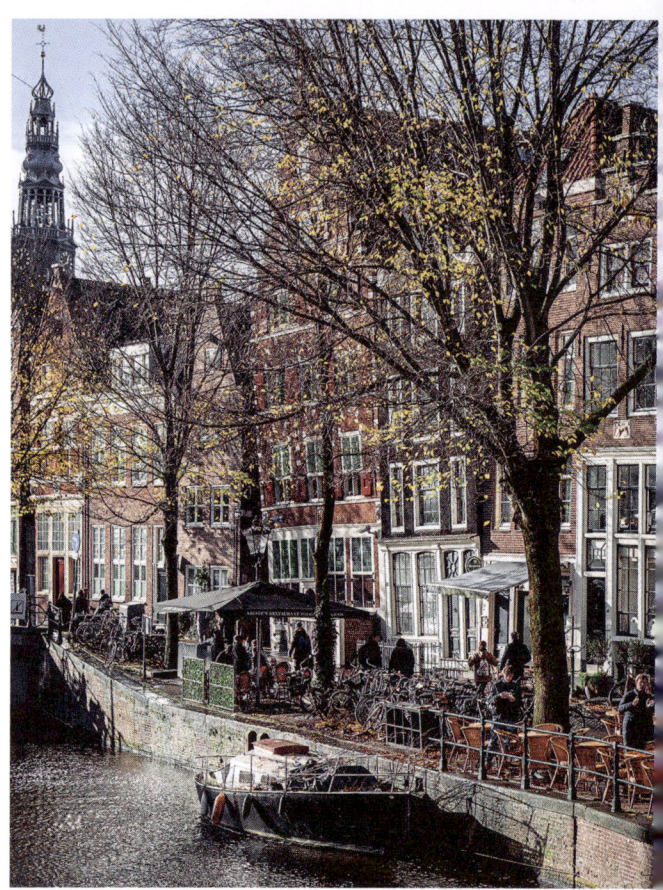
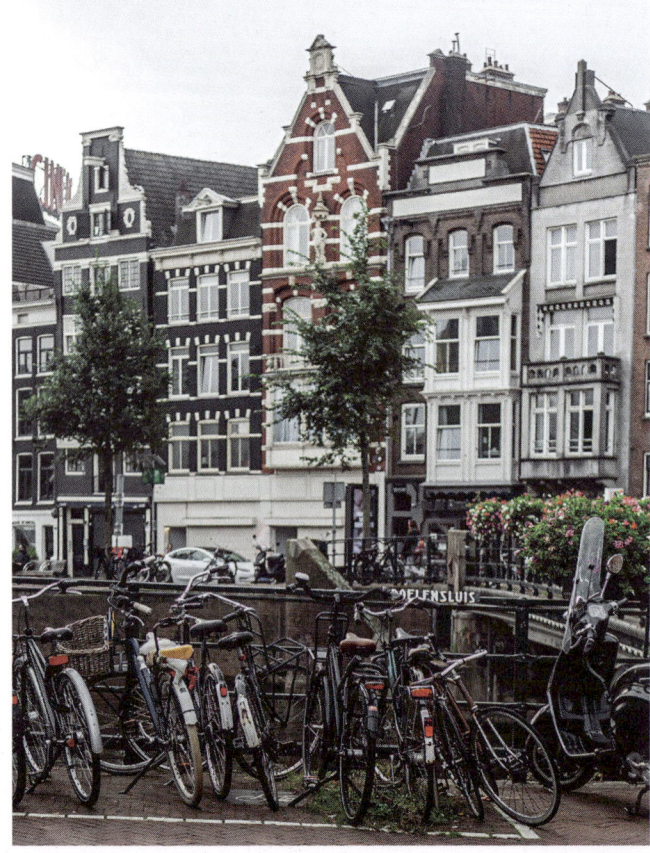
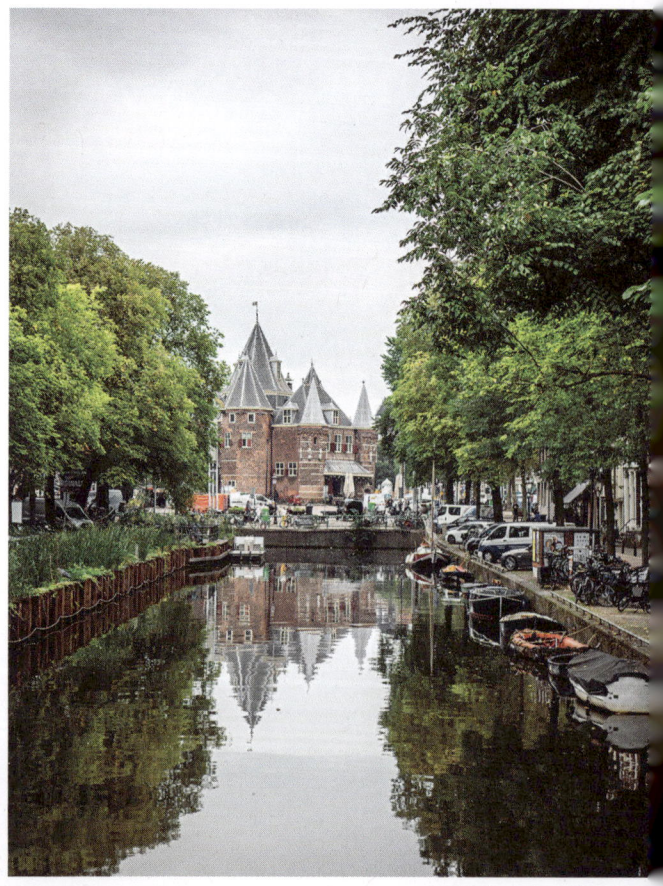

stuccoed image of God the Father and the Holy Spirit, portrayed as a dove. Devotional statues flank the ornate baroque style, and gilt-topped wooden columns are cleverly painted to resemble marble. Above the altar hangs a large oil painting: 'The Baptism of Christ' by Jacob de Wit, completed in 1716 and added some fifty years after the chapel was initially built. Opposite the altar is an organ explicitly constructed for the church in 1794 by Hendrik Meyer.

The building became a museum in 1888, making it the second oldest in Amsterdam after the Rijksmuseum. While the hidden church is the chief reason to visit, Our Lord in the Attic reveals how a successful seventeenth-century merchant lived and worked. Living and dining areas, bedrooms and kitchens have been beautifully restored with delft tiles and period furnishings. At the same time, other rooms hold a variety of religious objects dating from the Golden Age to the nineteenth century. Colour, light and furnishings exude an atmosphere of the time. You will find a lovely little gift shop and a great cafe overlooking the quiet canal.

Museum Rembrandthuis, **Jodenbreestraat 4**
For a remarkable insight into the life and work of one of Amsterdam's most prolific artists, plan a visit to Rembrandt House Museum. Purchased by the artist in 1639, he moved in with his wife, Saskia van Uylenburch, and stayed there for nineteen turbulent years, producing many of his great works there. His former home has been reconstructed to look as it did when they lived there. Temporary exhibitions featuring artists who were influenced or inspired by him are on display.

You could refuel after your visit at *Café de Sluyswacht*. It is famous for its lovely bright terrace and views over *Montelbaanstoren* and *Nieuwmarkt*.

Other notable places in the district:

Nieuwmarkt
This lively hotspot by night and market by day has existed since the fifteenth century. Alone in the middle, you will spot the historic *De Waag*. The multiturreted Waag is a landmark building built in 1488; it has served

various purposes over the years, including as a city gate, a weighing house, a guild hall, and a site for public executions. Farmers from around the city came to have their goods weighed to be taxed accordingly. After the weigh house closed in 1800, the building served as a fire station and then as two city museums. Today it houses a restaurant, a maker space, and a range of cultural and educational activities.

Waterlooplein Market
Amsterdam's oldest and largest flea market, it dates back to 1893. The market spread between the Leprozengracht and Houtgracht in the former Jewish Quarter, and has long been at the centre of Amsterdam's bohemian culture. Held from Monday to Saturday, it sells everything from vintage cameras to second-hand books and the latest fashion; every stall is unique. It also offers delicious street food and lovely views.

Explore beyond the borders of the Oude Zijde and east of the Amstel river to discover the tranquil residential area called De Plantage. The green spaces of the award-winning city zoo *Artis* (Plantage Kerklaan 38–40) and botanical gardens *Hortus Botanicus* (Plantage Middenlaan 2A) are at its heart.

ADDRESSES OF NOTE

National Opera & Ballet, **Amstel 3**

De L'Europe, **Nieuwe Doelenstraat 2–14**

Mendo, **Nieuwe Doelenstraat 10**

Stephen & Penelope, **Nieuwe Hoogstraat 29**

Tim Cantor Galleries, **Nieuwe Hoogstraat 6H**

Antiquariaat Kok, **Oude Hoogstraat 18**

Theewinkel Het Kleinste Huis Amsterdam, **Oude Hoogstraat 22**

Droog, **Staalstraat 7B**

In 't Aepjen, **Zeedijk 1**

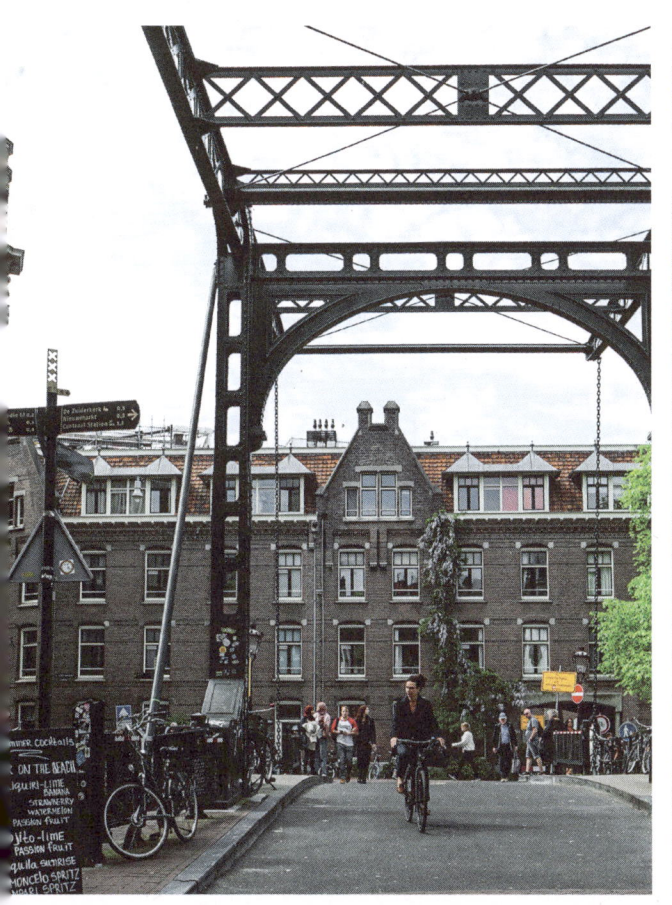
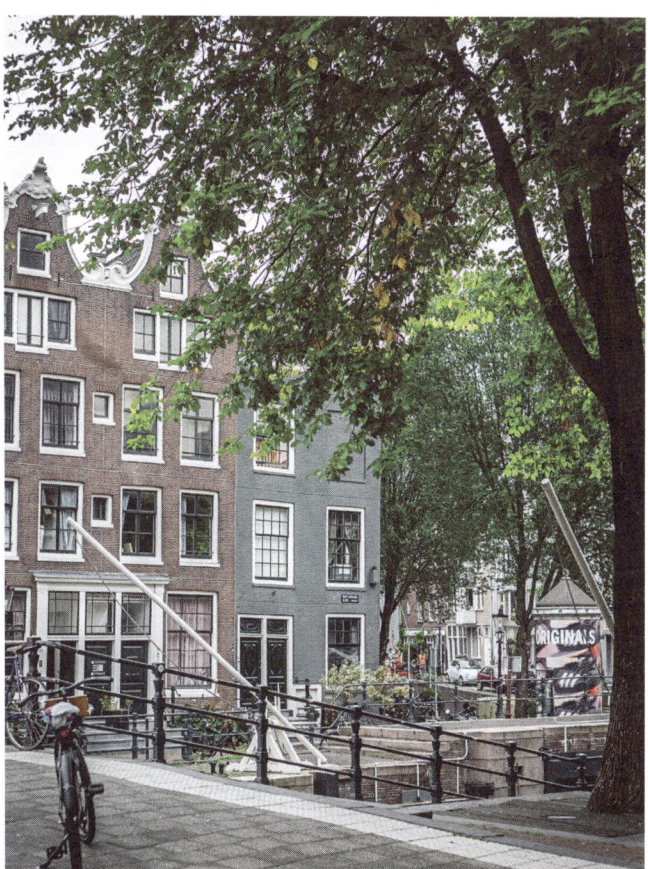

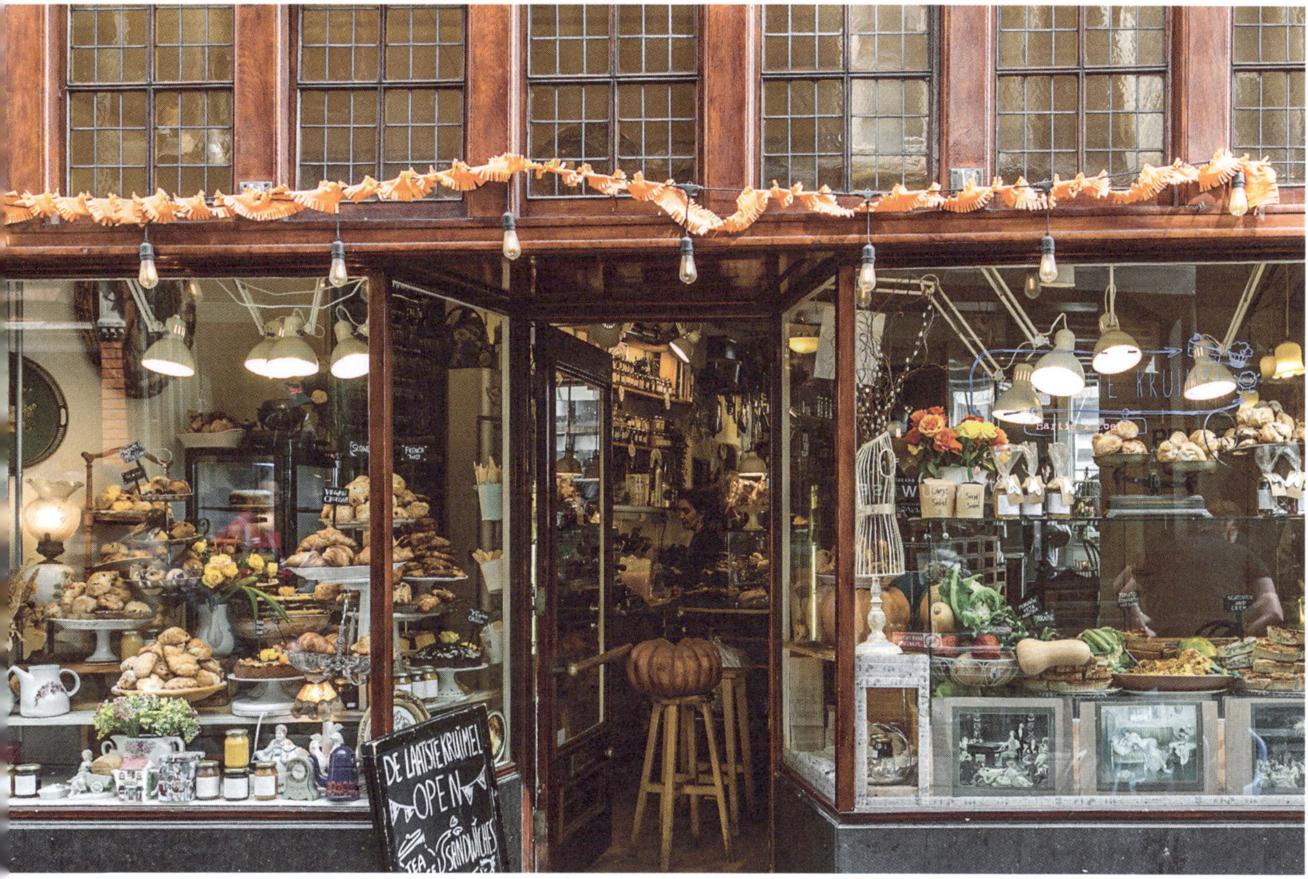

De Sluyswacht, **Jodenbreestraat 1**
Museum Rembrandthuis, **Jodenbreestraat 3**
Portugese Synagoge, **Mr. Visserplein 3**
Oude Kerk, **Oudekerksplein 23**
The Book Exchange, **Kloveniersburgwal 58**
Café de Jaren, **Nieuwe Doelenstraat 20**
Grand Hotel Amrâth, **Prins Hendrikkade 108**
Vent du Nord, **Staalstraat 16H**
ARTIS, Plantage **Kerklaan 38–40**
Dutch Courage, **Zeedijk 12**
Hortus Botanicus, **Plantage Middenlaan 2A**
H'ART (Hermitage) **Museum, Amstel 51**
House with Globes, **Amstel 49**

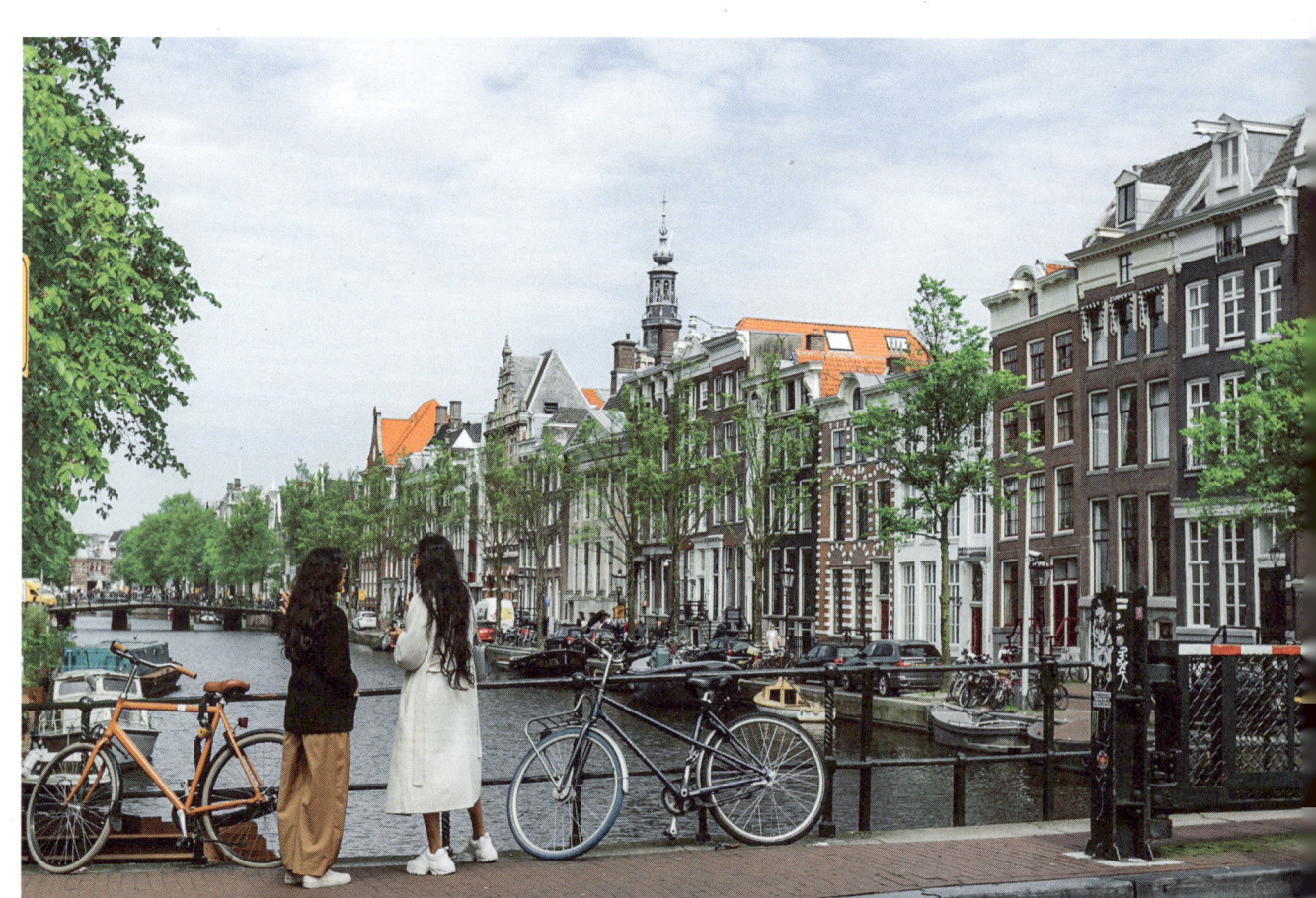

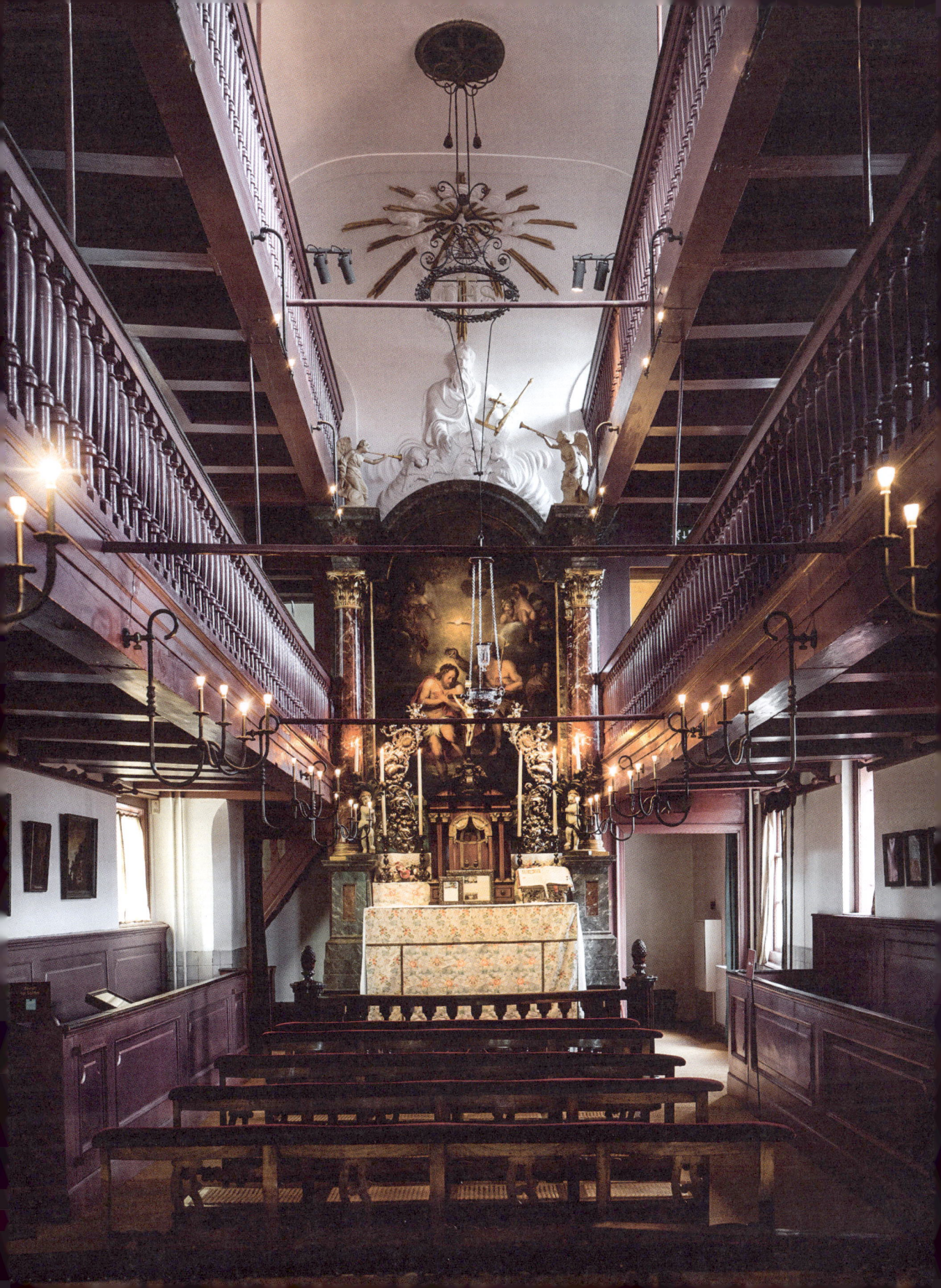

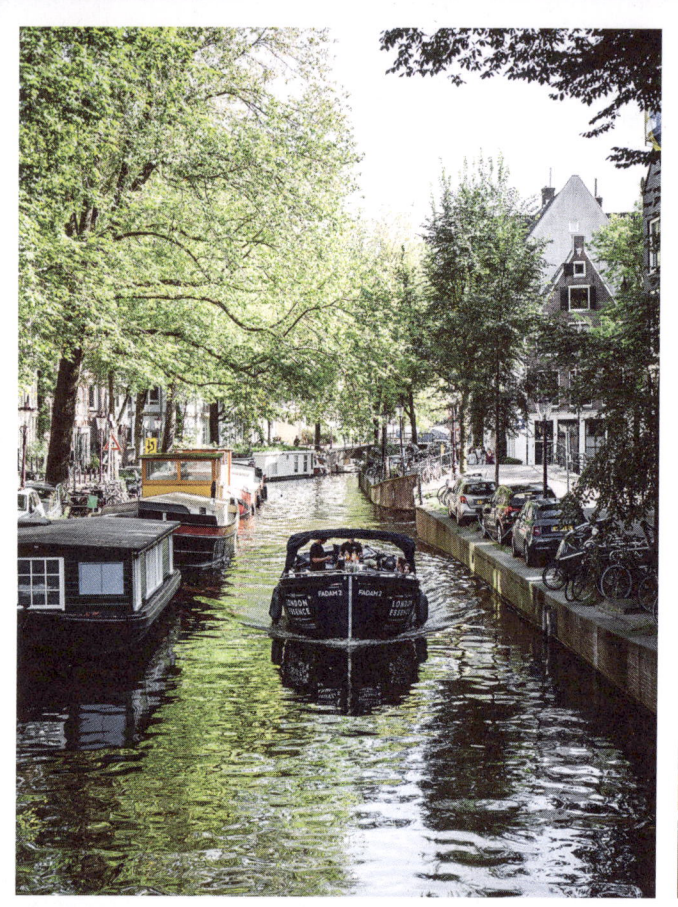
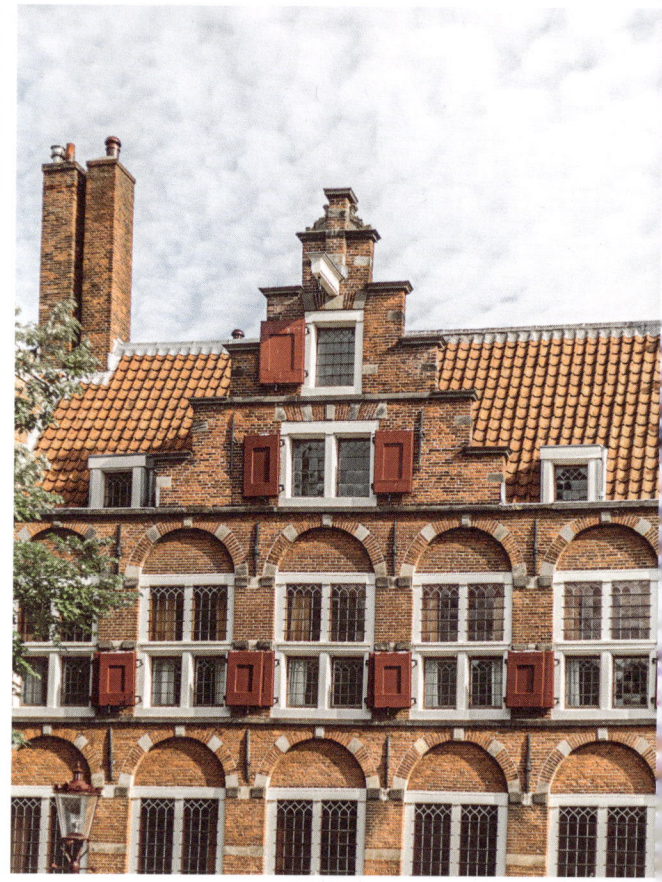
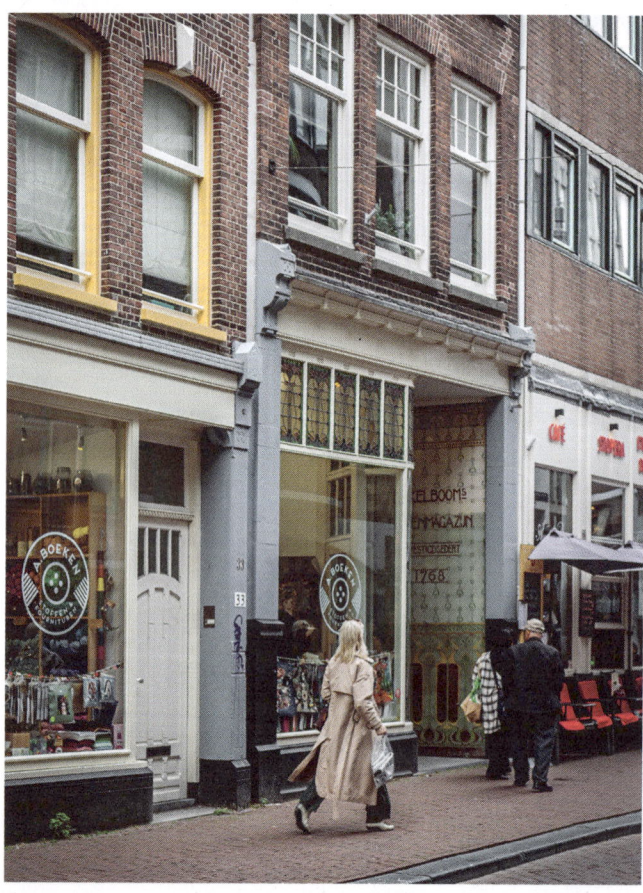
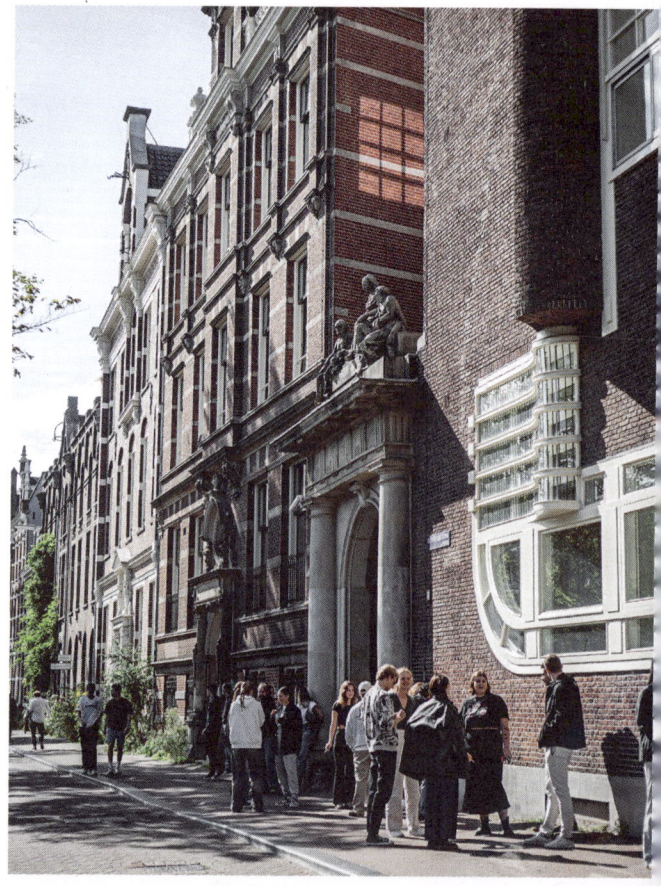

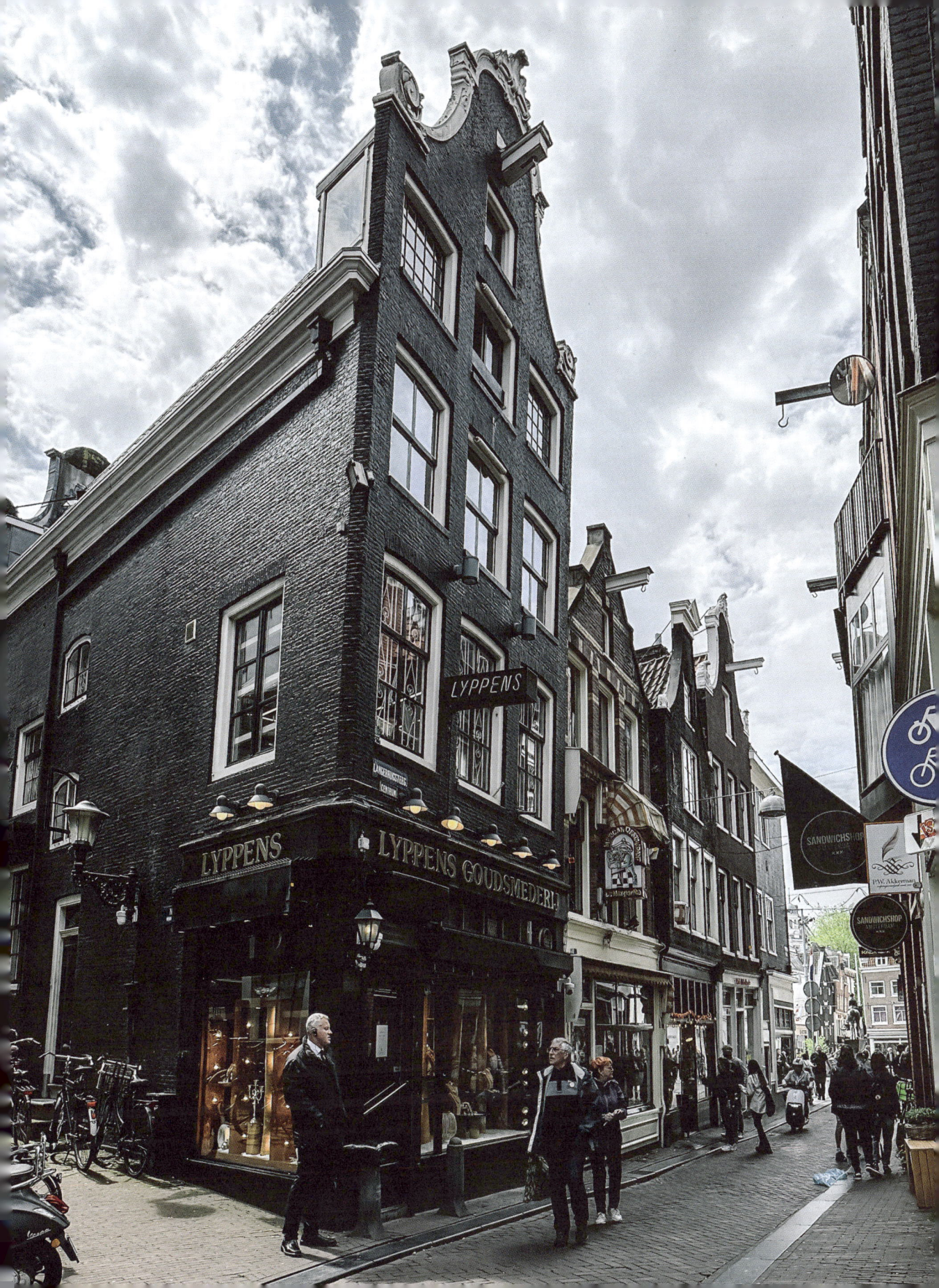

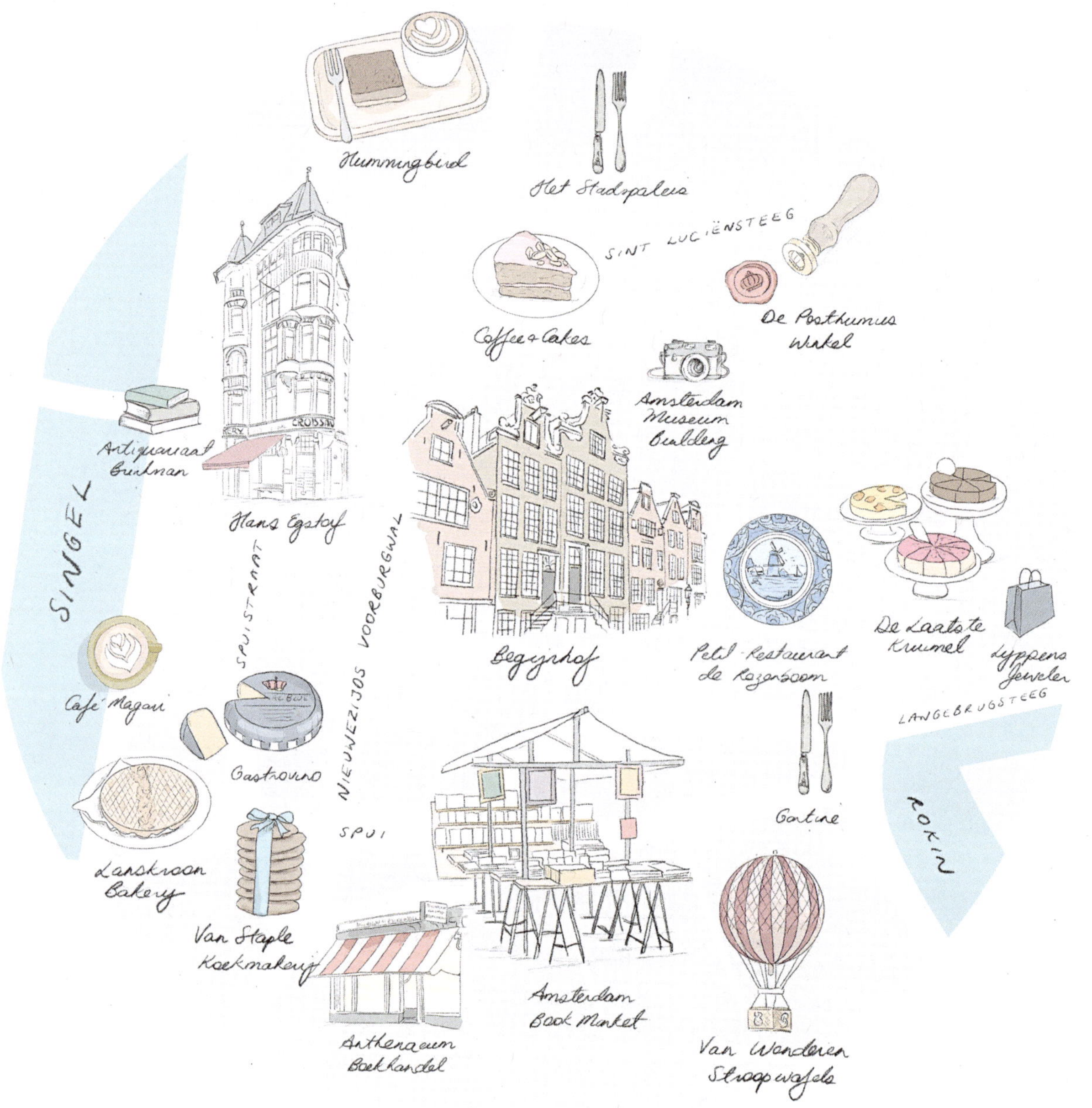

NIEUWE ZIJDE

#prettycityamsterdam

LYPPENS JEWELER Langebrugsteeg 8
DE POSTHUMUS WINKEL Sint Luciënsteeg 25
GASTROVINO Spuistraat 330

COFFEE & CAKES Sint Luciënsteeg 21
HUMMINGBIRD AMSTERDAM Spuistraat 217
CAFÉ MAGARI Singel 379A

HANS EGSTORF Spuistraat 274
LANSKROON BAKERY Singel 385
VAN WONDEREN STROOPWAFELS Kalverstraat 190
VAN STAPELE KOEKMAKERIJ Heisteeg 4
DE LAATSTE KRUIMEL Langebrugsteeg 4

Begijnhof, Amsterdam Museum Building

GARTINE Taksteeg 7
HET STADSPALEIS Nieuwezijds Voorburgwal 277
PETIT-RESTAURANT DE ROZENBOOM Rozenboomsteeg 6

AMSTERDAM BOOK MARKET Spui Square
ATHENAEUM BOEKHANDEL Spui Square
ANTIQUARIAAT BRINKMAN Singel 319

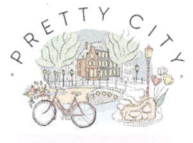

NIEUWE ZIJDE

Lively day and night, alongside its neighbour Oude Zijde, Nieuwe Zijde is the city's historical, geographic and tourist heart. With Oude Zijde to one side and Singel to the next, it's a compact area and best known for being home to Dam Square and its lively shopping streets: Damrak, Rokin, Nieuwendijk and Kalverstraat. It's the busiest part of town for visitors, and a walk around if you don't know where you are going can be overwhelming, so here's a little itinerary to help you find its best bits.

Start at *Central Station*; also known as Amsterdam Centraal, it is one of the most beautiful buildings in Amsterdam. It has a rich history dating back to the nineteenth century. The original station building, designed by architect P.J.H. Cuypers, was officially opened in 1889. It was constructed on three artificial islands and combines Gothic and Renaissance Revival architectural styles. The station has undergone several renovations and expansions over the years to accommodate the growing number of passengers and to modernise its facilities. In recent years, significant efforts have been made to restore and preserve the historic elements of the station while also integrating contemporary design and technology. Its iconic waterfront location makes it a prominent landmark in Amsterdam's cityscape.

Take some time to admire the ornate details and try not to let the chaos of trams, buses and bikes overwhelm you.

Walking directly ahead from the Central Station (it will be behind you), crossing over the tram tracks and avoiding bikes, trams and cars, you will find the Damrak houses on the left-hand side, around 500m from the station. Often referred to as the dancing gingerbread houses of Damrak, these elegant canal houses are part of the oldest part of the city and an excellent addition to an otherwise chaotic strip. Take some time to admire their distinct characteristics: crooked structures that lean gracefully thanks to an uneven settlement by the stilts they were built on at the beginning of the seventeenth century.

Continue to walk directly past tourist shops, a bureau de change and sex museums until you reach Dam Square, a lively and historic square, home to the *Royal Palace*, which dates back to 1648 and the Dutch Golden

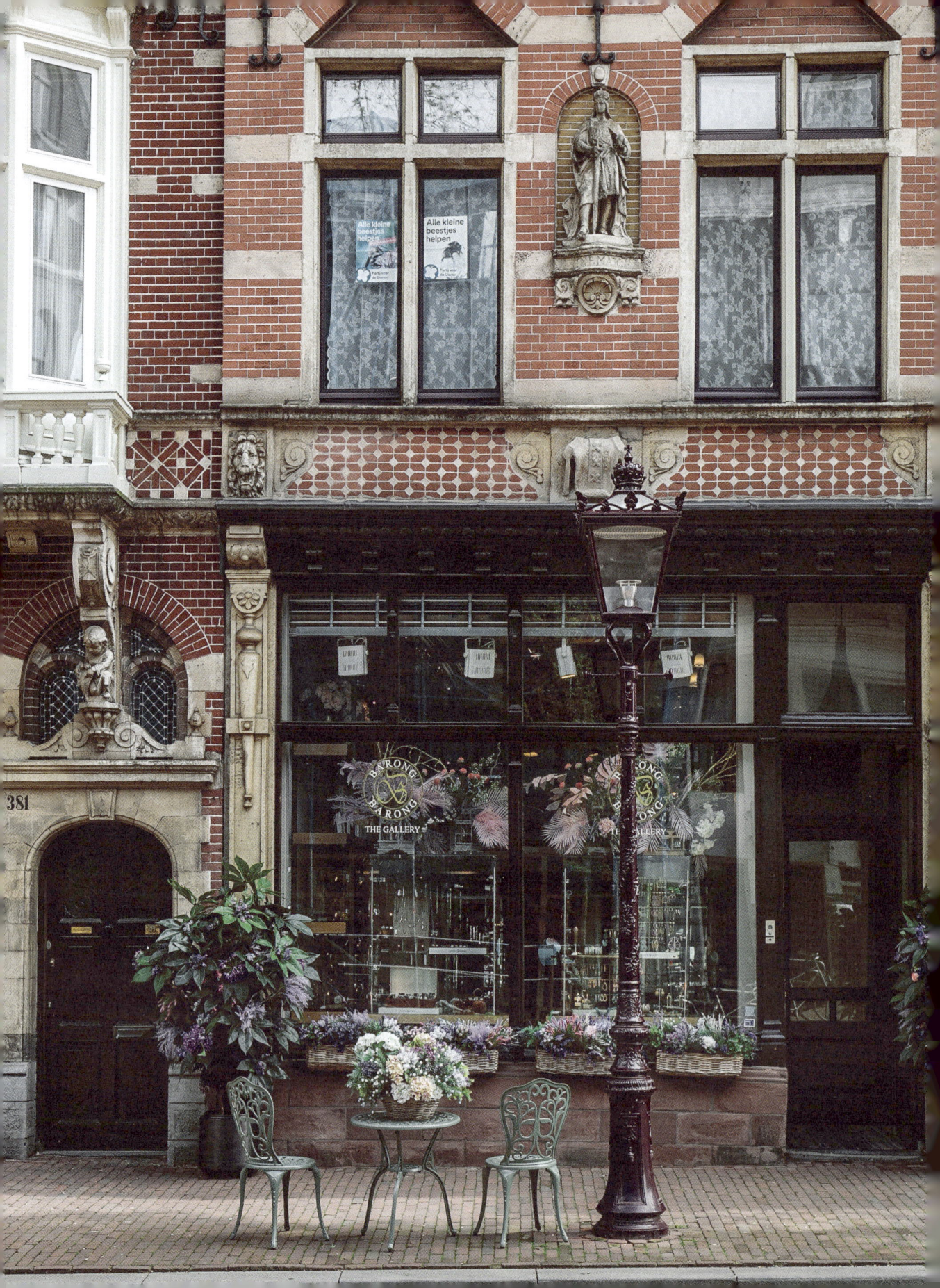

Age. The Royal Palace is an iconic landmark with impressive architecture, imposing decorations and a rich history. It's open to the public for most of the year and, although it is no longer the home of the Dutch royal family, it is worth visiting to admire the grandeur of the building and to learn about its significance in Dutch culture and history.

Head east from Dam Square towards the Royal Palace, then continue south on to Raadhuisstraat. From there, turn left on to Nieuwezijds Voorburgwal, a former canal lined with beautiful seventeenth-century buildings, many of which have been preserved and restored to their former glory. Halfway along the southern part of Nieuwezijds Voorburgwal, the street curves westwards; at that location, the buildings on both sides of the street are slightly recessed, creating a somewhat larger space. This area was formerly used as a car park and is colloquially called *Postzegelmarkt* (Post Stamp Market), after the collector markets that are held here. Recently the area has been converted into a small but beautiful public park as part of the development project Oranje Lopu. The results are absolutely lovely. Grab a drink and a bite to eat at *Het Stadspaleis*, housed in the most beautiful little wooden structure – once a police post, then a public toilet, now a friendly cafe. Order their smoked salmon bagel and have it outside on their cosy terrace.

Other buildings along Nieuwezijds Voorburgwal include the *Huis Bartolotti*, a stunning example of Dutch renaissance architecture, and the *Ronde Lutherse Kerk*, a round church that stands out among the surrounding buildings. The former main post office is now the *Magna Plaza*. Across from the Royal Palace on the corner with Raadhuisstraat, *W Hotel* can be found in a 1930s telegraphy building. Dutch psychiatrist Tina Strobos, who helped rescue over 100 Jewish refugees as part of the Resistance during the Second World War, lived with her family at Nieuwezijds Voorburgwal 282.

The back of the *Begijnhof* rectory is visible on or around Nieuwezijds Voorburgwal 373, in Old Dutch neo-renaissance style, featuring portrait medallions of seventeenth-century writer Joost van den Vondel, and priest and theologian Leonard Marius (from around 1885, by A.C. Bleys). The area also features the imposing *Oude Turfmarkt*, home to several important institutions, such as the *Allard Pierson Museum* and the University of Amsterdam's special collections library.

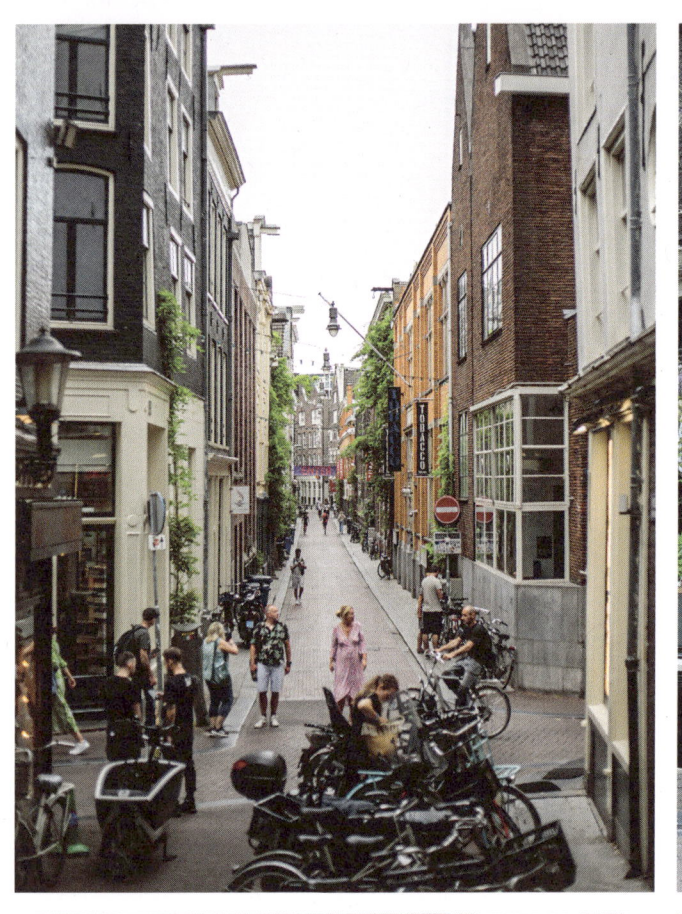
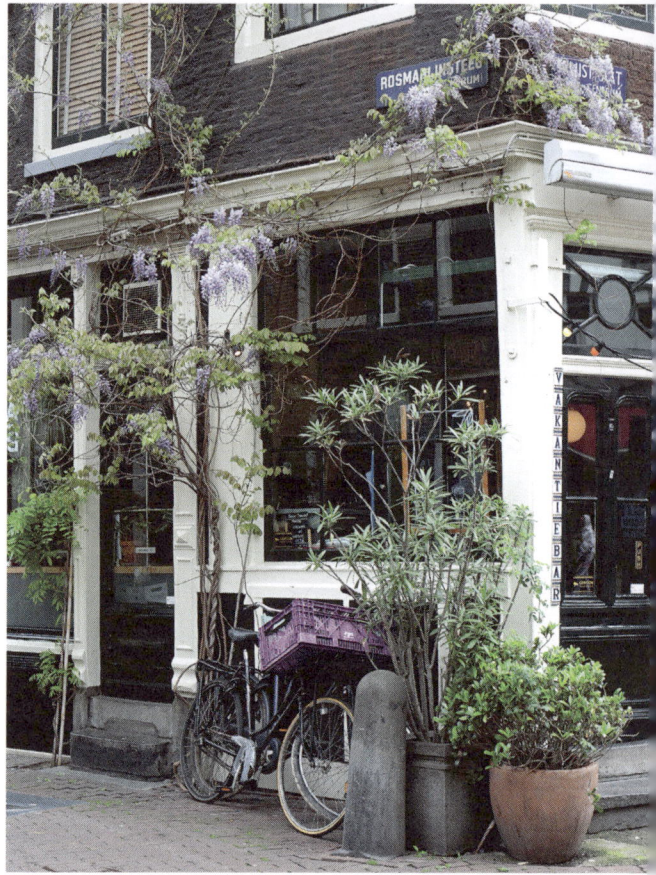
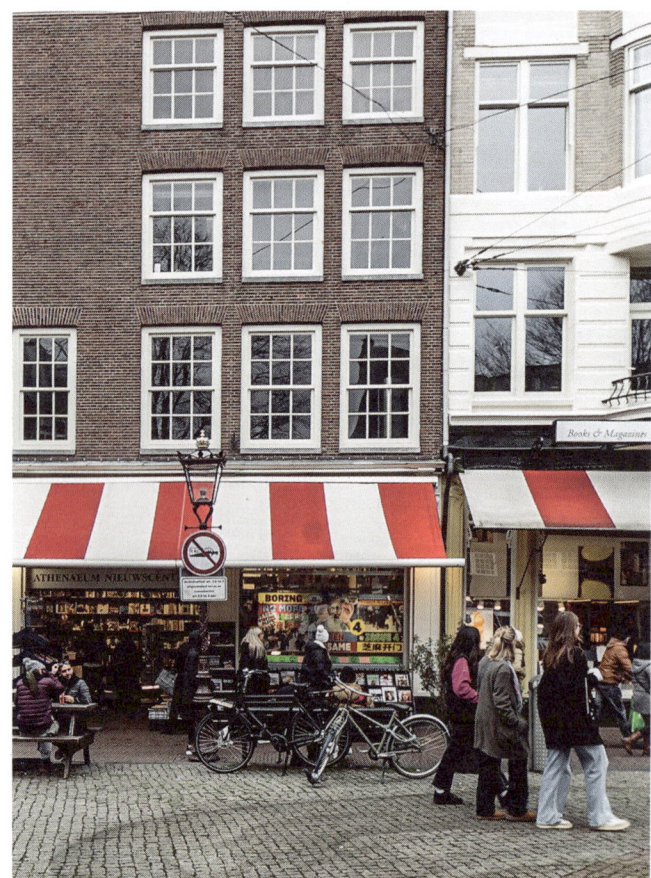
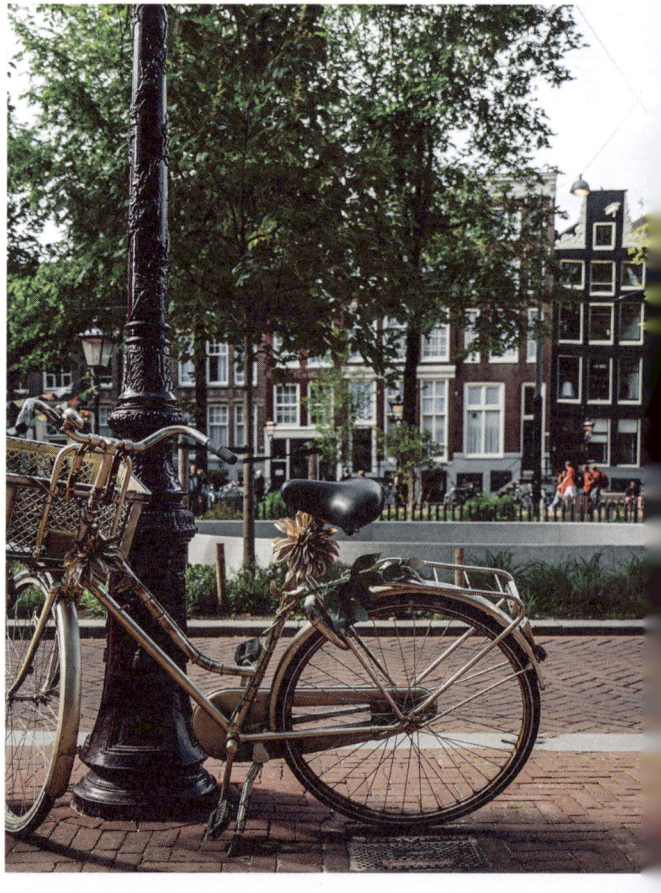

From here, walk over to Sint Luciënsteeg, a narrow street that runs from Kalverstraat to Nieuwezijds Voorburgwal. Walking up the short stretch, you will see another lovely little cafe, *Coffee & Cakes Amsterdam*, in front of you at number 2. Stop for another drink or a piece of delicious carrot cake and, once refuelled, pop in next door to one of the most elegant shops in Amsterdam. *De Posthumuswinkel*, established in 1865, is a specialist shop selling wax seals and stamps like no other. Back outside in the small square that flanks the street, look up at the large number of facade stones. The entrance gate to the *Amsterdam Museum* is at number 27, which was the Sint Luciënklooster in the Middle Ages and the Burgerweeshuis from 1579.

Continue your walk towards Nieuwe Voorburgwal until you come to *Begijnhof*.

Antiquariaat Brinkman is a short walk away at Singel 319, a very cosy old-worldly store specialising in old and rare books and scholarly works. Originally a second-hand bookstore dating back to 1938, it has been in the hands of Henk Brinkman since 1954. Take some time to browse the beautiful store, soak up its *gezellig* atmosphere, and buy a tome or two before returning to the canal. The temptation would be to continue across the bridge and over to The 9 Streets, but there is still so much to see here in Nieuwe Zijde that we will continue our tour.

As you walk south along this stretch of the Singel, admire the beautiful views of the canals, bridges and sights beyond, and turn left into a lovely tiny alley, Heisteeg. You'll come to *Van Stapele Koekmakerij*; you may have to join a very long queue but please don't hesitate to step inside the tiny shop. It is like stepping into Amsterdam's days of yore. Worth visiting for the aroma alone, they sell one thing and one thing only: a cookie with a crisp, rich outside rounded off with soft white chocolate inside. They are best enjoyed immediately while they are still warm, but you should take a leaf out of my book: take a box home and freeze them so they can be enjoyed on those days you yearn for a walk around Amsterdam.

From here, head back south along the Singel to see some of the best views of the canal and turn left into Spui. Of course, there is a much quicker route to Spui from Heisteeg, but I love the charming atmosphere of these short detours. With beer on your mind, you could make a beeline for *Café Hoppe*, a landmark brown cafe on Spui Square that has been open since

1670. You could soak up the ambience from one of the partly covered terrace tables or sit inside for something cosier.

Stroll east on Spui towards bustling Kalverstraat; when you hit the busy Kalverstraat, turn right into the narrow and historic Langebrugsteeg. The Langebrugsteeg has a rich history dating back several centuries. This little street, lined with merchants' houses and warehouses, in the city's heart has long been a bustling street, especially during the Dutch Golden Age. It was a vital link between the city's canals and markets, crucial in Amsterdam's economic activities. Today, Langebrugsteeg retains its historic charm while being a popular destination for shopping, dining and exploring the city's vibrant culture. The street is home to many shops, cafes and restaurants, making it a lively and dynamic part of Amsterdam's urban landscape. Whether you're interested in its historical significance or its modern-day attractions, Langebrugsteeg offers a fascinating blend of past and present for all to enjoy. Don't miss *Lyppens Jeweller* at number 8 or the cute little De Laatste Kruimel cafe at number 4. Pop in for a melt-in-your-mouth scone or a delicious soup. Take a seat inside or take your goodies to a nearby canal instead. Other options for food and drink include *Café 't Gasthuys* on Grimburgwal, or you could walk over to *Petit-Restaurant de Rozenboom* or *Gartine* on Taksteeg for some great Dutch classics.

Appetite sated, cross over the Grimburgwal canal and take a left on to Oudezijdes Achterburgwal. You will find Oudemanhuispoort (Old Man's Gate) on your right; walk through the old gate and under the arches of the University of Amsterdam, where you will find a tiny book market, open every day except Sundays, where booksellers have been selling used and antique books, prints and maps since 1879.

Finish your tour with a rest back out on the banks of the Oudezijdes Achterburgwal canal; as you sit here on the very peaceful southern stretch, it is hard to imagine that a bit further north, where this canal dissects De Wallen, it is full of sex shops, brothels and peep shows. These contradictions make Amsterdam unique, and finding the quieter parts to enjoy is all the more rewarding.

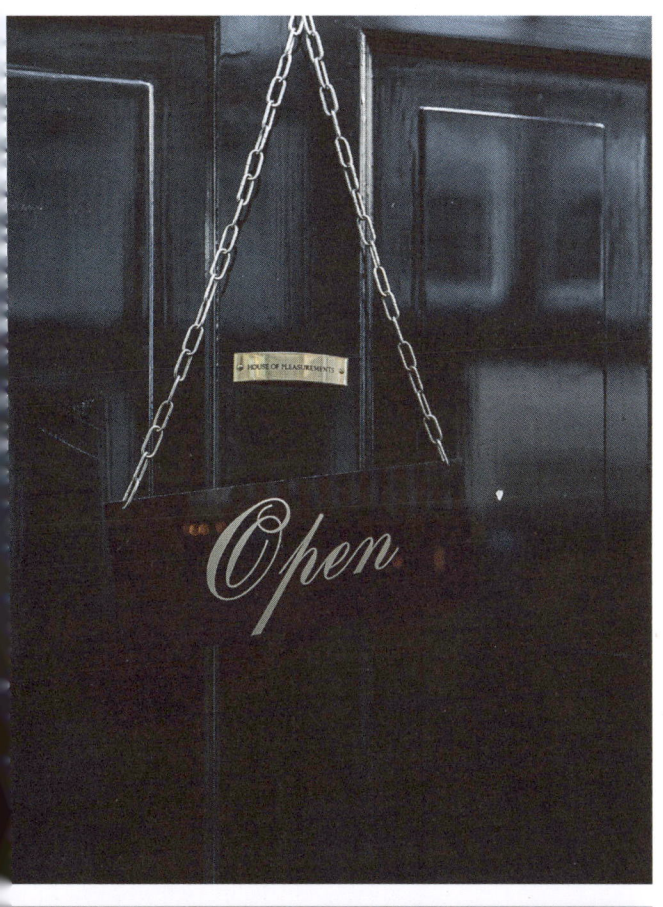
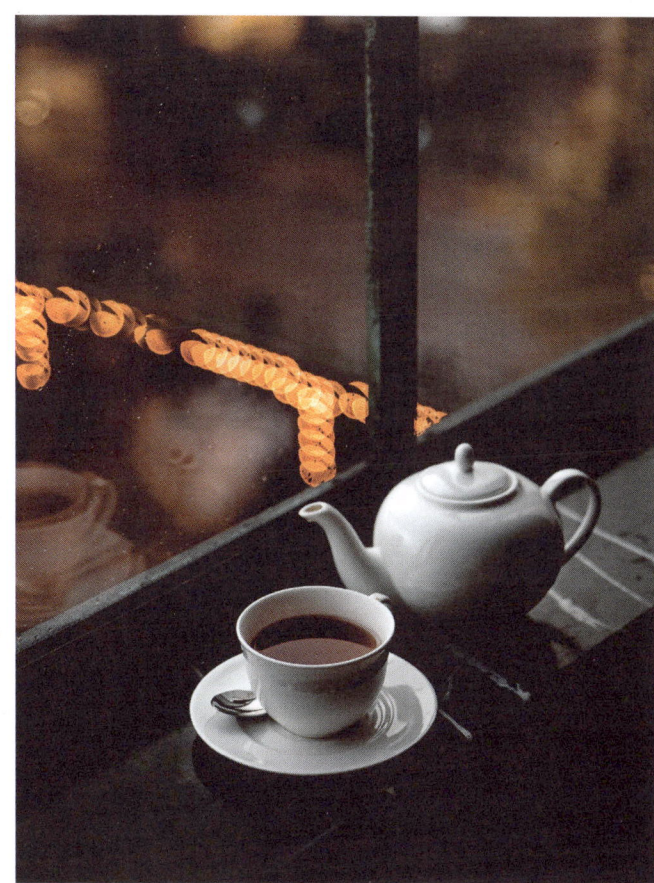
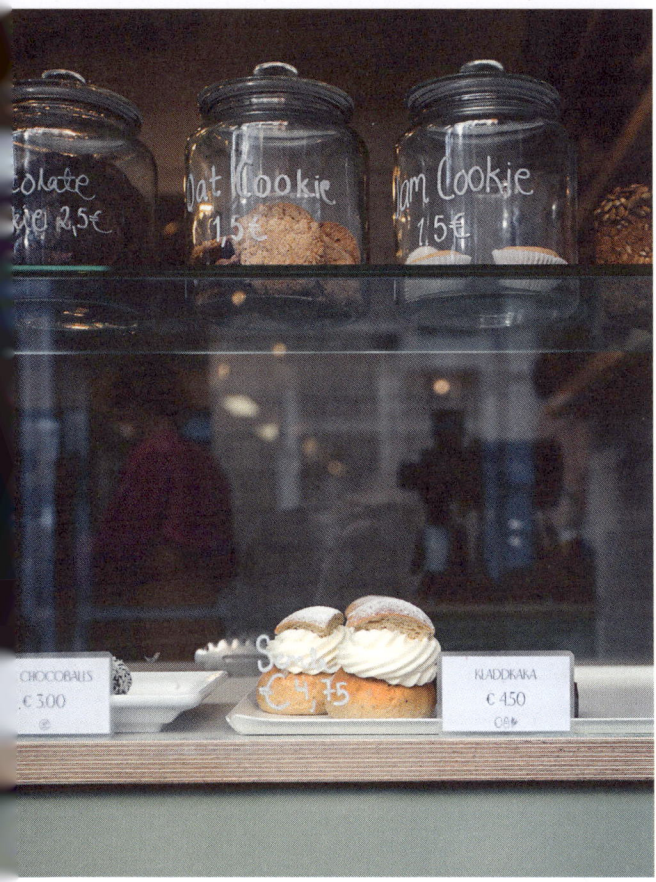
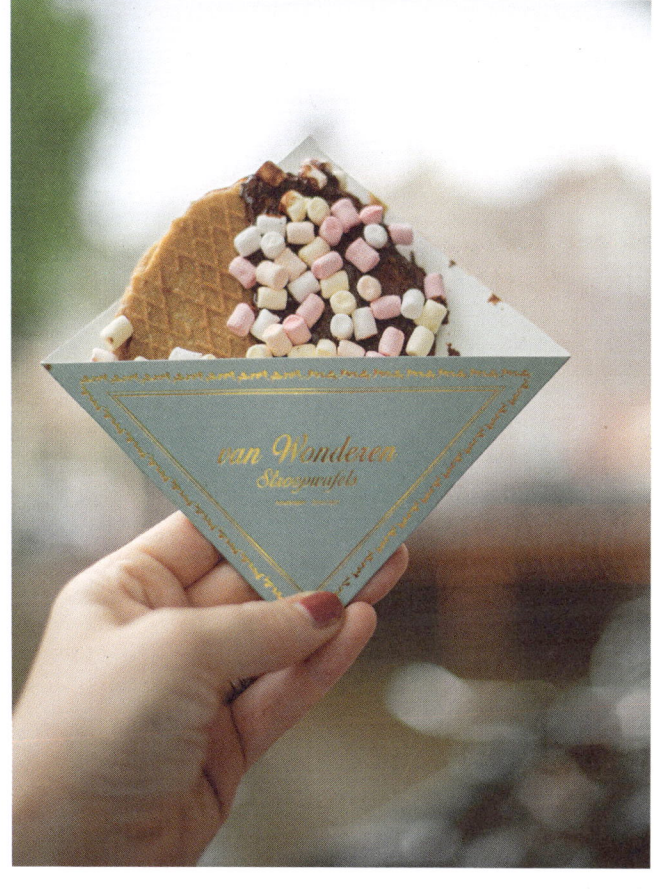

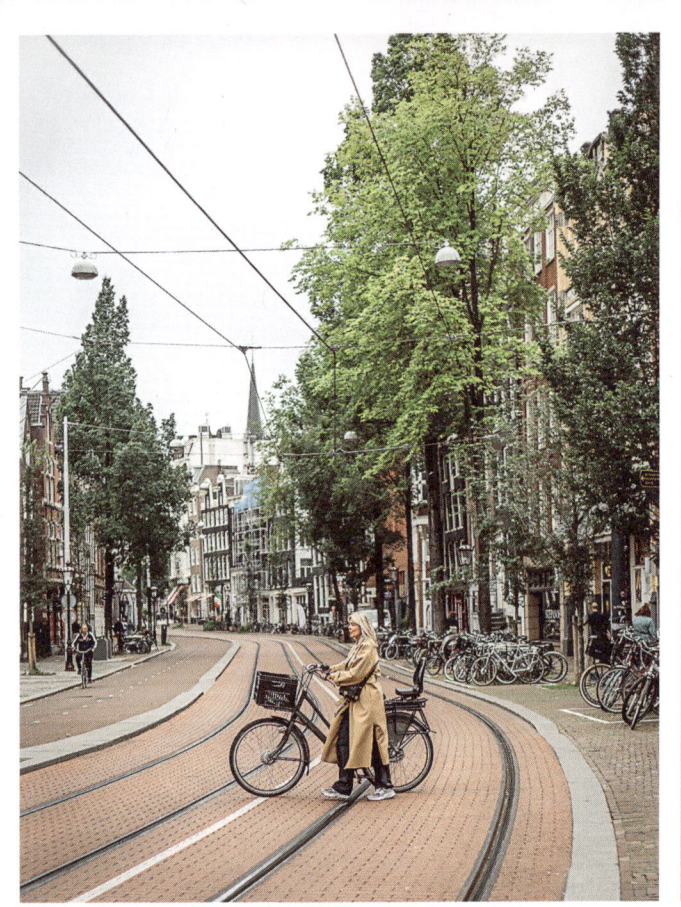
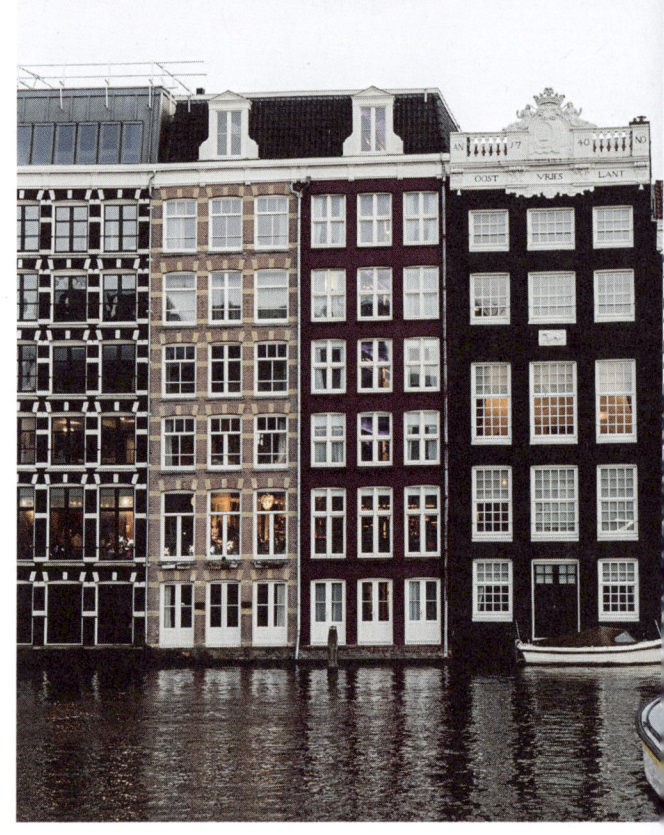
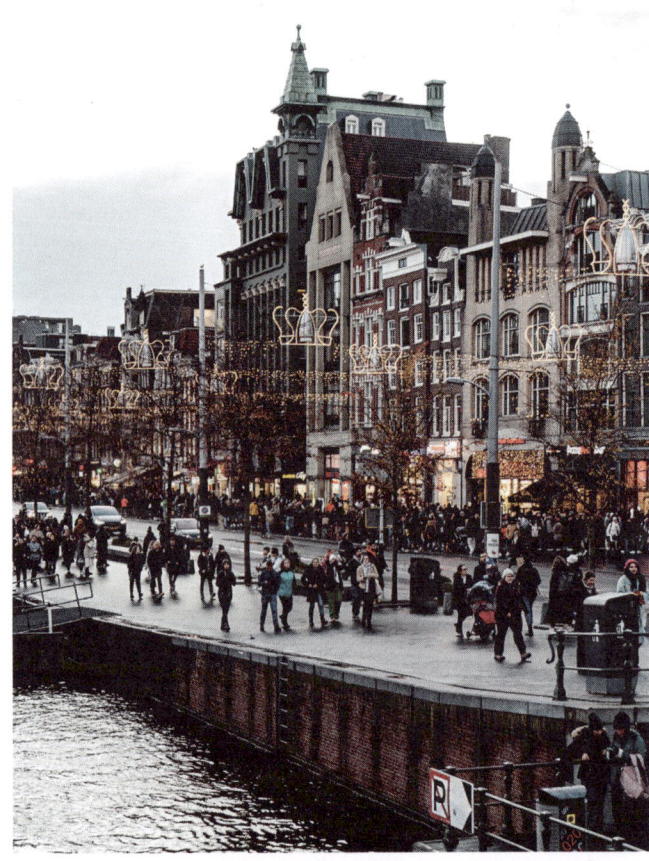
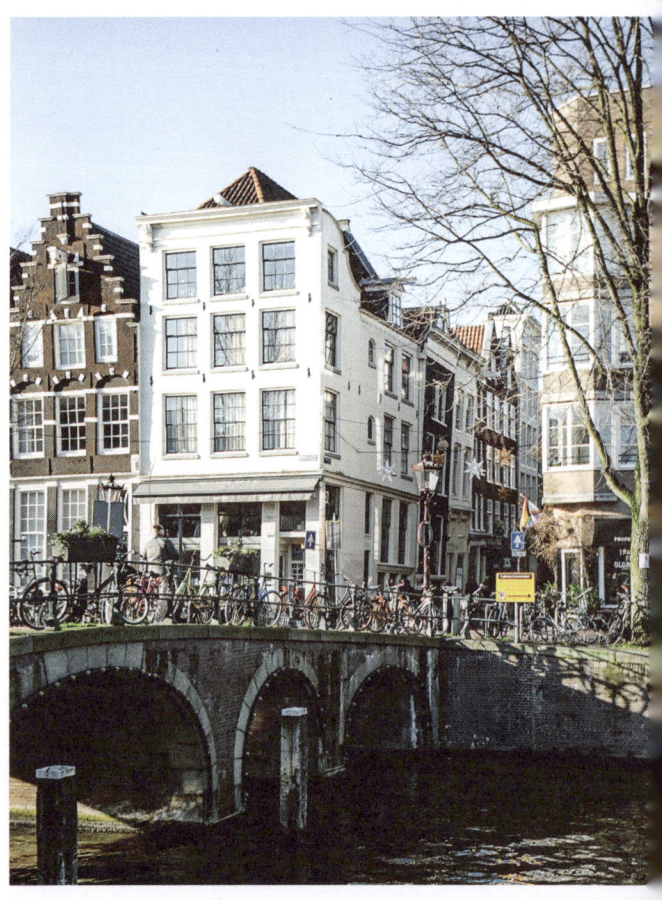

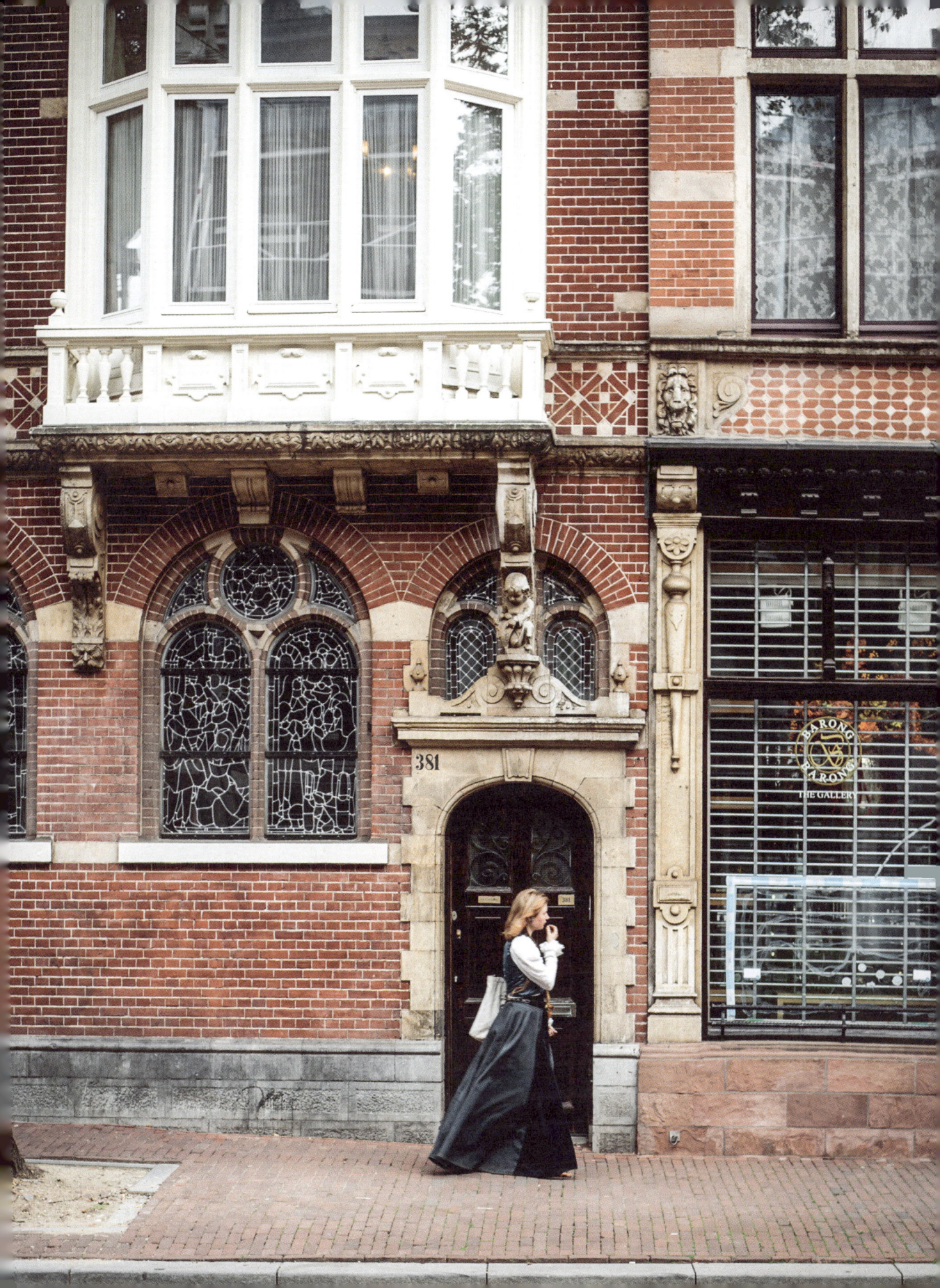

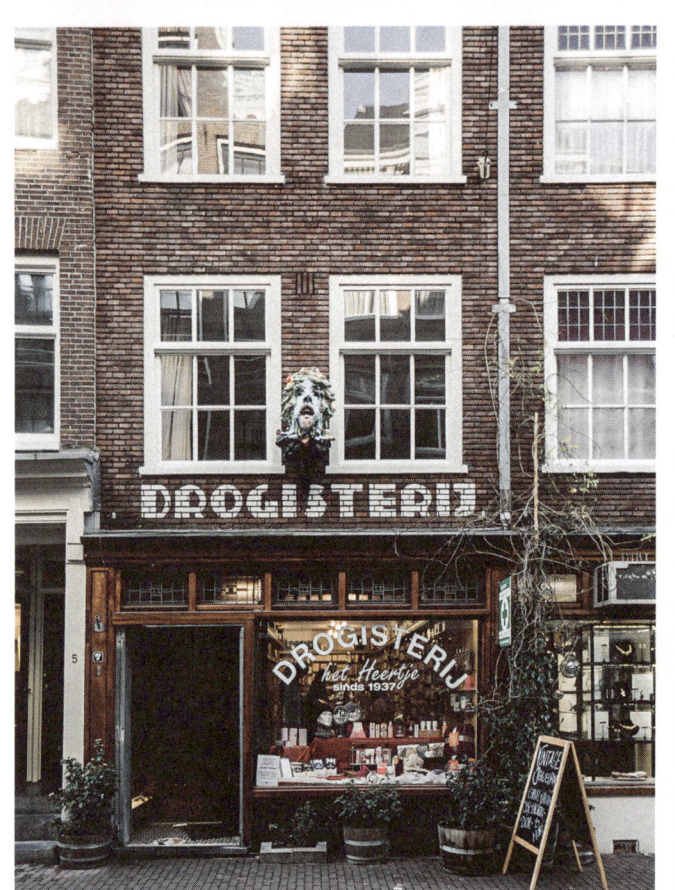
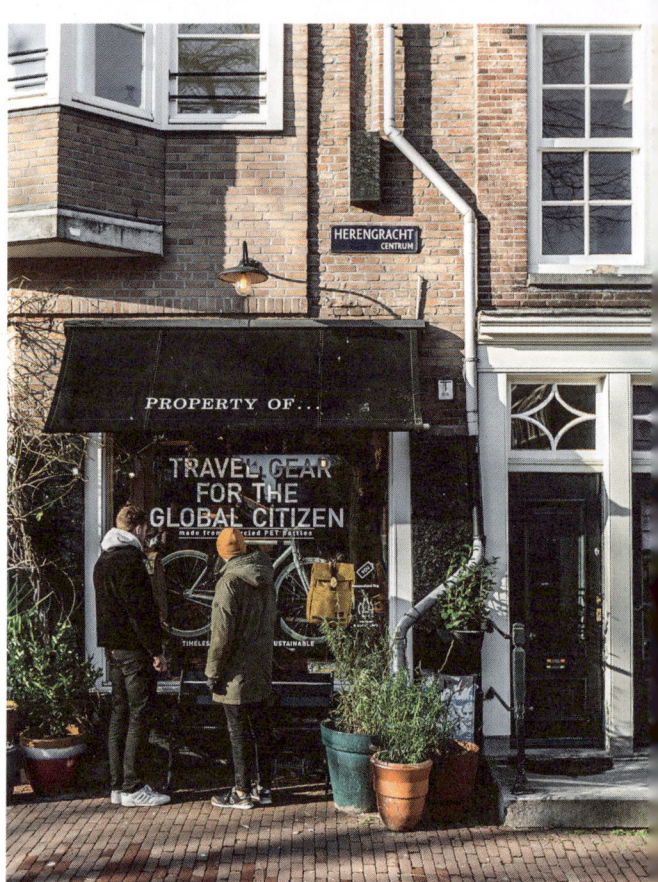

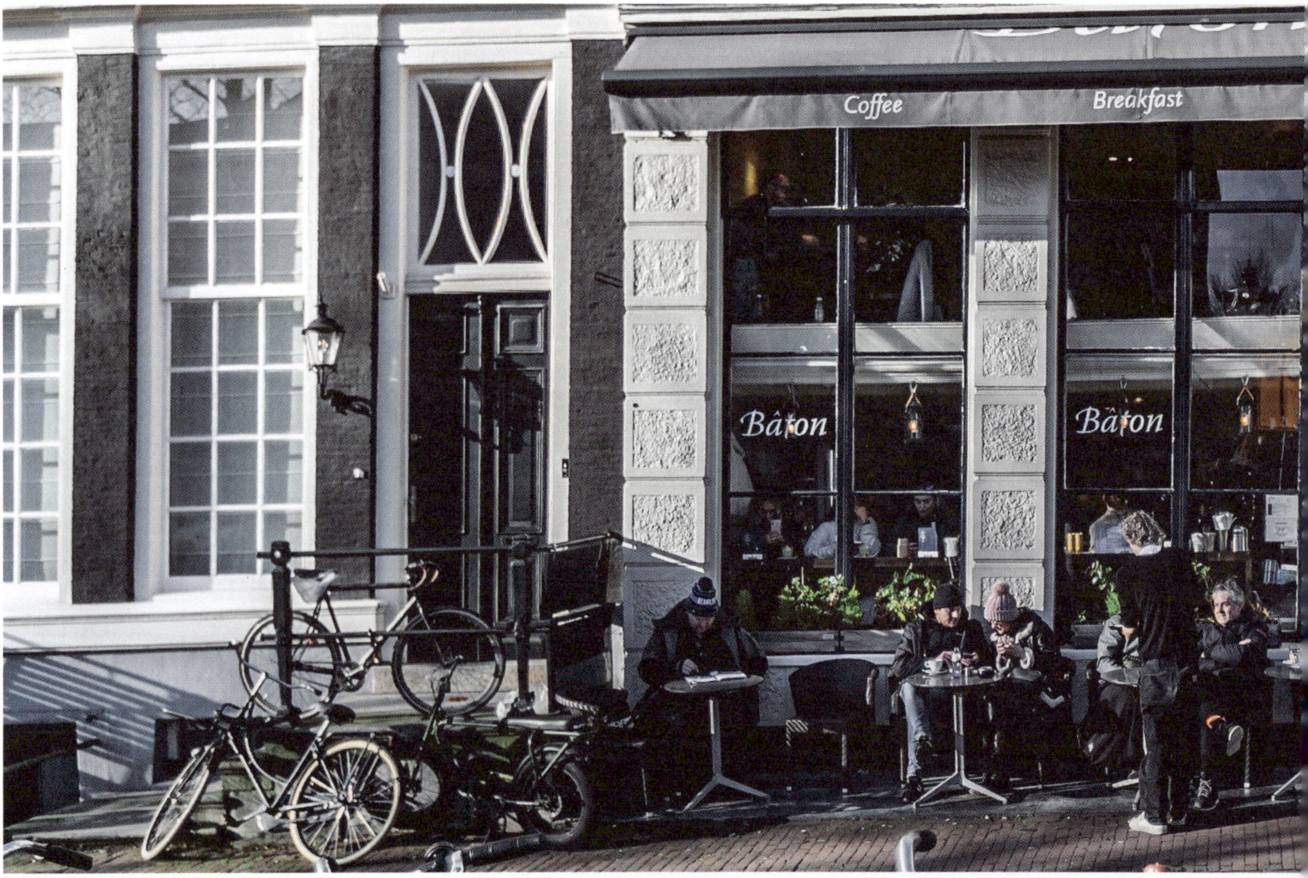

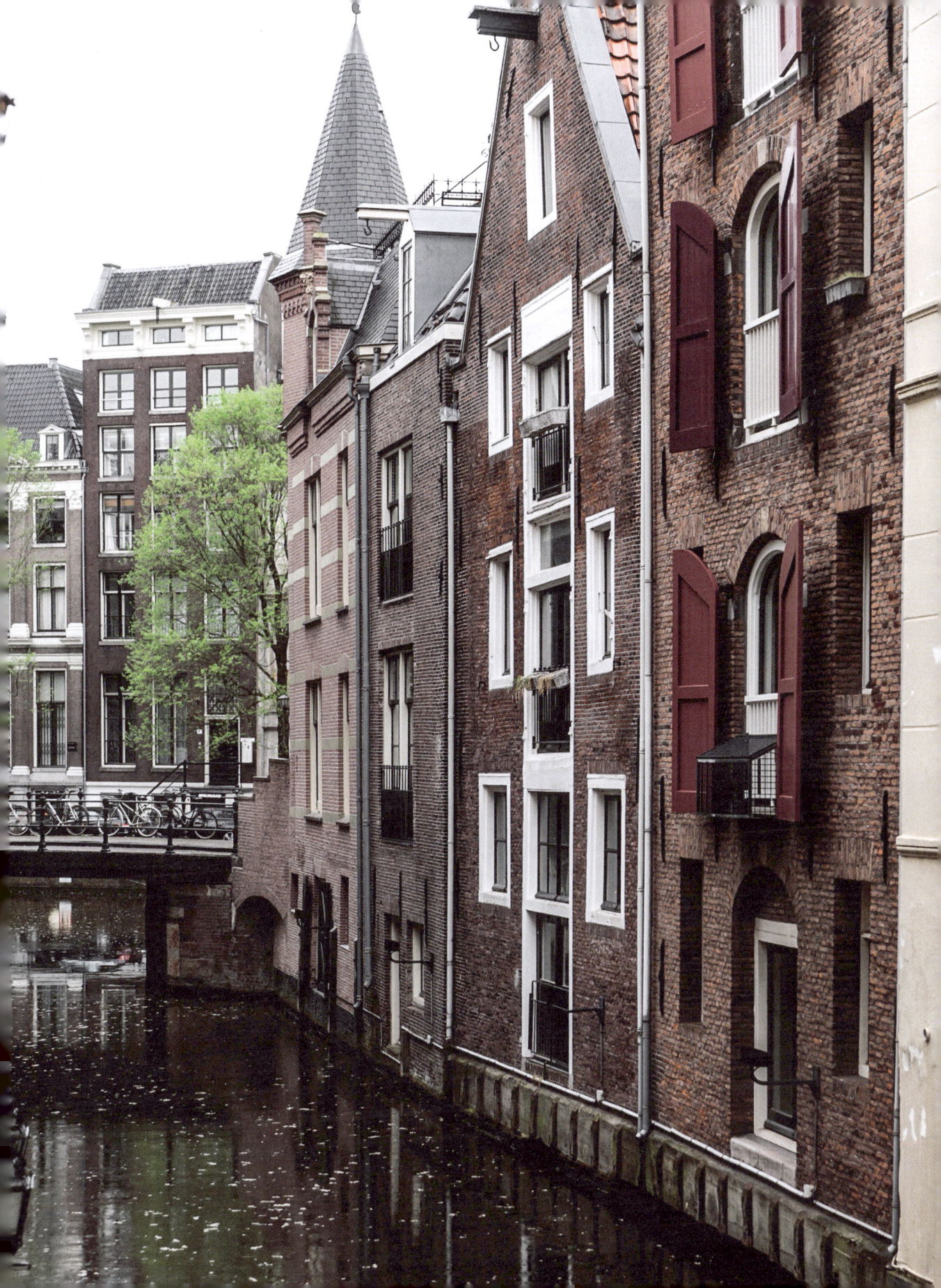

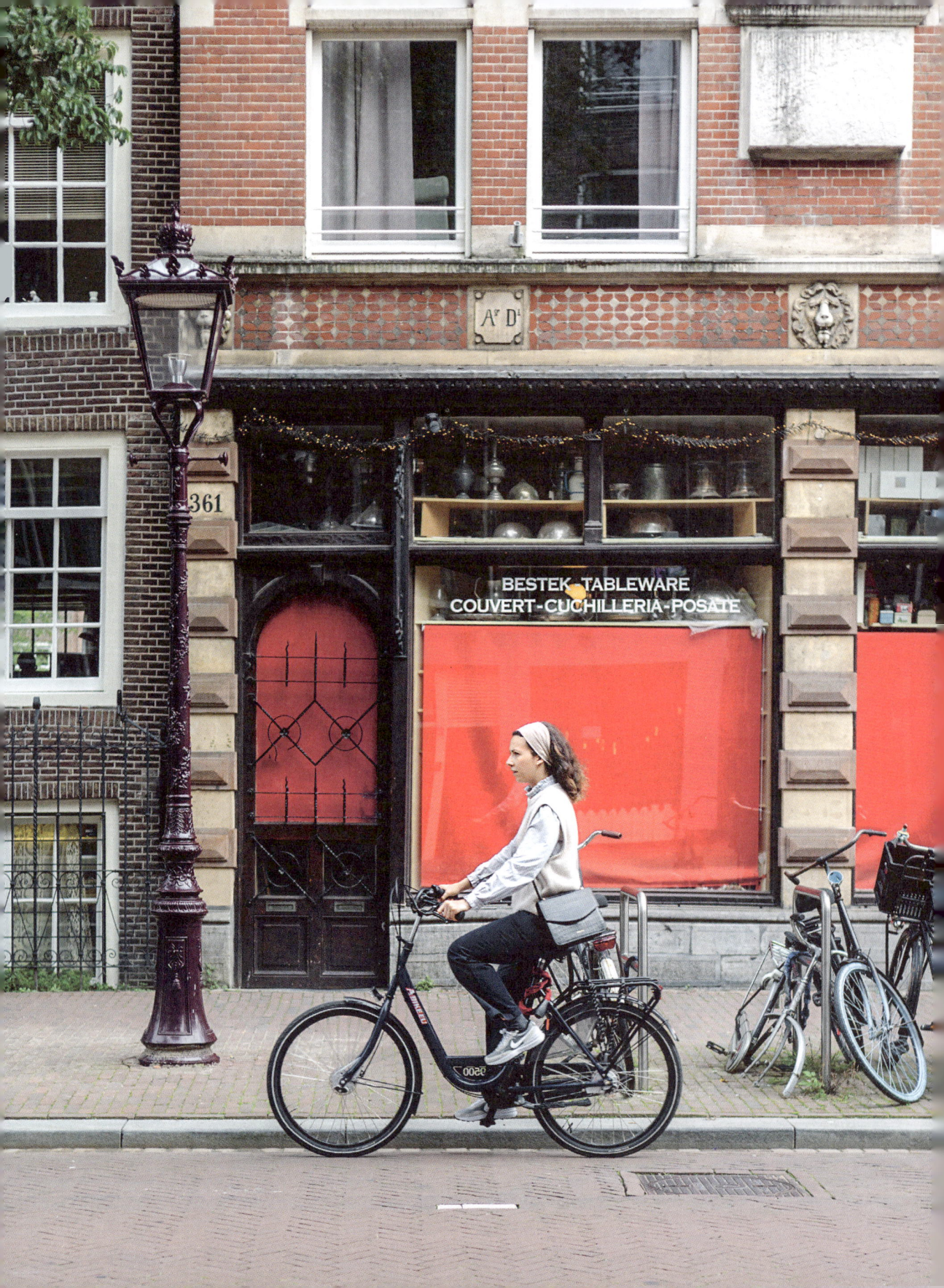

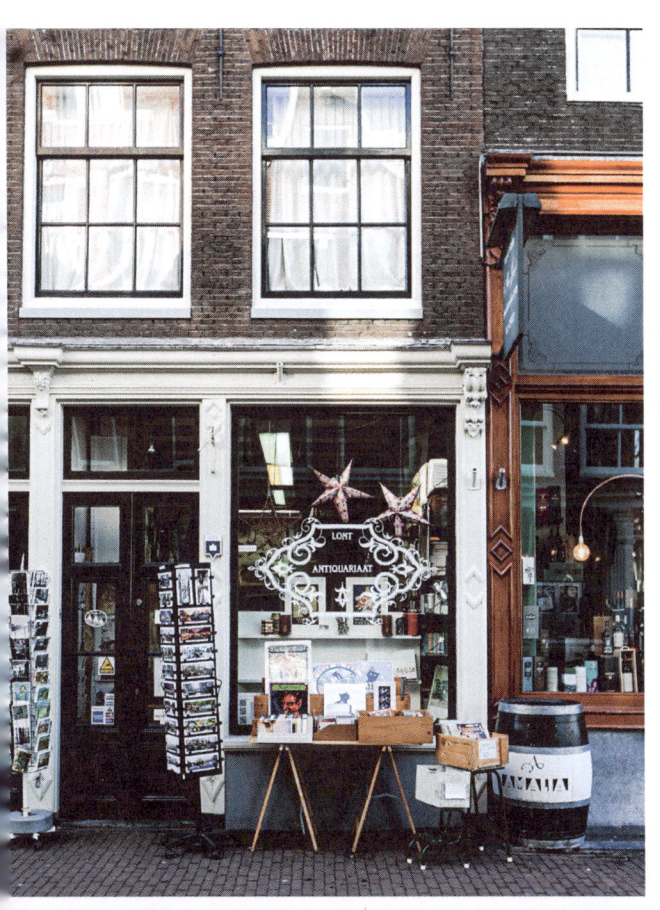
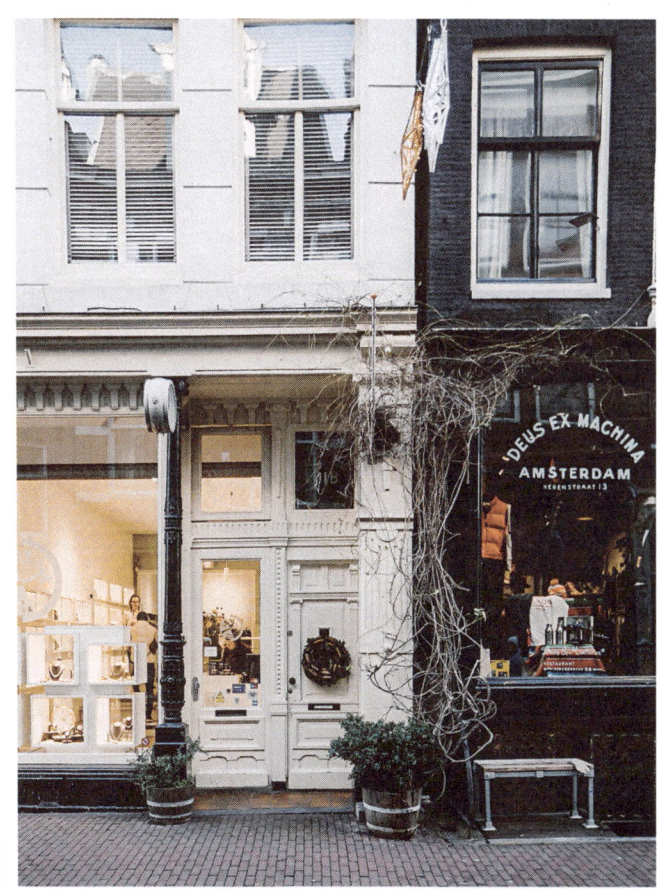
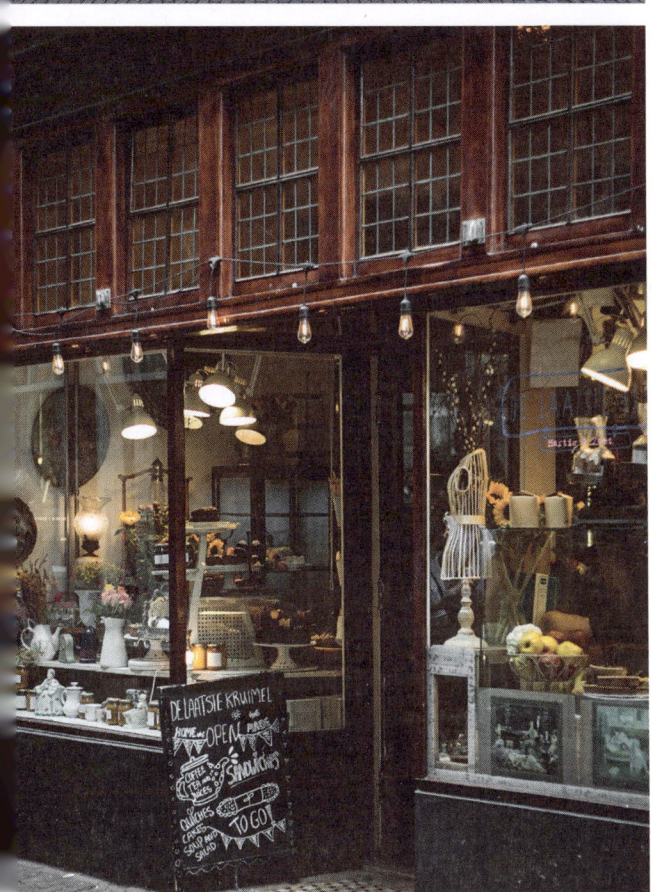
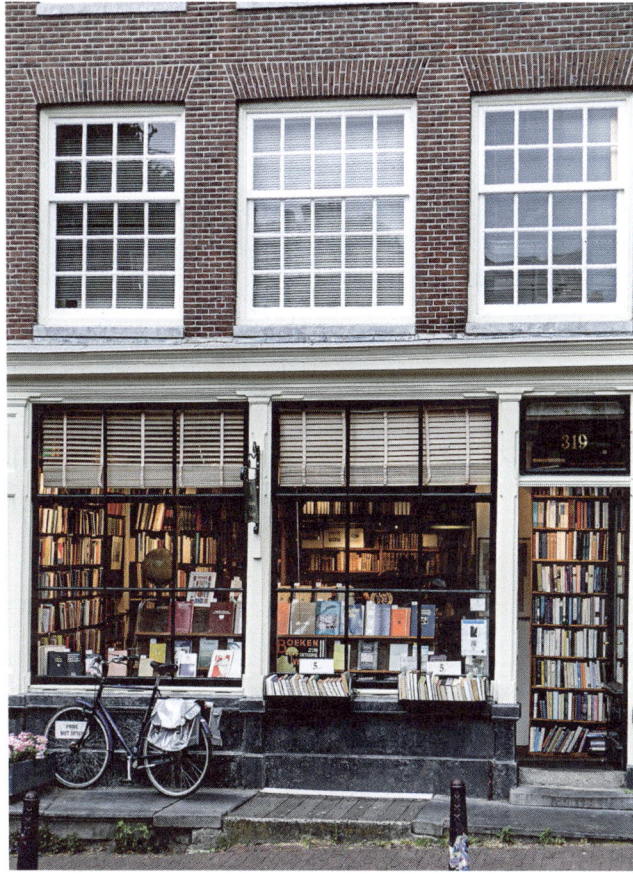

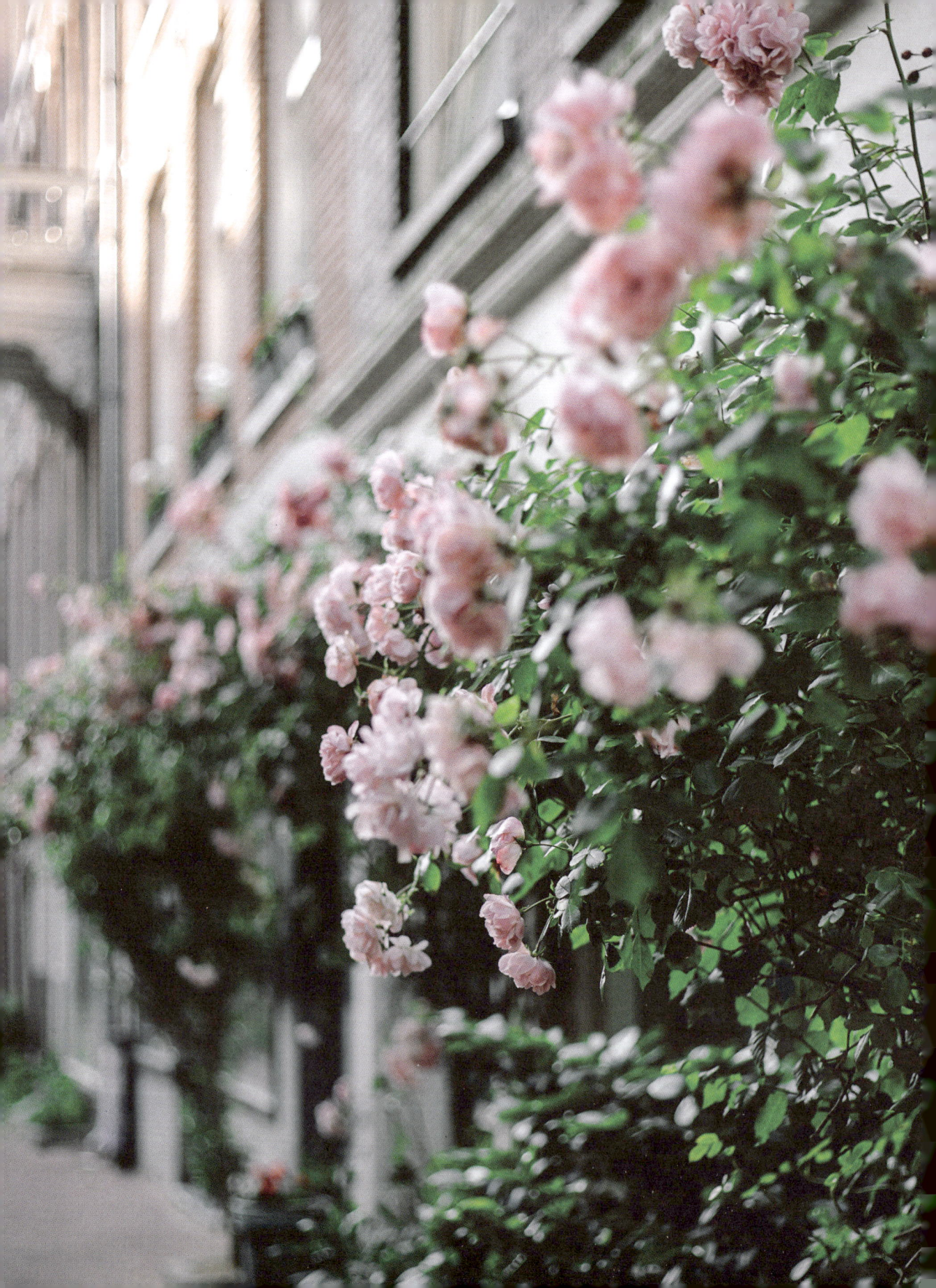

PART IV

PRETTY CITY AMSTERDAM THROUGH THE SEASONS

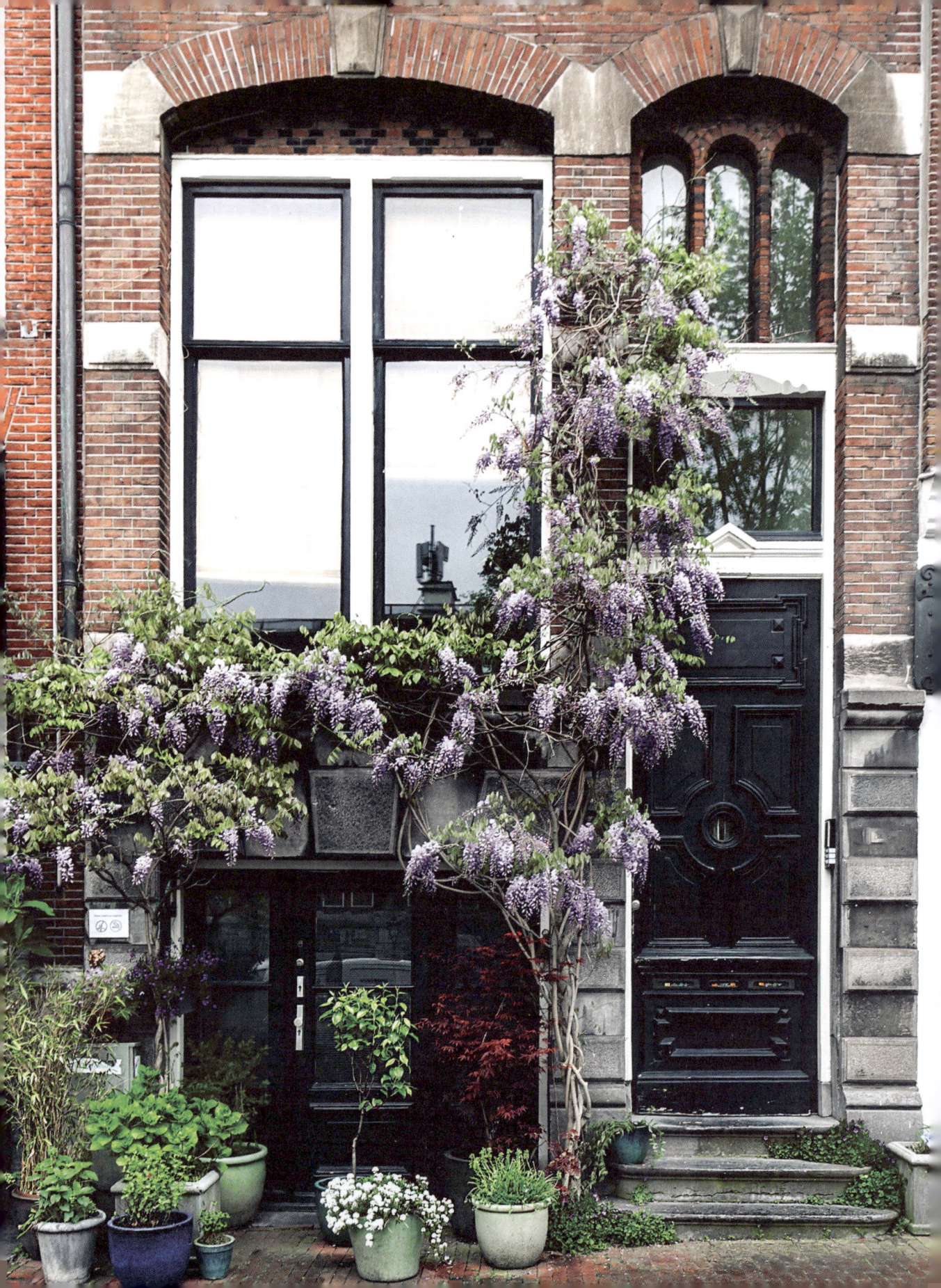

AMSTERDAM IN SPRING: A VIBRANT CITY BLOOMING WITH CULTURE AND BEAUTY

As the winter chill dissipates, Amsterdam undergoes a breathtaking transformation, welcoming the arrival of spring with open arms. The city's iconic canals and cobblestone streets come alive with a burst of colour as tulips and other vibrant blooms adorn every corner.

FLORAL SPECTACLE AT KEUKENHOF GARDENS

One of the most captivating aspects of Amsterdam in spring is the world-renowned Keukenhof Gardens, often referred to as the 'Garden of Europe'. Spanning over 32 hectares, this botanical paradise showcases a mesmerising display of tulips in various hues, alongside daffodils, hyacinths and other spring flowers. Visitors are treated to a sensory feast as they meander through meticulously landscaped gardens, capturing Instagram-worthy moments at every turn.

CULTURAL EXTRAVAGANZA AND FESTIVALS

Spring in Amsterdam is not just about nature's splendour; it also marks the onset of various cultural events and festivals celebrating art, music and heritage. The Konigsdag (King's Day) festivities on 27 April paint the city in a sea of orange as locals partake in lively street parties, flea markets and open-air concerts.

Remembrance and Liberation Day fall one day after another on 4 and 5 May, and they commemorate all who died in global conflicts and, of course, the freedom from Nazi occupation after the Second World War. A moment of silence occurs at 8 p.m. on the 4th.

AL FRESCO DINING AND OUTDOOR PURSUITS

The arrival of spring heralds an opportunity for residents and visitors to savour the city's culinary delights amidst picturesque outdoor settings.

Amsterdam's charming cafes and restaurants set up inviting terraces along the canals and squares, providing the perfect backdrop for indulging in delectable Dutch cuisine or simply sipping a refreshing beverage while basking in the sun. Furthermore, outdoor enthusiasts can partake in bike rides through blooming parks such as Vondelpark or a leisurely canal cruise to admire the city's springtime splendour from a unique vantage point.

In conclusion, Amsterdam in spring is a captivating tapestry of natural beauty, cultural richness and outdoor pursuits. Whether revelling in the kaleidoscope of floral wonders at Keukenhof Gardens or immersing oneself in the city's vibrant cultural scene, springtime in Amsterdam is a daily delight.

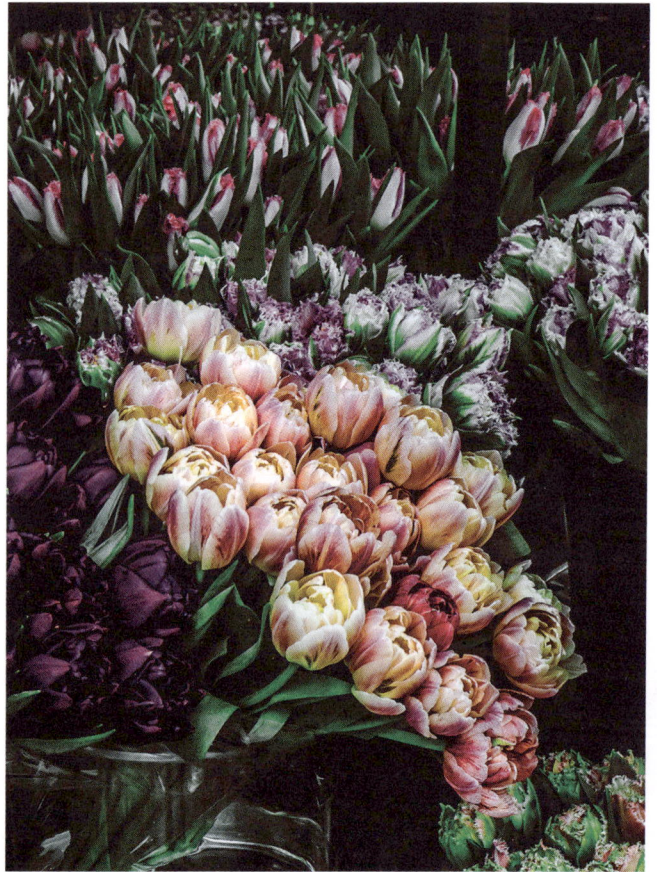
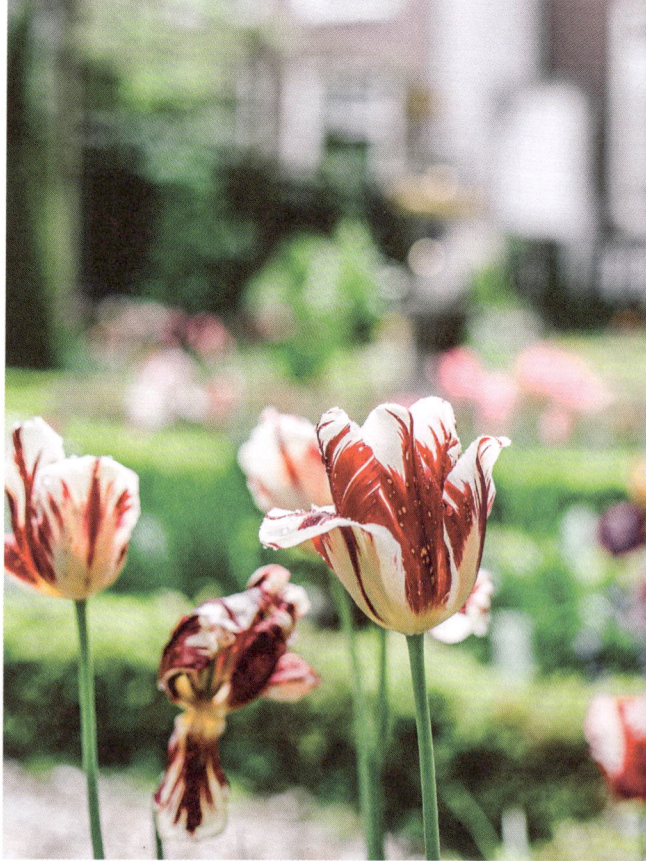

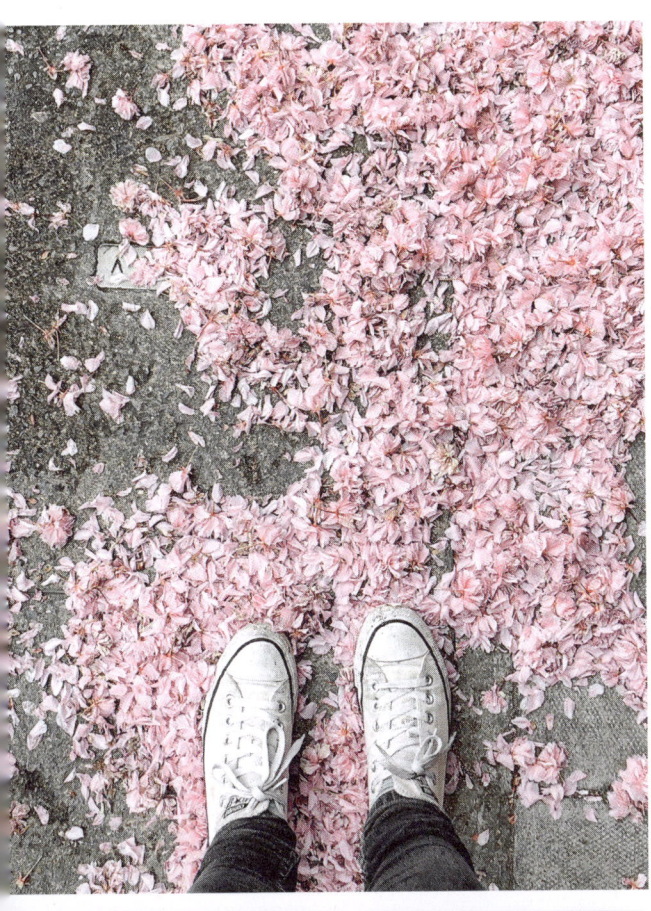
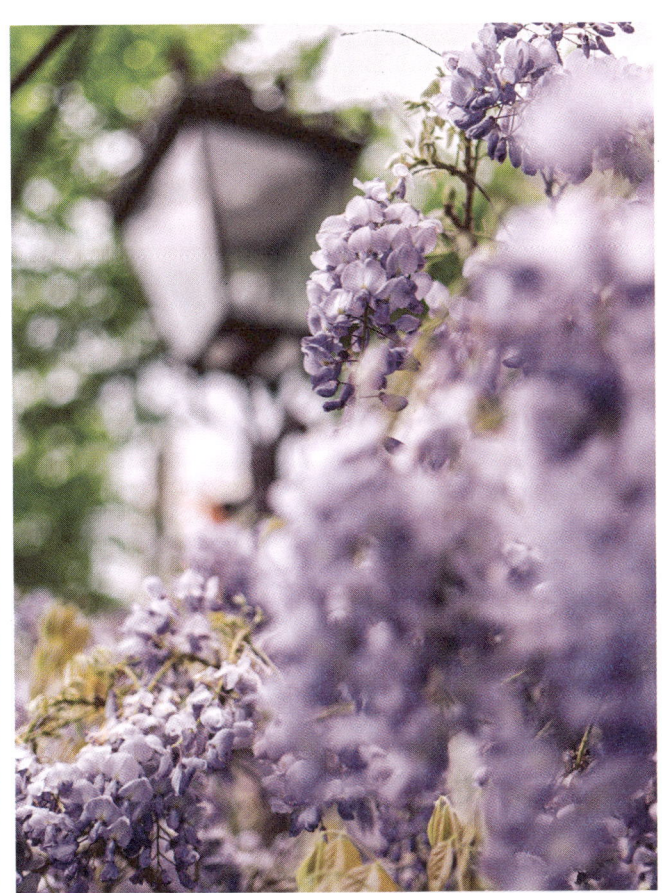
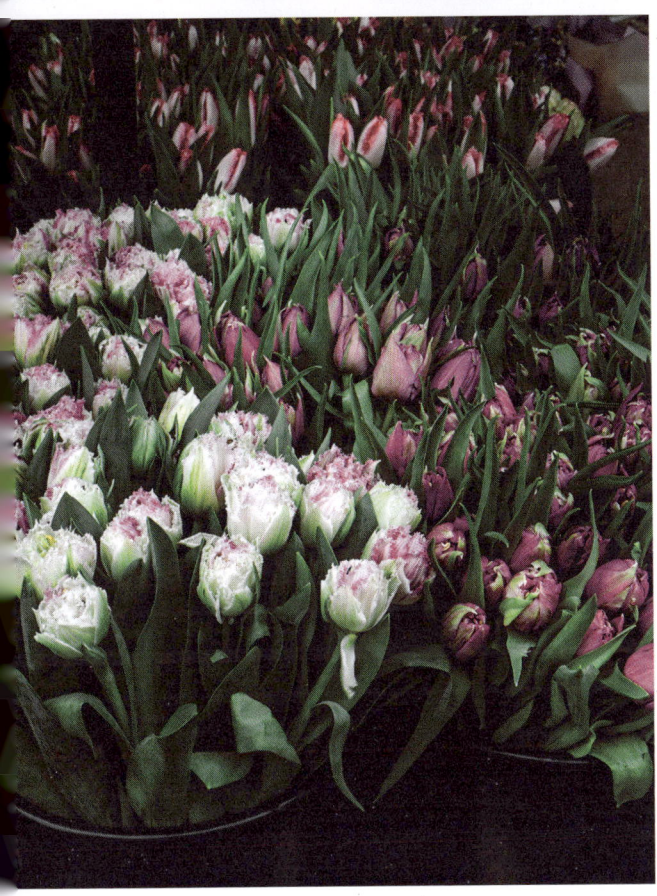
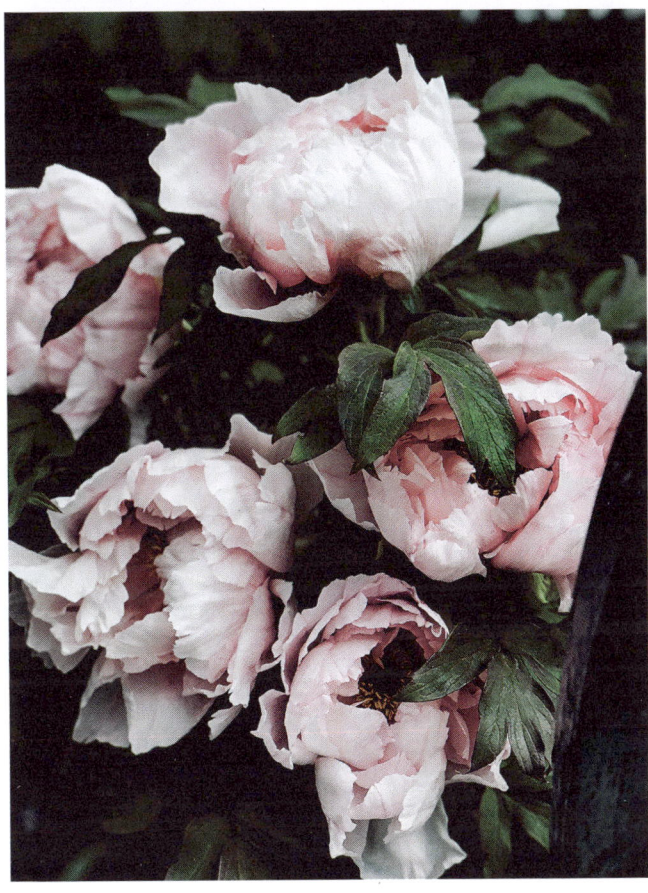

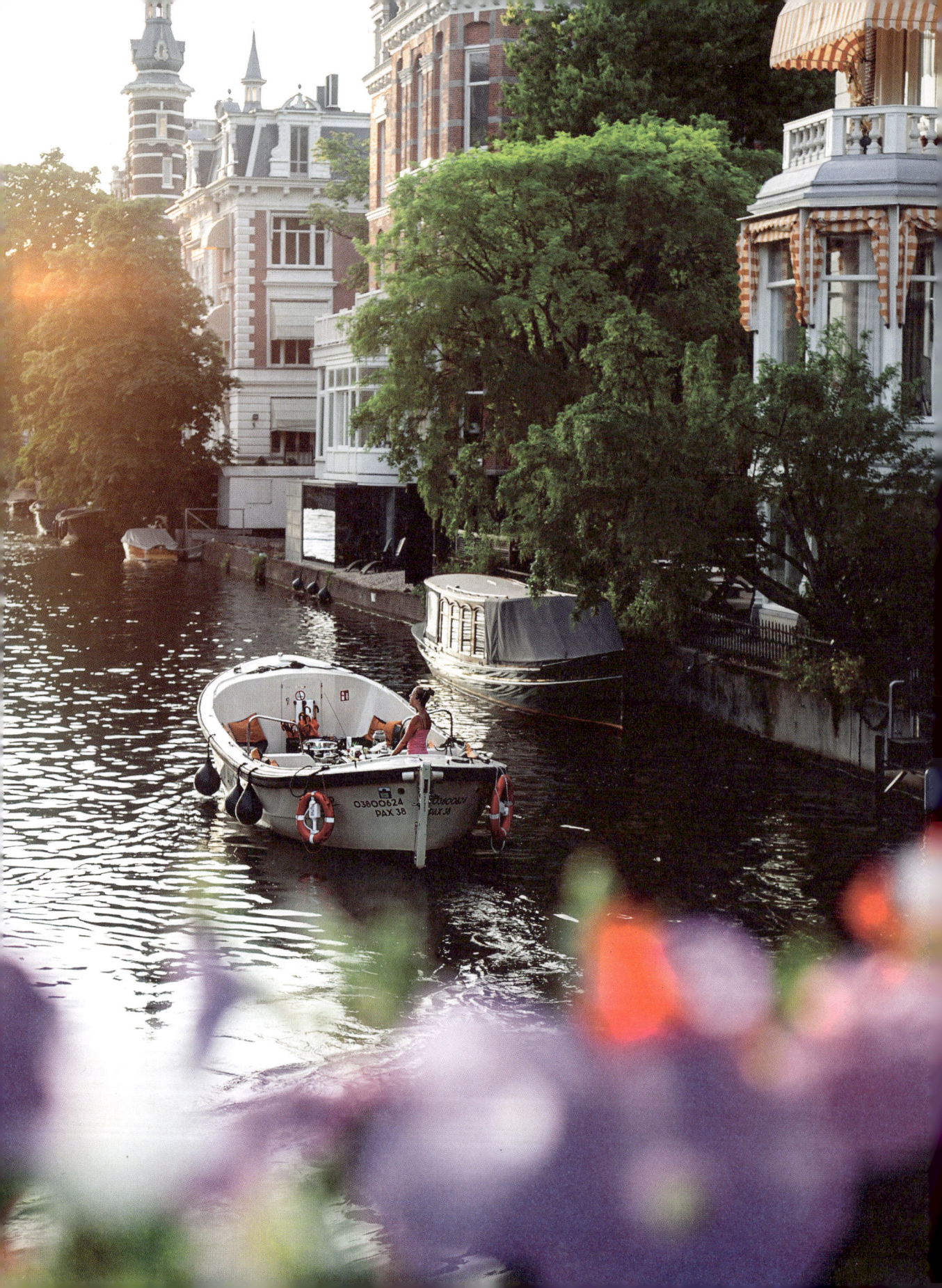

AMSTERDAM IN SUMMER: A GUIDE TO ENJOYING THE CITY'S VIBRANT SEASON

Amsterdam is a vibrant and picturesque destination that comes alive during the summer months. From its iconic canals and historic architecture to its lively festivals and outdoor activities, Amsterdam offers many experiences for visitors seeking to make the most of the sunny season. Whether you're a culture enthusiast, a nature lover, or a food aficionado, there's something for everyone in this charming city during the summer. Let's delve into the various aspects that make Amsterdam an ideal summer destination.

EXPLORING THE CITY'S LUSH GREEN SPACES

Amsterdam boasts abundant lush parks and green spaces perfect for strolls, picnics, or simply basking in the sun. Vondelpark, the city's most famous park, is a sprawling oasis where visitors can unwind amidst verdant lawns, serene ponds and enchanting rose gardens. The Amstelpark and Westerpark offer idyllic settings for outdoor relaxation and recreational activities, making them ideal destinations for nature enthusiasts and families alike.

CRUISING ALONG THE SCENIC CANALS

The summer season provides an excellent opportunity to experience Amsterdam's iconic canals in all their splendour. Embarking on a leisurely canal cruise allows visitors to admire the city's picturesque waterfronts, historic bridges and charming houseboats while soaking up the warm sunshine. Whether opting for a guided tour or renting a private boat, exploring Amsterdam from its waterways offers a unique perspective and an unforgettable way to appreciate the city's architectural marvels.

IMMERSING IN CULTURAL FESTIVITIES

Summer in Amsterdam is synonymous with cultural events and festivals celebrating art, music and local traditions. The Holland Festival, a prominent arts festival held annually from May to June, showcases an eclectic mix of performances encompassing theatre, dance, music and visual arts. Furthermore, the Open Garden Days provide exclusive access to hidden urban gardens and courtyards across the city, allowing visitors to marvel at exquisite floral displays and horticultural wonders. Mid-August brings the Grachtenfestival: a glorious celebration of classical music on the beautiful canals.

INDULGING IN CULINARY DELIGHTS

Amsterdam's culinary scene flourishes during the summer, with numerous outdoor markets, food festivals and al fresco dining options awaiting gastronomes. The city's vibrant street-food culture comes alive with various delectable offerings ranging from traditional Dutch snacks to international delicacies.

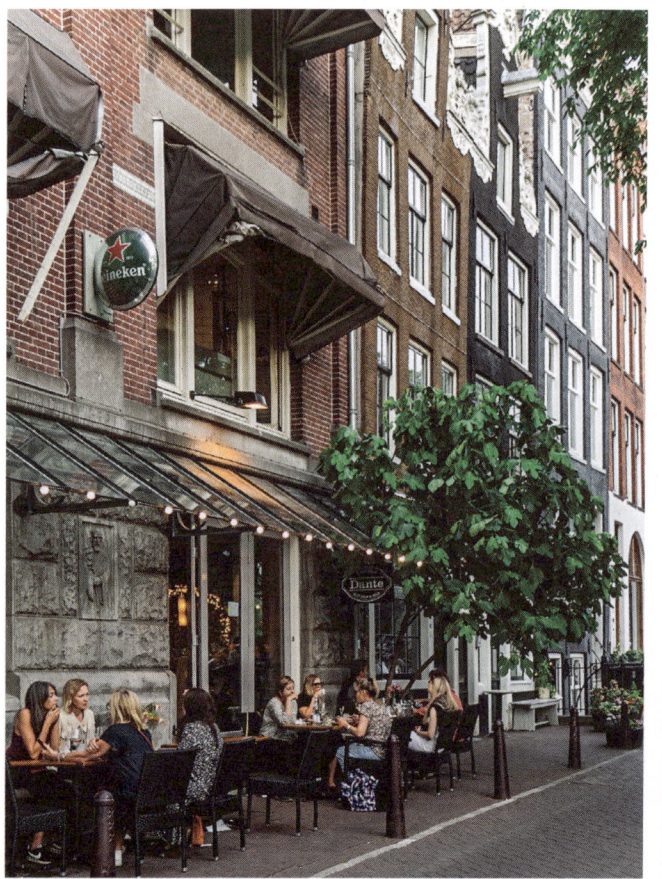
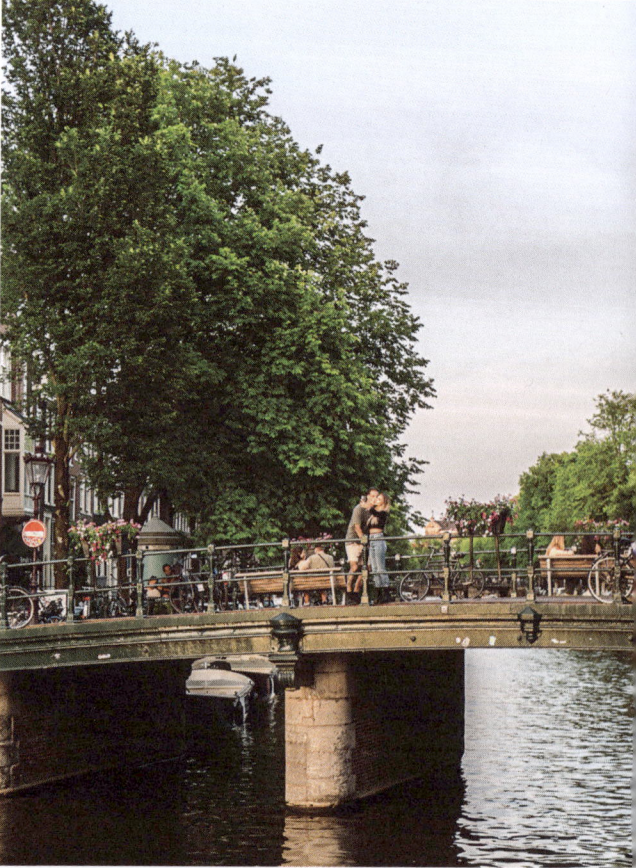

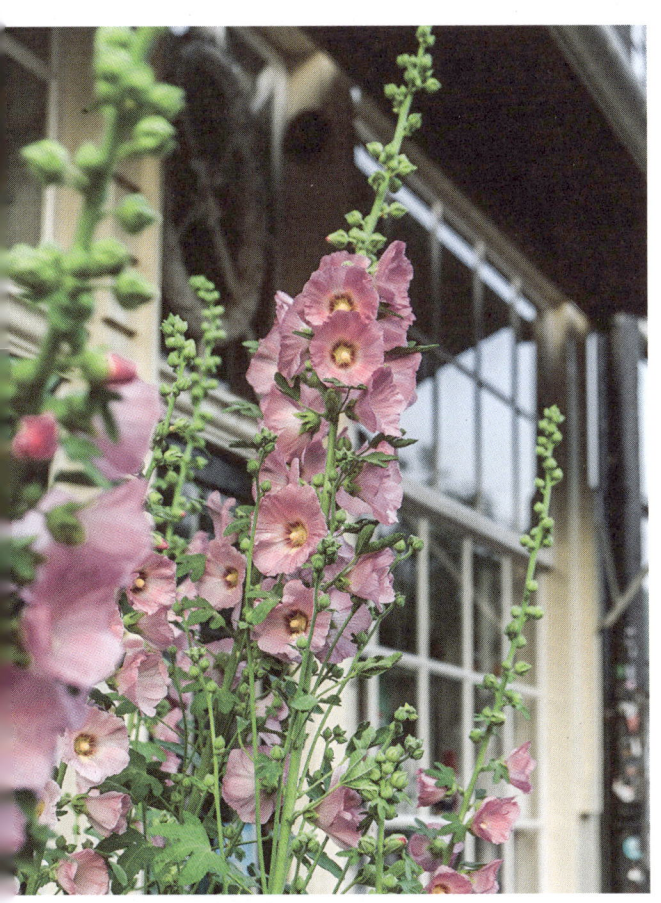
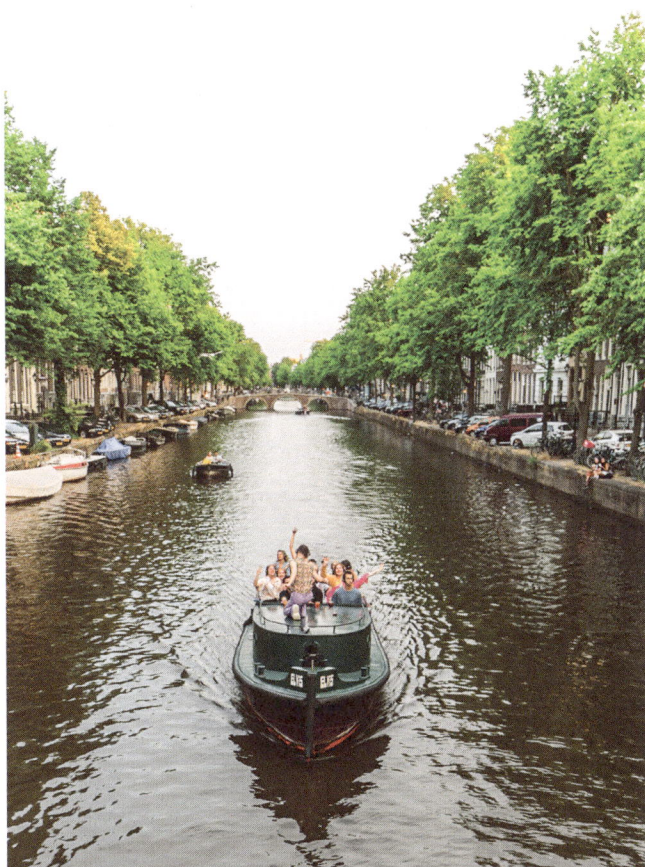
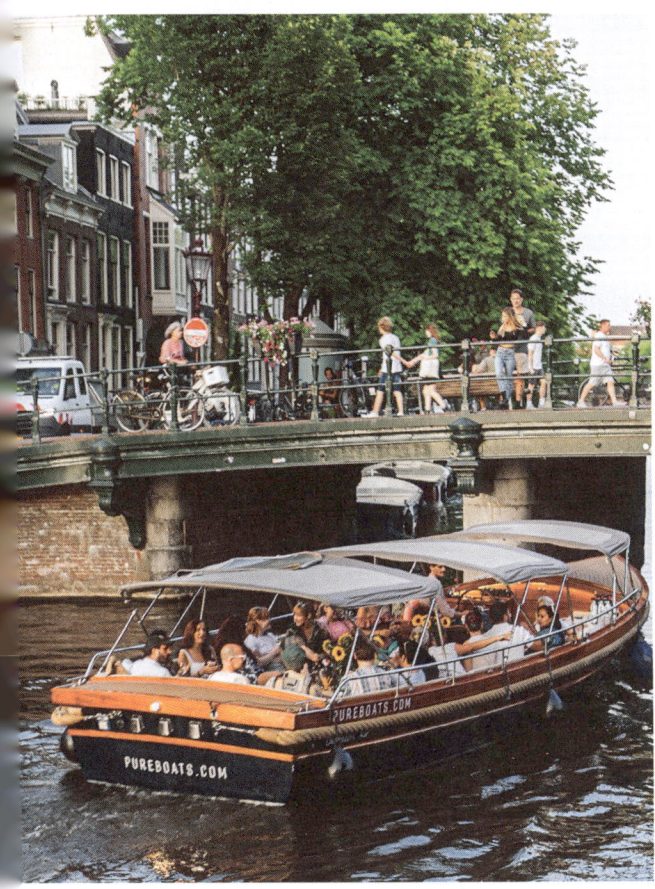
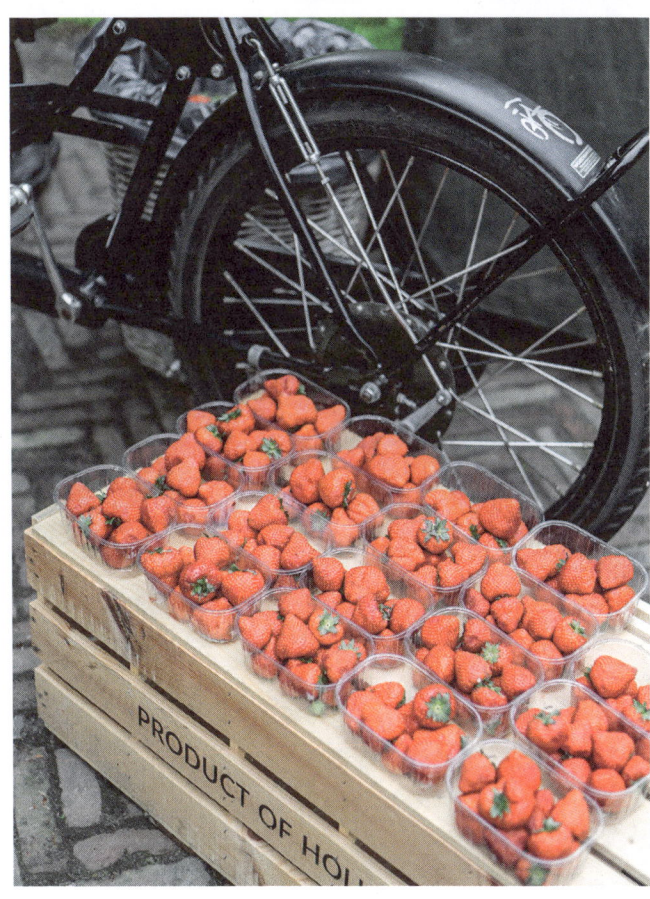

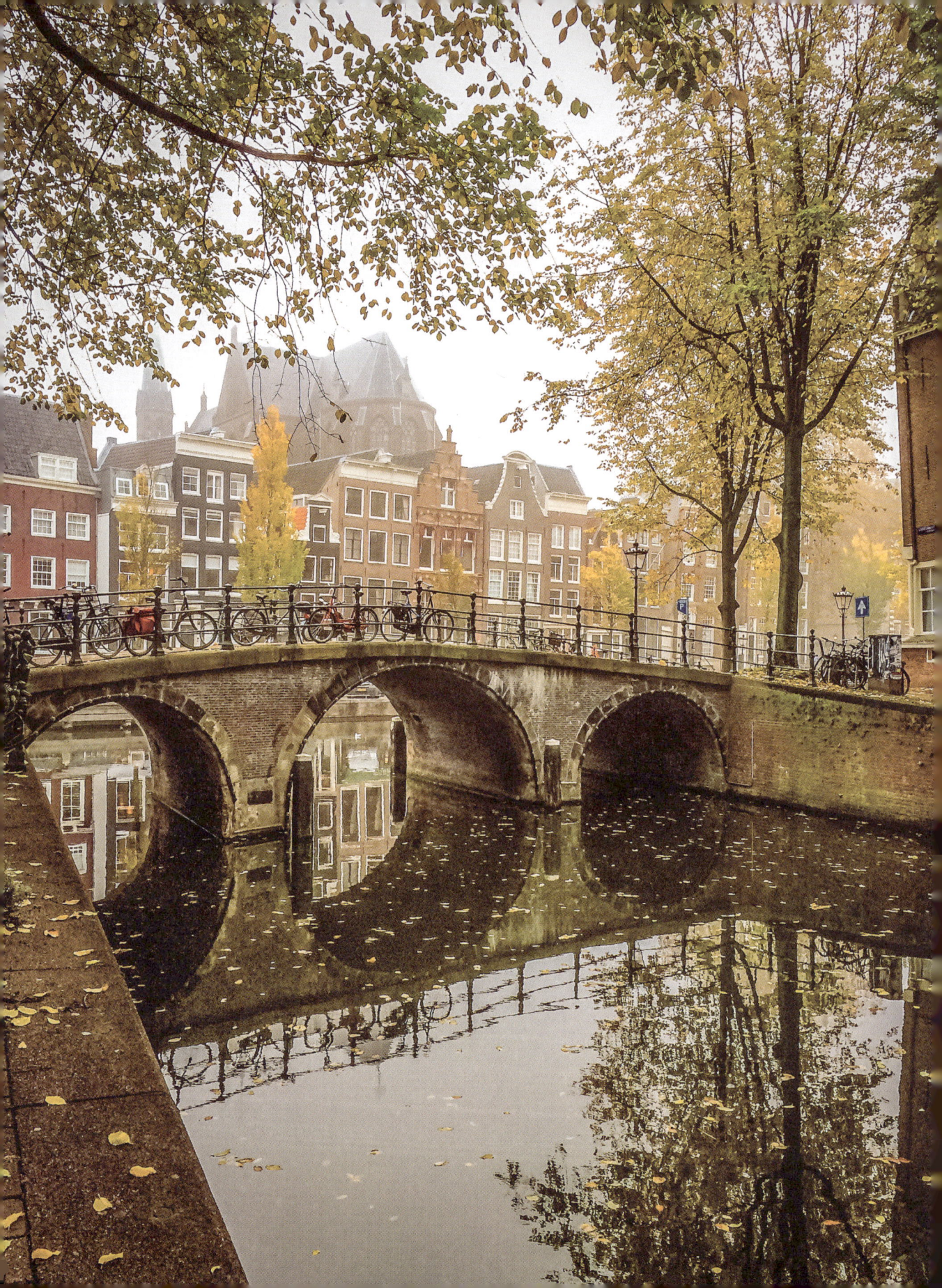

AMSTERDAM IN AUTUMN: EMBRACING THE SEASONAL SPLENDOUR

As the vibrant hues of summer gradually fade, Amsterdam undergoes another stunning transformation, welcoming the enchanting season of autumn. The Dutch capital, renowned for its picturesque canals, historic architecture and cultural richness, takes on a new allure as the autumn foliage adorns its streets and parks. From the iconic Vondelpark to the charming Jordaan district, Amsterdam becomes a tapestry of golden, amber and crimson tones, offering a captivating experience for locals and visitors alike.

EMBRACING NATURE'S PALETTE

In autumn, Amsterdam beckons nature enthusiasts and leisure seekers to revel in the city's natural splendour. The city's parks, such as the sprawling Vondelpark and the serene Sarphatipark, become veritable havens of tranquillity and scenic beauty. The lush greenery gives way to a kaleidoscope of autumnal colours, creating a picturesque setting for strolls, picnics and outdoor activities. The gentle rustle of fallen leaves underfoot and the crispness of the air evoke a sense of nostalgia and warmth, making it an ideal time to immerse oneself in the city's natural charm.

CULTURAL DELIGHTS AMIDST AUTUMN FESTIVITIES

Beyond its natural allure, Amsterdam in autumn offers a rich tapestry of cultural experiences and seasonal festivities. The city's renowned museums, including the Van Gogh Museum and Rijksmuseum, provide an immersive journey through art and history, offering respite from the occasional drizzle that characterises the season. Additionally, autumn heralds the arrival of cultural events such as the Amsterdam Dance Event (ADE) in October, where electronic music enthusiasts converge for a week-long celebration of creativity and innovation.

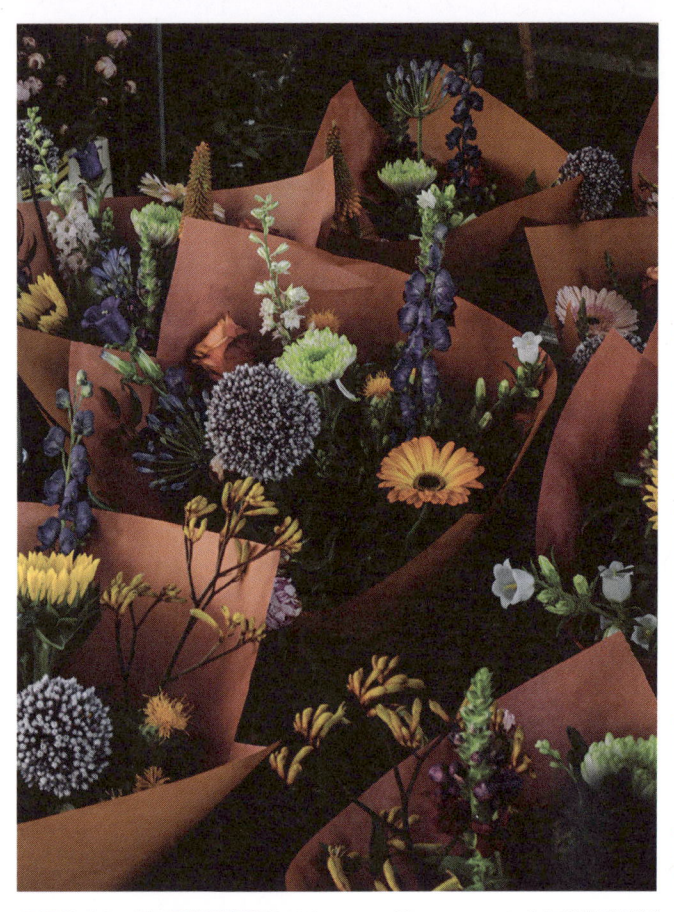
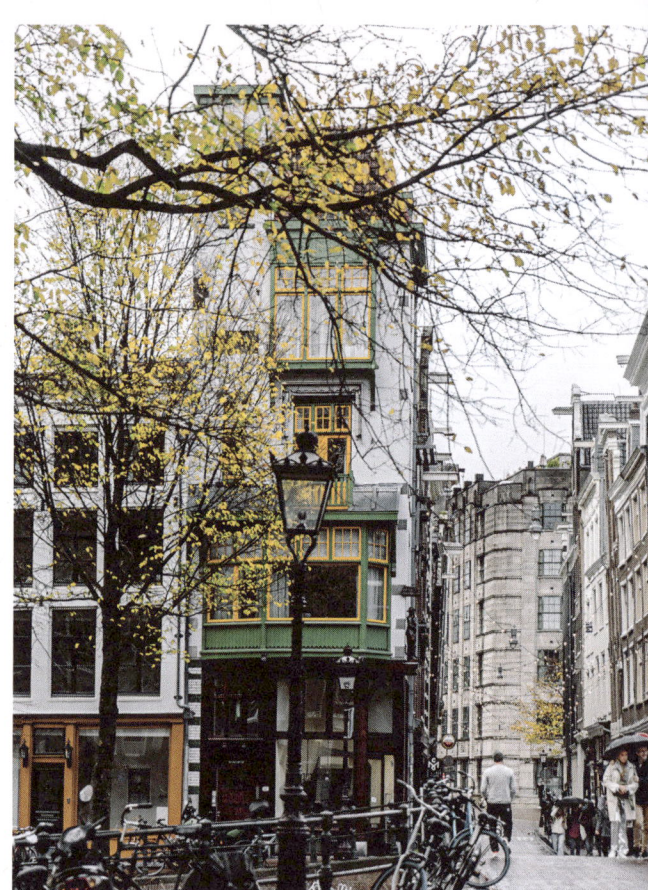
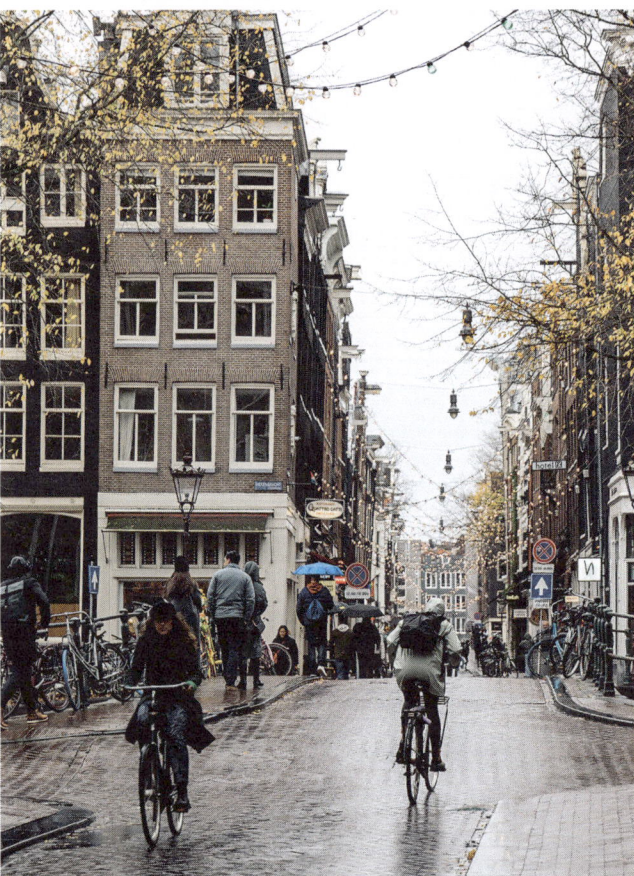
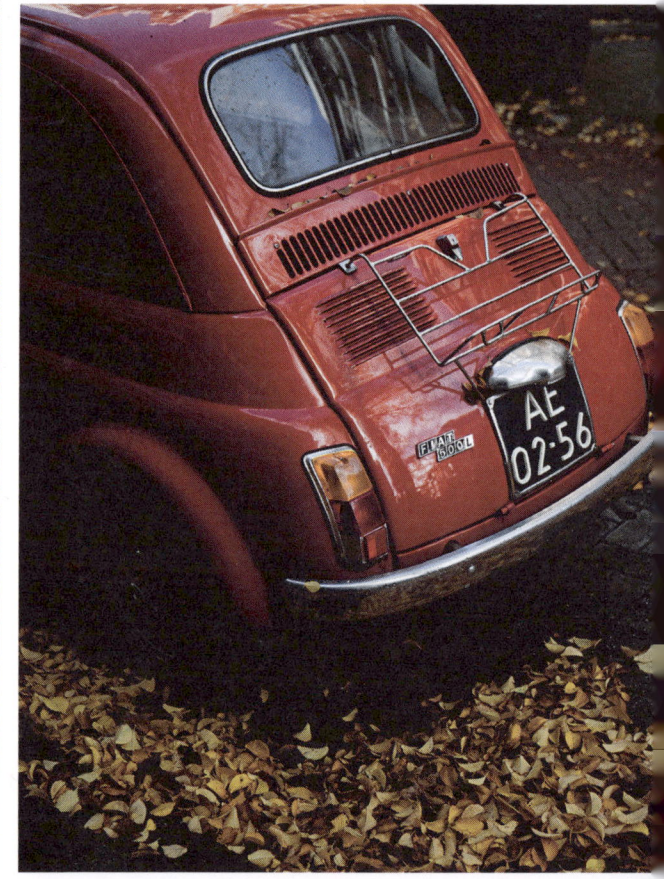

CULINARY EXPLORATION AND COSY RETREATS

Autumn in Amsterdam also presents an opportunity to indulge in culinary delights that reflect the season's bounty. Cosy cafes and restaurants across the city embrace the harvest season by offering delectable dishes featuring locally sourced ingredients. From hearty stews and freshly baked apple pies to aromatic pumpkin soups, Amsterdam's culinary scene comes alive with flavours that capture the essence of autumn. Furthermore, as the temperatures dip, the city's charming cafes and canal-side eateries provide inviting retreats where one can savour a steaming cup of Dutch hot chocolate or unwind with a glass of mulled wine.

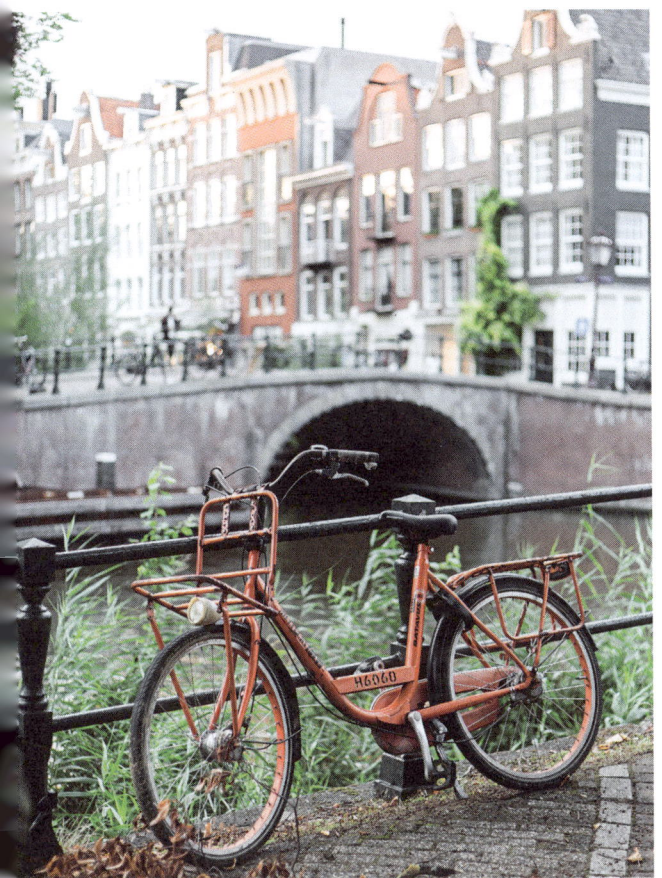
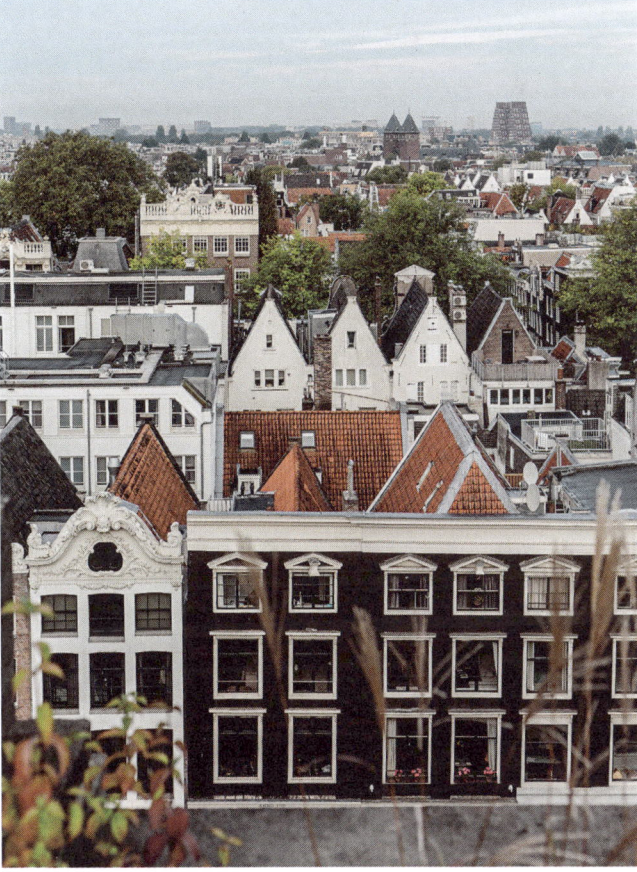

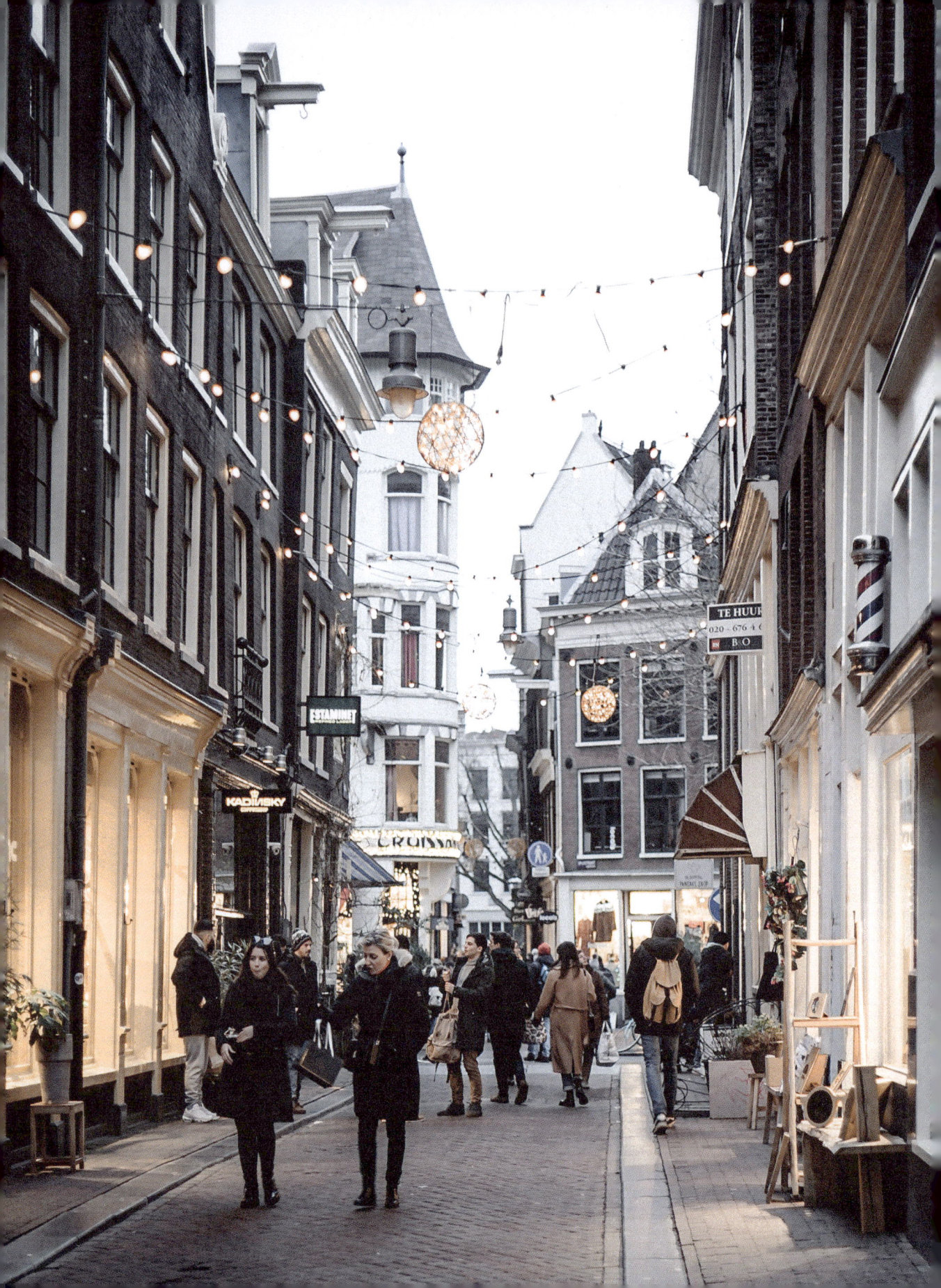

AMSTERDAM IN WINTER: A CHARMING ESCAPE

While it is often associated with springtime tulips and summer festivals, the city holds a unique charm during winter. From enchanting light displays to cosy cafes and seasonal festivities, Amsterdam offers a delightful escape for visitors seeking a winter wonderland experience.

WINTER ILLUMINATIONS AND FESTIVE MARKETS

As the winter season descends upon Amsterdam, the city transforms into a mesmerising spectacle of light and colour. The annual Amsterdam Light Festival illuminates the iconic canals and streets with captivating art installations and light sculptures, creating a magical ambience for evening strolls. Additionally, festive markets such as the Winter Parade and Christmas markets at Leidseplein and Museumplein offer an array of seasonal treats, handcrafted gifts and traditional Dutch delicacies, inviting locals and tourists alike to immerse themselves in the holiday spirit.

COSY RETREATS AND CULINARY DELIGHTS

Amsterdam's winter charm extends to its cosy retreats and culinary offerings. The city's quaint cafes and snug brown bars provide the perfect setting to savour hot chocolate, mulled wine and hearty Dutch cuisine. Visitors can relish the warmth of inviting interiors while indulging in stroopwafels, poffertjes and oliebollen – traditional Dutch delights that are particularly cherished during winter. Furthermore, Amsterdam's diverse culinary scene comes alive with seasonal menus featuring comforting dishes that showcase the rich flavours of the winter harvest.

CULTURAL EXPERIENCES AND INDOOR ATTRACTIONS

While outdoor activities abound in Amsterdam during winter, the city also boasts an array of indoor attractions that offer enriching cultural experiences. From world-class museums such as the Rijksmuseum and the Van Gogh Museum to immersive art exhibitions and theatrical performances, visitors can delve into the city's artistic heritage while seeking refuge from the brisk winter air. Additionally, music concerts, ballet performances and opera productions at renowned venues like the Royal Concertgebouw provide captivating entertainment options for those seeking to embrace Amsterdam's cultural tapestry.

WINTER WONDERLAND DAY TRIPS

Beyond the city limits, Amsterdam's surrounding countryside is a winter wonderland waiting to be explored. Charming towns such as Haarlem and Utrecht offer enchanting settings for leisurely day trips, where visitors can wander through cobblestone streets adorned with festive decorations and partake in seasonal events.

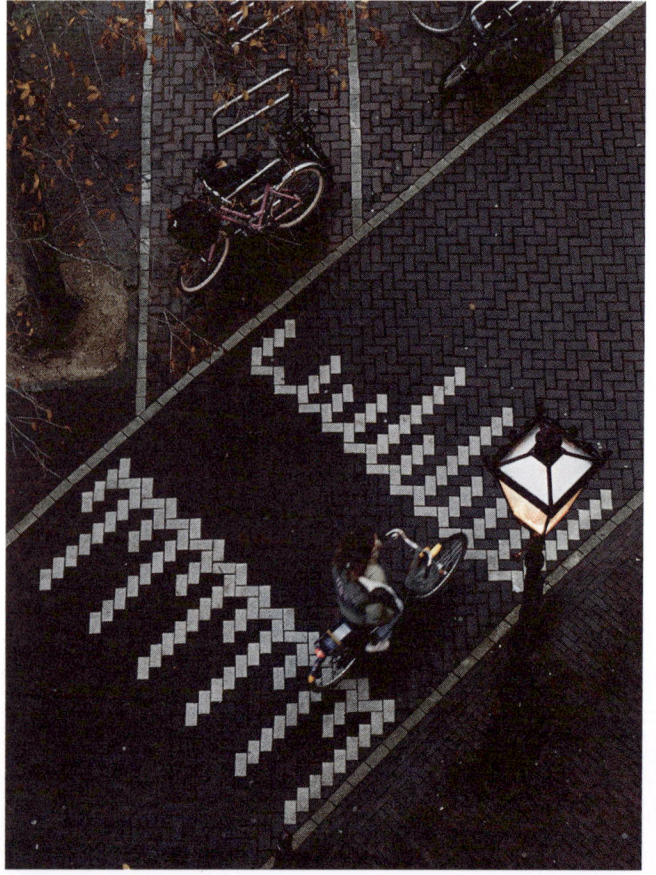
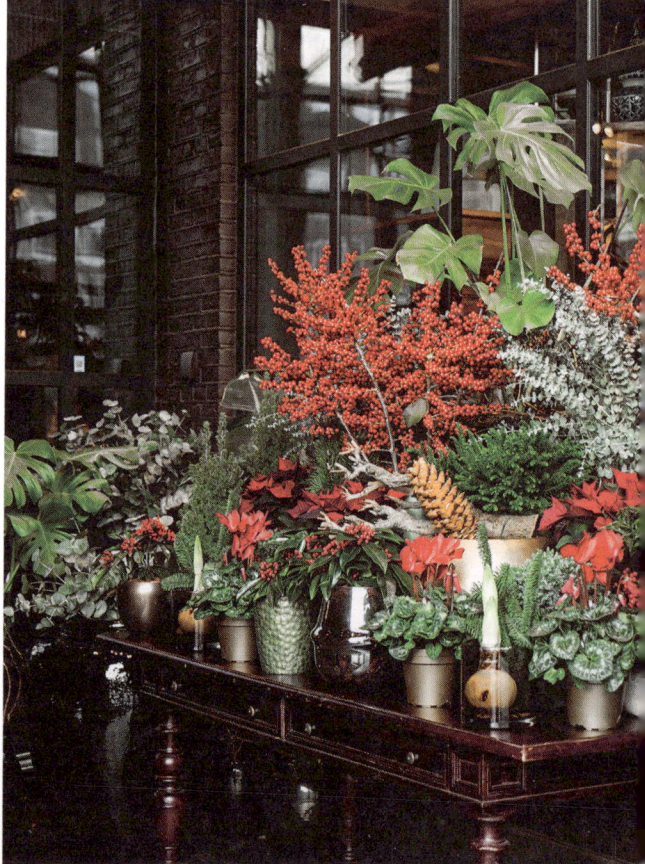

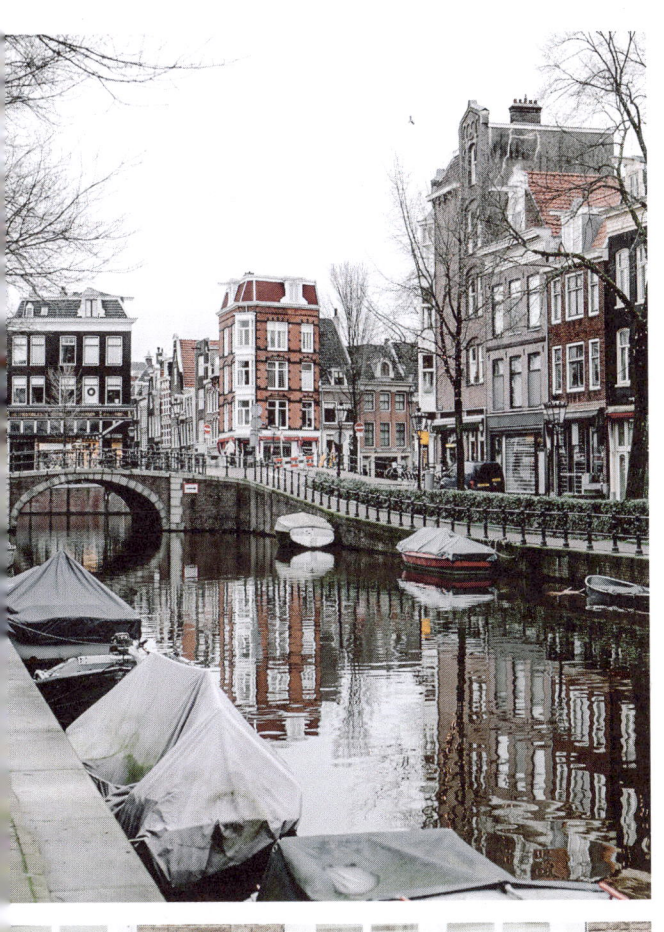
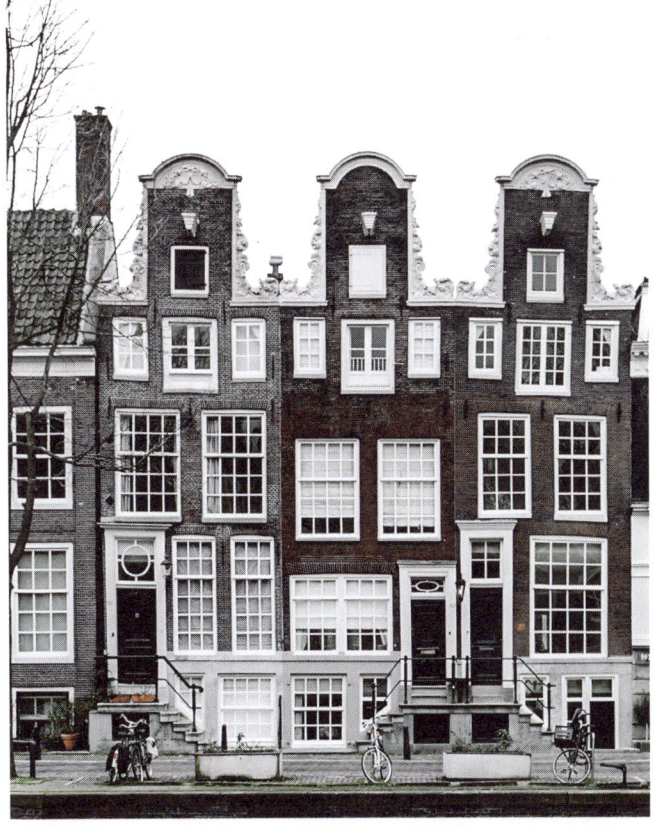
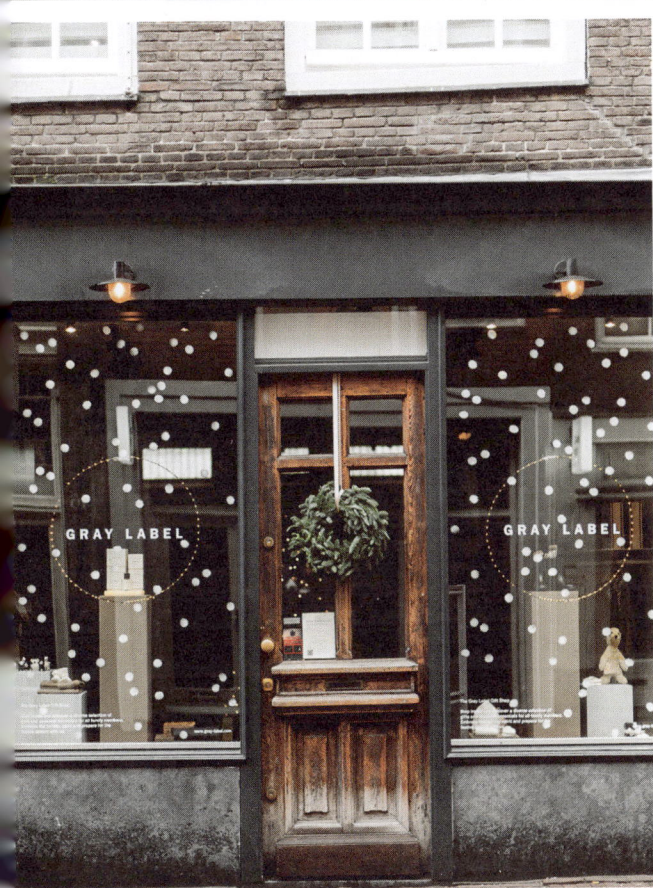
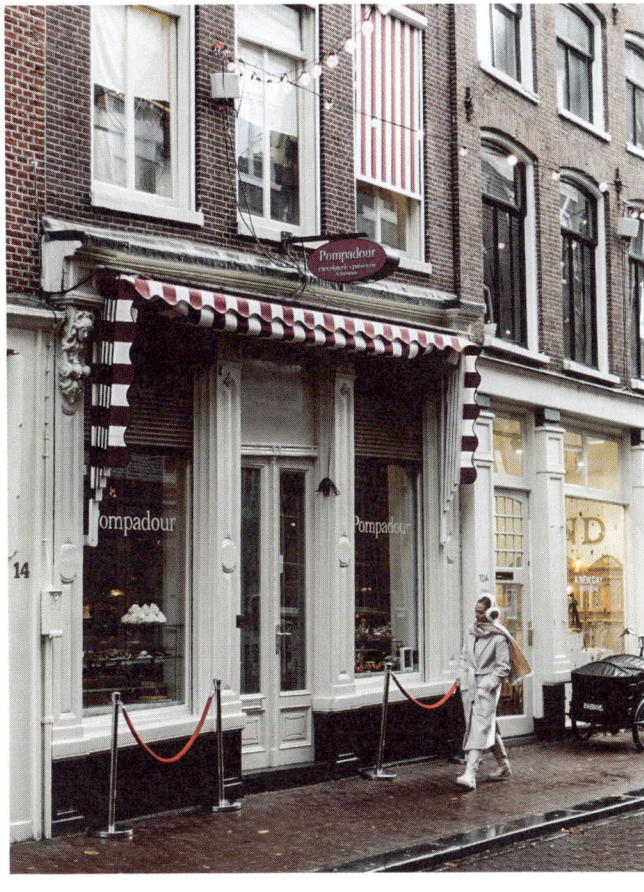

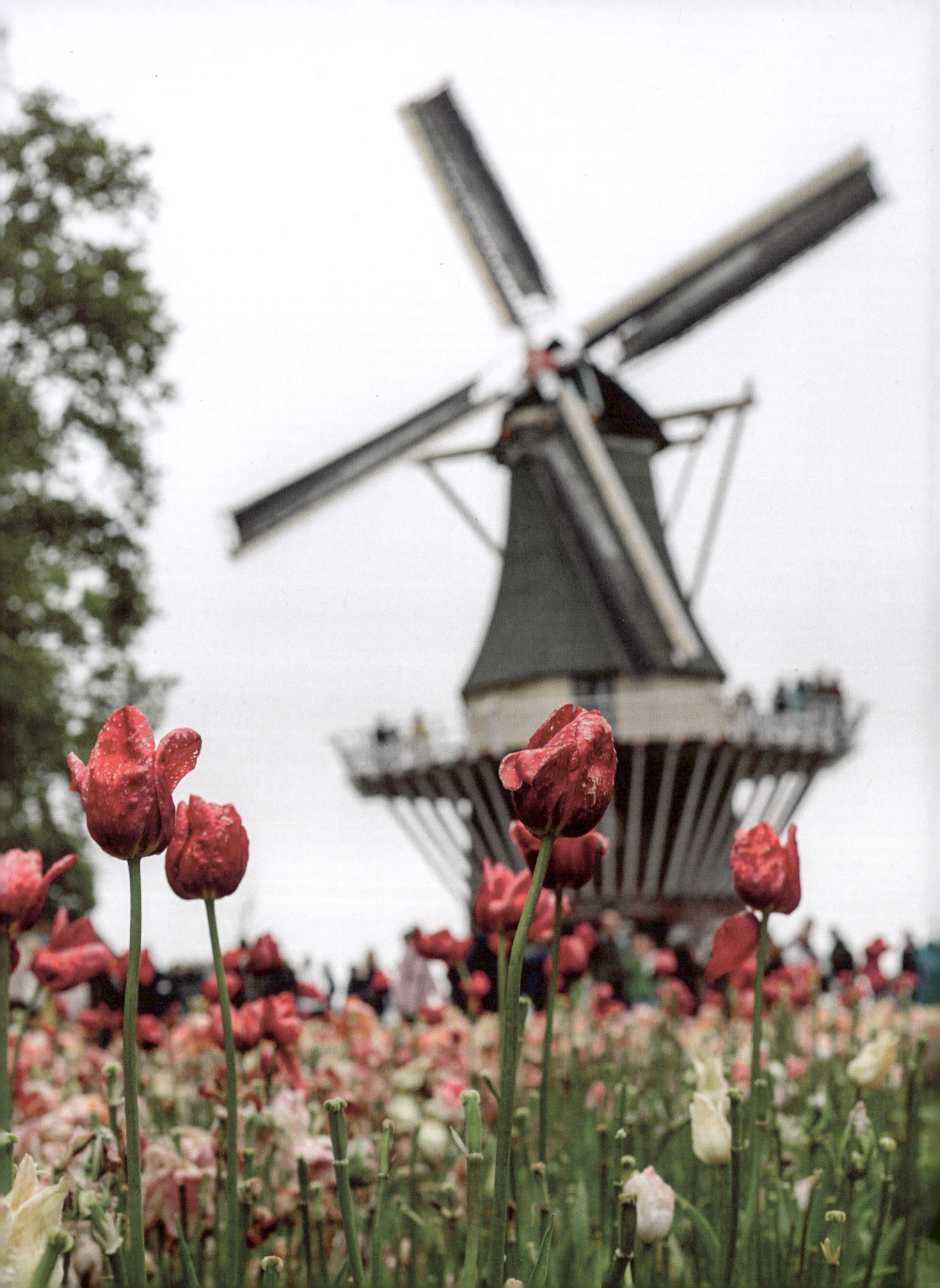

PART V

BUCKET LIST OF THINGS TO DO IN PRETTY CITY AMSTERDAM

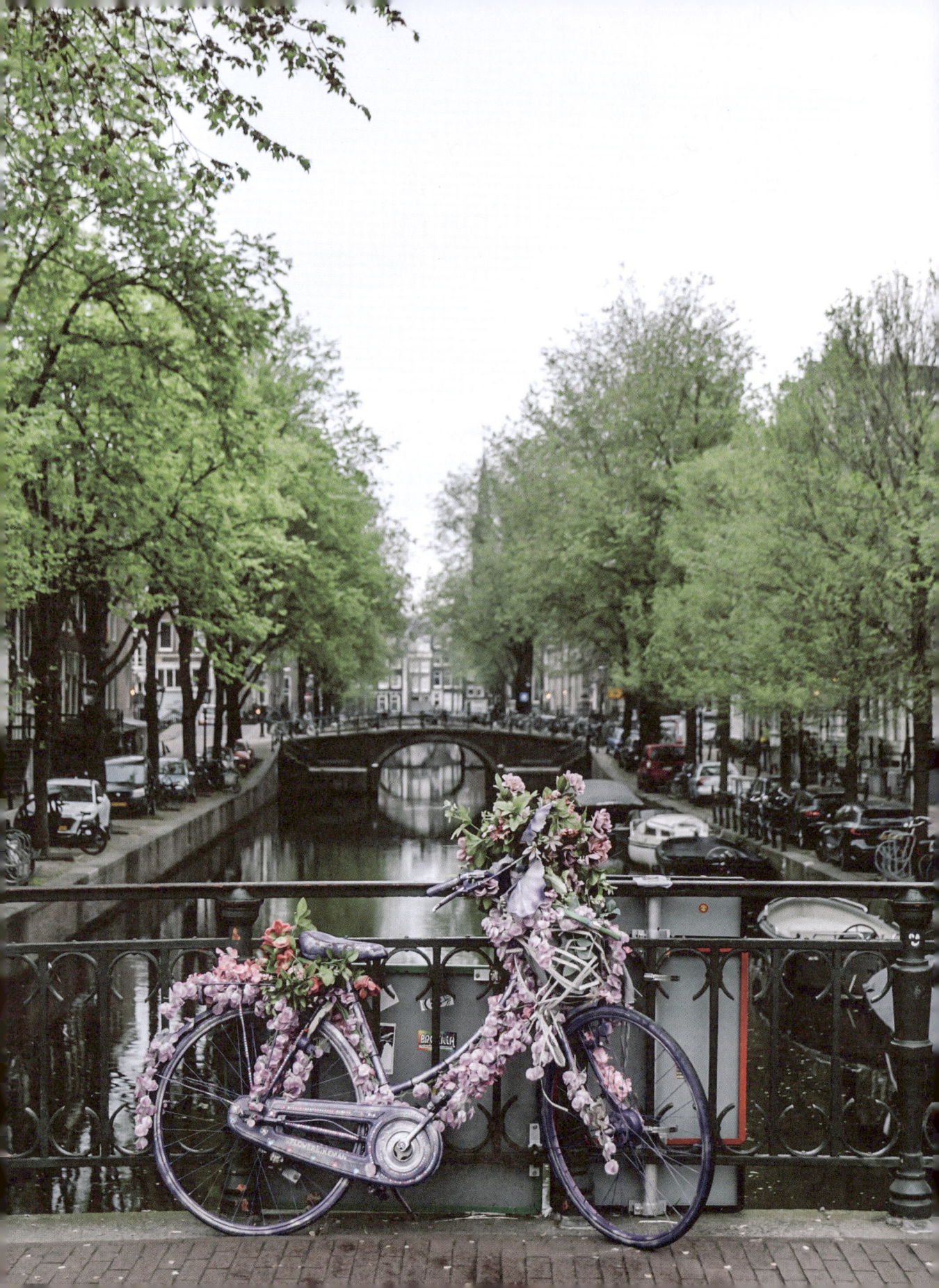

Amsterdam offers a plethora of experiences for travellers. From its picturesque canals and historic architecture to its rich cultural heritage and eclectic culinary scene, Amsterdam is a city that captivates the hearts of visitors worldwide. Whether you're a history buff, an art enthusiast, a foodie, or simply someone seeking adventure, Amsterdam has something for everyone. Here's a curated bucket list of must-see attractions and activities to make the most of your visit to this enchanting city.

CRUISE ALONG THE ICONIC CANALS (GRACHTENGORDEL)

One of the quintessential Amsterdam experiences is taking a leisurely cruise along its iconic canals. Cruising these waterways offers a unique perspective of the city's elegant gabled houses, charming bridges and bustling waterfronts. Whether you opt for a guided tour or rent a pedal boat to navigate the canals at your own pace, exploring Amsterdam from the water is an absolute must-do.

WALK ALONG THE ICONIC CANALS (GRACHTENGORDEL)

Follow my guided walks in the chapters that cover the canal belt to uncover the best of the area. Every canal in Amsterdam has its very own unique charm but Prinsengracht left its mark on me. On one of my trips I spent a whole afternoon walking the entire Prinsengracht (the outermost stretch of the Grachtengordel), which spans 3 miles, intersects with three bridges and offers a lovely way to get your bearings. I started at Reguliersgracht and ended with an apple pie and whipped cream at *Café 't Papeneiland*. This doesn't sound like far, but it took a while to complete, given my tendency to stop to chat to the locals, mooch in so many of the lovely shops along the way and, of course, stop to take the odd photo or two.

MUSEUMS

Immerse yourself in art and history at one of the many museums (note that tickets must be bought in advance). The best-known museums in Amsterdam – the *Rijksmuseum* and *Van Gogh Museum* – are definitely worth a visit, even if you have before, but bear in mind they get very busy.

Along Keizersgracht you will find the much quieter *Museum Van Loon*, a meticulously preserved seventeenth-century canal house. Here you can get a glimpse of the life of the Van Loon family, one of the founders of the Dutch East India Company.

Grachtengordel Museum: discover the history of Amsterdam and its quintessential museum located in a wonderful seventeenth-century canal house on Herengracht.

Houseboat Museum: experience first hand what it is like to live on a Amsterdam canal. Located in the Hendrika Maria, it's not open all year round, so do check the information page on their website for more details (houseboatmuseum.nl).

Het Rembrandthuis: step back in time to the seventeenth century and into the former home of Amsterdam's most famous artist, Rembrandt van Rijn.

Museum ons Lieve: visit the second-oldest museum in Amsterdam (Rijksmuseum is the oldest). The facade of a canal house in the Old City centre hides a seventeenth-century church in its attic. After the Protestant Reformation, when Catholic churches were banned, this church came into being and was used for over 200 years.

THE FOOD SCENE

Amsterdam's food scene is a delightful fusion of traditional flavours and innovative culinary concepts. Experience the city's vibrant food markets, such as *Albert Cuyp Markt*, *Noordermarkt*, *Ten Katemarkt* or *De Foodhallen*, and savour its gastronomic offerings. Here you can sample various Dutch treats, from stroopwafels and herring to artisanal cheeses and bitterballen. The lively atmosphere and diverse food stalls make these markets a paradise for food enthusiasts. If you only have time for one, I would suggest you plan a trip to Jordaan for the Saturday market at Noordermarkt.

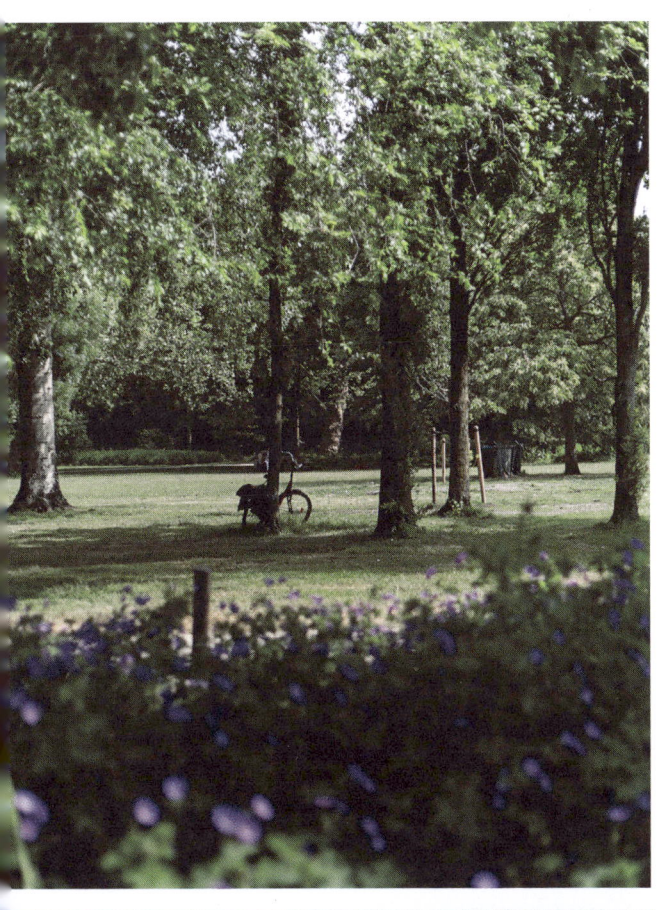
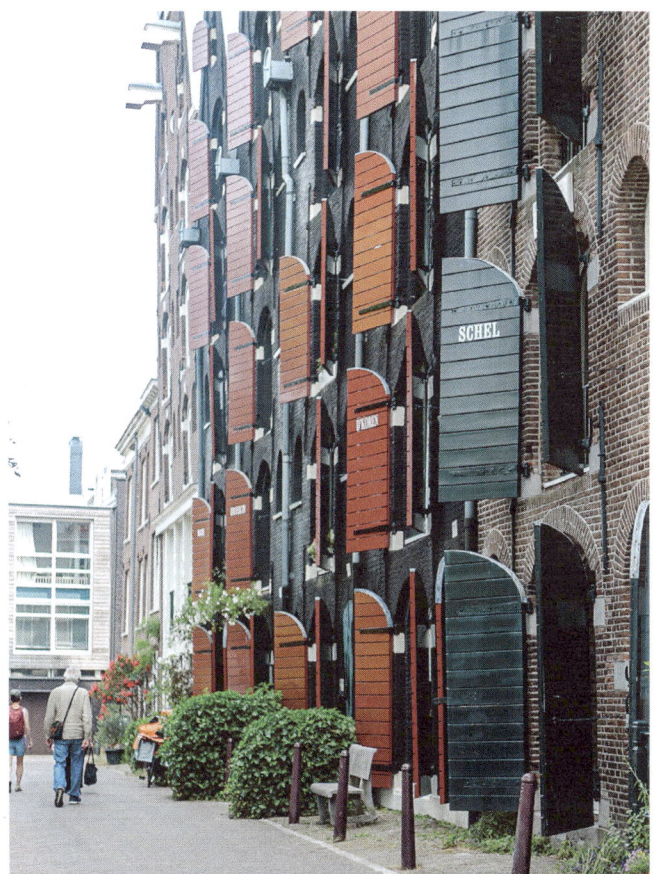
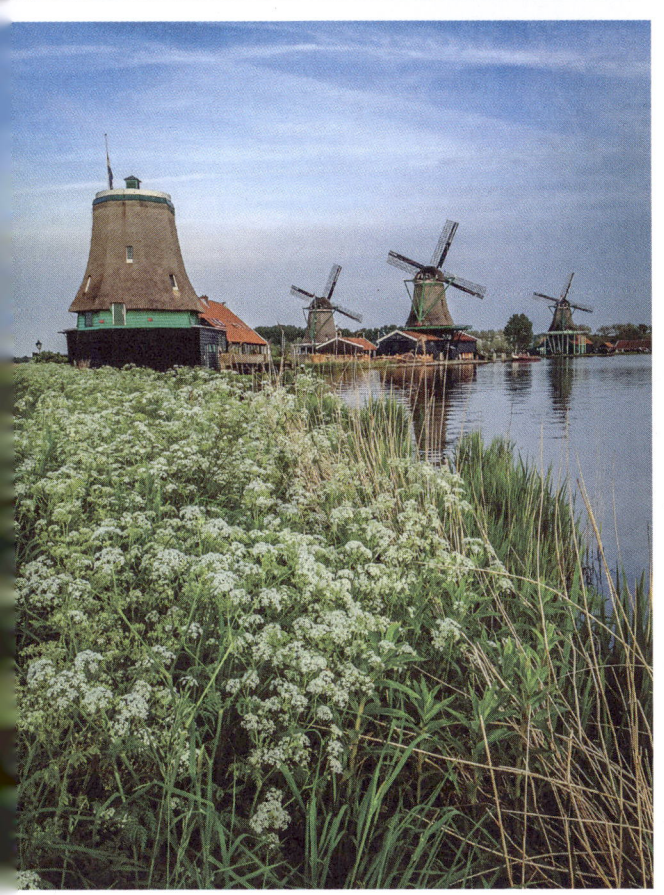
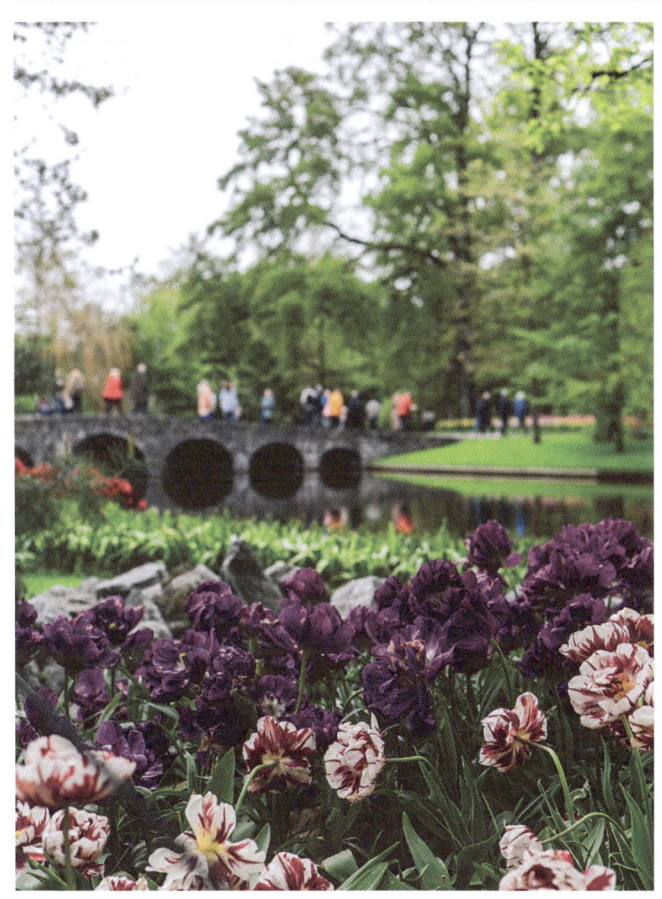

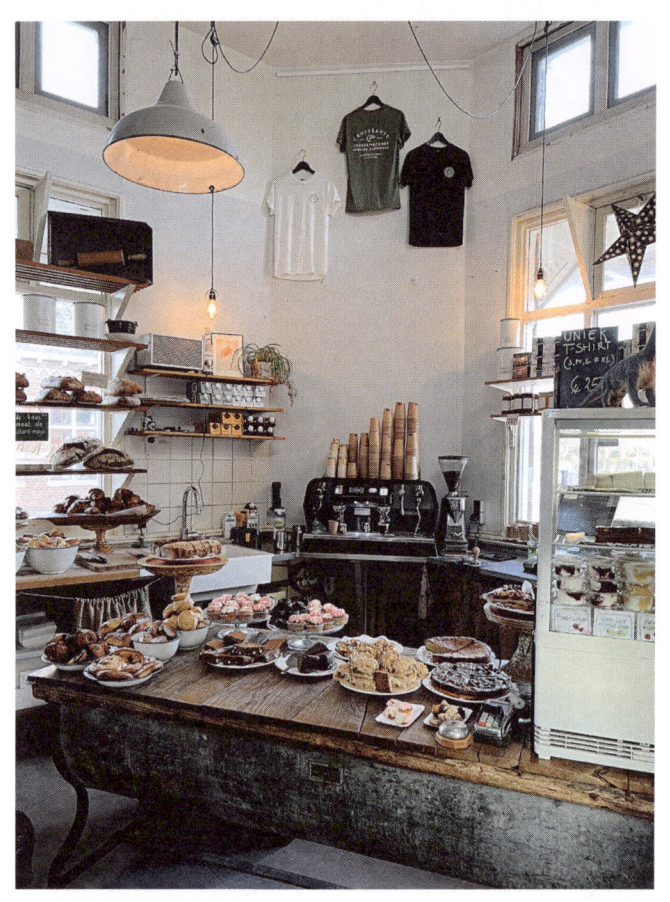
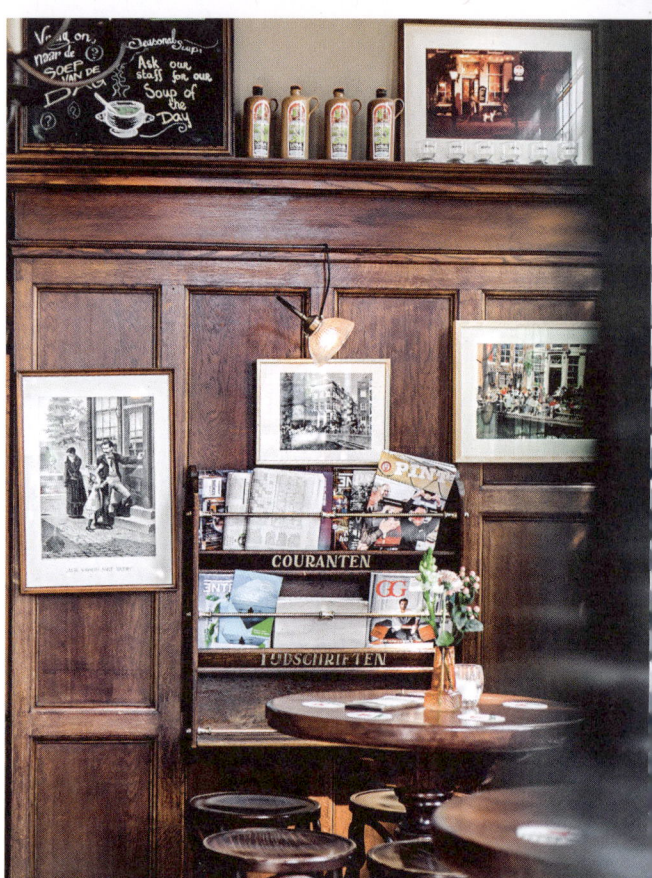
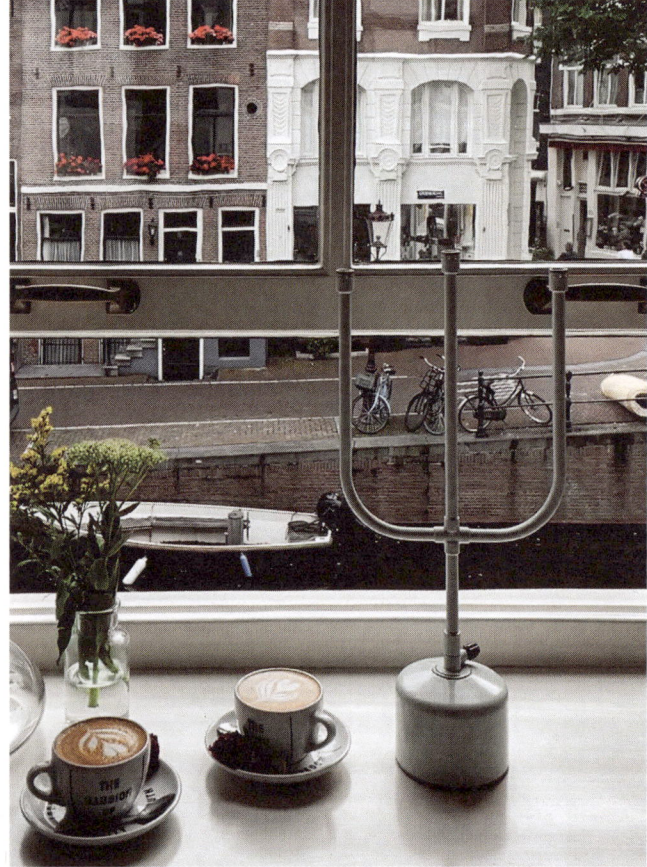
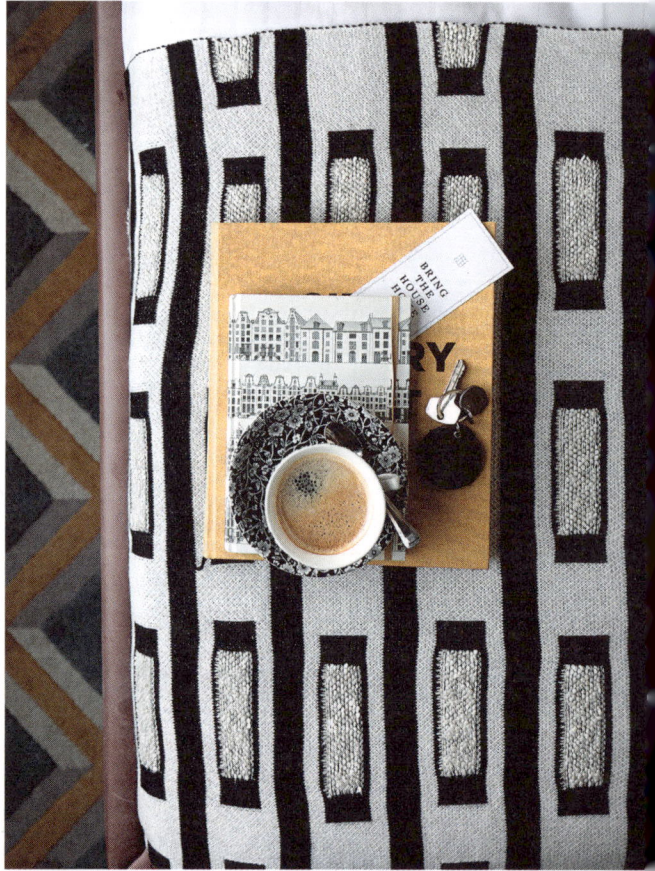

It's usually the fairy-tale canals and world-class museums that drive visitors to Amsterdam, but Morena, a content creator and brand marketing professional, advocates that a trip to the Dutch capital is worth it for the food scene alone. For her, the perfect day starts with a visit to one of Amsterdam's many artisanal bakeries. Her personal favourite is *louf* which boasts excellent sweet and savoury options, including their famous egg, Parmesan and chive Danish. Just a few minutes' walk away is *Salvo Bakehouse*, an authentic Italian bakery celebrating seasonal Italian flavours. If you're after a plant-based bakery, head to *SAINT-JEAN* whose baked goods are entirely vegan, including their famous pistachio cruffin. A ten-minute cycle or fifteen-minute tram ride will bring you to *Fort Negen* and *Ulmus*: two bakeries not to miss. While Fort Negen is famous for its seasonal cruffins, Ulmus excels at organic sourdoughs and sweet fruit Danishes. However, Morena's absolute favourite sweet treat in the city can be found at *Banketbakkerij Van der Linde*. This family-owned business has been serving the best homemade soft serve filled with fresh whipped cream since 1937.

For a leisurely brunch, head to *Staring at Jacob* for their famous chicken and waffles. *Lova* on Haarlemmerdijk is also excellent for a Latin American-inspired brunch, as is *Oficina* for a small and seasonal menu taking inspiration from around the world. For lunch or dinner, *De Kas* cannot be missed. Located in a greenhouse tucked away in the Frankendael Park in East Amsterdam, De Kas uses as much produce as possible grown from their very own gardens on site, so you know you'll always get the freshest, most seasonal ingredients.

Some of Morena's other favourite restaurants not to be missed are *Café Restaurant Metro*, *Café Binnenvisser* (and their signature celeriac and parsnip fritters), *Breda*, *Cantine de Caron* and *Cornerstore*. Celebrating small sharing plates and excellent wine lists, they all hit the perfect balance between laid-back and refined, creating dining experiences that are both relaxed and of high quality. For a truly magical culinary adventure that goes beyond the standard restaurant experience, she highly recommends *Vuurtoreneiland*, an uninhabited island north of Amsterdam accessible via a one-hour boat tour. Enjoy 360-degree views of the water, a six-course menu with the best ingredients and perfectly matched wine pairings.

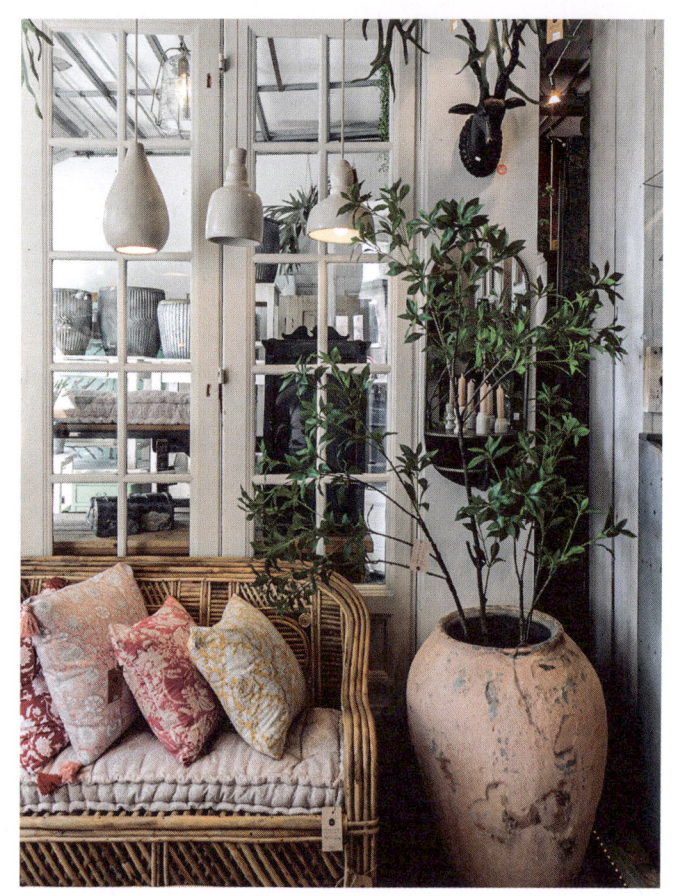
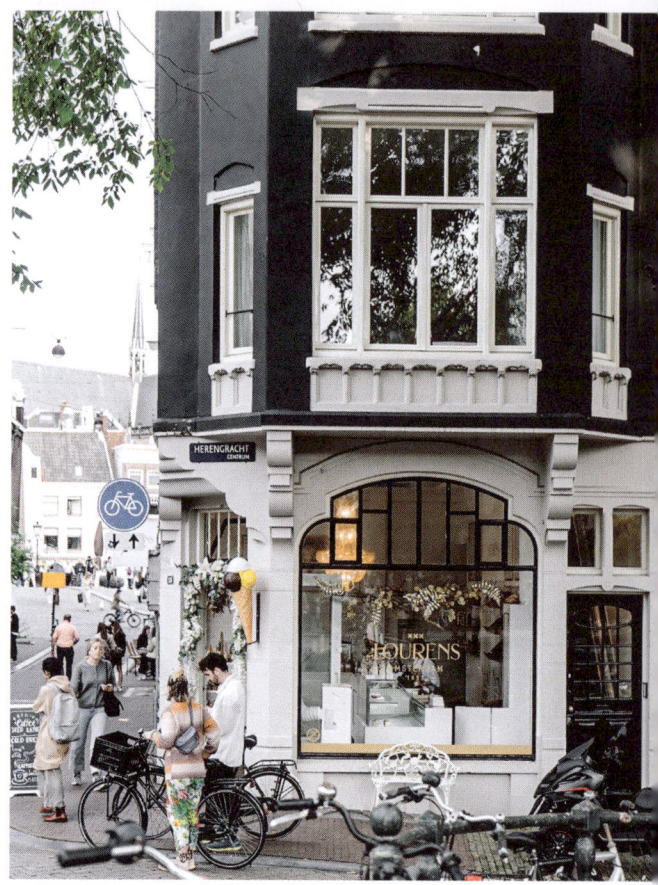
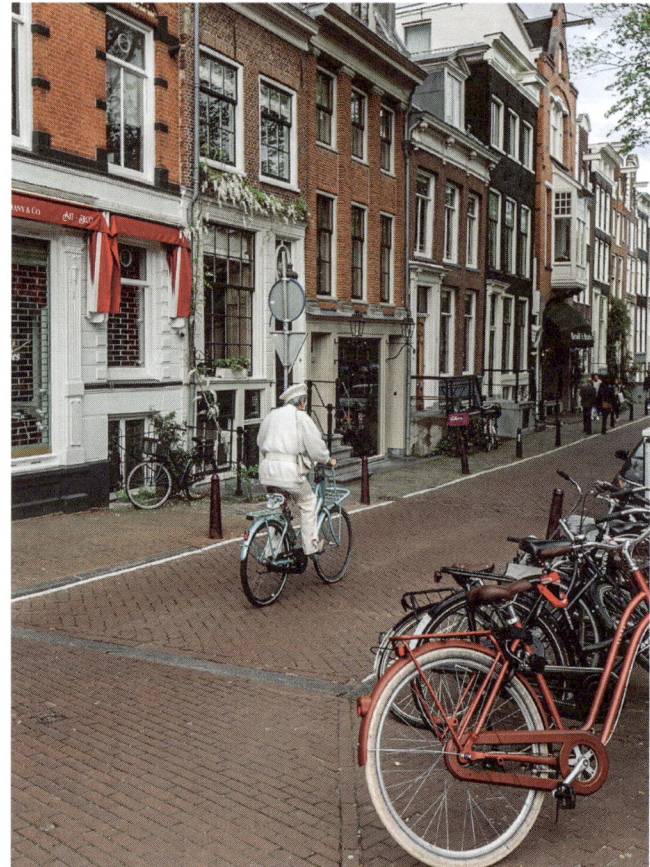
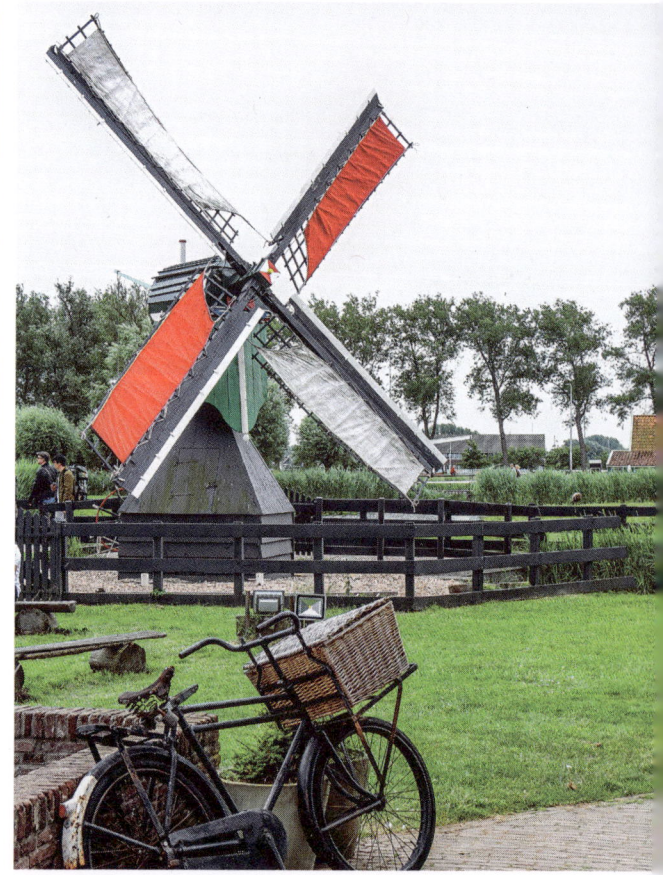

CYCLE THROUGH THE CITY LIKE A LOCAL

Amsterdam is renowned for being one of the most bike-friendly cities in the world, and cycling is ingrained in its culture. Joining the locals on two wheels is an excellent way to explore the city's charming streets and scenic parks. So rent a bicycle and pedal along the dedicated cycle paths.

For this segment I spoke with Julia Willard, a Paris-based photographer and very seasoned cyclist with strong ties to Amsterdam. Julia has over fifteen years' experience capturing the beauty of the Netherlands and she shares her beautiful photography on Instagram @FallingOffBicycles. Julia loves to explore Amsterdam by bicycle and has kindly provided an ideal itinerary for even the less experienced cyclists:

The recommended cycling route from Museumplein to Zaanse Schans by way of Vondelpark covers a distance of roughly 20km and takes just over an hour start to finish, but I recommend lingering in the park to take in all it has to offer. The route is mostly flat and therefore suitable for cyclists of all ability levels. Here is my recommended route.

From Museumplein, ride toward the centre of the Rijksmuseum, where you'll get to ride through the rib-vaulted passageway and where you can peek into the museum. You may even be able to enjoy musicians or singers taking advantage of the wonderful acoustics. When you exit the tunnel, you'll make an immediate left on to Stadhouderskade. Within a couple of blocks, you will see the beautiful gates to Vondelpark on your left. Take care to cross the street and the tram tracks with caution.

Enter Vondelpark and take your time cycling through the 47 hectares of this leafy expanse, which is home to a rose garden, open-air theatre, cafes, playgrounds, plants, trees and a wonderful network of ponds.

Take your time enjoying, and when you're ready to leave and move on to Zaanse Schans, take the exit to Kattenlaan next to the tennis courts.

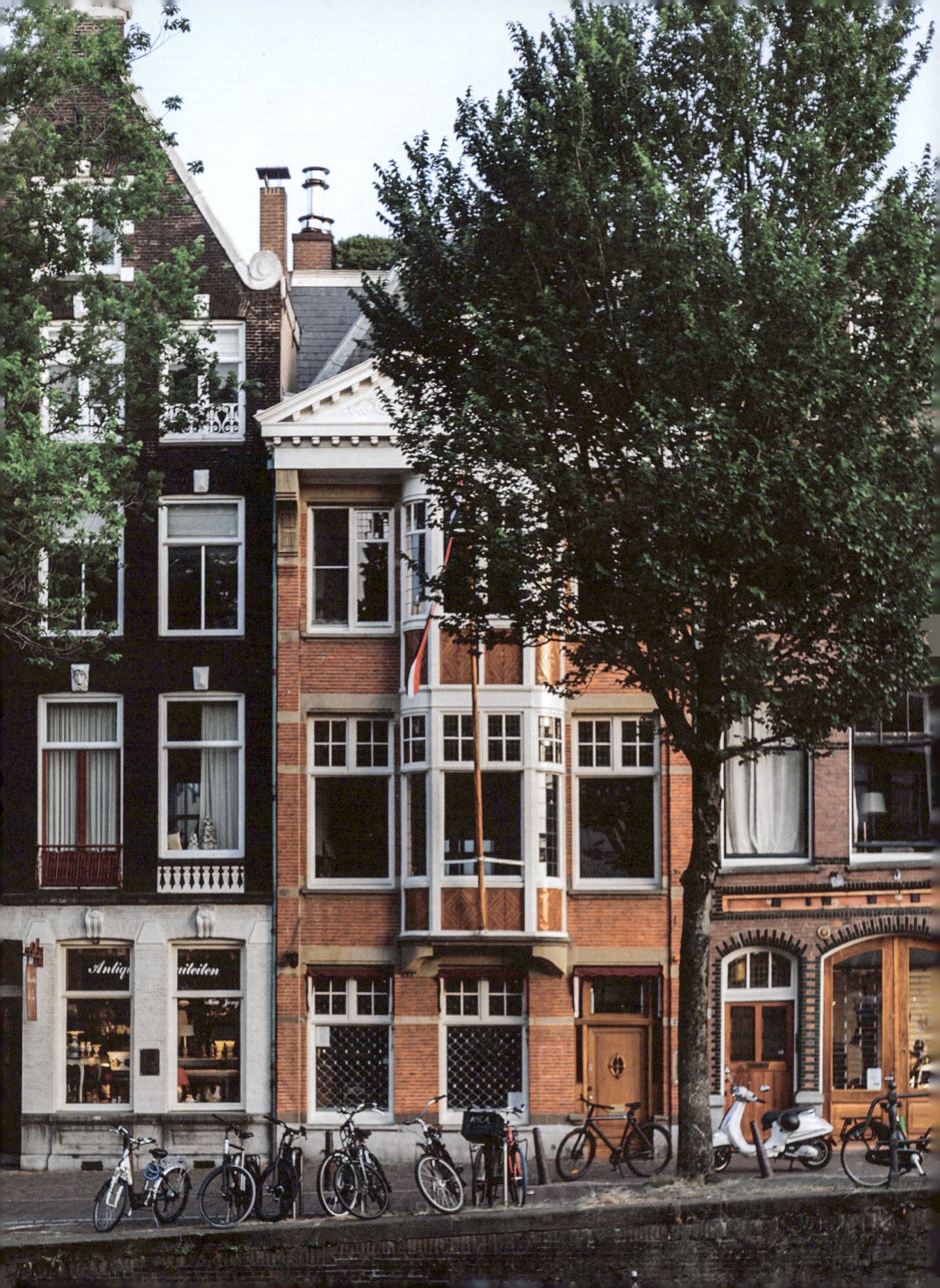

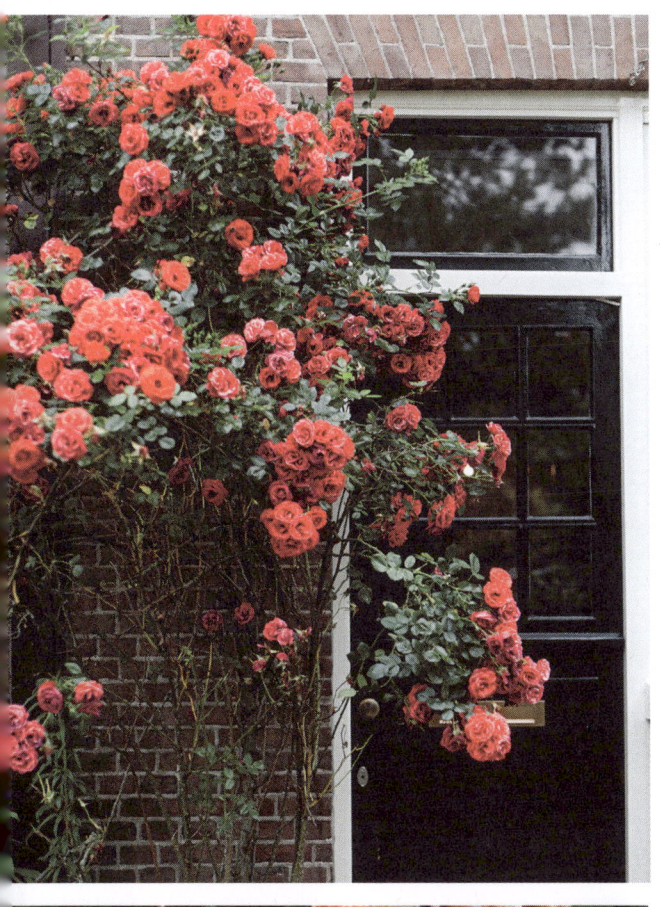
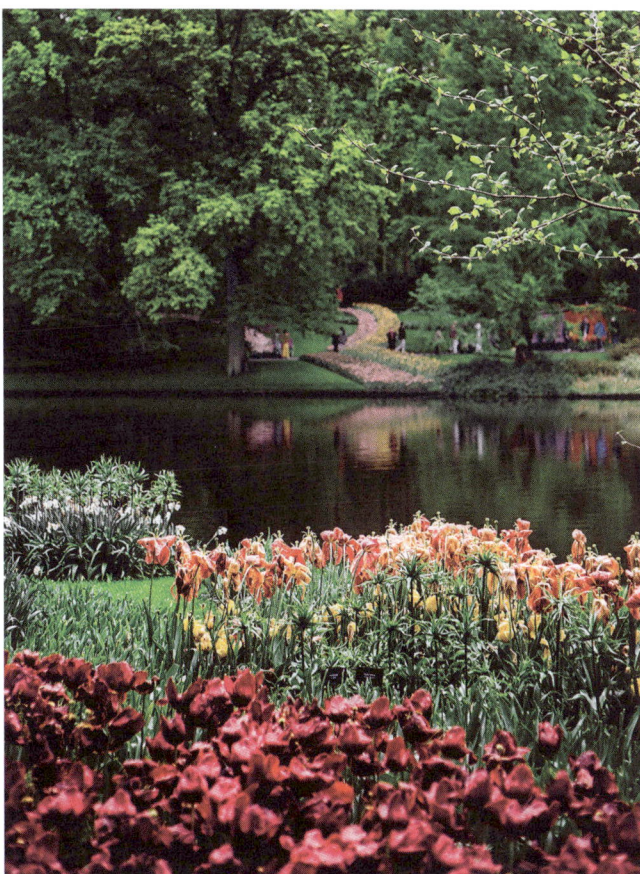
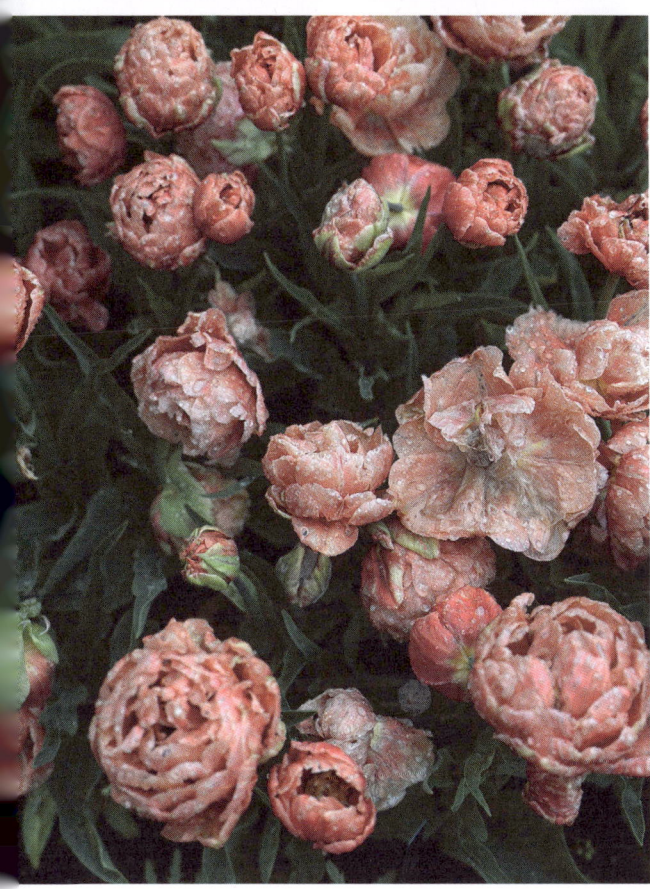
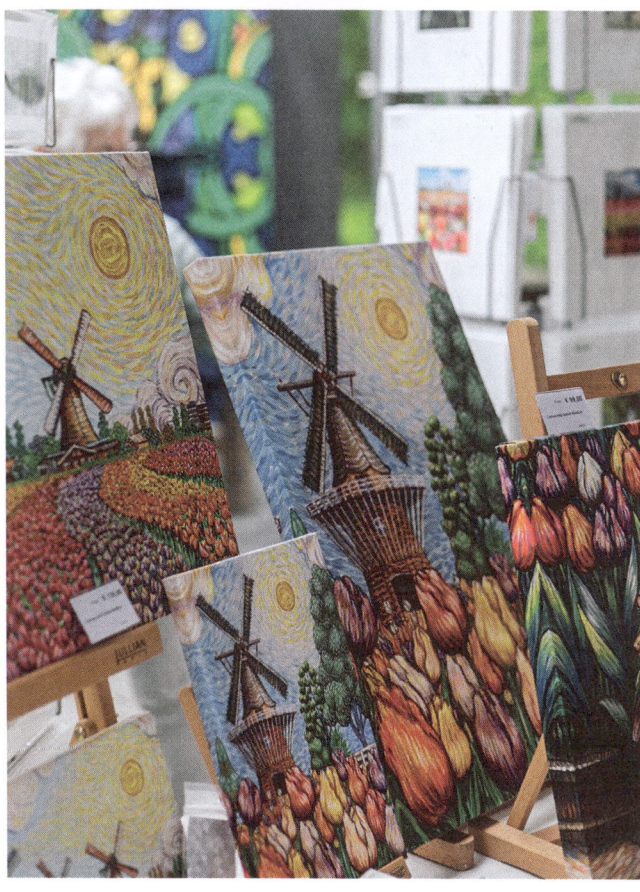

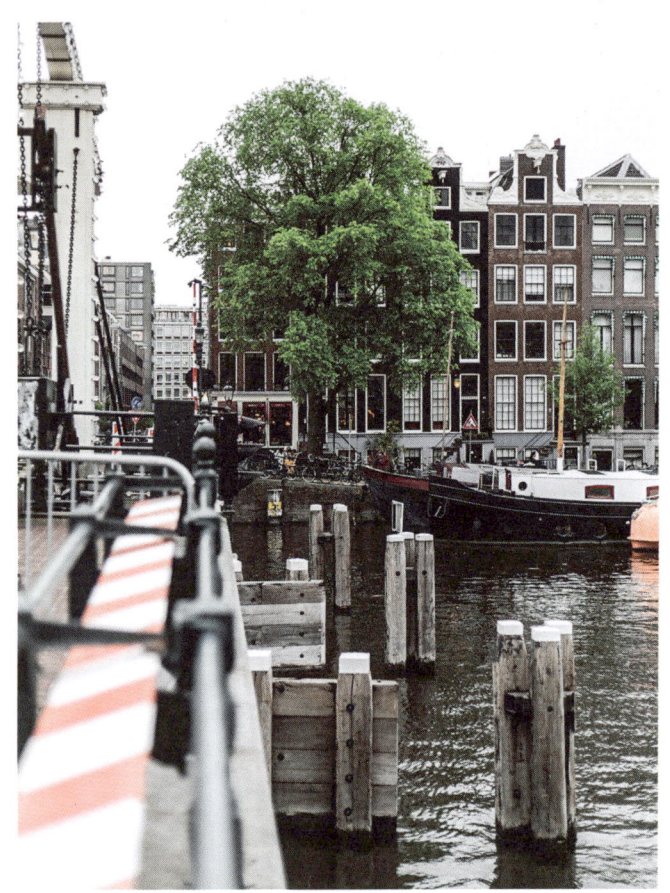
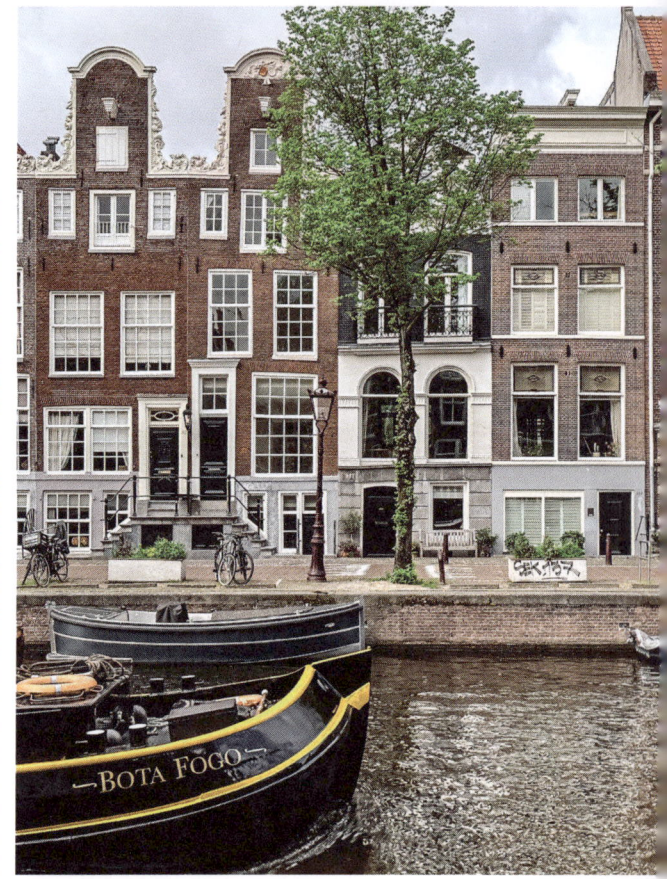
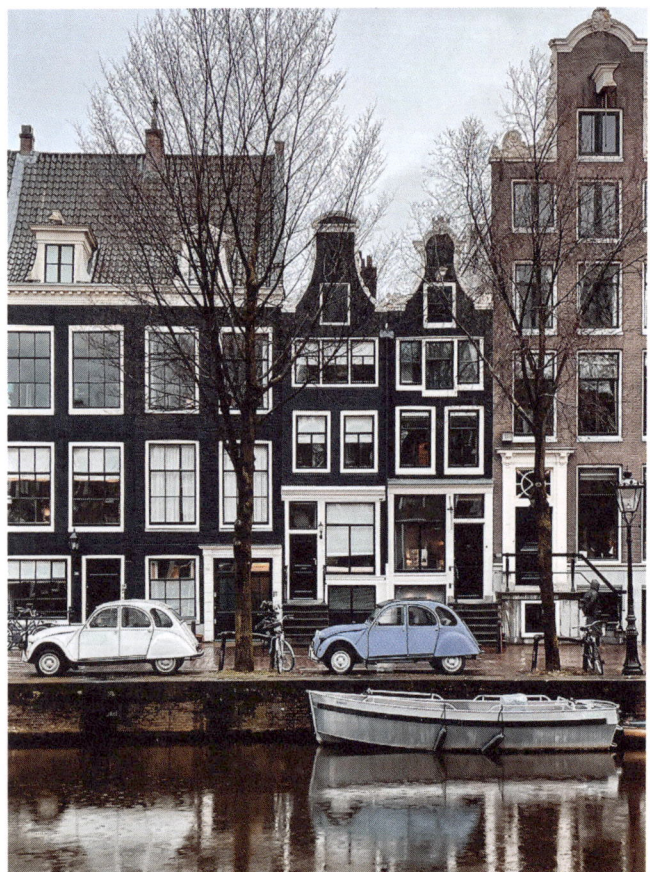
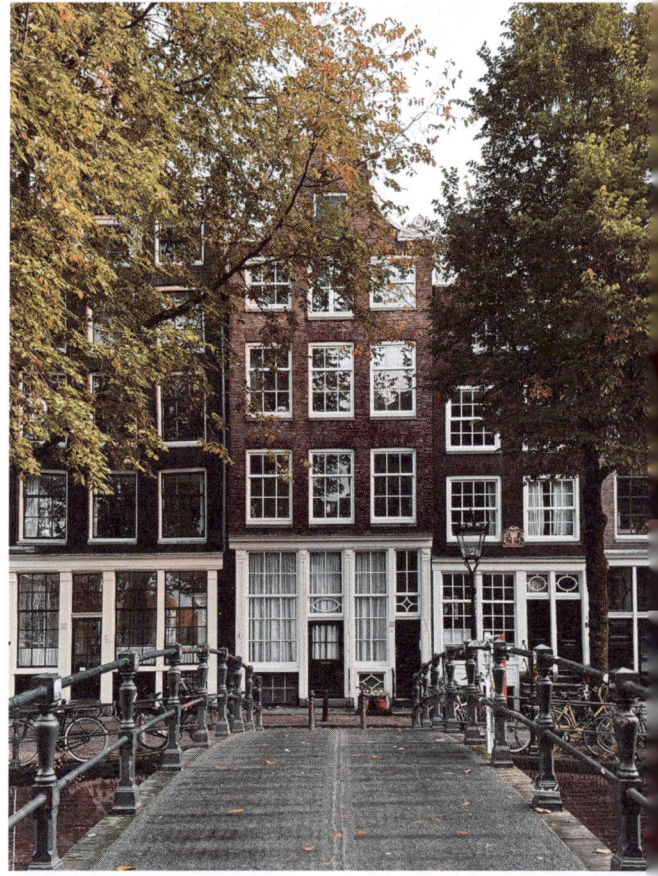

Turn right onto Overtoom and then take a quick left onto the cycle path on Jan Pieter Heijestraat. After 560m, you'll make a sharp left onto Kinkerstraat. After crossing the canal, you'll follow the fork to the right on to the Postjesweg bike path. After about 800m you'll turn right onto Jan Evertsenstraat and then meet Admiraal De Ruijterweg. Turn left then after a kilometre bear left to stay on the path at the fork. This street will become Haarlemmerweg. After 500m, turn right onto the G200 Brettenpad bike path. After about 800m, turn left on to cycleway Overbrakerpad. Remain on this path for about 650m. Turn right on to the bike path (part of the Stadhaven route).

Follow the path to make two left turns to then proceed onto Nieuwe Hemweg. After 110m, turn right. Follow the path for 380m until you arrive at the Hempont ferry dock. (Note there are restricted cycling hours here.)

When you exit the ferry, continue on Provincialeweg for 1.7km. At the end of the path, make a left on to Albert Heijnweg, then after 90m a right on to Guisweg. After crossing the Zaan (a body of water), turn left on to Kalverringdijk. Around here you'll see many signs for Zaanse Schans. As you continue to follow the path along Kalverringdijk for another couple hundred metres, you will arrive at Zaanse Schans.

The Zaanse Schans is a residential area in which the eighteenth and nineteenth centuries are brought to life. The area is perhaps best known for its historic windmills, barns, workshops and distinctive green wooden houses. The typical Dutch waterways that run through the village make for some spectacular reflection shots. Park your bike and stroll past the bakery museum, into the cheese museum or stop at the warehouse where clogs are made.

If you have time, make your way into the town of Zaandam and don't miss the Inntel Hotels Amsterdam Zaandam with the most extraordinary design. (I promise you'll want to see this!)

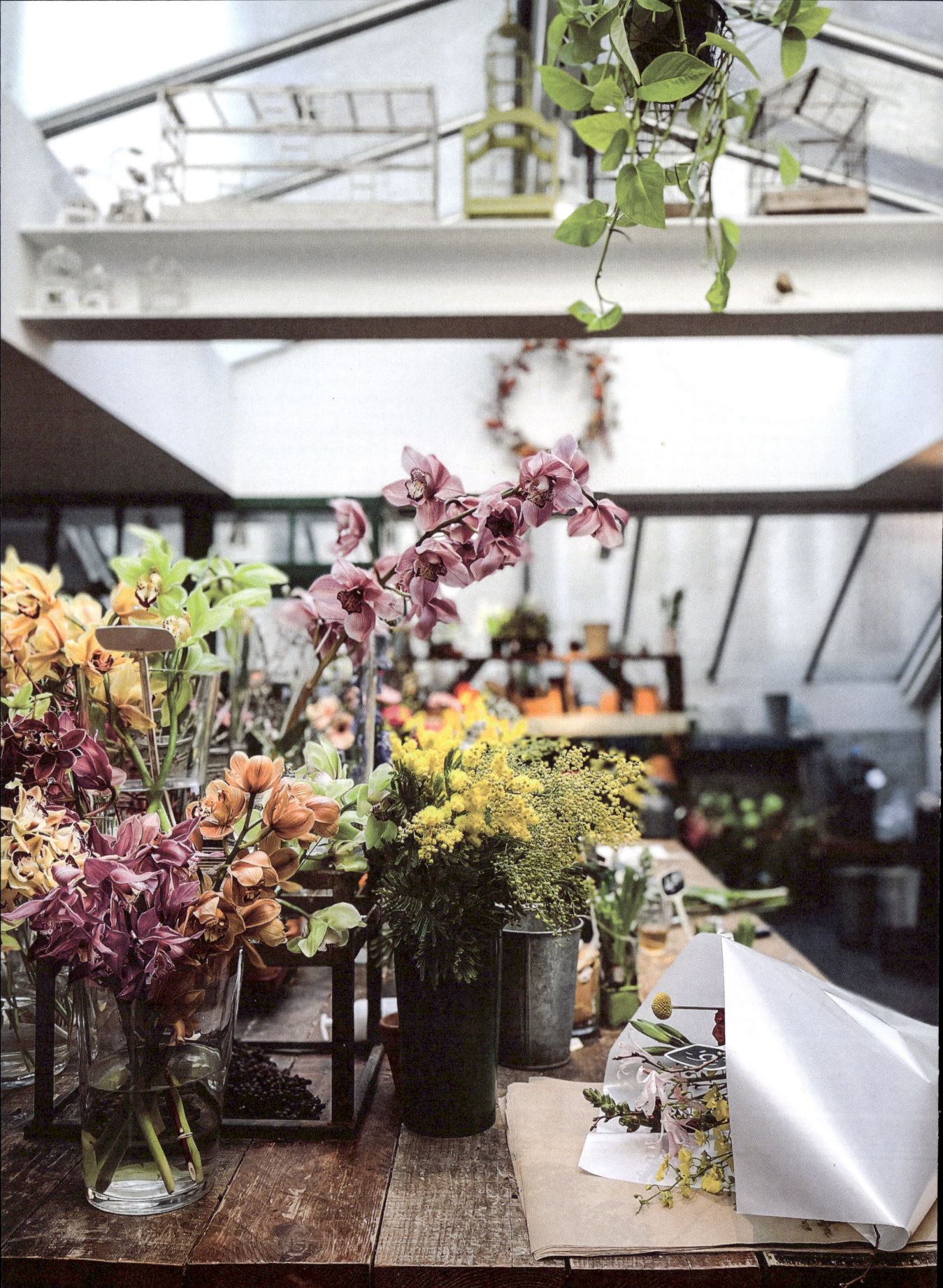

THE BEST OF AMSTERDAM

SPECIALITY SHOPS

Anna + Nina, Gerard Doustraat 94, 1072 and Herengracht 369, 1016
StoryTiles, Singel 410, 1016
De Weldaad Authentic Interior, Noordermarkt 35, 1015
De Posthumus Winkel, Sint Luciënsteeg 25, 1012
The Otherist, Leliegracht 6, 1015
Six and Sons, Haarlemmerstraat 41, 1013
LikeStationery, Prinsenstraat 24HS, 1015
COTTONCAKE, Eerste van der Helstraat 76HS, 1072
Wildernis, Bilderdijkstraat 165F, 1053
Pluk, Reestraat 19, 1016
Kramer Kunst & Antiek, Prinsengracht 807, 1017
Theewinkel Het Kleinste Huis Amsterdam, Oude Hoogstraat 22, 1012

BOOKSHOPS

Antiquariaat Brinkman, Singel 319, 1012
The Book Exchange, Kloveniersburgwal 58, 1012
The American Book Center, Spui 12, 1012
Athenaeum Boekhandel, Spui 14–16, 1012
Architectura & Natura, Leliegracht 22-H, 1015
Amsterdam Book Market, Het Spui, 1012 (Fridays)
Antiquariaat Kok, Oude Hoogstraat 18, 1012

BROWN BARS

Café 't Smalle, Egelantiersgracht 12, 1015
Café 't Papeneiland, Prinsengracht 2, 1015
Café de Pels, Huidenstraat 25, 1016
Café de Tuin, Tweede tuindwarsstraat 13, 1015
Café de Wetering, Weteringstraat 37, 1017
Café Thijssen, Brouwersgracht 107, 1015

CAFES

Back to Black, Weteringstraat 48, 1017
Bocca Coffee, Kerkstraat 96H, 1017
SAINT-JEAN, Lindengracht 158h, 1015
Rum Baba, Elandsgracht 134, 1016
Luuk's Coffee, Westerstraat 3, 1015
Winkel 43, Noordermarkt 43, 1015

RESTAURANTS

Jansz., Reestraat 8, 1016
Restaurant de Belhamel, Brouwersgracht 60, 1013
Gertrude, Bosboom Toussaintstraat 28-H, 1054
Oeuf, Daniël Stalpertstraat 36, 1072
Buffet van Odette, Prinsengracht 598, 1017
Balthazar's Keuken, Elandsgracht 108, 1016
Breda, Singel 210, 1016
Café de Parel, Westerstraat 266, 1015
Venus & Adonis, Prinsengracht 274, 1016
Toscanini and Toscanini Deli, Lindengracht 75, 1015
Café Parlotte, Westerstraat 182, 1015
Gartine, Taksteeg 7, 1012

HOTELS

Pulitzer Amsterdam, Prinsengracht 323, 1016
Soho House, Spuistraat 210, 3HG, 1012
Hotel 717, Prinsengracht 717, 1017
De L'Europe, Nieuwe Doelenstraat 2–14, 1012
Conservatorium Hotel, Paulus Potterstraat 50, 1071
Pestana Amsterdam Riverside, Amsteldijk 67, 1074
The Hoxton, Herengracht 255, 1016

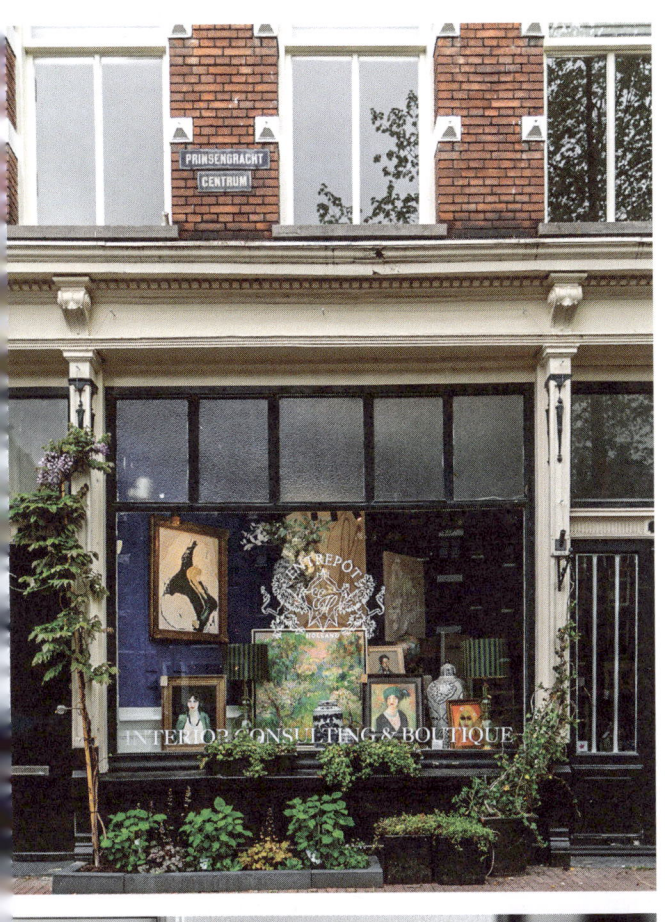
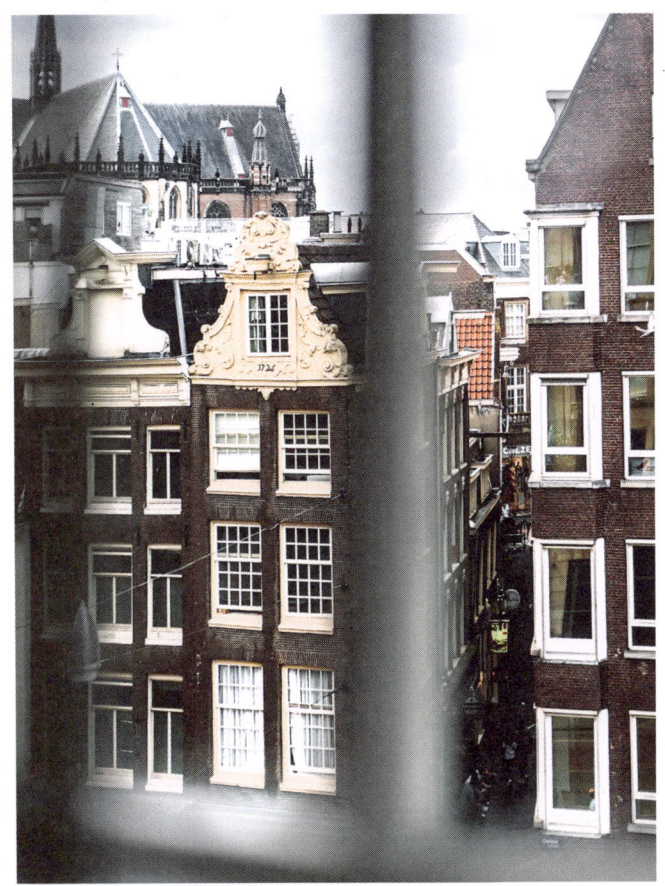
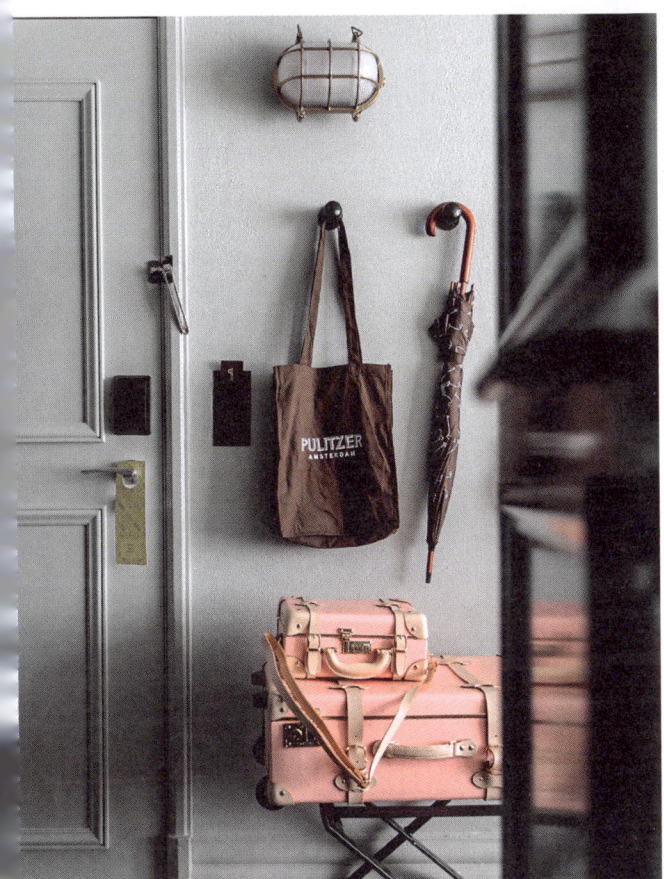
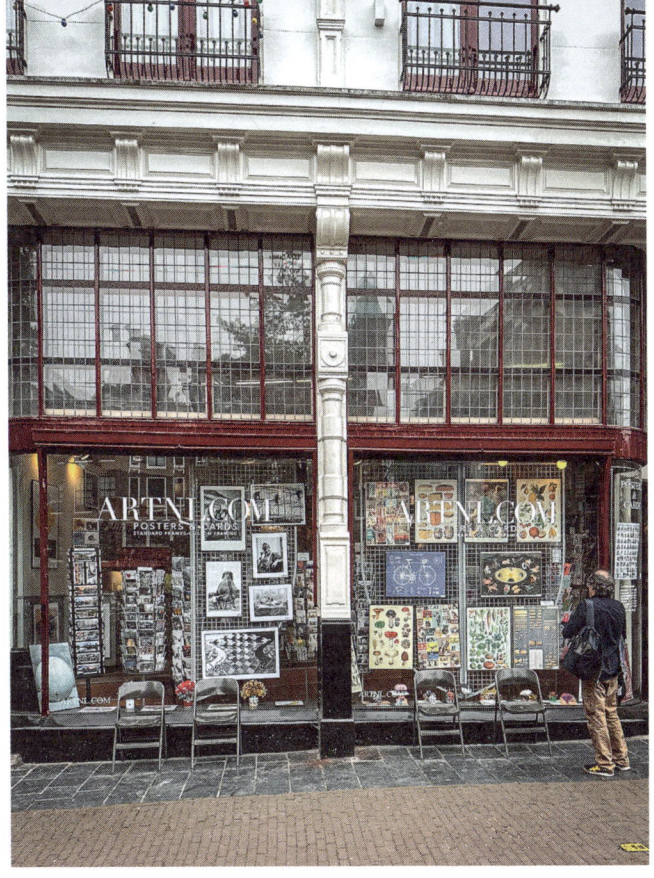

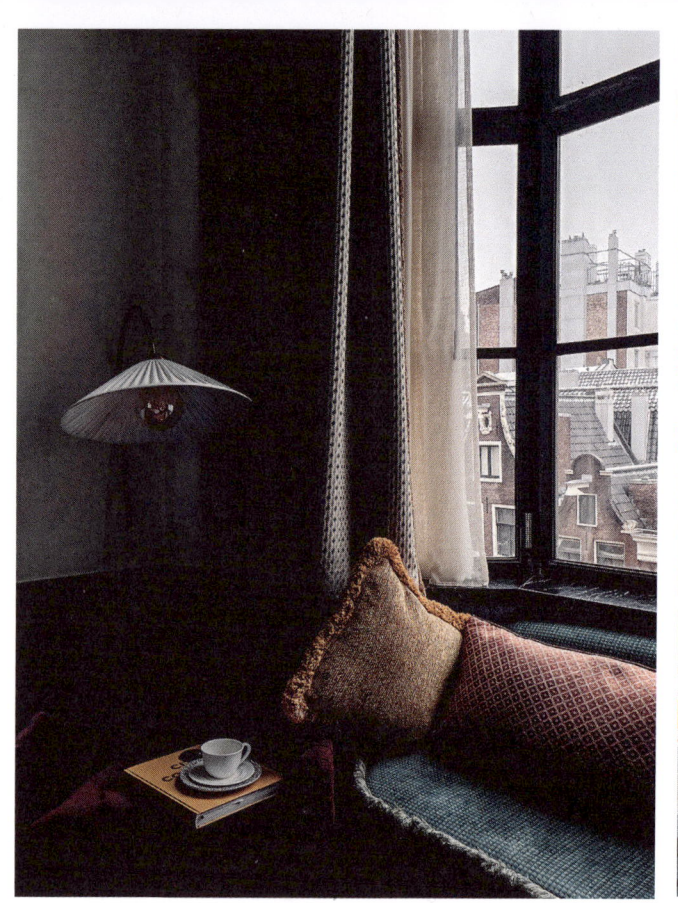
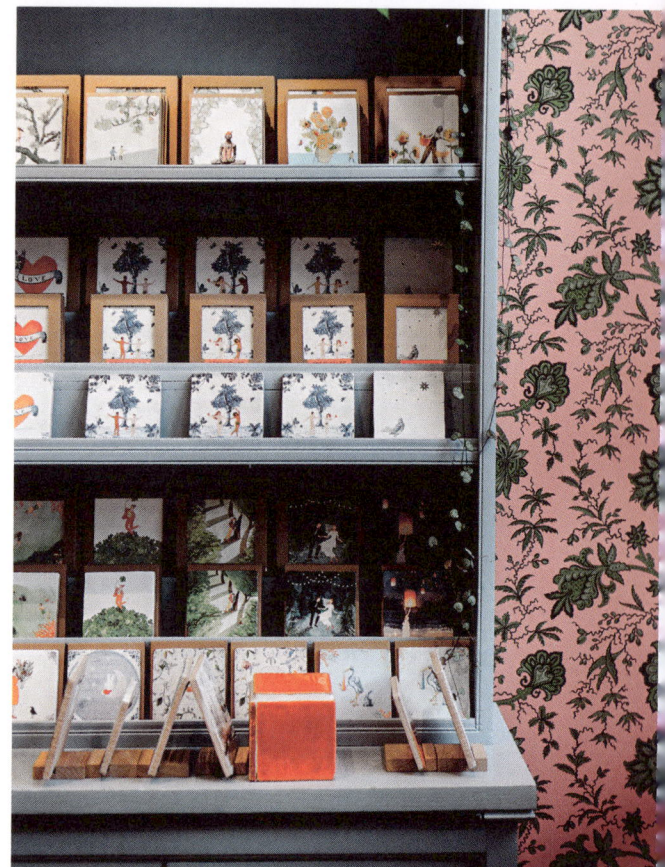

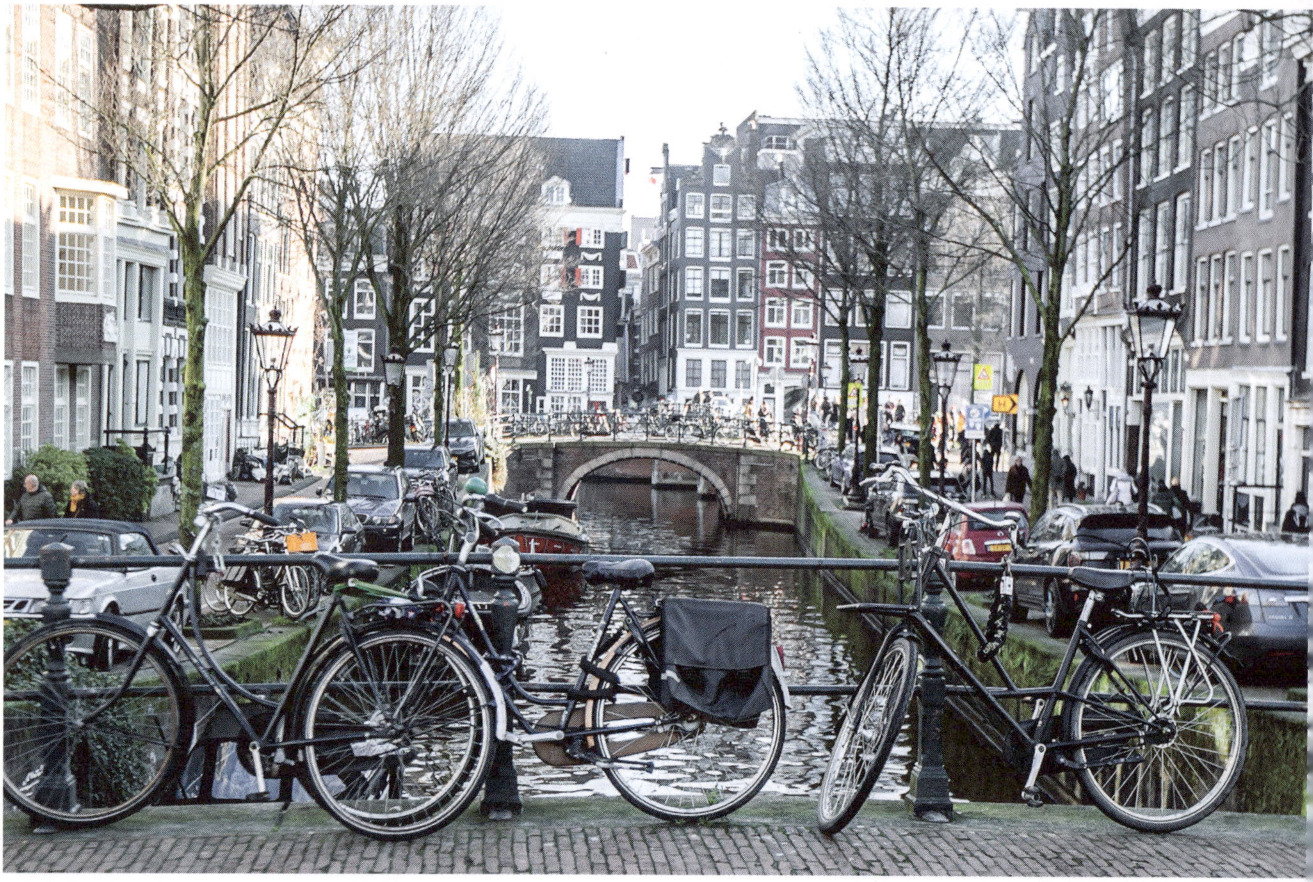

BAKERIES AND SWEET GOODS

Van Stapele Koekmakerij, Heisteeg 4, 1012
Ulmus, Cabralstraat 7, 1057
Iouf, Bilderdijkstraat 38, 1053
Levain et le Vin, Jan Pieter Heijestraat 168, 1054
Selma's, Herenstraat 35, 1015

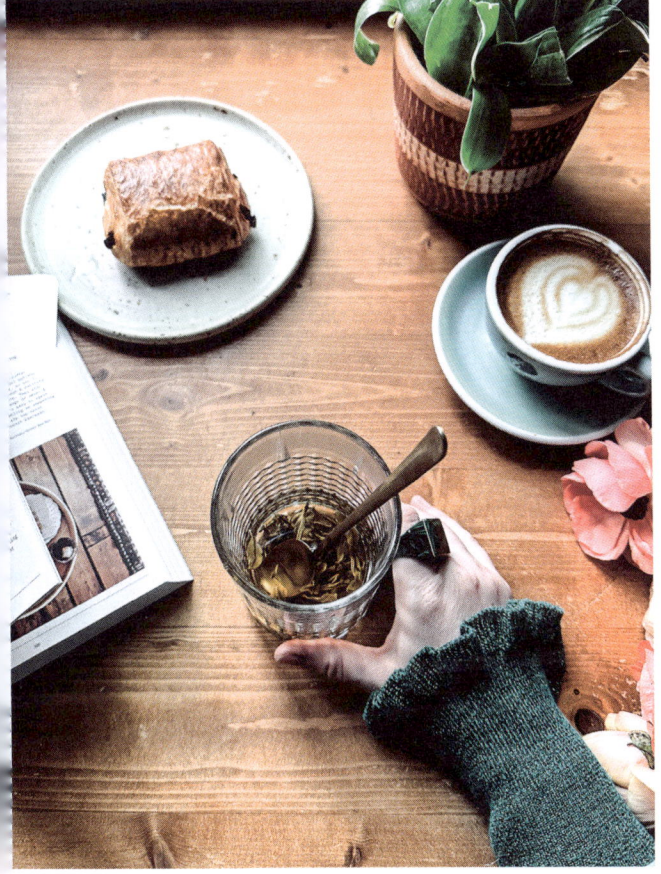
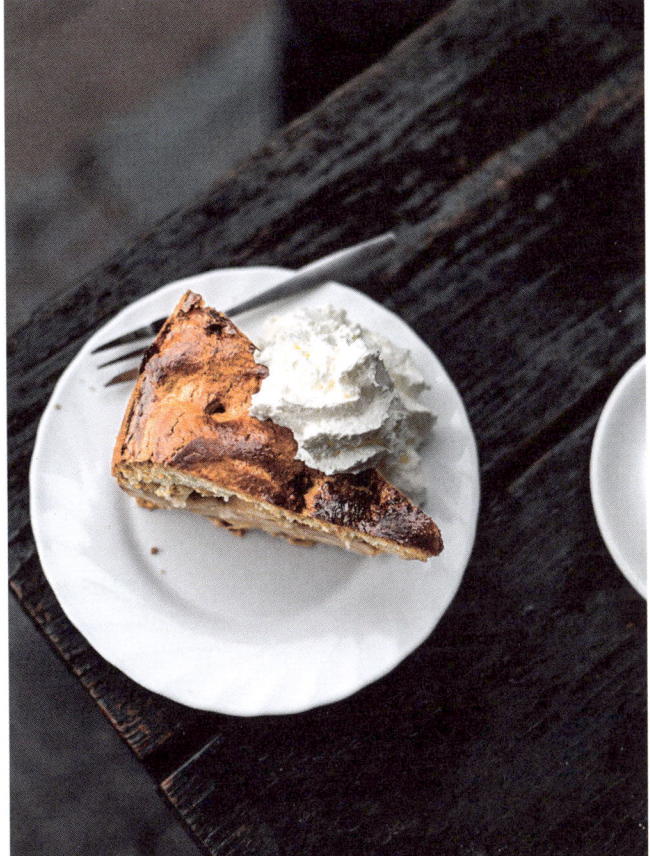

CONTRIBUTORS

All images © Siobhan Ferguson except:

Admira (@velvet.boulevard) fell in love with Amsterdam instantly for its architecture, culture, flower shops and cute cafes on every corner. It became her goal to call this city her home. Admira now works as a software engineer in Amsterdam and, beside her passion for computers and numbers, her greatest love is photography. She decided to start an Instagram account as a creative escape from her day job. She enjoys sharing her photography and impressions of the places she travels to, but, most of all, she loves sharing her love for Amsterdam and showcasing a side of it different from its reputation as a party city.

Back cover, bottom middle, pages 206 bottom left, 212 bottom left and right.

Julia Willard (@fallingoffbicycles) has over fifteen years of experience capturing the beauty of the Netherlands and beyond through her photography. Her first true muse, Paris, sparked her passion for photography, leading her to create Falling Off Bicycles, a photography company that reflects her adventurous spirit.

Having lived in three different countries, Julia has a deep love for exploring cities on her bicycle, allowing her to capture unique and authentic moments in her photography. Her current home in Paris, France, provides endless inspiration for her work, and she shares her daily life and discoveries through her lens via social media.

Pages 4, 192, 205 bottom left, 208 bottom right, 221 bottom, 224, 209 text contribution.

Morena Oliveira (@mformorena), based in Amsterdam for the last few years, is head of marketing at Lina Stores. Prior to working with Lina Stores, Morena worked with One Fine Stay and Culture Trip.

Pages 130, 135 bottom left, 206 top left, 207 text contribution.

Restaurant Venus & Adonis

Pages 102 top right, 107 top left.

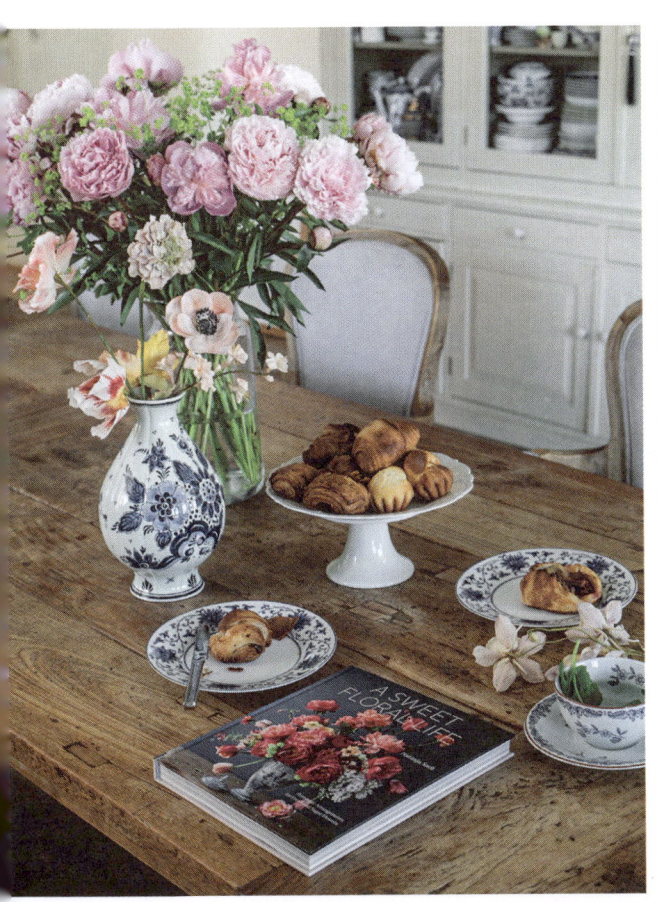
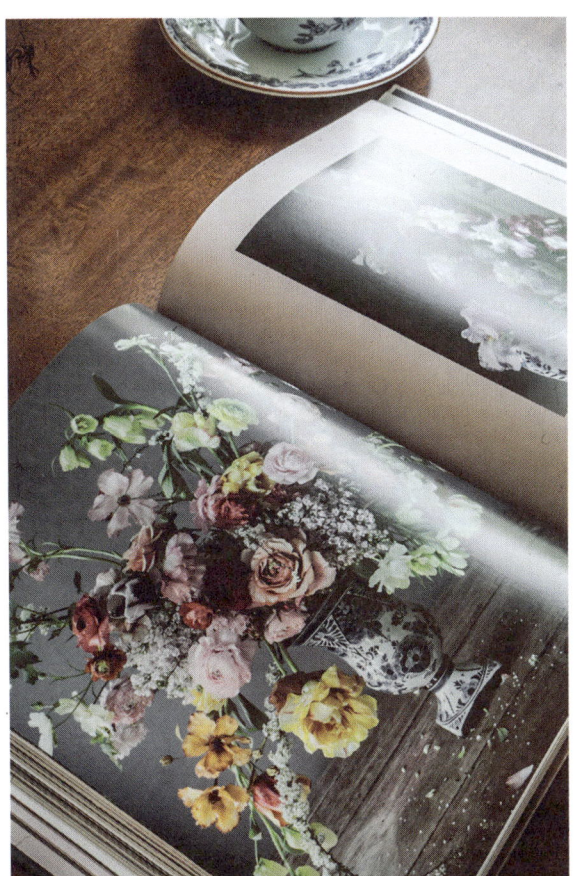

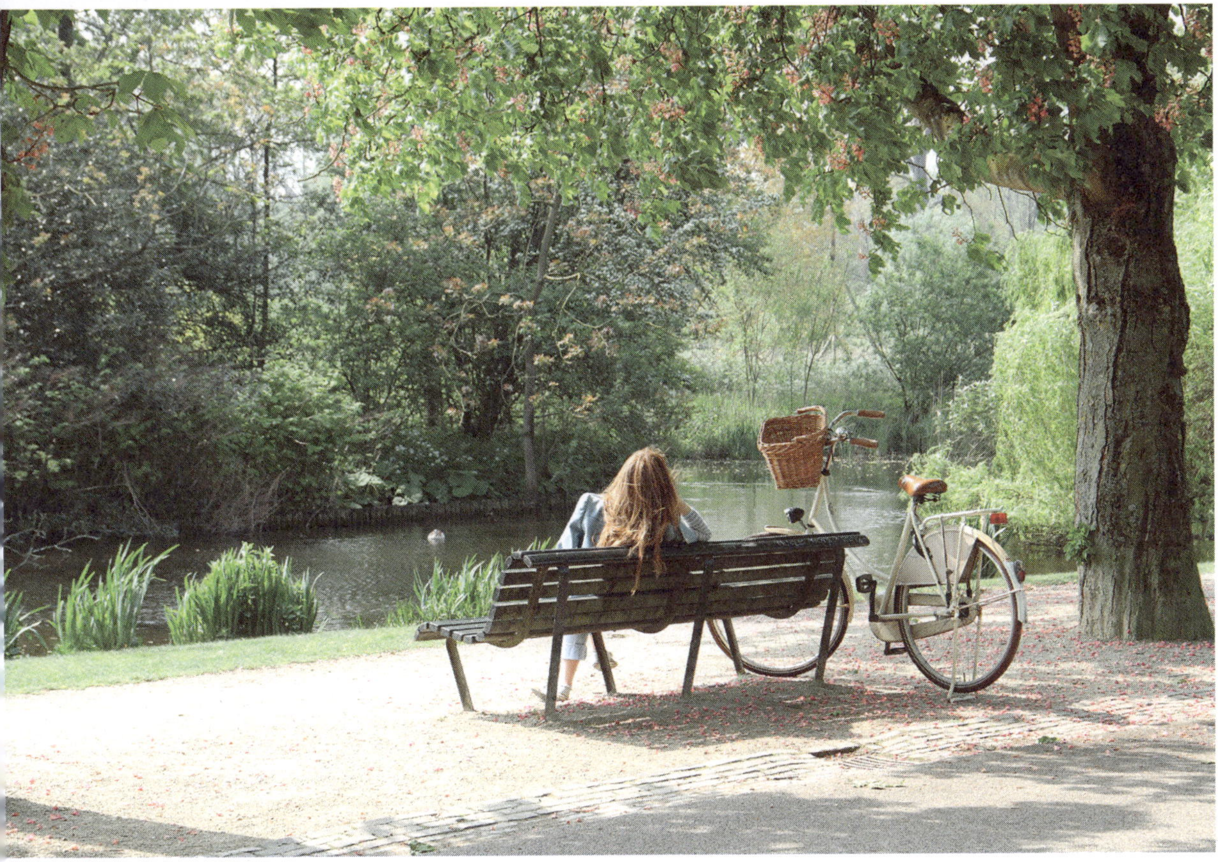

ACKNOWLEDGEMENTS

Thank you to my Instagram followers and all who continue to support my work. Thank you to my family for their constant support and encouragement. Thank you to the brilliant team at The History Press, especially Chrissy and Katie. A very special thank you to Holly Webber for once again producing a stunning set of illustrations for this book. To photographers Morena, Julia and Admira for their brilliant contribution to the chapters.

Thanks to all the lovely shop owners, cafe, restaurant and hotel staff, artists, locals and visitors who enhanced the story along the way. Finally, a special thank you to Eurostar for the gifted trip, Pulitzer Amsterdam for the gifted stay and Natasja Sadi (@cakeatelieramsterdam) for sharing your wonderful art and local insights.

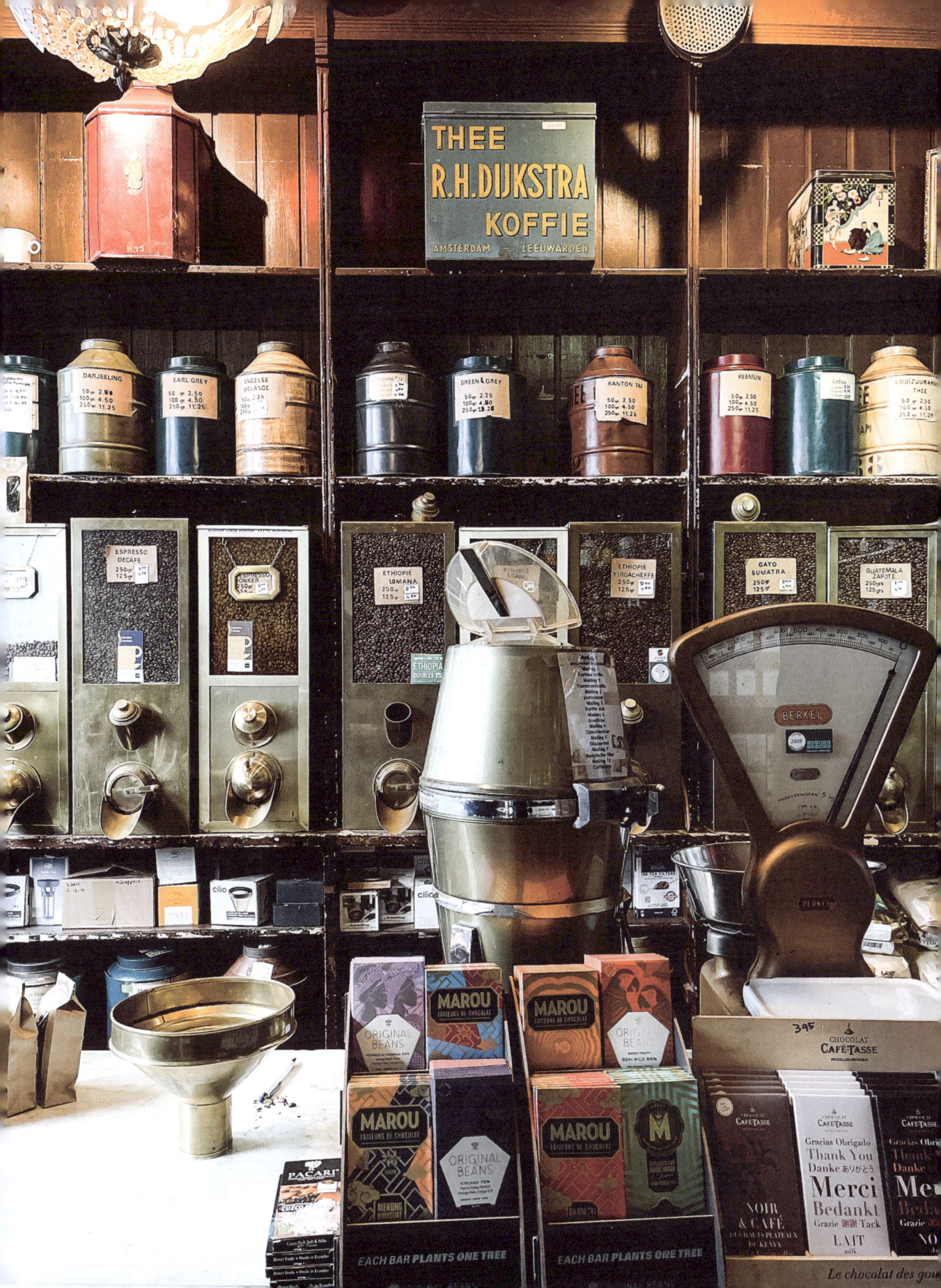

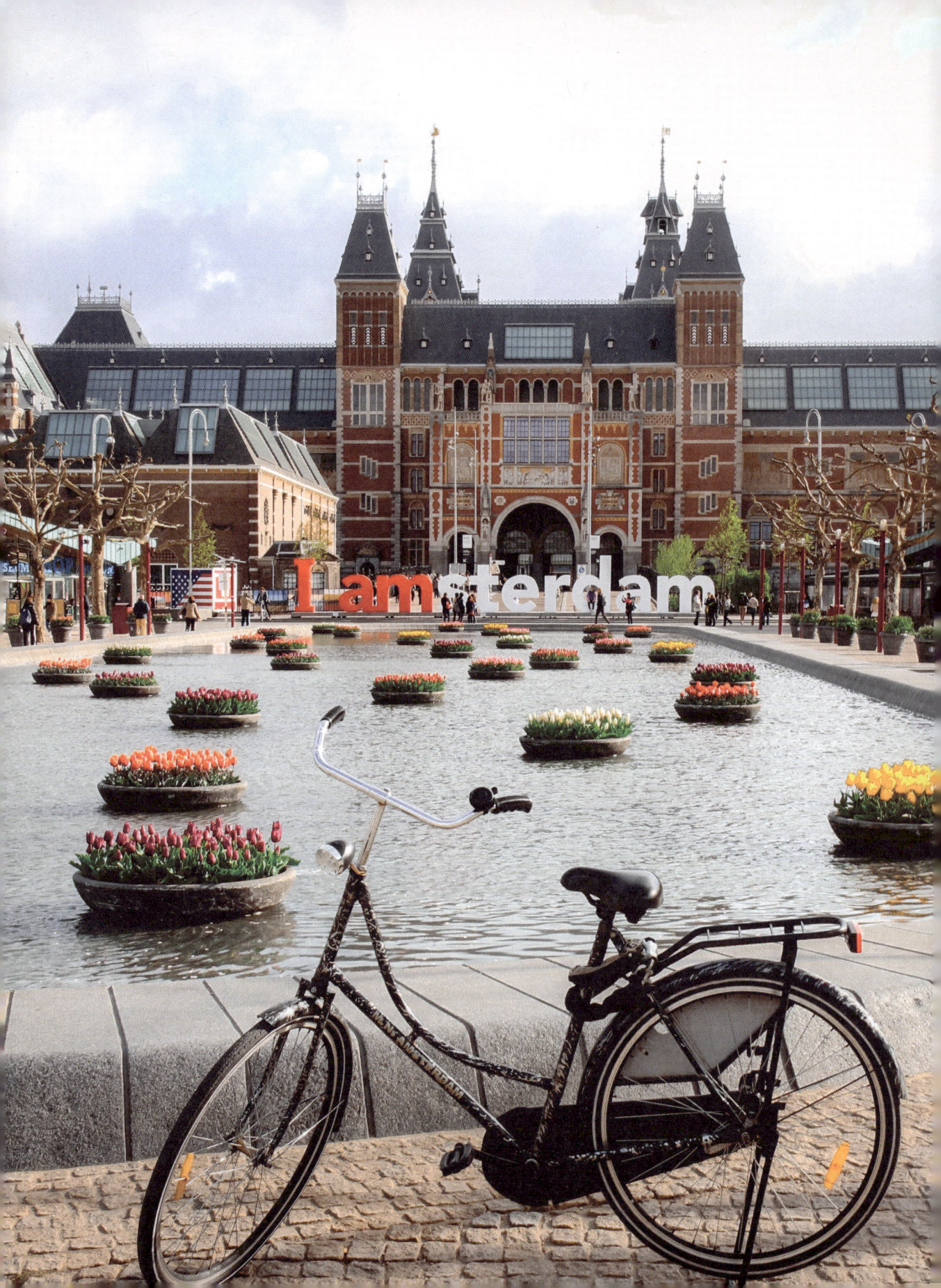

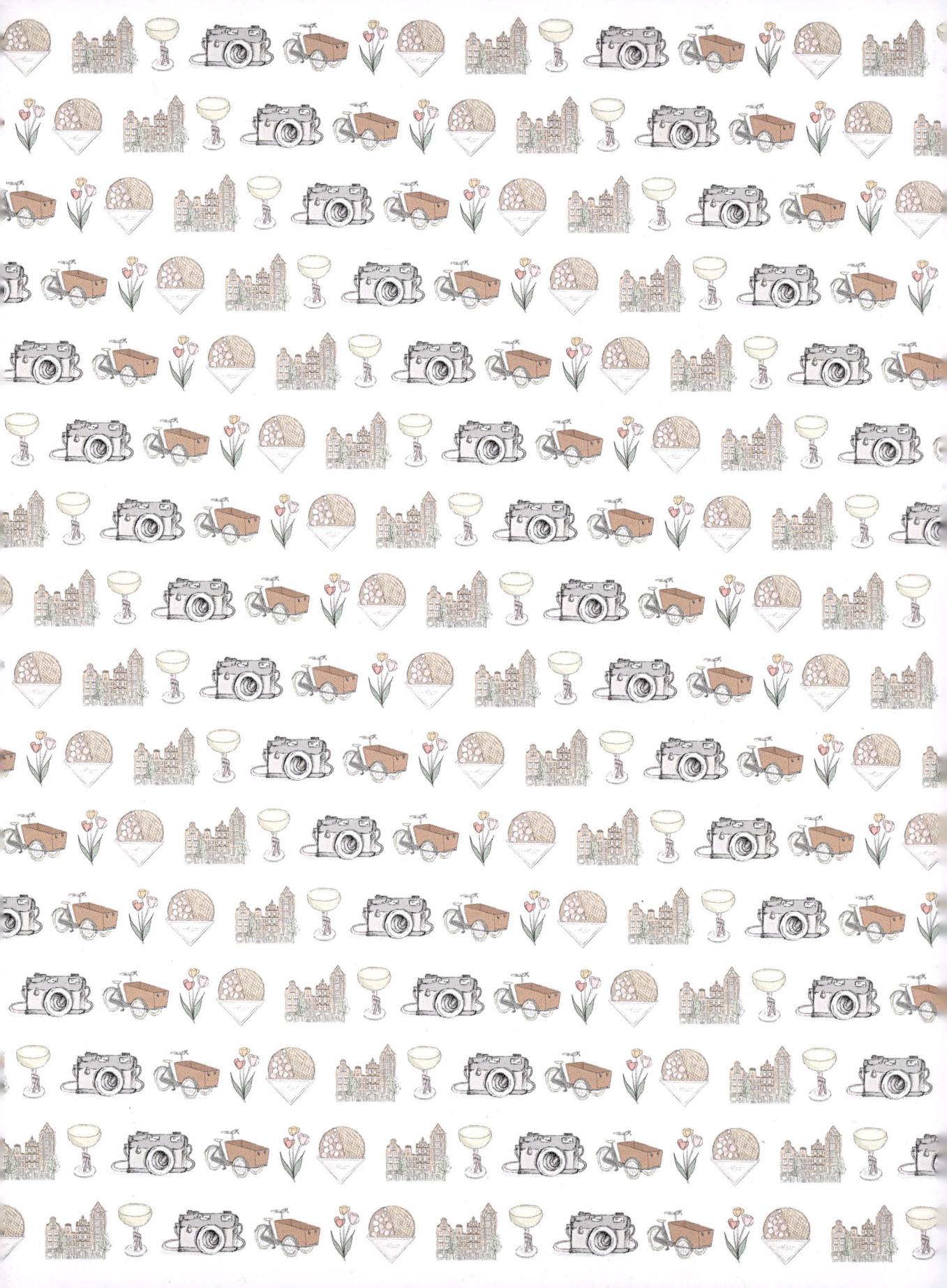